7000585509

UWE BRISTOL
WITHDRAWN
LIBRARY SERVICES

Cambridge Imperial and Post-Colonial Studies Series
General Editors: **Megan Vaughan**, King's College, Cambridge and **Richard Drayton**, King's College London

This informative series covers the broad span of modern imperial history while also exploring the recent developments in former colonial states where residues of empire can still be found. The books provide in-depth examinations of empires as competing and complementary power structures encouraging the reader to reconsider their understanding of international and world history during recent centuries.

Titles include:

Tony Ballantyne
ORIENTALISM AND RACE
Aryanism in the British Empire

Peter F. Bang and C. A. Bayly (*editors*)
TRIBUTARY EMPIRES IN GLOBAL HISTORY

Gregory A. Barton
INFORMAL EMPIRE AND THE RISE OF ONE WORLD CULTURE

James Beattie
EMPIRE AND ENVIRONMENTAL ANXIETY, 1800–1920
Health, Aesthetics and Conservation in South Asia and Australasia

Rachel Berger
AYURVEDA MADE MODERN
Political Histories of Indigenous Medicine in North India, 1900–1955

Robert J. Blyth
THE EMPIRE OF THE RAJ
Eastern Africa and the Middle East, 1858–1947

Rachel Bright
CHINESE LABOUR IN SOUTH AFRICA, 1902–10
Race, Violence, and Global Spectacle

Larry Butler and Sarah Stockwell (*editors*)
THE WIND OF CHANGE
Harold Macmillan and British Decolonization

Kit Candlin
THE LAST CARIBBEAN FRONTIER, 1795–1815

Nandini Chatterjee
THE MAKING OF INDIAN SECULARISM
Empire, Law and Christianity, 1830–1960

Esme Cleall
MISSIONARY DISCOURSE
Negotiating Difference in the British Empire, c.1840–95

T. J. Cribb (*editor*)
IMAGINED COMMONWEALTH
Cambridge Essays on Commonwealth and International Literature in English

Bronwen Everill
ABOLITION AND EMPIRE IN SIERRA LEONE AND LIBERIA

Róisín Healy and Enrico Dal Lago (*editors*)
THE SHADOW OF COLONIALISM IN EUROPE'S MODERN PAST

B. D. Hopkins
THE MAKING OF MODERN AFGHANISTAN

Ronald Hyam
BRITAIN'S IMPERIAL CENTURY, 1815–1914: A STUDY OF EMPIRE AND EXPANSION
Third Edition

Iftekhar Iqbal
THE BENGAL DELTA
Ecology, State and Social Change, 1843–1943

Leslie James
GEORGE PADMORE AND DECOLONIZATION FROM BELOW
Pan-Africanism, the Cold War, and the End of Empire

Robin Jeffrey
POLITICS, WOMEN AND WELL-BEING
How Kerala became a 'Model'

Miguel Bandeira Jerónimo
THE 'CIVILISING MISSION' OF PORTUGUESE COLONIALISM, 1870–1930

Miguel Bandeira Jerónimo and António Costa Pinto (*editors*)
THE ENDS OF EUROPEAN COLONIAL EMPIRES
Cases and Comparisons

Gerold Krozewski
MONEY AND THE END OF EMPIRE
British International Economic Policy and the Colonies, 1947–58

Zoë Laidlaw and Alan Lester (*editors*)
INDIGENOUS COMMUNITIES AND SETTLER COLONIALISM
Land Holding, Loss and Survival in an Interconnected World

Javed Majeed
AUTOBIOGRAPHY, TRAVEL AND POST-NATIONAL IDENTITY

Francine McKenzie
REDEFINING THE BONDS OF COMMONWEALTH 1939–1948
The Politics of Preference

Gabriel Paquette
ENLIGHTENMENT, GOVERNANCE AND REFORM IN SPAIN AND ITS EMPIRE 1759–1808

Sandhya L. Polu
PERCEPTION OF RISK
Policy-Making on Infectious Disease in India 1892–1940

Sophus Reinert and Pernille Røge
THE POLITICAL ECONOMY OF EMPIRE IN THE EARLY MODERN WORLD

Jonathan Saha
LAW, DISORDER AND THE COLONIAL STATE
Corruption in Burma c.1900

John Singleton and Paul Robertson
ECONOMIC RELATIONS BETWEEN BRITAIN AND AUSTRALASIA 1945–1970

Leonard Smith
INSANITY, RACE AND COLONIALISM
Managing Mental Disorder in the Post-Emancipation British Caribbean, 1838–1914

Miguel Suárez Bosa
ATLANTIC PORTS AND THE FIRST GLOBALISATION C. 1850–1930

Jerome Teelucksingh
LABOUR AND THE DECOLONIZATION STRUGGLE IN TRINIDAD AND TOBAGO

Julia Tischler
LIGHT AND POWER FOR A MULTIRACIAL NATION
The Kariba Dam Scheme in the Central African Federation

Erica Wald
VICE IN THE BARRACKS
Medicine, the Military and the Making of Colonial India, 1780–1868

Cambridge Imperial and Post-Colonial Studies
Series Standing Order ISBN 978–0–333–91908–8 (hardback)
978–0–333–91909–5 (paperback)
(outside North America only)

You can receive future titles in this series as they are published by placing a standing order. Please contact your bookseller or, in case of difficulty, write to us at the address below with your name and address, the title of the series and the ISBN quoted above.

Customer Services Department, Macmillan Distribution Ltd, Houndmills, Basingstoke, Hampshire RG21 6XS, England

The Ends of European Colonial Empires

Cases and Comparisons

Edited by

Miguel Bandeira Jerónimo
Institute of Social Sciences, University of Lisbon, Portugal

and

António Costa Pinto
Institute of Social Sciences, University of Lisbon, Portugal

Editorial matter, introduction and selection © Miguel Bandeira Jerónimo and António Costa Pinto 2015
Individual chapters © Contributors 2015

All rights reserved. No reproduction, copy or transmission of this publication may be made without written permission.

No portion of this publication may be reproduced, copied or transmitted save with written permission or in accordance with the provisions of the Copyright, Designs and Patents Act 1988, or under the terms of any licence permitting limited copying issued by the Copyright Licensing Agency, Saffron House, 6–10 Kirby Street, London EC1N 8TS.

Any person who does any unauthorized act in relation to this publication may be liable to criminal prosecution and civil claims for damages.

The authors have asserted their rights to be identified as the authors of this work in accordance with the Copyright, Designs and Patents Act 1988.

First published 2015 by
PALGRAVE MACMILLAN

Palgrave Macmillan in the UK is an imprint of Macmillan Publishers Limited, registered in England, company number 785998, of Houndmills, Basingstoke, Hampshire RG21 6XS.

Palgrave Macmillan in the US is a division of St Martin's Press LLC, 175 Fifth Avenue, New York, NY 10010.

Palgrave is a global academic imprint of the above companies and has companies and representatives throughout the world.

Palgrave® and Macmillan® are registered trademarks in the United States, the United Kingdom, Europe and other countries.

ISBN 978–1–137–39405–7

This book is printed on paper suitable for recycling and made from fully managed and sustained forest sources. Logging, pulping and manufacturing processes are expected to conform to the environmental regulations of the country of origin.

A catalogue record for this book is available from the British Library.

A catalog record for this book is available from the Library of Congress.

Typeset by MPS Limited, Chennai, India.

Contents

Acknowledgements

The editors of this volume wish to express their gratitude to several personalities and institutions for their support. First and foremost, we are obliged to acknowledge the fundamental support given by the Portuguese Foundation for Science and Technology to two research projects that are related to this collective volume: *'Portugal is not a Small Country': The End of the Portuguese Colonial Empire in a Comparative Perspective* (FCT-PTDC/HIS-HIS/108998/2008), coordinated by António Costa Pinto and in which Cláudia Almeida was of great importance, and *Internationalism and Empire: The Politics of Difference in the Portuguese Colonial Empire in Comparative Perspective (1920–1975)* (FCT-PTDC/EPH-HIS/5176/2012), coordinated by Miguel Bandeira Jerónimo. We would also like to mention the Institute of Social Sciences of the University of Lisbon, Brown University – namely the Department of Portuguese and Brazilian Studies, in the person of Onésimo Teotónio de Almeida, and the Department of History – and the Institute of Commonwealth Studies of the University of London, given their support which, at different moments, enabled the organization of meetings in which the majority of these papers were presented and debated: the international conference of 2011 in Lisbon, entitled *The End of the Portuguese Empire in a Comparative Perspective*; two panels at the American Historical Association annual conference in 2012 and 2013; and two conferences in Providence, at Brown University, in 2011 and 2012. A special reference is mandatory to the support given by the Luso-American Foundation for Development (FLAD).

Finally, the editors want to appreciate the excellent work made by the anonymous reviewers who critically assessed the texts in this volume and whose comments greatly improved it. The same happened with the multiple commentators who discussed these texts on many occasions: William Roger Louis, Martin Thomas, David Engerman, Jason Parker, David Ekbladh, Joseph Hodge, Corinna Unger, Taylor Sherman, Mairi MacDonald, Alexander Keese, Diogo Ramada Curto, José Pedro Monteiro, Andrew Zimmermann, and Perrin Selcer.

Notes on Contributors

Frederick Cooper is Professor of History at New York University and a specialist in the history of Africa, colonization, and decolonization. He is the author most recently of *Colonialism in Question: Theory, Knowledge, History* (2005), *Empires in World History: Power and the Politics of Difference* (with Jane Burbank, 2010), *Citizenship between Empire and Nation: Remaking France and French Africa, 1945–1960* (2014), and *Africa in the World: Capitalism, Empire, Nation-State* (2014).

John Darwin is Professor of Global and Imperial History at Oxford University and Professorial Fellow of Nuffield College. He is Director of the Oxford Centre for Global History from October 2014. His most recent books include *The Empire Project: The Rise and Fall of the British World System 1830–1970* (2009) and *Unfinished Empire: The Global Expansion of Britain* (2012).

Ryan Irwin is Assistant Professor of History at the University at Albany, State University of New York. He is the author of *Gordian Knot: Apartheid and the Unmaking of the Liberal World Order* (2012), and is currently writing a new book about liberal internationalism in the mid-20th century. His essays have been published in a variety of journals and periodicals, including *Diplomatic History, International History Review, Foreign Affairs, History Compass, Passport,* and *Kronos.* He has won several writing awards, including the Stuart L. Bernath Prize for an article published in 2009. He was previously a fellow at Yale University and the associate director of International Security Studies.

Miguel Bandeira Jerónimo is a research fellow at the Institute of Social Sciences, University of Lisbon, and Assistant Professor at the New University of Lisbon. He was a Visiting Assistant Professor at Brown University in 2011 and 2012 and a Visiting Scholar at King's College London in 2012–2013. His research interests focus on comparative histories of imperialism and colonialism. He recently published *A diplomacia do império* and edited *O império colonial em questão* (2012), co-edited *Portugal e o fim do colonialismo* (2014) and published *The 'Civilising Mission' of Portuguese Colonialism, 1870–1930* (2015).

John Kent is Reader in International Relations at the London School of Economics. He was a Series B editor of the British Documents on the End of Empire Project with three parts covering Egypt and the Defence of the Middle East 1945–1956 until the nationalization of the Suez Canal Company. He is the author of *The Internationalization of Colonialism Britain, France, and Black Africa 1939–1956* (1992), *International Relations Since 1945: A Global History* (2003, with John W. Young) and *America, the UN and decolonisation cold war conflict in the Congo* (2010) books on British, French, and American policy towards Black Africa and the relationship between British imperial policy and the early development of the Cold War. His next project is examining the incongruous relationship between defence strategy and foreign policy in the British (mis)management of decline.

Philip Murphy is Director of the Institute of Commonwealth Studies and Professor of British and Commonwealth History at the University of London. He has published extensively on 20th-century British and imperial history including a monograph on the Conservative Party and African decolonization (1995). Much of his published work has focused on the decolonization process in central Africa, with particular reference to the history of the Central African Federation. Many of his publications have also focused on the Commonwealth-wide role of the British monarchy and the implications of this for the UK's external relations, most notably his monograph *Monarchy and the End of Empire: The House of Windsor, the British Government and the Postwar Commonwealth* (2013). Since 2007, he has been co-editor of the *Journal of Imperial and Commonwealth History*.

António Costa Pinto is a research professor at the Institute of Social Sciences at the University of Lisbon, Portugal. He has been a visiting professor at Stanford University, Georgetown University, a senior associate member at St Antony's College, Oxford, and a senior visiting fellow at Princeton University and at the University of California, Berkeley. His research interests include authoritarianism, political elites, democratization and decolonization, transitional justice in new democracies, and the comparative study of political change in southern Europe. He published *The Nature of Fascism Revisited* (2011) and edited *The Last Empire. 25 Years of Portuguese Decolonization* (2003) *Dealing with the Legacy of Authoritarianism* (2011), and *Rethinking Fascism and Dictatorship in Europe* (2014).

Bruno Cardoso Reis is a research fellow at Institute of Social Sciences, University of Lisbon. He has been a visiting researcher at King's College London and a guest reader at a number of Portuguese universities since 2007. Recent publications include: 'The myth of British minimum force in counterinsurgency during the campaigns of decolonization', *Journal of Strategic Studies* (2011), pp. 245–279; 'Portugal and the UN: A rogue state resisting the norm of decolonization (1956–1974)', *Portuguese Studies* (2013), pp. 251–276; and *The Theory and Practice of Irregular Warfare* (co-edited with A. Mumford, 2013).

Luís Nuno Rodrigues is an associate professor at the Department of History of ISCTE, University Institute of Lisbon, and a researcher at CEI-IUL, Centre for International Studies. He is also the editor of the *Portuguese Journal of Social Science*. He has published several articles and books in Portugal and abroad. The Portuguese version of his PhD Dissertation on Portuguese–American relations during the Kennedy Administration was published in 2002 and won two national prizes in Portugal. His most recent book is *Perceptions of NATO and the New Strategic Concept* (2011, edited with Volodymyr Dubovyk) on worldwide perceptions of NATO, six decades after its creation.

Martin Shipway is Reader in Contemporary French and European History at Birkbeck, University of London. He is the author of *The Road to War: France and Indochina, 1944–1947* (1996/2003) and *Decolonization and Its Impact: A Comparative Approach to the End of the Colonial Empires* (2008), and has published numerous articles on French colonial policy and decolonization in Indochina, Madagascar, Algeria, and sub-Saharan Africa. He is currently working on the French 'official mind' and the late colonial state in the period of decolonization.

Sarah Stockwell is a senior lecturer at King's College London. Her books include *The Business of Decolonization: British Business Strategies in the Gold Coast* (2000) and the edited collection *The British Empire: Themes and Perspectives* (2008). With S. R. Ashton she co-edited *British Imperial Policy and Colonial Practice 1925–1945* (1996), the first volume in Series A of the *British Documents on the End of Empire,* and with L. J. Butler has recently edited *The Wind of Change: Harold Macmillan and British Decolonization* (2013). She is currently writing a book exploring British decolonization from the perspective of a range of domestic British institutions.

Crawford Young is Rupert Emerson and H. Edwin Young Professor Emeritus of Political Science at the University of Wisconsin-Madison, where he taught from 1963 till 2001. His major books include *Politics in the Congo* (1965), *Ideology and Development in Africa* (1982), *The Rise and Decline of the Zairian State* (1985), and *The African Colonial State in Comparative Perspective* (1994). More recently, he published *The Post-Colonial State in Africa: A Half-Century of Independence (1960–2010)* (2012). He served as President of the African Studies Association (1982–1983), which awarded him the Distinguished Africanist Prize in 1991.

Introduction – The Ends of Empire: Chronologies, Historiographies, and Trajectories

Miguel Bandeira Jerónimo and António Costa Pinto

The Ends of European Colonial Empires: Cases and Comparisons provides a plural assessment of the ends of the European colonial empires, made by some of the leading experts of the growing field – in quantity, quality, and scope – of decolonization studies.[1] The historiography of decolonization is still work in progress, vibrant in its plurality of analytical approaches, establishing productive conversations with other historiographies and disciplinary fields. It is a field of research marked by the emergence of novel intellectual concerns, political and ideological outlooks and also geopolitical vistas, as John Darwin illustrates in his contribution to this volume.[2] For example, the intersections between the scrutiny of the imperial and colonial endgames and *local* and *global* researches on the histories of the Cold War, of development, of labour, of human rights or of international organizations are being prolifically explored.[3] The establishment of a critical dialogue between historiographies of imperial endgames, geopolitical competition, and trajectories of globalization, for instance, entails many relevant advantages for each domain.[4] Of course, these historiographical dialogues may generate some problems.[5]

But whatever the relative importance granted to these historiographical and thematic intersections – and their political, economic, ideological, and cultural manifestations in history – it is crucial to emphasize their cross-fertilization (which we do below), illuminating the fertile outcomes and challenges they bring about, as many texts in this volume demonstrate.

Addressing different geographies and taking into account diverse *chronologies* of decolonization, this collection also highlights the specificities of each imperial configuration and respective *colonial situations*. Accordingly, it offers a variegated empirical assessment of almost

1

all European imperial endgames, focusing, with few exceptions, on the African continent.[6] The importance, indeed the necessity, of endorsing the advancement of ampler analytical exercises that can include and compare other cases of imperial disintegration – for instance, those related to the post-First World War period, to the Japanese and Soviet 'empires' or the 'American empire' – must be acknowledged, even if the selection of cases in this book does not respond to this need.[7] The chronological and geographical widening and enhancement of the comparative study of imperial formations, its emergence, consolidation and eventual dissolution, is a crucial endeavour that must be continuously promoted.[8]

Despite its focus on the post-Second World War years, this volume nonetheless highlights inter-war legacies, for instance, of racialized and paternalistic outlooks, modalities of imperial reformism or economic *protectionist* preferences. It therefore proposes a cautious use of the widespread argument that posits that the Second World War was *the* fundamental critical juncture that entailed the most *significant* changes to the fate of European colonial empires. Notwithstanding that war's unquestionable relevance to the study of 20th-century imperialism and colonialism, which is demonstrated by the majority of the texts contained here, a different economy of continuity and change should perhaps be pursued in our efforts to understand the multiple and overlapping *chronologies* of decolonization.

With that in mind, this volume offers studies of particular historical events and processes that characterized the multiple trajectories towards imperial demise, elucidating their connection with wider, *global* historical processes, and enabling comparative insights into the similarities and differences between these events, and the processes and trajectories of decolonization. The consideration of historical contingency and local particularities is a fundamental correction to *general*, linear and simplistic narratives of decolonization and its main causes. In this volume, the supposed inevitability of the imperial endgame is confronted by a multiplicity of competing possibilities, a diversity of options and decisions that were at stake. The polyhedral nature of political, economic, ideological, and sociocultural imagination(s) of late colonialism and decolonization is recognized, not suppressed or reduced to a single analytical dimension (e.g. political or economic). Likewise, the fact that imperial endgames were dynamic, often contradictory and unstable historical processes that influenced each other to varying degrees is acknowledged in this work. For instance, the political, economic, and sociocultural continuities and discontinuities between imperial and postimperial and postcolonial regimes must be carefully pondered. They must not be taken for granted with hindsight, given the manifest result: the transfer of power or sovereignty. The imperial endgames, their repercussions and 'legacies', are unsuited to reductionist, nomological, and teleological approaches, or to ideological oversimplifications, all of which persist inside and outside academia. The ends of empire were plural and complex, and the imperial endgame was not an inexorable and inevitable process.

Among the many historical subjects held up to critical analysis in this volume, let us single out the following, without aiming to be exhaustive.

The circulation and diverse appropriation of idioms and repertoires of imperial rule is one of the central issues of this volume, including those that left their imprint in the *nature* of the late colonial state.[9] The same goes for the circulation and diverse appropriation of idioms and repertoires of protest and resistance, and self-determination.[10] For instance, the issue of state-sponsored violence that conditioned the 'late colonial shift' in many imperial formations merits a special place, marked as it was by longstanding modalities of colonial stereotyping, racial discrimination and civilizational rhetoric.[11]

Also worthy of attention is 'developmentalism'. In fact, another important historical issue explored in some of these contributions relates to the engagement between international doctrines of development and modernization and the late colonial period. This historical engagement was a central feature of late colonialism. It was certainly associated with post-war economic and political imperatives that affected the European imperial states,[12] whose need to reinvent their colonial and international legitimacy as *progressive* and *modern* polities, confronting the archaism of their administrative apparatus and the meagre social penetration of the infrastructural power of the colonial state, was evident.[13] It was also related to the *local* and *global* interference of competing Cold War 'modernities', constituting an informative example of the postcolonial 'legacies' and ramifications of late colonialism and decolonizing processes. The persistence of idioms and modalities of statecraft and governance (e.g. institutional and constitutional architectures, including an 'imported State'[14]); of disciplinary knowledge with global impact (e.g. *community development* or *development economics*, or the growing institutionalization of Social and Human Sciences and related engagement with imperial processes[15]); of experts and epistemic communities (e.g. related to aid, agricultural economics or labour[16]); of grand schemes of societal transformation; or of repertoires of violent repression are some examples. Accordingly, this volume deals with the 'transfers of power' but clearly goes beyond its associated traditional narrative. It certainly addresses the causes, motivations and contexts of the formulation of imperial policies to manage or resist decolonizing pressures, but it provides a diverse and multidimensional set of interrogations that evade the emphasis on strict political-diplomatic rationales.

As briefly noted above, renewed interest in the role played by international and transnational actors is also perceptible in many of these contributions, accompanying an historiographical turn that is also noticeably rewarding in the assessment of work by bodies such as the League of Nations or the International Labour Organization.[17] The role of the United Nations, for instance, is investigated in many texts.[18] Within this institution, alongside power politics and efforts to *nationalize* the international, the emergence of a community of international experts – who shared particular normative frameworks and therefore mitigated national affiliations – was a crucial process. For sure, positions that were in favour of the continuation of colonial solutions, or that merely pushed for their reform, existed in these international organizations. But the ways in which international organizations accommodated *global* decolonization idioms, *moments* and trajectories, and transformed their normative, institutional and policy-making frameworks, constitute a crucial context through which to observe the plural, circumstantial and often contradictory nature of the imperial endgames.

Finally, alongside aspects such as the role of information and intelligence – the prolongation and perhaps adjustment of the inter-war *empires of intelligence*[19] – or of metropolitan political systems in determining the strategies of imperial resilience or retreat, aspects which are also explored in this collection, another important theme that runs throughout many of these contributions is that of the Cold War (and other geopolitical undercurrents).[20] Despite the need to avoid reducing the history of decolonization trajectories to the historical dynamics of the Cold War, not least because coincidence is the weakest form of causation, the entanglements between both historical processes are of undeniable relevance, as several contributions to this volume show. Among other aspects, the assessment of the global consequences of the transformation of the geopolitical and ideological chessboard brought about by Cold War dynamics, with its own intricacies and hard-to-simplify manifestations, requires moving beyond the 'tendency to imagine decolonization as a bilateral relationship between an imperial power and (one) colonial territory', as John Darwin notes in his piece. The understanding of the intersection between the politico-diplomatic, technological, cultural, ideological and artistic *economies* of the Cold War and the plurality of imperial endgames requires refined analytical frameworks.[21]

The contributions to this volume also raise some important methodological and analytical issues.

On the one hand, the multilayered approach of these texts and the diversity of themes and processes they intersect open important comparative possibilities, indicating and enabling comparative avenues of enquiry. In political formations bursting, then and now, with ideologies of exceptionality, the promotion of comparative exercises is perhaps the finest corrective available. The attention to common patterns and to distinctive paths enables understandings that counterbalance clear-cut differentiations between cases and *essentialized* versions of imperial formations (e.g. planned versus disordered trajectories of decolonization), and question the numerous doctrines of exceptionality – of the imperial venture and of its demise, sometimes portrayed as the ultimate evidence of the putative 'civilizing mission' guiding imperial powers – that still predominate in the historical, political and sociological assessment of the end of European colonial empires (e.g. the British Westminster-based constitutionalism versus the Portuguese isolationism). Moreover, the use of a comparative lens, or the exploration of comparable insights that these texts enable, also permits the appreciation of processes of interimperial and intercolonial cooperation and competition, therefore further questioning singular and exceptional self-serving national narratives.

On the other hand, these texts demonstrate, in varying degrees and with different emphases, the advantages of integrating discrete scales of analysis to understand the trajectories of the late colonial state and decolonization, assessing their co-constitution, their interconnections and interdependence, and evading, or at least questioning and complicating, the replication of the propensity to emphasize one of two prevailing explicative and interpretative decolonization models: the metropolitan and the peripheral (or *nationalist*). In association with the mobilization of a multidimensional approach (one which critically relates the historical dynamism of the colonial situations, of the metropolitan circumstances and of the geopolitical and international landscapes), an aspect already noted briefly, these texts also show the importance of an integrated study of the intersections between: international constraints and opportunities (e.g. those entailed by the dynamics of international organizations' engagement with imperial formations or by the changing nature of imperial and colonial sovereignties' political legitimacy); metropolitan and imperial pressures, strategies and decisions (e.g. the evaluation of the political, economic, social and cultural costs and benefits of an imperial permanence and the related sociopolitical mobilization of domestic constituencies regarding imperial and colonial affairs); and colonial situations (e.g. the changing aspects of the relationship between imperial authorities and plural modalities of colonial rule and colonial societies).[22]

This book is therefore a plural and multilayered collective effort which, alongside the promotion of historiographical dialogue as highlighted above, enables the assessment of international, transnational, metropolitan, and colonial approaches' advantages and shortcomings, exploring the variegated analytical possibilities opened by their articulation.

The volume has three parts. The first – 'Competing Developments: The Idioms of Reform and Resistance' – highlights the contextual production, circulation, and appropriation of specialized knowledge over colonial realities. Here, Frederick Cooper reveals how the need to reform French and British imperialism in Africa, already pressing colonial bureaucracies before the Second World War, was fundamental to the emergence and transformation of the discipline of Development Economics and modernization theories. Miguel Bandeira Jerónimo and António Costa Pinto reinforce the importance of international and interimperial circulation of imperial idioms, but stress the diversity of their appropriation, adaptation, and modification by each imperial configuration. The particular combination of administrative and economic modernization, and resistance to political and civic incorporation of African populations, characterized the late colonial state in the Portuguese Empire. Martin Shipway offers an instructive example of the plurality of idioms and repertoires of imperial rule and colonial reform that coexisted after the First World War, while demonstrating the wide spectrum of possible actions offered to those engaged with imperial and colonial affairs in turbulent times. Through the contextualization and interpretation of Robert Delavignette's shifting perspectives and actions, the ambiguities and complexities of late colonialism are illuminated, the associated political and moral quandaries exposed.

In the second part ('Comparing Endgames: the Modi Operandi of Decolonization'), Crawford Young offers a comparison of the turbulent Belgian, Dutch and Portuguese decolonization trajectories, stressing the role of symbolic, identitarian and material dimensions in the metropolitan and imperial decision-making processes within the broader framework of global politics. Addressing the Portuguese, the French and the British cases, Bruno Cardoso Reis aims to demonstrate the role played by metropolitan 'political culture' and respective 'myths' of empire in the definition of imperial strategies. Sarah Stockwell explores, with some important comparative insights concerning Mozambique, the role of political and cultural aspects in the diffusion of the Westminster model (which entailed more than political institutions, bureaucracies or security services) in order to improve our understanding of the apparent institutional stability in the political transitions after the transfer of power in the British Empire in Africa. Philip Murphy questions the British Empire's supposedly serene transfer of power. He avoids the more obvious cases of insurgency, and focuses instead on the case of the Central African Federation, which is nonetheless understood comparatively – and demonstrates how the threat of violence was a crucial element in the processes of conflict and negotiation between the imperial power and the two most important colonial groups: white settlers and African nationalists.

In the third part ('Confronting Internationals: the (Geo)politics of Decolonization'), Ryan Irwin reveals how global and international transformations associated with the decolonization *moment* impacted on the ideological debates (for instance, on human rights), the organizational cultures, and the political decision-making processes in international organizations, particularly the United Nations, in a process marked by the moderation of pan-European ideas and interests. Exploring the career of Enuga Reddy, the connections between postcolonial geopolitics, international solidarities and networks, and international politics are illuminated and explained. Dealing with the Belgian case, John Kent examines the multiple ways in which Cold War dynamics and decolonization processes intersected. Taking the secession of Katanga (due to the combined role of political and economic colonial interests) and its international impact, Kent shows how imperial and colonial actors gave an instrumental use to the bipolar competition and conflict, aiming to further their own ends. Similar aspects are explored after the transfer of power. Luís Nuno Rodrigues shows how the relationship between Portugal and former imperial states was an important element in the definition of Portuguese imperial policies and strategies at a diplomatic level, challenging the traditional focus on certain traits of Portuguese 'political culture' associated with an authoritarian regime. The latter have tended to reinforce doctrines of national exception, in the Portuguese case one of supposed isolationism.

Finally, in his 'Last Days of Empire', John Darwin provides a critical overview of the volume's main arguments and proposals, highlighting some of the most important themes that connect its contributions.

Notes

1. A proof, and also a cause, of this enlargement and improvement of the field of decolonization studies is the International Seminar on Decolonization, organized by the National History Center, directed by William Roger Louis and funded by the Andrew W. Mellon Foundation. More than 100 young scholars interested in this field participated in the seminar.
2. For some recent comparative reassessments see Martin Shipway, *Decolonization and its Impact: A Comparative Approach to the End of the Colonial Empires*, Oxford: Blackwell, 2008; Martin Thomas, Bob Moore, and Larry Butler, *Crises of Empire: Decolonization and Europe's Imperial States, 1918–1975*, London: Hodder Education, 2008; Jost Dülffer and Marc Frey, eds, *Elites and Decolonization in the Twentieth Century*, Basingstoke, Palgrave Macmillan, 2011; Pierre Brocheux, ed., *Les Decolonisations au XXe Siècle: Le Fin Des Empires Européens et Japonais*, Paris: Colin Armand, 2012. For comprehensive assessments that place imperial endgames in a *longue durée* approach see John Darwin, *After Tamerlane: The Global History of Empire Since 1405*, New York, Bloomsbury Press, 2008, and Jane Burbank and Frederick Cooper, *Empires in World History: Power and the Politics of Difference*, Princeton, Princeton University Press, 2010.
3. For five examples only, one for each theme: Odd Arne Westad, *The Global Cold War: Third World Interventions and the Making of Our Times*, Cambridge, Cambridge University Press, 2005; Joseph Hodge, Gerald Hodl, and Martina Kopf, eds, *Developing Africa: Concepts and Practices in Twentieth Century Colonialism*, Manchester, Manchester University Press, 2014; Frederick Cooper, *Decolonization and African Society: The Labor Question in French and British Africa*, Cambridge and New York, Cambridge University Press, 1996; Roland Burke, *Decolonization and the Evolution of International Human Rights*, Philadelphia, University of Pennsylvania Press, 2011; Daniel Maul, *Human Rights, Development and Decolonization: The International Labour Organization, 1940–1970*, Basingstoke, Palgrave Macmillan, 2012. See below for further relevant references.
4. For a recent review of the most interesting research possibilities and advantages emerging from this dialogue between historiographies, see Martin Thomas and Andrew Thompson, 'Empire and Globalisation: From "High Imperialism" to Decolonisation', *The International History Review*, vol. 36, no. 1 (2014), pp. 1–29.
5. For a cautionary approach related to the intersection between decolonization and the Cold War see Matthew Connelly, 'Taking off the Cold War Lens: Visions of North–South Conflict during the Algerian War for Independence', *American Historical Review*, vol. 105, no. 3 (2000), pp. 739–769.
6. For another geography see, for instance, Marc Frey, Ronald W. Pruessen and Tan Tai Yong, eds, *The Transformation of Southeast Asia: International Perspectives on Decolonization*, Armonk, NY, M.E. Sharpe, 2003; and Christopher E.

Goscha and Christian Ostermann, *Connecting Histories: Decolonization and the Cold War in Southeast Asia, 1945–1962*, Stanford, Stanford University Press, 2009.

7. This is an extremely valid point raised by one of the anonymous peer reviewers of this volume. For an important contribution see Alfred W. McCoy, Josep Maria Fradera, and Stephen Jacobson, eds, *Endless Empire: Spain's Retreat, Europe's Eclipse, America's Decline*, Madison, University of Wisconsin Press, 2012.

8. The editors of this volume also acknowledge the near absence of the Dutch experience, which is only substantially addressed by Crawford Young's contribution. For some important contributions see: Bob Moore, 'Decolonization by Default: Suriname and the Dutch Retreat from Empire, 1945–1975', *Journal of Imperial and Commonwealth History*, vol. 28, no. 3 (2000), pp. 228–250; Christian Penders, *The West New Guinea Debacle: Dutch Decolonisation and Indonesia, 1945–1962*, Honolulu, University of Hawaii Press, 2002; Gert Oostindie and Inge Klinkers, *Decolonising the Caribbean: Dutch Policies in a Comparative Perspective*, Amsterdam, Amsterdam University Press, 2003; Marc Frey, 'The Indonesian Revolution and the Fall of the Dutch Empire: Actors, Factors, and Strategies', in Marc Frey, Ronald W. Pruessen, and Tan Tai Yong, eds, *The Transformation of Southeast Asia*, pp. 83–104.

9. For inspiration see John Darwin, 'What Was the Late Colonial State?', *Itinerario*, vol. 23, nos 3–4 (1999), pp. 73–82.

10. For a history of the early period see Jonathan Derrick, *Africa's 'Agitators': Militant Anti-Colonialism in Africa and the West, 1918–1939*, London, Hurst, 2008. See also Erez Manela, *The Wilsonian Moment: Self-Determination and the International Origins of Anticolonial Nationalism*, New York, Oxford University Press, 2007; Cemil Aydin, *Politics of Anti-Westernism in Asia: Visions of World Order in Pan-Islamic and Pan-Asian Thought*, New York, Columbia University Press, 2007; and Christopher Lee, ed., *Making a World After Empire: The Bandung Moment and Its Political Afterlives*, Athens, OH, Ohio University Press, 2010.

11. For the notion of 'late colonial shift' see Martin Shipway, *Decolonization and Its Impact*, 12–16. For some recent important contributions to the assessment of violence in late colonialism see: Sylvie Thénault, *Violence ordinaire dans l'Algérie coloniale. Camps, internements, assignations à residence*, Paris, Odile Jacob, 2012; and Fabian Klose, *Human Rights in the Shadow of Colonial Violence: The Wars of Independence in Kenia and Algeria*, Pennsylvania, University of Pennsylvania Press, 2013. The now classic works of Anderson and Elkins are fundamental references as well: David Anderson, *Histories of the Hanged: Britain's Dirty War in Kenya and the End of Empire*, London, Weidenfeld and Nicolson, 2005; Caroline Elkins, *Britain's Gulag: The Brutal End of Empire in Kenya*, London, Jonathan Cape, 2005. For coverage of an early period see Martin Thomas, *Violence and Colonial Order: Police, Workers, and Protest in the European Colonial Empires, 1918–1940*, Cambridge, Cambridge University Press, 2012.

12. Frederick Cooper, 'Reconstructing Empire in British and French Africa' and Nicholas J. White, 'Reconstructing Europe through Rejuvenating Empire: The British, French and Dutch Experiences Compared', in Mark Mazower, Jessica Reinisch, and David Feldman (orgs), *Post-War Reconstruction in Europe.*

International Perspectives. Past and Present Supplement, vol. 6 (2011), pp. 196–210 and pp. 211–236, respectively.

13. On international development see Frederick Cooper and Randall Packard, eds, *International Development and the Social Sciences: Essays in the History and Politics of Knowledge*, Berkeley, CA, University of California Press, 1997, and the recent Marc Frey, Sönke Kunkel, and Corinna R. Unger, *International Organizations and Development, 1945–1990*, Basingstoke, Palgrave Macmillan, 2014. For the notion of infrastructural power of the state see Michael Mann, 'The Autonomous Power of the State: Its Origins, Mechanisms and Results', *European Journal of Sociology*, vol. 25 (1984), pp. 185–213.

14. See Bertrand Badie, *The Imported State: The Westernization of Political Order*, Stanford, Stanford University Press, 2000; Julian Go, 'Modeling States and Sovereignty: Postcolonial Constitutions in Asia and Africa', in Christopher Lee, *Making a World After Empire*, pp. 107–140; Dietmar Rothermund, 'Constitutions et décolonisation', *Diogène*, vol. 4, no. 212 (2005), pp. 9–21; and Crawford Young, *The Postcolonial State in Africa: Fifty Years of Independence, 1960–2010*, Madison, University of Wisconsin Press, 2012.

15. For the history of Sociology's engagement with imperial formations, see Georges Steinmetz, ed., *Sociology and Empire: The Imperial Entanglements of a Discipline*, Durham, Duke University Press, 2013.

16. See: Joseph Hodge, *Triumph of the Expert: Agrarian Doctrines of Development and the Legacies of British Colonialism*, Athens, Ohio University Press, 2007; Veronique Dimier, *The Invention of a European Development Aid Bureaucracy: Recycling Empire*, Basingstoke, Palgrave Macmillan, 2014; Sandrine Kott, 'Une 'communauté épistémique' du social?', *Genèses*, vol. 71, no. 2 (2008), pp. 26–46.

17. On the League of Nations see, for instance, Susan Pedersen, 'Back to the League of Nations', *The American Historical Review*, vol. 112, no. 4 (2007), pp. 1091–1117; and Patricia Clavin, *Securing the World Economy: The Reinvention of the League of Nations, 1920–1946*, Oxford, Oxford University Press, 2013. On the International Labour Organization see Daniel Maul, 'Human Rights, Development and Decolonization', in Sandrine Kott, ed., *Globalizing Social Rights: The International Labour Organization and Beyond*, Basingstoke, Palgrave Macmillan, 2013 and Miguel Bandeira Jerónimo and José Pedro Monteiro, 'Internationalism and the *Labours* of the Portuguese Colonial Empire (1945–1974)', *Portuguese Studies*, vol. 29, no. 2 (2014), pp. 142–163. For a collection of texts that explore several international and transnational organizations and dynamics see Miguel Bandeira Jerónimo and José Pedro Monteiro, eds, *Os passados do presente: Internacionalismo, imperialismo e a construção das sociedades contemporâneas*, Lisboa, Almedina, 2014. For a rich overview see Akira Iriye, *Global Community: The Role of International Organizations in the Making of the Contemporary World*, Berkeley, University of California Press, 2004. See also Neta Crawford, *Argument and Change in World Politics: Ethics, Decolonization, Humanitarian Intervention*, Cambridge, Cambridge University Press, 2002.

18. On the United Nations see, for instance: Paul Kennedy, *Parliament of Man, The United Nations and the Quest for World Government*, London, Allen Lane, 2007; Glenda Sluga and Sunil Amrith, 'New Histories of the U.N.', *Journal of World History*, vol. 19, no. 3 (2008), pp. 251–274; Mark Mazower, *No*

Enchanted Palace: The End of Empire and the Ideological Origins of the United Nations, Princeton, Princeton University Press, 2009; and Mark Mazower, *Governing the World: The History of an Idea*, New York, The Penguin Press, 2012.

19. Martin Thomas, *Empires of Intelligence: Security Services and Colonial Disorder after 1914*, Berkeley, University of California Press, 2007.

20. See, for a summary, Mark Philip Bradley, 'Decolonization, the Global South and the Cold War, 1919–1962', in Melvyn P. Leffler and Odd Arne Westad, *The Cambridge History of the War*, Vol. 1, Cambridge, Cambridge University Press, 2010, pp. 464–485. See also Robert J. McMahon, ed., *The Cold War in the Third World*, Oxford, Oxford University Press, 2013.

21. John Darwin, 'Last Days of Empire', in this volume. This tendency is also visible in many works that lean towards the reduction of the *international* to bilateral relationships between states, for instance between 'great' powers and imperial ones (e.g. the United States and the United Kingdom, Belgium, or Portugal). The acknowledgement of the multifaceted and composite nature of the international is fundamental to studies of decolonization trajectories.

22. This is a suggestion made by Prosser Gifford and William Roger Louis that hasn't lost pertinence. See the 'Introduction' to their edited volume, *Decolonization and African Independence: The Transfers of Power, 1960–1980*, New Haven, CT, and London, Yale University Press, 1988, pp. ix–xxix.

Part I
Competing Developments: The Idioms of Reform and Resistance

1

Development, Modernization, and the Social Sciences in the Era of Decolonization: The Examples of British and French Africa

Frederick Cooper

For scholars, as for the leaders of colonial empires and anti-colonial activists, the period of decolonization was a moment of uncertainty. It was no longer politically possible to divide the world between advanced and primitive beings. Africa would no longer remain the exclusive domain of anthropologists, and anthropologists would be obliged to rethink what distinguished their domain of research. Historians of empire – whose job it had been to make known the accomplishments of whites in regions otherwise without history – were increasingly marginalized or obliged to convert themselves into historians of Africa or Asia. Sociologists, economists, and political scientists, for whom colonized territories had previously held little interest, saw opening before them a new world to discover – and a lack of theory with which to analyse it.

To understand the intellectual atmosphere of the 1950s and early 1960s in the various branches of the social sciences, one must first grasp the passions of the era: the opportunity to observe a fundamental change in world political order and the difficulties of rethinking its overturn. It was now possible to imagine a world without racial distinctions. Distinctions in level of development persisted, to be sure, but they could be overcome. If before the shock of the Second World and its aftermath such differences could be used to justify colonial tutelage, from the 1950s the political impossibility for a European state to continue to exercise trusteeship over an African territory became the rationale for a new range of interventions by the 'developed' world to accelerate the social and economic evolution of the 'underdeveloped' world.

The process of decolonization – beginning with the independence of India and Indonesia in 1946–47 through the independence of Algeria in 1962, of the Portuguese colonies (1975), and of the last British colonies

15

(Rhodesia/Zimbabwe, 1979) – generalized the sovereignty of nation states. This process established, for the first time in history, the formal equivalence of political units across the globe. But economic and social situations were a long way from such equivalence, and this gap between the former colonizers and the decolonizing territories became more apparent, more dangerous, and more in need of examination than before. The subject of this chapter is this moment of possibility and uncertainty. I will describe the new thinking about social and economic issues that emerged from the confrontation of colonial regimes and social and political movements from the late 1930s to the 1940s, and the response of social scientists to the transformed situation. I will concentrate on two examples: the foundation of a branch of economics focused on development and – at a higher level of generalization – modernization theory, including the analysis of 'industrialization' as basic to the way of life of the modern world. I will have something to say about anthropology and ethnographic fieldwork, for in this domain one sees a more nuanced history of social science's approach to the decolonizing world, but one which does not contradict the key idea of the era, that of modernization. The relationship of social science and social policy was ambiguous, for colonial policymakers in the post-war years wanted to claim they were acting on the basis of scientific knowledge, without the knowledge base being very secure. Indeed, new thinking about how to analyse social and economic change in colonial situations emerged first not in the academy but in colonial bureaucracies themselves. An implicit modernization theory shaped colonial policy making in French and British administrations in the 1940s. Scholars soon responded both to the new demands for expertise, particularly in economics, and the new framing of social problems for them to analyse.

That knowledge-base took time to develop, even as weighty decisions about economic and social policy had to be made every day. And scholars did not agree on the details of programmes, or more importantly on their political and intellectual significance. At one extreme, modernization theory rationalized new forms of power to replace the now suspect colonial form: those with scientific knowledge and the experience of already accomplished 'development' could legitimately guide those not so far along the path. At the other end, researchers kept complicating the picture of a smooth path from tradition to modernity, revealing the conflicts and complexity attendant upon change and suggesting different choices might be made, that new forms of human suffering were emerging and that power could be exercised in different ways. American variants on 'modernization theory' epitomise the former tendency, in which change appeared as a self-propelled, all-enveloping process, whereas the 'development' concept pointed to the need for particular actions to bring about change, and hence to the importance of debating exactly what those measures should be, who should be empowered to decide and whose interests would be served by them.

From today's perspective, all forms of evolutionary theory are suspect.[1] But one cannot understand the intellectual passions of the period 1945–60 without appreciating the importance in the South as well as the North of participating in a movement against the obstacles of the colonial system and towards opening to the great majority of people the possibility of their own actions improving their lives.

I will link my discussion of scholarly work to a narrative of social eruption in the late 1930s and 1940s, mounting conflicts in the vital economic centres of export-oriented colonies which forced a change in the direction of colonial politics. The new policies intended to gain control over the situation in turn provoked other sorts of tensions that placed increasingly difficult and costly burdens on the guardians of empire.

The administrator's Africa

Within French and British colonial administrations from the conquest to the Second World War, interventionist policies alternated with a more limited policy of surveillance built around the conservation of the particularity of African societies. Early in the colonial era came the arrogance of the 'civilizing mission' of the French Third Republic, the effort of missionaries to open the continent to Christianity, and the anti-slavery doctrines of British humanitarians; but alongside this came efforts to make Africa the object of all sorts of projects to exploit its human and material resources – railroads, mines, plantations and the intervention of experts in agronomy and medicine.[2] By the time of the First World War, both French and British officials had learned how difficult it was to implement these projects – to reform Africa or to exploit it. In the vast spaces of the continent, officials had to co-operate with the very leaders who were the object of transformation. Officials had not counted on the tenacity of African political structures or the dynamism of social groups, capable of deflecting social reconstruction in unintended directions. Sometimes, colonial regimes profited from unintended innovations, the growth of peanut production by peasants in northern Nigeria, for example, when the government had tried to promote cotton cultivation on the large plantations of the indigenous aristocracy.

Important changes in African economies did not await the invention of the word 'development'. But one should note the irony of colonial ideology in the 1920s: this was a period when peasant production of cocoa, coffee, peanuts and other crops was advancing in several regions, yet colonial governments were elevating the non-transformation of African societies into the central claim to the legitimacy of their rule. The responsible colonizing regime would, or so officials claimed, maintain the cultural integrity of African societies while slowly modifying them within their own terms. Such policies were consistent with the work of ethnographers – which became increasingly influential in the 1920s and 1930s – on the organization of particular African communities, but they did not imply the need for theories of evolution or transformation. The impact of medical-technical or ethnographic knowledge on the practice of colonial administration was varied and often ad hoc, but what counted most in the end was the authority of the white administrator who 'knew his natives'.[3]

For a time in the early 1920s, some leading figures of British and French colonial establishments had argued for a more ambitious colonial policy. In 1923 Albert Sarraut, the minister of the colonies in several governments, published a sweeping book, *La mise en valeur de l'Afrique Noire*, proposing a programme of state investment to obtain a more rational and more serious exploitation of the continent's resources. His British equivalent, Lord Milner, argued in 1919–20 for a more systematic effort to develop the infrastructure and resources of British colonies.[4] But these two projects, despite the influence of their authors, were rejected by their own governments, mainly because officials expected higher returns from investments within the metropolis, but also because other men of influence, such as Frederick Lugard, opposed them for fear that active development would upset the delicate equilibria of Africa societies and the delicate relations between white officials and African indigenous authorities.[5] It was the politics of 'indirect rule' that won the day, a colonial doctrine that celebrated the genius of colonial administrators to operate within the structures of kinship and chieftaincy, gently increasing peasant production while maintaining 'customary' law and 'customary' land tenure. In French Africa, policy-makers followed similar practices, if not the name of this policy. Some administrators thought African cultivators could be turned into something like French peasants via *colonisation indigène*, their 'nomadism' tamed by settlement on better land, with French training and supervision, irrigation and orientation toward marketable crops designated by knowledgeable officials. But the most notable such experiment, the

Office de Niger, was slow to develop the promised facilities, relied on questionable economic and agronomic assumptions, and was unable to get Africans to participate willingly, turning to coercion to acquire settlers and keep them from running away.[6] To the extent that after the First World War educated Africans had become more politically active in both French and British Africa, as they had in some territories, the politics of indirect rule were a reaction, an attempt to enclose Africans within cages labelled as 'tribes'.[7] The very people who could have been the vanguard of African progress under colonial rule were instead pejoratively labelled 'detribalized natives'.

The 1920s and 1930s were the golden age of ethnography. It is not necessary to reduce the ethnographic scholarship of this era to an annex of imperial ideology – ethnographers did their work within the limits of the possible, limits that were practical but also those of the imagination. Some regarded themselves as defenders of the integrity and values of African societies against the encroachments of white settlers and labour recruiters, but the social order they described – an Africa divided into 'tribal' units – acquired its own reality, even if this was the reality of an historical conjuncture rather than a timeless Africa. The famous book on The Nuer by E. E. Evans-Pritchard[8] brilliantly described a certain political organization of an apparently well-defined unit without acknowledging the fluidity and variability of its linguistic and cultural frontiers or that his fieldwork was done in the aftermath of a rebellion whose political effects therefore remained unexamined.[9]

British anthropology was making itself into a science. The thinking of its most notable figure, Bronislaw Malinowski, was more complex than the quest for the pure 'tribe', and he was interested both in social change and in the role anthropologists could play in improving colonial administration – something colonial administrators were not necessarily keen to see. The centrality of academic interests and the concerns of funders to support a science of humankind – as well as the need to tread cautiously in colonial waters – pushed the field towards systematic exploration of general principles of social organization and elucidation of human diversity. If the scientific spirit was thought to have a 'depoliticizing influence', as Malinowski claimed it would on his star African pupil, Jomo Kenyatta, this did not necessarily turn out to be the case. Kenyatta appropriated the language of functionalist anthropology, with its emphasis on the integrated way in which societies work, to assert the integrity of the Kikuyu people, who had made him into a spokesman in conflicts with white settlers and British authorities. Kenyatta was to show that a seemingly conservative vision of an ethnically bounded

Africa, consistent with the politics of indirect rule, could be turned into a language of assertion and critique.[10]

If academic anthropologists, by a combination of choice and necessity, kept a certain distance from the dynamics of a colonized continent, some administrators were becoming increasingly concerned with the question of knowledge. By 1929, some members of the imperial establishment were insisting that 'the time had come to substitute fundamental thinking for aimlessness and drift in the management of the Empire'.[11] But drift remained a basic characteristic of colonial rule, particularly in the revenue-starved Depression years. Nonetheless, the monumental survey of Africa, begun under Lord Hailey's direction and published in 1938, at least put the importance of research on Africa onto the imperial table. Hailey's paternalism and the scarcity of on-the-ground research, particularly into urbanization, wage labour, and political mobilization – limited the originality of the project, but not the identification of Africa as a place that needed careful examination.[12]

The knowledge question was posed somewhat differently in inter-war France. The work of early French ethnographer-administrators, such as Maurice Delafosse, was more open to historical analysis and to regional connections, particularly in West Africa, but their point of departure remained the particularity of African societies.[13] Certain intellectual-administrators, like Robert Delavignette or Henri Labouret, had a conception of Africans as peasants rather than as members of tribes. Even this conception had its romantic dimension – the reflection of a rural France that no longer existed – but their peasants were open to the market and to interactions, part of a community without being wholly enclosed within it.[14] But neither the anthropology of ethnic units nor this conception of an African peasantry opened to examination a fundamental aspect of the inter-war period: the complexity of African forms of agricultural production for export markets and the movement of workers toward mines in central or southern Africa or towards ports and urban centres throughout the African continent.

Certain new departures anticipated what would become stronger tendencies after the war, not so much among the most academically influential anthropologists as among good observers of social policy in action. For example, *Modern Industry and the African*, published in 1933 by a team under Merle Davis, sponsored by the Carnegie Foundation and the International Missionary Council, revealed the basic contradiction in a British policy that preached the conservation of African cultures, but risked destroying their 'integrity and solidarity' via a badly organized system of migratory labour in central Africa. Davis did not ask that colonial regimes simply leave Africans in peace. He advocated a policy of 'stabilization' on two levels: first, in the village, the integrity of which should be reinforced by the provision of agricultural services and schools; second, in the mines and mine towns. Without denying the risks, he saw the emergence of a permanent labour force in the mine towns, able to create a real family life, as preferable to the perturbations of circular migration.[15]

The British administration did not want to think about this critique. It preferred importing rural chiefs to mine towns – to supervise the affairs of 'their' people – and repatriating migrants once their contracts were over. At this time, almost all scholarly study of this and other regions focused on rural societies, but ethnographic fieldwork was beginning to shed light on the realities of migration. Audrey Richards published in 1939 *Land, Labor and Diet in Northern Rhodesia* in which she asked why the Bemba ate badly. She did not quite answer her own question, but she asked if the response was located within the framework of the tribe or in the absence from the village of young men for part of their lives.[16]

The anthropologist Godfrey Wilson pushed further. His book of 1940 used statistics and personal observation to examine a mine town. His title, *The Economics of Detribalization in Northern Rhodesia*, took the phrase then used for something that should be avoided to point to something that already existed. He showed that 40 per cent of men lived in the town with their wives and 70 per cent of them had been there for a long time. He insisted that social policy should take social reality into consideration: a stabilization policy was necessary to manage the tensions and bad conditions associated with the stabilization that had already taken place. Two observations are necessary: there was little follow-up from anthropologists of the region for a decade, and the British administration – in principle concerned with the social problems of the Copperbelt – did not follow Wilson's advice until considerably later.[17] In spite of the opening of an institution for ethnographic research in central Africa, the Rhodes Livingstone Institute, the mines forbade researchers from access to their properties, and researchers had to turn to rural, ethnically defined units of study. The administration would somewhat later – and scholars considerably later – begin to speak of stabilization as an official policy, not as a reality created by Copperbelt workers themselves.[18]

The modernization of colonialism

Godfrey Wilson did not convince the government to change its mind, but the process he described had its consequences. There was a wave of strikes and urban riots in much of the British Empire after 1935. The largest strikes took place in ports, sugar plantations and oil fields in Jamaica, Guyana, Barbados and Trinidad (British West Indies), but also in the copper mines of Northern Rhodesia in 1935 and again in 1940. There were general strikes in Mombasa and Dar es Salaam in 1939, a railway workers strike in the Gold Coast and many other places during this period. One can read in the archives of the Colonial Office how shocked and embarrassed senior officials were by these events. The Copperbelt strikes jumped from mine to mine, with the participation of town dwellers, including women, beyond the miners themselves. The strikes entailed mass demonstrations and led to considerable police violence, resulting in deaths among the strikers.[19]

The first Copperbelt strike solidified the desire of the administration to prevent detribalization. But in London, the strike wave, embracing the West Indies as well as parts of Africa, was a question of Empire. A series of investigating commissions began work, and the Colonial Office asked the territorial administrations to think about creating labour departments. The Colonial Office struggled to understand the situation within the terms of their colonial policy. The model of tribal society gave them little indication what to do. The strikes brought to their minds another set of images, associated with the working classes and underclasses of European cities.

The secretary of state for the colonies hoped to redefine the problem. He used the anxiety within the government to argue for making a gesture, which he saw as opening the door to a more vigorous colonial policy. The central concept he invoked was 'development', a word sometimes used to describe investment in the colonies intended to produce a return to British interests, but now linked to the word 'welfare'. The new law the Colonial Office proposed would become the Colonial Development and Welfare Act of 1940. What was new in this act was the use of the metropolitan government's own budget – the taxes collected from British citizens – for projects not intended to produce profits, for municipal water supplies, for building schools and for providing sub-market lodging to workers. The Colonial Office was breaking with the old colonial doctrine – the rule in France as well – which held that no colony should be a drain on the metropolitan budget, that each should pay its own bills. Now the Colonial Office was arguing that social improvements should raise productivity in the long term, but the development process should proceed without expectation of direct return. A top official wrote in private that the argument for long-term economic benefits was intended to please the Treasury, but that, 'I feel, however, that so far as the Colonial Office is concerned our real aim should be the more general one of turning the African into a happier, healthier more prosperous individual in which case all the other subsidiary objects will automatically be attained'. The colonial secretary added, 'if we are not now going to do something fairly good for the colonial empire, and something which helps them to get proper social services, we shall deserve to lose the colonies and it will only be a matter of time before we get what we deserve'.[20]

The secret paternalists of the Colonial Office obtained their law in 1940, under the shadow of general strikes and riots. In reality, they had to wait until the end of the war for the disbursement of useful quantities of funds, but the underlying principles of the development era were in place from then on. During the war, each colony received orders from London to start planning for a concerted development effort. Planning was of fundamental importance to the Colonial Office for two reasons: first, given the spirit of rationalism and painful recent experience, the anarchy of the market was insufficient to guarantee that the standard of living in colonies would actually progress; and second, the state's role in planning was vital to distinguish the government's intentions from the possible interpretation of development as heightened exploitation of the colonies. What was less clear was the knowledge-base on which planning was to rest. The early plans came from officials in the colonies who were, to all intents and purposes, generalists. The Colonial Office itself had some economic talent, such as Sydney Caine, who had graduated from the London School of Economics, but by training and instincts its orientation was toward laissez-faire economics. During the war, it had created a Colonial Economic Advisory Committee, which called upon a range of British economists, a few of whom, such as W. A. Lewis, had begun to think seriously about the particular conditions of underdeveloped economies (see below).[21]

The French parallel to the Colonial Development and Welfare Act came after the war, in the form of the Fonds d'Investissement et de Développement Économique et Social (FIDES – Economic and Social Development Investment Funds), enacted in 1946. Strikes and urban riots in French Africa did not yet have an amplitude comparable to the experience of the British Empire, but the development idea was a response to the uncertainties of the imperial conjuncture in a somewhat different sense. After the failure of the Sarraut plan to garner support, the Popular Front proposed its plan, which also never received funding. Vichy too had its plan, but it was pure fantasy – a call for a thorough remaking of colonial economies, put forward at the very time when

French West Africa was blockaded and the economy in a shambles. The reality of the political economy of Vichy was sordid and not very new: an escalation in the use of forced labour, with not much output to show for it.[22]

At the Brazzaville Conference of 1944, French colonial officials talked at length about the need to turn a new page, to reformulate the principles of the French Empire. There was high-minded talk of building an economy *au service de l'homme* (at the service of man), of making the goal *l'amélioration du sort de l'indigène* (improving the lot of the native) and of *une économie dirigée et planifiée* (a managed and planned economy), but even the officials present with the most experience of economic affairs did not get specific about how an economy was to be directed.[23] The conference discussed the need to simultaneously improve the French economy and raise the standard of living of colonial peoples, but the ideas that emerged were prudent, timid even: the texts of debates reveal that officials thought of Africans as peasants to the depths of their souls who must remain that way, freed of the abuses of forced labour and excessive taxation to produce more effectively within the frameworks of their traditional societies. Any support for industrialization would be 'prudent'. Even the plan to improve infrastructure was justified on the grounds that it would reduce the need for manual labour, notably in transport, and hence the size of the working class. Forced labour was severely criticized, but officials were so fixated on the idea Africans would not work for wages (after a half-century of colonial tutelage) that they feared any programme of improving public works would fail without it. They gave themselves another five years to phase out forced labour.[24]

The conference was still under the influence of men whose expertise was above all in claiming to know 'the native'.[25] The idea of an Africa that was very African, very peasant and very traditional, still resonated strongly among senior officials, and this idea was a severe constraint on their imagination, even when they self-consciously sought to articulate a colonial policy they could regard as progressive.[26] Some officials argued that because the African was necessarily a peasant, the government had to act directly to transform him; others agreed that the African was necessarily a peasant, but concluded the government should therefore leave him alone, in his own milieu, waiting for a gentle social evolution.[27] From such positions, it was hard to think through what a strategy of development would look like.

Two processes helped the administration get out of its malaise. First, the political reforms the government initiated with the goal of reinforcing the unity of the French Empire – giving people in colonial territories a small number of representatives in the Paris legislature – led to electoral campaigns and the election of African deputies, including Léopold Senghor and Félix Houphouët-Boigny. Forced labour quickly proved unable to tolerate the light of an African electoral campaign and a parliamentary debate: the African presence changed the political dynamics. Second came the workers' presence. The general strike in Senegal in January–February 1946 signalled that the idea proletarianization could be avoided was impossible. A working class already existed and it was capable of acting. Officials, in the midst of the strike, realized they could only regain control and authority if they figured out a way of managing the presence of such a class and if they could mount a programme of development that provided liveable conditions in African cities.[28]

Whatever the notions of progress of some officials in Paris and London, FIDES and the Development and Welfare Act followed upon social movements initiated by Africans and represented an attempt to seize the initiative. The new approach signalled that the imperialism of the post-war era would be an imperialism of knowledge and planning, as well as of capital.

It is necessary to pause for a moment to look at the sociology implicit in official developmental thinking between 1946 and 1950, and at how officials lost control of the implications of that sociology. In the debates at Brazzaville, the sociology of Africa was clear enough: the population was divided into two categories: peasants and *évolués* (evolved). The category of wage worker appeared only insofar as officials asserted the absence of Africans within it. It was this sociological conception that proved useless after the strike of 1946 and the social movements that followed. From then on, two sociological visions were in competition. The first was an industrial sociology advocated by the Inspection du Travail, whose influence was increased by the resolution of the Senegalese strike of 1946. Inspectors were trained at both the École Coloniale Supérieure and the ministry of labour, the latter the source of their special expertise. They knew the techniques for defining the labour problem and regulating labour issues within such a framework: the most important part of their training was in the experience of European bureaucracies in handling social and economic problems as they arose, and the notion that European practices could be applied generally. In order to bring the 1946 strike to a close, the labour inspector, sent in haste to Dakar, used established formulas as a basis for negotiation: a scale of wages with six levels plus an off-scale (*hors catégorie*), an exact copy of the system recently implemented in France.

The essential task of the labour inspectors after 1946 was to construct a working class distinguished from other social categories and differentiated internally. The inspectors were happy to see Africans join unions and for unions to negotiate with employers' organizations. For them, the particularity of African cultures had no interest. The inspectors regretted the lack of skill in the workforce and the absence of experience with the world of work, and they wanted the workforce to become stable, skilled, and accustomed to the rhythms of industrial work. One can read in the annual reports and correspondence of the inspectors the hope that if one pretended an African worker was just like any other worker, he would become one.[29]

But if one reads the reports of civil servants in the economic sections of the ministry of overseas France, one finds another sort of discourse: one about Africans outside the world of wage labour. The cultivation methods of Africans are described as *nomadisme agricole* (nomadic cultivation). Officials complain about the rigidity of land tenure systems and the passivity of cultivators. In a conference about economic plans, officials insisted one had to teach African farmers everything. A governor spoke of the archaisms of rural populations, of their resistance to change. What is surprising in these reports from around 1950 is that another part of the administration was congratulating itself on the large increase in cocoa and coffee production in the Ivory Coast. The local administration knew African producers – farmers employing wage labour and tenant farmers to grow export crops – were responsible for this economic success.[30] This inconsistency in forms of knowledge was at the core of officials' early frustration with how their development project was going: officials with local knowledge could see evidence of adaptability and expanded output on the part of African cultivators, but officials in Paris were thinking of an agricultural revolution that was falling short, given the limits of new resources, shortages of skilled labour, and the sheer vastness of the domain they thought had to be radically transformed.[31]

So it was in British Africa as well. Labour officers, a bit ahead of their French homologues, deployed a sociology of work based on the idea of a working class distinguished from the backward population of the bush, benefiting from decreased turnover (stabilization), training, union organization, and living with their families in towns, where a new generation would be born, well fed and watched over by doctors and teachers, and where they would be better able to adapt to the conditions of urban capitalism. One sees in their texts the same prejudices about the capacity of rural communities to improve their farming techniques, the same view of lack of ambition. The head of the economic bureau of the Colonial Office put it this way:

> Broadly, there can be little doubt that the social structure throughout most of our African territories acts as a pretty heavy brake on change ... African systems of land tenure and the cultural routines associated with them, if maintained to the full in their traditional form, would effectively prevent any rapid technical change, possibly any change at all.[32]

As in France, thinking within the administration was compartmentalized: the experts in economic planning ignored the evidence of increased cocoa production from smallholders in Nigeria and the small-scale coffee production of Tanganyika. The colonial secretary instead called for a British-led agricultural revolution in Africa.[33] Prejudices of this sort had serious consequences on the ground: programmes to promote soil conservation among supposedly ignorant cultivators in Kenya, Tanganyika and Rhodesia, brutally implemented by British agronomists, led to rebellions in these areas.

Here we have a central problem in colonial-style developmentalism. The concept came from a vision of the future, an ethnocentric notion to be sure, but one that was being opened to Africans who wished to reform themselves. Development would lead directly from the backwardness of the African past to a modern future. What was missing in official development discourse in the 1940s was the present, with its dynamism and possibilities as well as constraints.

Yet developmentalist thinking in colonial administrations existed in an unacknowledged dialogue, particularly with the leaders of African social movements. The impetus behind the new departures in industrial sociology and economic planning followed upon the wave of general strikes and urban confrontations, and once European bureaucracies had articulated their new, forward-looking vision, African trade unionists seized this language to make their own claims. The idea of the universal worker represented a useful basis for African union leaders to claim wages and benefits equal to those of other workers. That is exactly what happened in French West Africa: the labour movement's slogan became *à travail égal, salaire égal* (equal pay for equal work). Inspectors could not deny the logical validity of such claims within their own understanding of the place of the worker within the French system; they could simply try to soften them, to limit their effects. Labour unions and the Labour Inspectorate quickly agreed on the importance of writing a labour code, the former to guarantee certain rights to their members – the 40-hour week, the right to strike – and the latter to ensure a rational treatment of labour questions, to have clear rules for regulating conflicts and clear definitions of those benefits workers were entitled to and what they could negotiate for.

Employers – well aware of the danger of raising labour costs – were ideologically trapped, linked to the state and its imperial ideology to assure its presence in Africa, dependent on the Labour Inspectorate to settle disputes, and thus unable to avoid the implications of a universalistic sociology of work, shared by the inspectorate and the unions. The employers succeeded in slowing down the drive to write a labour code – it passed the French legislature in 1952 – but it could not soften its principles. One component of workers' demands since 1946 had been for family allowances for all wage workers without distinction of origins – a right obtained by French workers in 1932. Labour inspectors accepted the logic of this demand, for they wanted to encourage the reproduction of a working class within an urban and industrial milieu, not in rural villages. In 1950, African civil servants won equal family allocations to those of European French civil servants, and in 1956 a system of family allocations for the private sector was instituted, based on the structure of the metropolitan system, with rates which, while not equal to those in metropolitan France, constituted an important addition to the wage packets of workers with children. This system was implemented after much discussion within colonial institutions and serious mobilizations by the West African labour movement.[34]

British officials tried to avoid the question of family allowances for fear of exactly the kind of politicized debate that occurred in French Africa. But the British administration could not ignore the underlying issue, for it too wanted to ensure the reproduction of a working class far away from the backwardness of rural Africa. The doctrine of family wages was a response to this imperative and to the demands of workers in places like Kenya. The calculation of minimum wages was supposed to take into account family needs. Efforts were made to encourage a bigger spread in wage hierarchies, so that more senior workers would earn enough to support a family without recourse to cultivation by family members.[35] The reality was always more complicated than this, for men and women did not necessarily want to separate themselves from rural Africa even if in some instances they had the means to do so.[36]

In any case, between 1945 and 1960, wages in most colonies increased and material conditions for wage workers improved. The labour movement had made use of a developmentalist ideology to turn a discourse about the necessity of organizing work along European models into a series of demands for improving their living conditions.

African political leaders in the 1950s would also turn developmentalist discourse in a direction favourable to them. For development to be in the interest of African people, they would argue, it was necessary for an African government to make the decisions about what development policy should be, for if not there was a danger development would simply mean an escalation of exploitation. The colonial government's conception of development as a technical problem, best implemented by people with the requisite knowledge, was thus answered by a politicizing argument: development as a question of choices to be made by those with the most at stake.[37]

This kind of politics opened up a door in the imaginations of colonial officials, a door through which they would in the end pass. When it became clear that the post-war efforts to find a new basis for the legitimacy of colonial regimes would not end conflict, when the economic results expected from development initiatives proved unrealistic and when the interventions of colonial states into social questions produced more conflict than stability, the universalistic reasoning of development thinking permitted the leaders of empire to envisage another sort of future.

Development and modernization were at the same time a programme to be directed by a government and a meta-historical tendency affecting the entire world. African social and political movements had indicated, very clearly, their continued interest in economic and social progress. It was slowly becoming possible for colonial officials to convince themselves Africa could become independent and that the development project would continue. What has just been described does not constitute an explanation of decolonization, but rather an explanation of how decolonization could become imaginable within European bureaucracies. With the dominant idea of the 1920s and 1930s of Africa as an ethnographic repository, as the domain of tradition, decolonization was not imaginable. Within developmentalist thinking in the 1950s, such a change remained difficult but imaginable.[38]

The other side of official developmentalism was its rigid vision of untransformed African society. Here one sees much continuity from the ethnographic era, but with one major change. Before the war, the backwardness of African populations was a given, but with the new developmentalist spirit, backwardness became an act of defiance, a sign of the ill will of Africans who refused the opportunity now being offered. African primitivism became an explanation for why development plans did not work out as well as anticipated. One can read in official archives a bitterness towards those who seemed to be refusing the developmentalist framework, even where – as in the case of major strikes – officials were willing to treat other forms of collective action as falling within acceptable frameworks of confrontation and negotiation.

The worst example of such a reaction came with the British response to the rebellion among the Kikuyu of Kenya, beginning in 1952, that they named Mau Mau. If retrospective explanations of this rebellion gave prominence to the rapid economic growth of the late 1940s – squatters chased from land by white settlers seeking to exploit it more systematically, African landowners not acknowledging obligations to take in people from their village returning from the settler farms, peasants victimized by mismanaged agricultural reform efforts – the government and the press at the time treated the rebellion as a resurgence of African primitivism. There was indeed an anti-modern dimension to the rebel movement, but one situated more in a conflict-ridden present than in a purely Kikuyu past. The rebellion began at a time when the British government was congratulating itself for removing racial restrictions on coffee cultivation and for several reform projects: it thought it had taken the road towards progress. Its reaction to the rebellion was furious: brutal suppression, the use of concentration camps to re-educate Kikuyu. The irrationality, the excess of this reaction revealed the fragility of the ideology of modernization. The other face of colonial administrations' openness to change was this inscription of atavism and wilful backwardness on Africans who did not choose the right road.[39]

Alongside this image of the anti-modern Africa we find another basic aspect of decolonization: the refusal of responsibility. The British governor of Eastern Nigeria during the period (1955) when African political leaders were taking charge of budgetary matters as part of the programme of self-government reacted this way to cost overruns and financial scandals in the new government: 'Inevitably the people are going to be disillusioned, but it is better that they should be disillusioned as a result of the failure of their own people than that they should be disillusioned as a result of our actions'.[40] One finds more such evidence in the archives: official awareness that decolonization had not been well planned, a calculation that the cost of development in colonies would exceed the economic returns, a fear that the failures of development and the conflicts to which it led would get out of control, all this in the shadow of Algeria and Suez.[41]

The British and French willingness to devolve power to African leaders in their sub-Saharan territories – decisions made for many of the major colonies by 1956–57 – thus reflected the hope that economic and social evolution had already created irreversible ties to Western states and a desire to ensure it would be Africans who had to assume the burden and responsibility for the failures, disappointments and conflict that emerged.[42] In economic and social terms, the results of the developmental colonialism of the 1950s were not purely negative. This was a period of rapid export growth, of improvement in the wages paid to workers in key sectors, of rapid expansions of schools, extension of the road network and sharp drops in infant mortality. But the contradictions were evident as well, above all the impossibility of totally transforming social institutions, the disarticulation of African economies, and the enormous disparities of opportunity for different people within the African continent. It was the project of economic development that was especially fragile, with its prefabricated vision of a modern Africa. If one begins at the end, one never arrives.

The modernization of the social sciences

Now we turn to the question of the social sciences. It is important to be clear about the dates. The break in colonial economic policy comes with the development plans: 1940 in the case of the United Kingdom and 1946 for France. The new labour policy – the attempt to reduce reliance on the back-and-forth movement of migratory workers and create a 'stabilized' working class living with families in workplace and cities – dates to 1946 in French Africa and 1945–47 in British Africa. In this era, one finds a variety of projects in the agricultural domain – from the teaching of new techniques, to programmes to provide credit, to the formation of farmer co-operatives – plus a number of grandiose projects such as the ground nut scheme in Tanganyika or the cotton and later rice schemes of the Niger Office. That many such projects failed and that the real dynamism in agriculture remained with small-scale farmers is another question: this was a period of state activism.

It was thus very soon after the war that one sees a push by the French and British states towards programmes of modernization. The theory of modernization in the academic milieu is an affair of the 1950s.[43] A curious aspect of this period is that the imperialism of knowledge was being pressed even before the knowledge was in place. There were, in the 1940s, no experts in development economics, and orthodox economists were more often than not opposed to interventionist policies in colonies, even in an era of Keynesian policy at home. The British policy of pushing for family wages, for example, was implemented against the advice of economists in the Colonial Office, and the most forward-looking economist of the 1940s, W. A. Lewis, resigned from one of the Colonial Office's wartime advisory committees because the orthodox considered his ideas 'political' rather than 'economic'.[44]

As far as fieldwork-based studies of the crucial sites of change in Africa are concerned, one has to wait for 1950 to find the birth of urban anthropology: there is a ten-year gap between the pioneering work of Godfrey Wilson and the development of an anthropological school that studied the themes he pointed to.[45] That is why I am insisting the direction of influence went from the bureaucracy to the academy and not the other way around. An implicit theory of modernization grew up in colonial administrations before a systematic version was spelled out by social scientists, and the key loci for articulating this implicit theory were commissions of inquiry into strikes and other events in Africa and reports by labour inspectors.

Administrations needed expert advice. They could call on agronomists or public-health specialists with some experience in the tropics, and for social engineers they had to turn to people like labour inspectors who had practical experience in Europe. Among economists, it took time for the profession to develop the expertise to engage in planning. Still, theoretical innovations beginning in the early 1950s would come to have great influence on framing knowledge of change in Africa. I will emphasize two: a branch of modernization theory that focused on industrialization as the key arena of transformation and development economics. I will also look at anthropology in the 1950s to show how on-the-ground research could complicate the picture being drawn by the advocates of modernization.

First, industrialization. I will take as an indicative text the book *Industrialization and Labor: Social Aspects of Economic Development*, by the influential American sociologist Wilbert Moore, published in 1951. Industrialism, to Moore, meant something more than the organization of factories. It was a mode of life. Moore thought industrialization was transforming the entire world and that it demanded a response from every society, including those he labelled primitive. Industrialization demanded a rationalist perspective, sensibility to universal logic, the will to adapt to labour markets and systems – necessarily hierarchical – of discipline in factories. For Moore, the transition to industrialism was necessary but not easy; he acknowledged some people would fail to make the transition. 'The world is not peopled by economic men', he wrote. Adaptation depended on local traditions, and on the means by which communities were integrated into industrialization. Primitive societies, however, were not homogeneous, and cracks in their solidarity – the tension between young men and their elders, for example – gave rise to motivations for a part of the society to take an interest in industrial life. Industrialism for Moore was a package of necessary phenomena which he did not wish to take apart: rationalism and hierarchy would always be part of the industrial world. Resistance would be futile, even if adaptation would yield inequality. Those who did not adapt would be poor and marginalized.[46]

Others went further than Moore. Clark Kerr, considered the doyen of the field of industrial sociology in the United States, wrote in 1960: '[W]hether a society has been matrilineal or patrilineal, whether based on family or tribal ownership of land, whether responding to the Protestant ethic or the Bantu ethic, or whether it goes through a prior commercial revolution or not, it ends up following the logic of industrialism'.[47] Africa, in such a vision, stood as the epitome of traditional and backward: it represented the clay to be made into industrial society.

This universalizing, homogenizing argument was at the core of modernization theory. At their most ambitious, modernization theorists posited that the most important aspects of social life varied together. Industrialism was not limited to industry: it was a way of life. Such theories owed much to the work of American sociologist Talcott Parsons, who developed the notion of pattern variables, whose covariance charged the process of modernization. Modernization proceeded along several key axes:

- from a subsistence economy to an economy of exchange and industrialization;
- from rural to urban society;
- from a political system of subjects to one of citizens;
- from ascriptive notions of status to notions of status based on achievement;
- from extended to nuclear kinship units;
- from religious ideologies to secular ideologies;
- from diffuse, personalized relationships to contractual ones.[48]

What was strong about such theorization was precisely what was vulnerable: the association of the variables with each other, the notion that modernity constituted a package.

These arguments were consistent with the structural-functional analysis then in vogue in both sociology and anthropology. But instead of treating a unit, like the tribe, as the universe in question, modernization theory addressed a global system whose structures adapted to perform the functions demanded by the integrity of the system.

Such theories may appear to us as arrogant, teleological, and ethno-centric. A stereotype of the West took the place of dynamic analyses of actual on-going societies. As Kerr wrote, 'the best place to start is with a view of the end result; for industrialism is a great magnet which is drawing all human life to it and ordering the orientation of this life'.[49]

In W. W. Rostow's *The Stages of Economic Growth*,[50] the idea of a passage from tradition to modernity is tied to an argument that Western govern-ments were obliged to promote and sustain such a process, hence the word 'manifesto' and the opposition between the communist version of modernization and one based on capitalism and electoral democracy. It was the fall of colonial empires that opened underdeveloped countries to this competition between systems, each with its version of modernization.

But in 1951 as in 1960, it is important to point to another aspect of such theories: their refusal of racism, their conception of the pos-sibility of a modernization open to all. For scholars, as much as for bureaucrats, the period after 1945 was one of upheaval. Old certitudes about the order of the world no longer worked. For sociologists such as Moore or Kerr, here was a new domain of inquiry. But what they did with this domain was a kind of intellectual pacification. They wished to incorporate it into what was already known, to tell formerly colonized peoples that they were welcome to the modern world but had to accept it as it was. Neither Moore nor Kerr had done fieldwork in Africa or other colonial territories, but they relied on reports from the front lines of colonial modernization, from labour inspectors, the International Labour Bureau, and – although the work was equivocal on the questions at hand – on the studies of anthropologists such as Audrey Richards. However frail their own knowledge-base, they did not hesitate to tell the people of the decolonizing world what their future was.

There is something very American about all this, a disdain for all the old obstacles to progress, from tradition to racism, and an absence of reflection upon the particularity of this universalistic conception of change.[51] This tendency reached its apogee with Kerr and Rostow. Applied to Africa, the romance of modernization reflected a notion that America's restless urge to remake itself would rub off on a continent held by Europeans in bondage and just beginning to open itself to participation in an interactive world in which the United States would play a shaping role. At a meeting of American elites from business, gov-ernment, philanthropic foundations and academia, coming together in 1958 to discuss the US's relation with Africa, the anthropologist Walter

Goldschmidt referred to 'the slumbering giant of Africa' that was just awakening. 'America has a moral interest in Africa', he insisted, an interest reflecting the importance of people of African descent to the population, but also 'an interest in the kind of place that Africa will become'. Political scientist Rupert Emerson applauded the 'emergence of modern, forward-looking nationalist movements'. Still, Africa was just beginning to come out of its 'tribal' nature: it was 'developing', 'emergent', 'new'. The assembly's report applauded 'self-determination' and stressed the positive role the US could play in the development of African economies and the advancement of education.[52]

But this desire to look towards a new world is also evident in the writings of French labour inspectors and British labour officers, with the difference that Kerr wrote with perfect certitude while colonial officials in the 1940s and 1950s saw the world through anxious eyes. And over time, the fact that branches of the social sciences, such as sociology and political science, had strong traditions of empirical research meant the simplistic nature of these theories would be criticized within the scholarly tradition that gave birth to them.[53]

Let me turn now to theoretical work that was crucial to the founding of the sub-field of development economics. The most important point is the departure from orthodox economics, with its vision of a single universe of transactions. Development economics accepted the idea of such a universe, but insisted that it took work to get into it. There were certain prerequisites for a functioning market economy. The underdeveloped economy would remain a special case until it reached a certain level or acquired certain capabilities so that normal rules would then apply. A foundational article of development economics was Paul Rosenstein-Rodin's 1943 study on eastern Europe. He set out a theory known since as the 'big push': it was necessary to concentrate resources, more than a capital market would allocate, to a backward region in order for it to be able to come out of its structural constraints. A version of this theory was part of the first development plans: a push had to come from outside to provide the infrastructure and organize the human resources that would, in time, enable an underdeveloped economy to respond adequately to demand for its products.[54]

The elaboration of a rigorous theory of transition came later, above all with the publication in 1954 of an article by W. A. Lewis, 'Economic Development with unlimited supplies of labor'.[55] Lewis first defined a backward sector as one in which the marginal product of labour was zero or negative, that is where the physical or institutional capacity of the sector was such that one could remove a labourer without any

reduction in production. Then he posited a capitalist sector. To transfer labour power from the backward to the advanced sector it was not
necessary to pay the worker the marginal product of his labour, as in
orthodox theory, but only a wage sufficient for his subsistence plus a
small supplement to make displacement worth his bother. Ordinarily,
one would expect that as the capitalist sector began to grow, wages
would rise with demand. But not in these circumstances. Wages could
be kept at the same level until the entire labour surplus of the backward
sector had been absorbed into the capitalist sector. At that point, the
economy becomes normal and wages follow the marginal product of
labour. This was a dualist theory, the basic premise of which was a neat
division between sectors. Progress consisted of eliminating the excess
of labour power in the backward sector by concentrating resources in
increasing production in the capitalist sector.

What is striking here is the parallel between an economic argument
starting with the notion of a marginal product of labour as zero and a
sociological argument that accepts the notion of a society as primitive.
Lewis always distinguished capitalist dynamism from colonial plantation economies, which he regarded as another form of backwardness.
For him, the reinvestment of profits in the capitalist sector drove the
transfer of labour from somewhere it was under-utilized to somewhere it
fostered economic dynamism. The dynamic sector was not specifically
urban. It was not 'traditional' and it was not 'European', but it was a
zone of economic modernization within a once colonized society. Lewis
was careful to distinguish appropriate policies for areas where labour
was not in surplus, and he saw most of Africa in this light. There, the
development drive should focus within the rural economy, but the
thrust of his argument was the same: bringing new techniques and
resources to a sector where it would do the most good: 'what we have
to do for agriculture in Africa is mainly to fertilize African farming; to
bring it knowledge, tools, water, better varieties, and better organization; and to seek the strategic points where these new ideas may most
easily be absorbed'. This would cost money, and the money to get Africa
over the hump where it could participate fully in the normal operations
of a market economy would have to come from outside – from the
United Kingdom first of all.[56] Lewis's work had much influence in shaping the sub-discipline of development economics, and it became a basic
tool of economic planners; his career would be crowned by the Nobel
Prize in economic science in 1979. The theory was especially interesting because of the man who devised it. Lewis was a black man born in
the British West Indies. He was a student in London in the 1930s when

he volunteered his services to anti-colonialist organizations and wrote a series of pamphlets denouncing the planter class of the West Indies and advocating education and political liberation in the colonies.[57] He advocated the reduction of global inequality and the incorporation of excluded peoples into the world economy. He did not romanticize traditional cultures: he thought they exhibited a 'low cultural level' and that their literary or musical accomplishments were of interest only to anthropologists. However, he thought people coming from such a milieu should have their place in the modern world.[58]

Lewis, while embarking on a distinguished academic career – the first black man to hold a professorship at Manchester University – brought his expertise to the situation faced by impoverished colonial regions in British Africa and the West Indies. He advised the Colonial Office during the war and – despite his severe criticism of its cautious policies – was called upon repeatedly in the post-war years to offer advice. But he offered his knowledge and reputation to the first African leaders who were edging towards power. Shortly before the publication of his famous article, he worked for the government of Kwame Nkrumah, the leader of the Gold Coast in its phase of self-government en route to total independence, and he produced for it a plan for the industrialization of the country. He later returned to Ghana after its independence in 1957 as an economic advisor.[59] Lewis was a theorist of the end of empire, an advocate of eliminating structures that constrained colonized people's future and of freeing them to enter a modern economy.

If one looks at development as the imposition of Western categories on other peoples, what does it mean when the supposed universalism of the West is not exactly the invention of Europeans? Are Lewis's theories insufficiently exotic or insufficiently revolutionary to be regarded as more than derivative of Western social science, even if Lewis has as good a claim as anyone to be the inventor of the branch of science in question?[60] Or should one regard the science to which he contributed as a creation of neither the West nor of the 'South', but as part of a historical process that entailed the redefinition of the categories of political life?

Development economics never was the orthodoxy that is now much criticized. Even before the consolidation of a new sort of expertise under the influence of Lewis and others, a different argument came to the fore from Latin American economists, above all from Raúl Prebisch, an Argentinian, and his colleagues at the Economic Commission for Latin America. At the end of the 1940s they began to argue that growing exchange between developed and underdeveloped countries was not in the interest of both parties. Unequal exchange, they insisted, enriched the rich and impoverished the poor unless the national economies of underdeveloped states followed their own routes.[61] Meanwhile, economists from North America argued over whether 'balanced growth' or 'unbalanced growth' should be the goal of development planning, whether certain sectors should be promoted over others. Over the years, these debates gave rise to discussions about the possibility of 'durable' or 'sustainable' development.[62] In France, some influential economists of the 1950s linked to social-Catholic movements, notably Louis-Joseph Lebret, advocated a 'humanist' economics and influenced the first planners in several African states at the time of independence. Other economists took a more social, more demographic approach to the development question.[63] Meanwhile, economists born in 'underdeveloped' countries, like Lewis, took different positions in such debates, some favouring a pure market-driven approach, others being extremely critical of the current economic system.[64]

If Lewis's writings reveal the different aspirations behind the ideals of economic and social modernization, they are not at all ambivalent about the contents of modernization: education, improved productivity, fuller integration into world markets, industrialization, higher incomes, more investment. But the complexities and ambiguities of modernization were concerns to influential intellectuals and scholars in the 1950s. Let me turn to two other interventions, one coming from fieldwork-based social science, the other from anti-colonial intellectuals, African and European. The texts in question come from the same general period as the writings of Moore and Lewis. The first comes from a colloquium sponsored by the United Nations Education, Science, and Cultural Organization (UNESCO) and held in Abidjan in 1954 and published two years later as *Social Implications of Industrialization and Urbanization in Africa South of the Sahara*.[65] The anthropologists and sociologists who were present, including such leading researchers of the 1950s as Georges Balandier, Paul Mercier, Aidan Southall, J. Cyde Mitchell, A. L. Epstein and E. Hellmann, accepted the reality of a new Africa: urban, in the process of industrializing. But the main themes of their work were the instability of employment of unskilled migrants, poverty, slums and shanty towns, the vulnerability of women. The ideal-type family of the labour inspectors – wage-earning man, woman at home – did not correspond to the urbanization they were observing.

The Africanist and anti-imperialist journal *Présence Africaine* published a special edition in 1952 on the labour question, and it shared several elements of the critical vision of the sociologists: a focus on the poverty of Africa, on the insecurity of workers, but also on the hopes for equality and improvement of living conditions on the part of workers and their organizations. The founder of the journal, Alioune Diop, also tried to place the European model for workplace change in a context: the European obsession with exactitude, with the control of time and the control of people. This was, in short, a colonizing vision. He was seeking a critical engagement with European social thought, not an acceptance or a rejection. He was at the same time seeking a basis for improving the living conditions of workers and to examine critically the social basis of urban life. He advocated the 'co-responsibility' of Africans and Europeans in the management of urban affairs.[66]

Both publications contained contributions from the French anthropologist Georges Balandier, who identified with both the scientific work of UNESCO and the political project of *Présence Africaine*.[67] Balandier, with Paul Mercier, was the pioneer of Francophone urban anthropology, as A. L. Epstein, Max Gluckman, and Clyde Mitchell were for the Anglophone equivalent.[68] We should note the dates. Balandier went to Dakar in the late 1940s to conduct a more or less classic study of Lébou fishermen. There, he discovered what he later described as an Africa different from that of his *maîtres ès sociétés primitives* (masters of primitive societies). He was particularly eager to get away from the *intemporalité des peuples interrogés* (timelessness of peoples in question) in the anthropology of his day, including that of the highly influential Marcel Griaule. Working within the bounds of the ethnic group, as with Griaule's Dogon, and with the notion of traditional religion or philosophy, missed the dynamic situation Balandier saw before him.[69] It was first the intellectuals of Dakar who captured his imagination, then the slum dwellers of Brazzaville. In 1951, before the publication of his Brazzaville research, he wrote a remarkable article, 'La situation coloniale: approche théorique'. The lived reality for Africans was the colonial situation a political system as particular as that of any African 'tribe'. A central organizing principle of the system was racism.[70]

What is curious is the faintness of the echoes this intervention had in the anthropological literature in subsequent years. Even though colonialism was a central issue of French politics in the years after 1951, it was not a central theme of academic study. Even Balandier changed direction, making urbanization the focus of his research throughout the 1950s.[71] He cited Wilbert Moore in his own writing, but his focus was on precisely what the grand theories of modernization preferred not to examine seriously: the precariousness of urban life, the enormous difficulties of adaptation, and the continued ties between rural and urban milieux.[72] This view of profound discontinuity and devastating social costs led him to emphasize the distinct problems of the 'third world' rather than the direct path from tradition to modernity that moderniza-tion theorists envisaged.[73]

Anglophone urban anthropology brought out the same themes, with a somewhat more optimistic view of them. The timing of urban research was similar: early research concentrated on the towns of the Copperbelt, with the most important publications emerging after 1957 and extending into the 1960s. In other words, both French and British anthropologists were studying the consequences of the modernizing imperialism put in place in the late 1940s and of the way Africans built their social worlds in complex dialogue with that vision. Epstein and Mitchell used the same word as Balandier did in 1951 – 'situation' – but they, like Gluckman who had used it earlier still, were more concerned with specific local situations than with the notion of a total situation that Balandier's treatment of colonialism entailed.[74] The Copperbelt anthropologists argued that the African could in certain circumstances be a townsman, in others a tribesman, moving between the two with difficulty, perhaps, but able nonetheless to find ways of organizing social life in these different situations. Urbanism and industrialism were not displacing other sorts of life: it was not a question of a movement from tradition to modernity. Uncertainty about the direction of change and the precariousness of living conditions along the way was much greater than modernization theory allowed, but with this complexity came the possibility of creating new forms of social and cultural life in African cities.[75]

Conclusion

Now, we can re-read these studies of modernization – complex and simplistic versions – with another sensibility. At the time, the language of colonial officials, trade union leaders, political activists, and scholars expressed a new sense of possibility for the people of the colonized world, even if the end point and the process were ambiguous. For social scientists, the kinds of social norms that had been the focus of debate within Europe over the past several decades – the organization of social life to give the large majority of people a chance to attain a socially acceptable standard of living, to obtain education, to form families, to survive outside the web of familial and village structures – could now be made available to people of all origins. And by the 1950s, the most important of all victories seemed to be within reach of the populations of French and British colonies: the chance to manage their own political affairs. For many city dwellers, especially wage workers and their families, the stake in modernizing social organization was quite concrete: the possibility of living as a family near a place of work, schools for children, health services, and the prospect of a pension on retirement.

By 1955 or 1960 there was much evidence to indicate that the trend was towards making such aspirations feasible for at least a portion of the African population. There seemed to be a world consensus that it was desirable for all people, whether once subordinated to the exigencies of colonization or not, to have access to minimal services and maximal opportunities. Now, at the beginning of a new century, it seems as if what looked in the 1950s and 1960s like a beginning was in fact a high point. For a copper-miner in central Africa, the idea of a salary sufficient for a family to live decently and a pension sufficient for an honourable retirement – once a realistic aspiration – has become a cruel disappointment, as James Ferguson has shown in his remarkable study of that region in the 1990s. The economic crisis of the 1970s and its sequels put an end to the possibility of continual improvement. Inflation has eaten up the pensions and the savings of those who benefited from the wage increases and 'modern' social institutions put in place after the 1950s. The only hope of retired copper-miners has become a return to the soil or petty commerce, now harder to live off than ever. This situation is experienced with disappointment and pain by a generation of workers who once had confidence – as did the scholars who observed them – in the project of reorganizing the colonial labour system, of opening opportunities for schooling, of providing health services.[76]

For scholars today, the question that comes to mind is no longer about what kind of social science an era of decolonization demands, but what kind of social science is needed for an era that people in Africa are experiencing as one of marginalization and despair? The relevance of such a question is not simply the consequence of the fact of poverty. Its importance follows upon a particular historical trajectory, and it is there that the tragedy of contemporary Africa lies. However critical one is of the pretensions of social theory in the era of modernization, it contained within its divergent strands a sense of possibility of a world in which neither race nor dependent political status constrained the imagination. This sense of possibility was fundamental to the aspirations of social and political movements across Africa at and immediately after the moment of independence, and the most observant social scientists at the time understood its importance. Already in the 1950s, alongside a triumphalist vision of 'modernization' spreading around the world, there appeared a more cautious understanding of 'development' as a process that demanded resources and sacrifice, that could cause dislocation and vulnerability as well as give people new options, that did not lead all people in the same direction. Most important, political actors in the decolonizing world – from political elites, to trade unionists, to members of a rural co-operative – could see in the language of development a way of making claims and articulating aspirations, of challenging local patriarchs or national authorities, and of insisting that the benefits of global interaction should come to them. The arrogance of the development idea came not from its assumption that one part of the world had something to offer another, but from the detachment of such a notion from a politics of assertion and transformation, when inequality became static hierarchy. Looking at a moment of possibility in the era of decolonization can serve to remind us of the importance of looking for new openings, in both political and scholarly practice.

Acknowledgement

This chapter was originally published in *Revue d'histoire des sciences humaines* in 2004.

Notes

1. For two examples of rejections of development thinking, see A. Escobar, *Encountering Development: The Making and Unmaking of the Third World*, Princeton, NJ, Princeton University Press, 1995 and W. Sachs, ed., *The Development Dictionary: A Guide to Knowledge as Power*, London, Zed, 1992. Different points of view on the development question are evaluated in F. Cooper and R. Packard, eds, *International Development and the Social Sciences: Essays in the History and Politics of Knowledge*, Berkeley, CA, University of California Press, 1997.
2. For the example of medicine and sanitation, see J. P. Bado, *Médecine coloniale et grandes endémies en Afrique 1900–1960: Lèpre, trypanosomiase humaine et onchocercose*, Paris, Karthala, 1996, and M. Vaughan, *Curing their Ills: Colonial Power and African Illness*, Cambridge, Polity, 1991.
3. The periodization of French and British colonial policy remains a subject of debate. For the sequence of interventionist approaches before the First World War followed by a more conservative approach oriented towards ethnic units, I am following my own work on the history of development (cited above). See A. Phillips, *The Enigma of Colonialism: British Policy in West Africa*, London, Currey, 1989, and A. Conklin, *A Mission to Civilize: The Republican Idea of Empire in France and West Africa, 1895–1930*, Stanford, CA, Stanford University Press, 1998. See also C. Coquery-Vidrovitch, 'La mise en dépendance de l'Afrique Noire: Essai de périodisation, 1800–1970', *Cahiers d'Études Africaines* 16, 1976, pp. 5–58.

4. A. Sarraut, *La mise en valeur de l'Afrique Noire*, Paris, Payot, 1923; S. Constantine, *The Making of British Colonial Development Policy 1914–1940*, London, Frank Cass,1984, pp. 44–56; C. Cotte, 'La politique économique de la France en Afrique Noire (1936–1946)', unpublished doctoral thesis, Université Paris VII, 1981; J. Marseille, *Empire colonial et capitalisme français: Histoire d'un divorce*, Paris, Albin Michel, 1984; C. Coquery-Vidrovitch, D. Hémery and J. Piel, *Pour une histoire du développement*, Paris, l'Harmattan, 1988.

5. Frederick Lugard, a pioneer of colonization in East Africa in the 1890s, achieved lasting recognition as the ruler of northern Nigeria during the next decade, where he pioneered methods of working with indigenous authorities. He later codified his practices as 'indirect rule'. See F. Lugard, *Dual Mandate in Tropical Africa*, London, Blackwood, 1922.

6. M. M. van Beusekom, *Negotiating Development: African Farmers and Colonial Experts at the Office du Niger, 1920–1960*, Portsmouth, NH, Heinemann, 2002.

7. Conklin, *A Mission to Civilize*, 1998.

8. E. E. Evans-Pritchard, *The Nuer, a Description of the Modes of Livelihood and Political Institutions of a Nilotic People*, Oxford, Clarendon, 1940.

9. See also the important re-examination of the Nuer in a deeper historical context by S. Hutchinson, *Nuer Dilemmas: Coping with Money, War, and the State*, Berkeley, CA, University of California Press, 1996, and, on British anthropology generally, the dissertation for the École des Hautes Études en Sciences Sociales by B. de L'Estoile, *L'Afrique comme laboratoire: Expériences réformatrices et révolution anthropologique dans l'empire colonial britannique (1920–1950)*, Paris, Éditions de l'ÉHÉSS, 2004.

10. Malinowski's phrase is cited in G. Stocking, Jr, *After Tylor: British Social Anthropology 1888–1951*, Madison, WI, University of Wisconsin Press, pp 995, 412, which is an excellent starting place for a discussion of the overall issue. For the politicizing of Malinowskian anthropology, see J. Kenyatta, *Facing Mount Kenya: The Tribal Life of the Gikuyu*, London, Secker and Warburg, 1938.

11. H. A. L. Fisher to a meeting at Oxford, 1929, cited in H. Tilley, *Africa as Living Laboratory: Empire, Development and the Problem of Scientific Knowledge, 1870–1950*, Chicago, University of Chicago Press, 2011.

12. L. Hailey, *An African Survey*, London, Oxford University Press, 1938. The second edition, in 1945, was also timid on such issues as the labour question. See Tilley's study of the entire project of which Hailey's survey was a part.

13. On inter-war French ethnography, there is an important literature. See, for example, B. de L'Estoile, 'Science de l'homme et 'domination rationnelle': Savoir ethnologique et politique indigène en Afrique coloniale française', *Revue de Synthèse* 4, nos. 3–4, 2000, pp. 291–323; E. Sibeud, *Une science impériale pour l'Afrique? La construction des savoirs africanistes en France 1878–1930*, Paris, Éditions de l'ÉHÉSS, 2002; A. Conklin, 'The new "ethnology" and "la situation colonial" in inter-war France', *French Politics, Culture and Society* 20, pp. 29–46; C. Blanckaert, *Les politiques de l'anthropologie, discours et pratiques en France (1860–1940)*, Paris, l'Harmattan, 2001. In general, see S. F. Moore, *Anthropology and Africa: Changing Perspectives on a Changing Scene*, Charlottesville, VA, University of Virginia Press, 1994.

14. See, especially, Robert Delavignette's personal explanation of the connections between his native Burgundy, the Sudan, and his administrative and intellectual career: R. Delavignette, *Soudan-Paris-Bourgogne*, Paris, Grasset, 1935.

15. M. J. Davis, ed., *Modern Industry and the African: An Enquiry into the Effect of the Copper Mines of Central Africa upon Native Society and the Work of Christian Missions Made under the Auspices of the Department of Social and Industrial Research of the International Missionary Council*, London, Macmillan, 1933. Davis was a specialist on 'social and industrial research' with the Missionary Council, and his inquiry included a sociologist, an economist, a historian and mission-based educators. They spent July–December 1932 in Africa.

16. A. Richards, *Land, Labour and Diet in Northern Rhodesia: An Economic Study of the Bemba Tribe*, London, Oxford University Press for International African Institute, 1961 [1939].

17. G. Wilson, 'An essay on the economics of detribalization in Northern Rhodesia', *Rhodes-Livingstone Papers*, Livingstone, Rhodes-Livingstone Institute, 1941.

18. R. Brown, 'Passages in the life of a white anthropologist: Max Gluckman in Northern Rhodesia', *Journal of African History* 20, 1979, pp. 525–554; J. Ferguson, *Expectations of Modernity*, Berkeley, CA, University of California Press; W. A. Lewis and M. Gersovitz, eds, *Selected Economic Writings of W. Arthur Lewis*, New York, NY, New York University Press, 1983.

19. This paragraph and those which follow are based on F. Cooper, *Decolonization and African Society: The Labour Question in French and British Africa*, Cambridge, Cambridge University Press, 1996.

20. George Creasy, Minute, 30 November 1939, to 'Draft outline of statement of policy-, and MacDonald, Minute, 14 January 1940, CO 859/19/7475, Public Record Office (PRO), London.

21. On the ideological need to emphasize planning, cf. Ernest Bevin (Foreign Secretary), Memorandum, 4 October 1947, PM/47/139, PREM 8/456, PRO. On the difficulties of the Colonial Office in coming to grips with the problems of economic development during and immediately after the war, see Cooper, *Decolonization*, 1996, pp. 111–124, 202–216. See also J. M. Lee and M. Petter, 'The Colonial Office, war and development policy: Organization and the planning of a metropolitan initiative, 1939–1945, *Commonwealth Papers* 22, London, Maurice Temple Smith, 1982.

22. Even if the Vichy development plan was stillborn, the debate about it was interesting, as the ministry in Vichy called for the unrestrained development of African resources, with no attention to the situation of Africans, whereas the Government General in Dakar warned Vichy that use of manpower was already close to what indigenous communities could tolerate and there was a danger of destroying peasant production altogether. Marseille's argument that the Vichy plan represented a more radical break from the *pacte colonial* than either the Popular Front or the Free French plans is valid only at the level of Vichy's fantasy. In practice, Vichy's development effort did little other than increase the brutality of forced labour. See Marseille, *Empire colonial*, 1984; Cooper, *Decolonization*, 1996, chapter 4.

23. This was a conference of officials, not economists, but those present included the director of economic affairs at the Commissariat des Colonies and the director of public works, both of whom kept the conversation both general and cautious.

24. Transcripts of Brazzaville debates on questions linked to development may be found, in Séance des 2–3 février 1944, Rapport de la Commission de l'Économie Impériale, séance du 1er février 1944, AP 2295/2, Archives

d'Outre-Mer, Aix-en-Provence (AOM); Rôle et place des Européens dans la colonisation, 20 janvier 1944, and, Direction Générale des Affaires Politiques, Administratives et Sociales, Programme générale de la Conférence de Brazzaville, 28 décembre 1943, AP 2201/7, AOM, Mahé, Rapport sur l'industrialisation des Colonies, transcript of séance du 7 février 1944, AE 101/5, AOM; *La conférence africaine française.* Brazzaville, 30 January–3 February 1944, Brazzaville, Éditions du Baobab, 1944, 60–61. See also Cotte, *La politique économique*, 1981, pp. 58–63.

25. This was especially true of Governor General Félix Éboué, one of the convenors of the conference, who kept insisting on the limits of what could be expected from natives, so much so that another official had to remind the conference attendees that 'the purpose of our colonization is to civilize'. See Eboué's remarks on the session of 2 February 1944 and those of Governor Saller on 3 February, both in AE 101/5, as well as Eboué's earlier explanation of his views from his circular of 8 November 1941, later published as F. Éboué, *La nouvelle politique indigène pour l'Afrique Équatoriale Française*, Paris, Office Français d'Édition, 1941.

26. The idea of Africans as essentially peasants figured not only among progressive administrators – such as Delavignette or Labouret, or the more paternalist Éboué – but also with Vichy's Gouverneur Général, Pierre Boisson. See P. Boisson, *Contribution à l'œuvre africaine*, Rufisque, Imprimerie du Haut Commissariat de l'Afrique Française, 1942.

27. This put officials in a quandary, for even a conservative approach to increasing production demanded better infrastructure, which demanded labour – which they were not convinced a 'free' market would supply. Governor-General Cournarie to Minister of Colonies, 3 September 1945, K 324 (26), Archives of Senegal.

28. Cooper, 'Conditions analogous to slavery: imperialism and free labor ideology in Africa', in Cooper, F., Holt, T., Scott, R., eds, *Beyond Slavery: Explorations of Race, Labor, and Citizenship in Postemancipation Societies*, Chapel Hill, University of North Carolina Press, 2000, pp. 134–148; id., 'The senegalese general strike of 1946 and the labor question in post-war French Africa', *Revue Canadienne d'Études Africaines* 24, 1990, pp. 165–215.

29. Here are some examples of the goals cited by the inspectors: 'cause labour stabilization', 'facilitate better labour performance', 'improve family stability', 'gradually [move towards] a more European-style life', 'give the African worker a decent material life'. AOF, *Inspection du Travail, Rapports Annuels,* 1946, 1947, 1948. For a detailed analysis of the Inspectors' discourse, see F. Cooper, *Decolonization*, chapters 5 and 7.

30. AOF, *Inspection du Travail, Rapport Annuel,*1951; *Sénégal, Rapport Économique,* 1947; Gouverneur Général, Bernard Cornut-Gentille, *Mémoire sur l'exécution du plan d'équipement en Afrique Équatoriale Française pendant les exercices 1947–1948 et 1948–1949*, Brazzaville, Imprimerie Officielle; M. Moreau, à la Conférence d'Études des Plans, 29 November 1950, Compte rendu, AE 169, AOM; 'Observations et conclusions personnelles du Gouverneur Roland Pré, Président de la Commission d'Étude et de Coordination des Plans de Modernisation et d'Équipement des Territoires d'Outre-Me', May 1954, typescript, AOM.

31. See the revealing discussions among officials from the department of economic affairs in Paris and local officials in the Conférence d'Études des

Plans, 28 November–1 December 1950, AE 169, ANSOM, and Inspecteur Général de la France d'Outre-Mer, Bilan du Premier Plan du développement économique et sociales des Territoires d'Outre-Mer, 1952, AE 749, ANSOM.

32. Sydney Caine, Minute, 23 April 1946, CO 852/1003/3, PRO.
33. Secretary of State Creech Jones, Circular Despatch, 22 February 1947, CO 852/1003/3, PRO.
34. Cooper, *Decolonization*, 1996, chapter 7.
35. Ibid, chapter. 8, and for more detail on the Kenyan case, F. Cooper, *On the African Waterfront: Urban Disorder and the Transformation of Work in Colonial Mombasa*, New Haven, CT, Yale University Press, 1987.
36. Lisa Lindsay, in a study of Yoruba families during the period in which work on the Nigerian railways was being transformed by the state, shows that workers used their gains to sustain a system of family labour and kinship quite different from what the administration had in mind. L. Lindsay, *Working with Gender: Men, Women, and Wage Labor in Southwest Nigeria*, Portsmouth, NH, Heinemann, 2003.
37. On the politicizing and depoliticizing tendencies in the debates about development, see Cooper and Packard, *International Development*, 1997. For an interesting example of an African political party accepting the notion of development and then using it to assert the need for African control over its implementation, see van Beusekom's discussion of the US-RDA in the French Soudan, in Van Beusekom, *Negotiating Development*, 2002, pp. 171–172.
38. Cooper, *Decolonization*, 1996, chapters 10–12.
39. J. Lonsdale and B. Berman, *Unhappy Valley: Conflict in Kenya and Africa*, vol. 2: *Violence and Ethnicity*, London, James Currey, 1992; T. Kanogo, *Squatters and the Roots of Mau Mau, 1905–1963*, London, James Currey, 1987; D. Throup, *Economic and Social Origins of Mau Mau, 1945–1953*, London, James Currey, 1987.
40. Governor Clement Pleass to Thomas Lloyd, Colonial Office, 6 August 1955, CO 554/1181, PRO.
41. The British government's negative cost-benefit analysis of its African colonies may be found in a series of Cabinet documents from 1957, in CAB 134/1555 and CAB 134/1556, PRO. A related, but public, assessment in the French case, became known as cartierisme, after 'En France Noire avec Raymond Cartier', *Paris Match*, 11 August and 1 September 1956. See also Cooper, *Decolonization*, 1996, chapter 10; Marseille, *Empire Colonial*, 1984.
42. 'Future Constitutional Development in the Colonies', 6 September 1957, CPC (57) 30, CAB 134/1556, PRO.
43. D. C. Tipps, 'Modernization theory and the comparative study of societies: A critical perspective', *Comparative Studies in Society and History* 15, 1973, pp. 199–226.
44. W. Arthur Lewis, minute offering his resignation, 30 November 1944, CO 852/586/9, PRO.
45. Some of the earliest studies of urban situations were notable for the information they provided, but did not shape the field of anthropology as did the later work of Georges Balandier or Clyde Mitchell (cf. below). Cf., for example, E. Hellmann, *Rooiyard: A Sociological Survey of an Urban Native Slum Yard, Rhodes–Livingstone Papers 13*, Cape Town, Oxford University Press, 1948; S. van der Horst, *Native Labour in South Africa*, London, Cass, 1971

[1942]; I. Schapera, *Migrant Labour and Tribal Life: A Study of Conditions in the Bechuanaland Protectorate*, London, Oxford University Press, 1947; M. Grévisse, *Le centre extra-coutumier d'Élisabethville*, Bruxelles, CEPSI, 1951; A. Doucy and P. Feldheim, *Problèmes du travail et politique sociale au Congo Belge*, Bruxelles, Librairie Encyclopédique, 1952; J. Guilbot, *Petite étude sur la main-d'œuvre à Douala*, Yaoundé, Imprimerie du Gouvernment, memorandum du Centre IFAN Cameroun, 1947.

46. W. F. Moore, *Industrialization and Labor: Social Aspects of Economic Development*, Ithaca, NY, Cornell University Press for The Institute of World Affairs, 1951, pp. 3, 6, 48, 188, 192–198.

47. C. Kerr, J. T. Dunlop, F. Harbison, and C. A. Myers, *Industrialism and Industrial Man*, Cambridge, MA, Harvard University Press, 1960, pp. 187–192; C. Kerr, 'Changing social structures', in W. E. Moore and A. S. Feldman, eds *Labor Commitment and Social Change in Developing Areas*, New York, NY, Social Science Research Council, 1960, pp. 348–349, 350, 351, 357, 359.

48. D. Lerner, 'Modernization: Social aspects', *International Encyclopedia of the Social Sciences*, New York, NY, Crowell Collier, 10, pp. 386–394; T. Parsons, *Structure and Process in Modern Societies*, New York, NY, Free Press 1960; T. Parsons, 'Evolutionary universals in society', *American Sociological Review* 29, 1964, pp. 339–357.

49. Kerr, 'Social structures', 1960, pp. 348–349.

50. W. W. Rostow, *The Stages of Economic Growth: A Non-Communist Manifesto*, Cambridge: Cambridge University Press, 1960.

51. For the place of modernization theory within American politics and foreign policy, see M. E. Latham, *Modernization as Ideology: American Social Science and 'Nation Building' in the Kennedy Era*, Chapel Hill, NC, University of North Carolina Press, 2000. Robert Vitalis argues that American internationalism drew on the notion of 'race development' among certain scholars that dates to the pre-First World War era and which was turned into a critical look at European colonies in the 1930s. R. Vitalis, 'International studies in America', Items, 2002, pp. 3–4, 12–16.

52. W. Goldschmidt, 'Africa in the twentieth century', in W. Goldschmidt, ed., *The United States and Africa*, New York, The American Assembly, 1958, p. 9; Emerson, 'The character of American interests in Africa', in Goldschmidt, op. cit, 1-231958, 15; American Assembly, 'Final report of the thirteenth American Assembly', in Goldschmidt, op. cit., pp. 241–244. The report reflects the general consensus of those attending, and the book also contains papers by the leading political scientists, economists, and anthropologists then working on Africa.

53. See Tipps, 'Modernization theory', 1973. For an example of a political scientist's critique of the modernizers' version of African political development, see A. Zolberg, *Creating Political Order: The Party-States of West Africa*, Chicago, IL, Rand-McNally, 1966.

54. P. H. Rosenstein-Rodan, 'Problems of industrialisation of Eastern and South-Eastern Europe', *The Economic Journal*, 53, 1943, pp. 202–211. For another example of the tentative demarcation of a domain of inquiry into underdeveloped economies, see H. W. Singer, 'Economic progress in underdeveloped countries', *Social Research*, 16, 1949, pp. 1–11. An historical overview may be

found in H. W. Arndt, *Economic Development: the History of an Idea*, Chicago, IL, University of Chicago Press, 1987.

55. W. A. Lewis, 'Economic development with unlimited supplies of labour', *The Manchester School*, 22 1954, pp. 139–191. Lewis later wrote that his early interest was in industrial economics and he only became systematically interested in development in 1950. Then and later he was also interested in world economic history. Autobiography on website of Nobel Museum [www.nobel.se/economics/ laureates/1979/lewis-autobio.html]. See Robert Tignor, *W. Arthur Lewis and the Birth of Development Economics*, Princeton, Princeton University Press, 2006.

56. W. A. Lewis, 'A policy for colonial agriculture', in W. A. Lewis, M. Scott, M. Wright and C. Legum, *Attitude to Africa*, Harmondsworth: Penguin, 1951, pp. 71–73.

57. See for example, W. A. Lewis, *Labour in the West Indies*, London, Fabian Society, 1939.

58. W. A. Lewis, 'The economic development of Africa', in C. W. Stillman, ed., *Africa in the Modern World*, Chicago, IL, University of Chicago Press, 1955, pp. 97–122.

59. W. A. Lewis, *Industrialisation and the Gold Coast*, Accra, Government Printer, 1953. Lewis's experience in Ghana led him to write a book severely critical of African political leaders, especially for anti-democratic tendencies that emerged soon after independence. However, he remained committed to the opportunity for young Africans to do better than their elders, and he retained – unlike others who became disillusioned with Africa's economic progress – his beliefs that sound policies of economic development could improve people's lives in ways that a free market could not. From his days as a student until the end of life, he thought that the actions of powerful men – be they West Indian planters or African authoritarian rulers – could make things worse, but that the actions of thoughtful, knowledgeable people within democratic systems could make things better. See W. A. Lewis, *Politics in West Africa*, Toronto, Oxford University Press, 1965; W. A. Lewis, 'The state of development theory', *American Economic Review*, 74, pp. 1–10. For a collection of influential writings and a full bibliography, see M. Gersovitz, ed., *Selected Economic Writings of W. Arthur Lewis*, New York, New York University Press, 1983. For another study by a 'colonized subject' that had a formative influence on the social sciences in Africa, see K. A. Busia, *Report on a Social Survey of Sekondi-Takoradi*, London, Crown Agents for the Colonies, 1950.

60. See the references in Note 1 for dismissive arguments about development as Western modernization. A more interesting analysis of science and colonialism comes from Gyan Prakash, who brings out different modes of thought among Indian scientists, but he still insists on contrasting them to an apparently singular form of 'Western' reason. G. Prakash, *Another Reason: Science and the Imagination of Modern India*, Princeton, NJ, Princeton University Press 1999.

61. Economic Commission for Latin America, *Economic Survey of Latin America 1949*, New York, United Nations, 1951.

62. For examples of the vitality of development economics in the 1950s, see A. N. Agarwala and S. P. Singh, *The Economics of Underdevelopment: A Series*

of Articles and Papers, Delhi, Oxford University Press, 1958. See also Arndt, *Economic development*, 1987.

63. L. J. Lebret, *Dynamique concrète du développement*, Paris, Éditions Ouvrières, 1956. For other points of view among French economists and demographers at the time, see A. Sauvy, 'Introduction à l'étude des pays sous-développés', *Population*, 6, 4, 1951, pp. 601–608; F. Perroux, *Programmation régionale de théorie économique*, Paris, Presses Universitaires de France, 1960. See also M. Diouf, 'Senegalese development: From mass mobilization to technocratic elitism', in F. Cooper and R. Packard, eds, *International Development and the Social Sciences: Essays in the History and Politics of Knowledge*, Berkeley, CA, University of California Press, 1997, pp. 291–319.

64. One could compare, for example, the neoliberal position of the Indian economist Deepak Lal with that of the defender of a socially focused notion of development, the Indian economist Amartya Sen, and with that of the Egyptian critic of the world capitalist system Samir Amin. The divergences of approach are a theme of Cooper and Packard, *International Development*, 1997.

65. UNESCO, *Social Implications of Industrialization and Urbanization in Africa South of the Sahara*, Paris, UNESCO, 1956.

66. A. Diop, 'De l'expansion du travail', *Présence Africaine*, 13, 1952, pp. 7–17. Among other articles in this issue, one should note G. Balandier, 'Urbanism in west and central Africa: The scope and aims of research', pp. 297–315; K. B. Gnasounou Ponoukoun, 'La vie d'un militant syndicaliste', pp. 355–358; P. Naville, 'Note sur le syndicalisme en Afrique Noire', pp. 359–367; H. Labouret, 'Sur la main-d'œuvre autochtone', pp. 124–136; J. C. Pauvert, 'La notion de travail en Afrique Noire', pp. 92–107; P. Mercier, 'Travail et service public dans l'ancien Dahomey', pp. 84–91; M. Leiris, 'L'expression de l'idée de travail dans une langue d'initiés soudanais', pp. 69–83; A. S. Tidjani, 'L'Africain face au problème du travail', p. 108; D. Palme, 'La femme africaine au travail, *Présence Africaine*', 13, 1952, pp. 116–123.

67. G. Balandier, 'Le travailleur africain dans les "Brazzaville noires",' *Présence Africaine*, 13, 1956, pp. 315–330.

68. P. Mercier, 'Aspects de la société africaine dans l'agglomération dakaroise: Groupes familiaux et unités de voisinage', *Études Sénégalaises*, 5, 1954, pp. 11–40; P. Mercier, 'La vie politique dans les centres urbaine du Sénégal: Étude d'une période de transition', *Cahiers Internationaux de Sociologie*, 27, 1959, 55–84. For other examples of sociological inquiry, see G. Savonnet, 'La ville de Thiès: Étude de géographie urbaine', *Études Sénégalaises*, 6, 1955; Y. Mersaider, 'Budgets familiaux africains: Étude chez 136 familles de salariés dans trois centres urbains du Sénégal', *Études Sénégalaises*, 7, 1957.

69. G. Balandier, *Histoire des autres*, Paris, Stock, 1977, p. 52; G. Balandier, 'De l'Afrique à la surmodernité: Un parcours d'anthropologue, Entretien avec Georges Balandier', *Le Débat*, 118, p. 52. Marcel Griaule's large œuvre includes *Masques Dogon*, Paris, Institut d'Ethnologie, 1938, and *Dieu d'eau: Entretiens avec Ogotemmêli*, Paris, Éditions du Chêne, 1948.

70. G. Balandier, 'La situation coloniale: Approche théorique', *Cahiers Internationaux de Sociologie*, 11, 1951, pp. 44–79.

71. Balandier's focus on the urbanization problematic is already clear in his article 'Le développement industriel de la prolétarisation en Afrique Noire',

L'Afrique et l'Asie, 20, 1952, 45–53. Evident as well is his insistence that one should not assume that Africa urbanization and industrialization would follow a European trajectory but had to be studied on its own terms: '[I]l reste difficile d'approcher les problèmes du travail africain avec nos critères européens. Il faut insister sur la nécessité absolue de les étudier (véritablement) en fonction des particularités bio-psychologiques, sociales et culturelles ...' (p. 53). See also F. Cooper, 'Decolonizing situations: The rise, fall and rise of colonial studies, 1951–2001', *French Politics, Culture and Society*, 20, 2002, pp. 47–76.

72. G. Balandier, *Sociologie des 'Brazzaville' noires*, Paris, Colin, 1955; Balandier, 'Étude interdisciplinaire' 1958.

73. G. Balandier, *Le Tiers-Monde. Travaux et documents*, Paris, Presses Universitaires de France, 1956.

74. For the pioneering work on the micro-sociological version of the 'situation' (as compared to Balandier's macro-sociological one), see M. Gluckman, *Analysis of a Social Situation in Modern Zululand*, Manchester, Manchester University Press, 1958.

75. J. C. Mitchell, 'Urbanization, detribalization and stabilization in Southern Africa: A problem of definition and measurement', in UNESCO, *Social Implications*, 1956, pp. 693–711; A. L. Epstein, *Politics in an Urban African Community*, Manchester, Manchester University Press, 1958, pp. 46, 224–240; M. Gluckman, 'Anthropological problems arising from the African industrial revolution', in A. Southall, ed., *Social Change in Modern Africa*, London, Oxford University Press, 1961, p. 69; J. C. Mitchell, 'The Kalela Dance', Lusaka, Rhodes-Livingstone Institute, *Rhodes-Livingstone Papers*, 27, 1957. See also L. Schumaker, *Africanizing Anthropology: Fieldwork, Networks, and the Making of Cultural Knowledge in Central Africa*, Durham, NC, Duke University Press, 2001.

76. Ferguson, *Expectations*, 1999. See also Lindsay, *Working with Gender*, 2003 J. Ferguson, 'Decomposing Modernity: History and Hierarchy after Development,' in Ania Loomba, Suvir Kaul, Antoinette M. Burton (eds.), *Postcolonial Studies and Beyond*, Durham, Duke University Press, Durham 2005, pp. 166–181.

2
A Modernizing Empire? Politics, Culture, and Economy in Portuguese Late Colonialism

Miguel Bandeira Jerónimo and António Costa Pinto

Introduction

The politics and policies of late colonialism in the Portuguese empire were characterized by a repressive developmentalism, a particular combination of enhanced coercive (symbolic and material) repertoires of rule, programmed developmental strategies of political, economic and socio-cultural change, and processes of engineering of socio-cultural differentiation. At its core, as Frederick Cooper noted, was a 'repressive version of the developmentalist colonial state'.[1] The late imperial and colonial states aimed to co-ordinate policies of imperial resilience in a context of widespread evolving colonial and international pressures which were contrary to their existence, or pressing for their substantial reform.[2] They were the institutional loci in which the entangled policies of repressive developmentalism evolved, in which there was a coalescence between idioms, programmes, and repertoires of colonial social control and coercion (for instance, the schemes of resettlement, civil and military, of the African population and the strategies of counter-insurgency) – related, but not reducible, to the colonial wars and to the militarization of colonial societies; idioms, programmes, and repertoires of colonial development and modernization (for instance, the developmental plans of the 1950s and 1960s); and idioms, projects, and repertoires of imperial and colonial social engineering (for instance, the *indigenato* regime or the nationalized version of the doctrine of welfare colonialism and its languages and programmes of native welfare and native social promotion).

As a consequence, the analysis of Portuguese late colonialism must rely to a large extent on the understanding of the idioms, institutional design, and mechanics that brought the 'repressive version of the developmentalist colonial state' into existence, exploring its multifaceted nature, dynamism, and manifestation from historical and geographical perspectives. To do so it is crucial to recognize the importance of international, transnational, and inter-imperial connections and dynamics – for instance, the internationalization of doctrines of international development, the globalization and localization of Cold War dynamics or the role of international organizations in the definition of colonial social policies – that interacted with metropolitan and colonial processes.[3] An understanding of the role played by these international, transnational, and inter-imperial connections and dynamics is generally absent from the analytic framework used to examine the modus operandi of Portuguese late colonialism, its moral and political economies. The rhetoric of imperial exceptionality, constantly promoted by the Portuguese political and cultural elites, and the image of the regime's autonomy and international insularity, continually projected by Oliveira Salazar's authoritarian administration, certainly contributed to the existence of specific types of methodological, analytical and historiographical *nationalisms* – that is, the exclusive focus on a single national or imperial analytical framework, guided by an enquiry restricted to endogenous factors – which still prevail in the analysis of the country's national and imperial history, and still govern as well the traditional historiography of its international relations.[4] Beside entailing the understanding of certain metropolitan and colonial dimensions (for instance, the impact of the nature of the political regime or the particularities and dynamics of local societies), the examination of repressive developmentalism – as a form of coercive rule, as a model of planned political, economic, and socio-cultural order and change, and as a process of engineering socio-cultural differentiation – requires scrutiny of the ways in which the regime and its administrative apparatus gave instrumental use to significant international doctrines; that is, how the imperial and colonial states (its agencies and actors) interacted with, appropriated, incorporated, and transformed them for their own imperial and colonial political, economic, and socio-cultural ends.[5]

What were the fundamental doctrines and repertoires of rule developed and employed by the imperial and colonial states? For instance, what kind of new imperial models of legal and administrative orders were formulated to address the changing nature of the international legitimacy of imperial formations in the mid-20th century, a process certainly fuelled by transformations brought about by some intellectual and institutional transformations related to the impact and aftermath of the First World War?[6] In a different but related direction, what mechanisms and institutions of intelligence and information gathering were created and used to enhance colonial rule, especially in three types of investigative modalities: survey (e.g. classification of the colony's natural and human resources), enumerative (e.g. censuses) and surveillance (e.g. identification, knowledge about, and classification of each indigenous group into an array of grids, with a view to determining their temperament and ability to comply or resist colonial domination or repression).[7] What were the developmental strategies of political, economic, and socio-cultural change advocated and implemented by the imperial and colonial states? What were the main, modern, scientific, and experimental schemes of colonial development selected and promoted by them?[8] What were the principal policies of ethnic colonization or the modern modalities of population control devised to induce change within the colonial worlds? What were the idioms and ready-to-use models of imperial social change, born out of revisions of the long tradition of imperial statecraft or based on processes of transfer or imitation from other polities, imperial or not?[9] Finally, what were the key processes of engineering of socio-cultural differentiation programmed and deployed by the late imperial and colonial states? What were the politics and the policies of difference: that is, the strategies of socio-cultural and/or ethnic inclusion/differentiation used?[10] How did they evolve through time and how did they relate to international, metropolitan and colonial conditions, interacting with local and global transformations in the grammar of social integration and differentiation?

How did all these inter-related aspects impact upon the Portuguese, political, economic and socio-cultural late imperial strategies? How were these imperial strategies instrumental in the creation of political, economic, and ideological conditions to resist global decolonizing pressures, for instance by increasing the colonial empire's international and colonial projection as a legitimate, progressive, and exceptional imperial formation? How did they reflect and interact with international, transnational, and inter-imperial connections and dynamics? Obviously without aiming to provide an exhaustive assessment of their importance or to offer a comprehensive answer to them all, these are some of the main questions that this chapter aims to tackle while assessing the main characteristics of Portuguese late colonialism in Africa since 1945. The argument for a distinctive repressive developmentalism as the main feature of Portuguese late colonialism is therefore an attempt to answer some of these inter-related historical problems. It is also the main focus of this chapter.[11]

In the first part, we look at the origins and intents of the political, mainly administrative and juridical, reforms that aimed to transform the ways in which imperial and colonial affairs were managed at metropolitan and colonial levels. Two of the most important examples are addressed: first, the legal end of the colonial empire with the constitutional revision of 1951, which started a process of semantic decolonization, which possessed instrumental use at a diplomatic level; second, the constitution in 1959 of a new department at the overseas ministry to deal with political affairs, the Political Affairs Department (Gabinete dos Negócios Políticos, GNP) was a keystone of the new institutional network of information and intelligence gathering, which aimed to promote a new information empire which was considered more adequate in dealing with novel historical conditions. These examples demonstrate how an authoritarian political system strove to modernize its institutional architecture and related imperial policies in order to cope with the change and to seize the opportunities brought about by the post-Second World War international society, namely those that impacted, or could impact, on imperial and colonial affairs. They also reveal the progressive institutionalization of an 'imperialism of knowledge', similar to what defined, to varying degrees, the British and French Empires.[12] The post-Second World War informational redefinition of imperial and colonial politics and policies – which favoured planning, interventionist, and modernizing vistas in order to enhance social, economic, and political reform overseas and to appease international and local criticism – was an important aspect in Portuguese late colonialism, even if there was no endeavour such as the one undertaken in *An African Survey*.[13] What was nonetheless clear was the progressive institutionalization of new forms of scientific and specialized knowledge – economic, juridical, political, social, and psychological – as favoured tools for imperial consolidation and resilience. These forms were related to international, informational, circulatory regimes associated with international organizations and their normative frameworks, as well as with the national, international, and transnational epistemic communities that formulated them.[14]

In the second part, we address the ways in which the doctrines and projects of welfare colonialism surfaced in Portuguese late colonialism and we investigate the origins and intents of the fundamental economic developmental plans (*planos do fomento*) devised by the Portuguese authorities from the 1950s onward to modernize the colonial empire, modernize the colonial empire in economic and socio-political dimensions.[15] The development plans marked a significant moment of economic planning and tentative modernization of the Portuguese economy, while possessing a clear political reasoning and intent. In this second part we also highlight the emergence of schemes of ethnic colonization – the *colonatos* – and of schemes of (forced) native rural resettlement – *aldeamentos*. Both schemes had an encompassing modernizing rationale, integrating political (and military), economic and socio-cultural dimensions, and were fundamental to the process of consolidation of a developmental late-colonial state, being also related to the counter-insurgency schemes developed at the time.[16]

A new state of law, a semantic decolonization

Reinforcing processes visible from the 1930s onwards and following tendencies noticeable in other imperial and colonial formations in the period of the second colonial occupation (in the Portuguese case we might argue that it was indeed the first colonial occupation), the following decades were marked by renewed institutional, legal, and administrative frameworks, and by the intensification of government planning and economic intervention by the colonial state. This was visible in the establishment of languages and programmes for improved efficiency, productivity, and 'good [imperial and colonial] government', in the establishment of development plans, and in the formulation of new modalities of imperial legitimization.[17] As a result, and despite differences in causes, conception, and expected impact within and between imperial formations – good government debates could be associated with economic considerations (as in Portugal from the 1920s onwards) or political legitimation (domestic and/or international), or could be related to proposals for indirect rule or direct rule, for instance, as John Lee summarized when saying that in the 1930s British administrators' 'most perplexing dilemma was whether to aid the transformation of colonial society or to preserve the traditional order' – a renewed strategy of imperial rule emerged.[18]

The principles and dispositions inserted in the Colonial Act, the fundamental imperial legal 1930 framework of the New State, were repealed in 1951 with a constitutional revision that followed some precepts which had been argued for since the mid-1940s in certain political and governmental circles.[19] The 1951 constitution stated that the colonies were now overseas provinces: the concept of a Portuguese colonial empire was abandoned. Notwithstanding important differences, Portugal now had a version of Greater Britain and of *la plus grande France*, echoing old doctrines of national and imperial vital spaces, now reframed as 'Portuguese space', 'greater nation' or 'mission-space', with a view to reinvent national identity, reinforce mythologies of national and imperial exceptionality, and, perhaps more important, to counter-balance decolonizing pressures.[20] The principles of political assimilation and economic integration were reinforced, and a new era of political legitimation of the empire begun, both at home and abroad. Supported by a series of administrative and juridical procedures, semantic decolonization began, certainly in response to the accruing internal and external pressures that questioned the workings of the empire. As the former minister of colonies, José Ferreira Bossa, argued in 1944, during the meeting of the National Union (União Nacional),[21] a new juridical construction of the empire, was a sine qua non for imperial survival in new historical circumstances, turning the metropole and the former colonies into one single political and economic reality. The new framework should take the new historical circumstances into consideration, adapt to its signs, messages, and foreseen threats, and provide the instruments necessary to turn integration into a reality, at least formally.[22] It should also give substance to a rhetoric of exceptionality: the Portuguese empire-that-was-no-more was substantially different from other imperial formations. As Salazar stated in 1947, 'in the context of present convulsions we [must] present ourselves as a brotherhood of peoples, cemented by centuries of peaceful lives and Christian understanding'.[23] Moreover, in the Portuguese case, this new juridical construction of the empire was promoted as being much more that the verbal reform that characterized the similar operation made by the French in 1946. Contrary to what happened in the French case, however, the *indigenato* regime was not abolished and the pillar of the politics of difference within the Portuguese overseas provinces remained almost unchanged.[24]

However, the rhetoric of national (imperial and colonial) unity and exceptionality was insufficient and had to be reinforced by other type of mechanisms. The constitutional revision of 1951 set the tone, creating a putative pluricontinental nation with European and overseas provinces, with no colonies and, importantly, with no non-autonomous territories, an expression promoted at the United Nations (UN) to enlarge the reach of its enquiries over the forms of modern colonization.[25] The constitutional revision and the related Overseas Organic Law (1953) had an additional aim. These new juridical constructions were designed to create the institutional conditions for the overall modernization of the imperial system, stressing the unity of its means and ends and highlighting the importance of devising principles that acted in 'harmony with the necessities of the development and welfare' of the overseas provinces, as Article 159 of the constitutional revision stated. The language of welfare colonialism was added to the recipe, following early attempts to turn it into a mainstay of colonial programmes and policies in the 1940s. The emergence of a modernizing imperial policy supported by a scientific and technocratic rationale was needed to face the novel circumstances and tackle the impact, seen as potentially threatening, of urbanization, as Marcelo Caetano declared in 1945 while serving as colonial minister. Social change needed to be directed and administered by technicians with a practical spirit and an efficient will which could, among other things, monitor and control social dysfunctions while promoting a new type of economic relationship with the native population, especially in respect of the recruitment and use of African labour, an aspect mentioned as being crucial in the overall project of reforming the nature and practice of ethnic interaction in the colonial worlds, despite the above mentioned persistence of its long-standing discriminatory politics of difference.[26]

The 1950s also brought about other important changes at metropolitan and colonial levels. At a metropolitan level, the restructuring of the colonial ministry, namely the creation of the GNP in 1959, was crucial. This department was devised to be the centre of a new order of imperial and colonial information. A new empire of information, not only of intelligence, was mandatory. The GNP was designed to be the hub of political co-ordination and information-intelligence gathering and management. It was also an element of a larger network of departmental agencies that aimed to govern the colonial world in a new, more rational and technical, modern and scientific manner. This network comprised the foreign affairs ministry, the regime's political police – the International and State Defence Police (Polícia Internacional e de Defesa do Estado, PIDE) – which from 1957 established several agencies in the overseas provinces, the Centralization and Coordination of Information Service (Serviços de Centralização e Coordenação de Informações) and the Tourism and Information Centres (Centros de Informação e Turismo). With a wide network of informants, the creation of counter-insurgency militias (formed mainly by natives) in co-ordination with the overseas ministry, the army, and the PIDE (especially from 1961 onwards) became the backbone of the 'repressive version of the developmentalist colonial state'. The figures are noteworthy: in 1954 the PIDE had fewer than 100 research and intelligence officers in the colonies; in 1972 it had 1,700. The formation of this institutional network aimed to prepare the late-colonial state to cope with the evolving international and colonial circumstances.[27]

Another important example was the creation of 'study' sections, determined by the major ministerial reform of 1957, exclusively focused on the production of specialized knowledge about several imperial sub-ject-matters, some related to the modernizing projects which had been in development since the early 1950s. These were seen as instruments of ministerial modernization and would prove crucial in relation to the developmental plans we analyse below. In the same vein, as a result of the creation of the Portuguese single market in 1961, several important departments focusing on economic planning and integration were cre-ated from the 1950s onwards. In the 1960s they began to have branches overseas, as determined by the 1963 Overseas Organic Law that made the technical commissions for economic planning and integration mandatory.[28] Some of these changes were obviously related to the con-flicts at the imperial periphery, as could be seen at the extraordinary meeting of the Overseas Council in 1962, an important body which politically and ideologically evaluated the imperial and colonial affairs guiding the process of revising the Overseas Organic Law of 1963.[29]

In the colonies, from the late 1940s, the colonial state gradually acquired increased degrees of infrastructural power.[30] Before that, par-ticularly in the interior, its presence was confined to labour recruitment and tax-extraction expeditions, despite the efforts made in the 1930s, for instance in the creation of a professional colonial civil service with inspection and reporting procedures. The forms and mechanisms of ter-ritorialization of the colonial state's bureaucratic apparatus multiplied, noticeably emphasizing the creation of administrative agencies focused on the production of knowledge about colonial realities. These were devised to guide the economic developmental projects, as well as to boost the traditional aim of increasing tax revenue. The investigative modalities of the colonial state – especially in relation to the census, enumerative and surveillance modalities – were tentatively enhanced and were no mere by-product of the mounting anti-colonial forces or, from the early 1960s, of the related process of militarization of colonial societies. In 1940, the first general census in the colonial world was made, an important moment in the historical process of consolidation of state power. In Angola, ten departments were formed focused on financial and economic problems (from public works and the organiza-tion and central coordination of the coffee, cereal, and cotton produc-tion, to scientific domains such as geology and forestry). In the next decades, the state apparatus increased and enlarged significantly.[31]

The bureaucratization of the colonial world also included the forced incorporation of *mestiços* organizations into para-governmental agen-cies, thus controlling the process of their expected progression towards the constitution of political parties. The political dynamics at a colonial level were also seen as a marker of political development and modernization, which was determined by the nature of the articulation between the politico-administrative institutions of the colonial state and the native political and associative organizations.[32] The same operation was tentatively applied to the Catholic ecclesiastical and missionary structures, intending to turn them into the agencies of civilization under the all-encompassing imperial and colonial bureaucracies. However, as Henrique Galvão stated, the 'variety and multiplicity of the organs' and 'their dispersal' did not necessarily entail forms of co-ordination, given their 'constitution as monopolistic compartments'. He was critical of the functioning and efficacy of what he called the 'plethora of bureaucracy'. But he also recognized the need for a new order of colonial information and its respective management – a new empire of information – that was also crucial to meet the need to foster social change at a local level.[33] The instructions given to the *chefes de posto* (the most important officials representing the colonial state in the interior alongside the village *régulos*, the government appointed chiefs) clearly demonstrated the extent to which developmental principles should, in theory, be actively pursued. Indeed, responsibilities for promoting and disseminating agricultural techniques, sanitary standards, and gender role models were added to the traditional collection of the hut tax and labour recruitment.[34]

Engineering welfare, preserving inequality, and planning resistance

The rise of welfare colonialism was associated with the promotion of a rational colonial bureaucracy, of scientific methods of governance, and with the gradual global spread of models of planned and managed economic development and social and cultural modernization. It also entailed significant expansion in the scope of activity and scale of operation of the colonial state, requiring a significant transformation in the administrative, technical and specialized bodies that co-ordinated the colonial empire. In the Portuguese case, this expansion was partially justified by the increase in the colonial state's revenues – due to the expansion of the volume of revenues, the enlargement of the administration's geographies of taxation, and the colonial economic boom during the war – and by the progressive abandonment of the fiscal pact that prevented substantial metropolitan investment in the colonial world and required the colonies' self-sufficiency. Allocations to colonial development funds, especially those provided and managed by the empire-state, bolstered a novel phase in the economic role and a new appraisal of the economic value of the colonial worlds. Notwithstanding differences in scale and resources when compared to other empires, the Portuguese case was also characterized by this general tendency.[35] Simultaneously, the questioning of its legitimacy, both by the mounting anti-colonial nationalist movements and by growing international criticism, rose steadily. Indeed, despite signs of an increasing adequacy in the new imperial modus operandi, based on the promotion of a *mise en valeur*, welfare and developmental colonialism, according to declared discourses and policies,[36] and despite the resilience of doctrines of national-imperial exceptionality from the late 19th-century version of civilizing mission to the 1950s appropriation of Gilberto Freyre's luso-tropicalism,[37] the Portuguese Empire continued to be confronted by a barrage of criticism over its functioning, especially in relation to three inter-related issues. First, the condemnation was directed at the policies of native labour, which included the central role of the state's administrative and coercive machinery in providing it to private employers. Not even the legal suppression of forced labour in 1961 and 1962 appeased the vocal denunciations coming from states such as Ghana or organizations such as the International Labour Organization or missionary societies.[38] Second, the criticism continued to focus on the system of dual citizenship – the *indigenato* regime – which was abolished in 1961. However, the formal abolition did not prevent or halt the social, cultural, economic, and political consequences that its long-standing existence entailed. Inequality continued to be the (colonial) rule. Third, more generally, the overall shortcomings of its native policies, regarding education or health services, continued to be deplored. The doctrine of political, economic, and cultural integration, influenced by mainstream sociological thought, was constantly challenged by the realities of the imperial situation, characterized both by anti-colonial demonstrations and by demands for greater, local, colonial autonomy. The 'principles and methods to be used by the colonizing state to guide the relations with the native population in the colonies', as Silva Cunha defined native policy, a particular constituent of colonial policy, revealed its double nature. At the surface it seemed to embrace the tenets of modern and social welfare colonialism, and its specific languages of gradual equality. But it continued to rely essentially upon deep-rooted processes of engineering of social difference within the overseas provinces. If the civilizing mission was a mechanism for engineering inequality, welfare colonialism was in essence a form of managing it. The politics and the policies of multi-racial integration, as proclaimed by Adriano Moreira, a master ideologue and administrator of Portuguese late colonialism, hardly matched its proclaimed motivations and purposes.[39] The rhetoric of the Portuguese space, based on similar principles, was not accompanied by effective policies and discernible modernizing outcomes.[40]

Nonetheless, important efforts to transform colonial economies and to change their relationship with the metropole existed before the war. As a rule, Salazar's imperial economic policy replicated the basic terms of the metropolitan one.[41] The reduction of the deficit, the establishment of balanced budgets, and the promotion of self-financing colonies were the main goals. Until the late 1930s this was mainly attained via scarce investment. In 1935, the Economic Reconstitution Law included the development of the colonies as one of the three main pillars of overall Portuguese economic policy, side by side with national security and metropolitan development. In 1937 and 1938, colonial development plans were devised for Mozambique and Angola, based solely on local funds. Their main projects were related to public works, to communications and, importantly, to two irrigation and settlement schemes: one in the Limpopo Valley; the other in the Umbelezi.[42] In 1947, the Portuguese government invested PTE1 billion to encourage the development of the Tete Railway, which was crucial to local and regional economies. But it was not until the 1950s that the regime started to view the overseas provinces as spaces for development within a general plan of creating a single economic market.[43]

During the 1950s several developmental plans were devised to modernize the imperial and colonial worlds. Sharing some aspects of the British and French imperial developmental plans, but certainly occurring in different political and ideological circumstances, the formulation of an imperial developmental policy had the six-year development plan of 1953 as its first manifestation.[44] A smaller part of a developmental programme that had the metropole as its main beneficiary (circa 70 per cent of the funds applied), the colonial investments nonetheless signalled a major change in the political and economic rationales of the promoted imperial integration: the Greater Portugal.[45] The first development plan was the first Portuguese experiment in economic planning, which from the start articulated state-co-ordinated and state-controlled economic, political, and social rationales, merging factors such as ethnic colonization, labour and community resettlement, moral and spiritual elevation of the native communities (the old civilizational rhetoric now supported by modern instruments) and the methodical, scientific economic exploitation of the resources of the overseas provinces. At least in theory, it began a comprehensive project of managed social change, essentially guided by an economic rationale. Three-quarters of the funds invested in the first development plans were directed towards basic communicational infrastructures. No money was spent in social areas (e.g. education), either in Angola or Mozambique.[46] No particular section was devised to deal with the native communities, a fact justified by the putative existence of an egalitarian system, as Sarmento Rodrigues, the overseas territories minister, declared in 1953 during a series of speeches on the subject at the National Office for Information, Propaganda and Tourism (Secretariado Nacional de Informação, Propaganda e Turismo). The egalitarian rhetoric of a Greater Portugal impeded positive discrimination. The rhetoric of equality was the crucial instrument for the preservation of inequality, which was still legally established and legitimized.[47]

The second six-year plan (1959–64), which marked the duplication of the money spent in Mozambique (PTE41 million), began to include social items, 14 per cent in Mozambique and 6 per cent in Angola. However, these figures did not match the percentages being spent at roughly the same time in the Belgian Congo (20 per cent, 1950–59) or Uganda (22.5 and 25.8 per cent in the two development plans covering the same period). The old focus on plantation economies or in intensive agriculture, based on unskilled and forced native labour, continued, either within the Portuguese colonies or governing the functioning, large, regional market of labour migration which directed African labourers to the South African mines, to Tanganyika, Nyasaland, or to the Rhodesias. The civilizing-mission rhetoric that promoted labour as the most efficient social device that could lead the natives to enter the 'civilization guild' still prevailed. Likewise, colonial education was never a priority, except in the domain of ideology and propaganda, despite the increasing provincial governmental budgets in Angola and Mozambique and the steady increase in their surplus. As we will see, the social dimension would be aimed via methods associated with plans of rural settlement and the establishment of spaces of development and modernization.[48]

Another point needs to be stressed here: foreign investment was crucial to the colonial economy and to the series of developmental plans being devised. Contrary to what is frequently stated and oft repeated, the importance of foreign investment in the imperial and colonial worlds predates the 1965 law that regulated it.[49] The Benguela Railway, the Angola Diamond Company (which accounted for 5 per cent of the local government's revenue in 1966), the Sena Sugar States and the

Niassa Companies were under the control of British, South African, and Belgian interests. Moreover, as the Economic Survey of the Organisation for Economic Co-operation and Development (OECD) of 1966 concluded, the modernization and development plans and processes in Angola and Mozambique were scarcely related to Portuguese private capital and were products of state and foreign financing. In 1959, the constitution of the National Development Bank (Banco de Fomento Nacional), which replaced the National Development Fund (Fundo de Fomento Nacional), created a financial institution exclusively focused on the development of the metropole and the overseas provinces (where the first branches were opened in 1960), reinforcing the local financing system, especially in Angola, where the existing Angola Development Fund was complemented by the creation of the Bank of Angola in 1946. The Overseas National Bank (Banco Nacional Ultramarino) was no longer alone in the overall imperial banking system. This was both a symptom and a cause of economic overseas developmentalism.[50]

The first six-year developmental plan (1953–58) did not include a significant contribution from foreign investment. It relied essentially on local contributions comprising metropolitan loans, but its funding came from the National Development Fund. Since its creation in 1952, this fund provided circa $25 million to be used in the Portuguese overseas territories. The investment in the 1950s plan – on transport, electric power, irrigation, and rural settlement schemes (*colonatos*) – was also partially promoted by the economic processes unleashed and partially sponsored by the Marshall Plan. The second plan (1959–64) contained 25 per cent external funding, rising to 34 per cent in the third plan (1968–73).[51] In this process, the role played by the US was crucial. Between 1962 and 1968, the Export-Import Bank alone contracted loans to Portugal to the value of $73.3 million. Directly or indirectly, US banking interests were also involved in the financing of developmental plans in Angola and Mozambique. The case of Gulf Oil in Angola is illustrative. In 1969 it paid $11 million to the Angola government, more or less half of the Angolan defence budget at a time of war. As Rebocho Vaz, governor of Angola from 1966–1971, clearly stated, oil and derivatives were 'the nerve-centre of progress'. Moreover, we might add, co-operation with foreign interests in the overall strategies of development and progress was also a vital element of political survival.[52]

The role of direct or indirect foreign investment in the post-war Portuguese colonial empire needs to be further investigated. Demonstrating the limitations of an analysis of colonial economic developmentalism that is based on national capitalism is certainly fundamental. The cartography of imperial and colonial sovereignties is not equivalent to the cartography of capitalist investment in the imperial and colonial worlds. The questioning of the prevailing methodological nationalism also depends on these assumptions.[53] European efforts at post-war colonial development and programmes of colonial modernization depended on programmes such as the Economic Cooperation Act (1948), the Point IV (1950) and similar financing schemes associated with the European colonial world (and more broadly to the Marshall Plan agenda). For instance, the Marshall Plan enabled two major loans for investment in Mozambique in 1950 and 1953, directed to the Port of Beira and to the Limpopo railway line. Whether based on direct investment, state-driven or private, or based on programmes of technical assistance that involved the circulation of knowledge, technologies, and personnel, the role of these factors in the Portuguese imperial efflorescence of the 1950s and 1960s was certainly important and needs to be inserted at the core of studies looking at the historical dynamics and eventual demise of the empire. Their contribution to the overall formation of political and economic conditions that strengthened the Portuguese imperial and colonial stand must be acknowledge and properly assessed. For example, they enable the understanding of the post-war evolution of American foreign policy – its geo-strategic and economic rationales – towards the European colonial empires, and the evaluation of how this evolution promoted the continuation and reinforcement of imperial solutions. Technical assistance, direct and indirect investment, public and private funding, technological and institutional transfers, experts' circulation and knowledge diffusion were fundamental to the post-war economic development and modernization of the Portuguese Empire, enhancing and reinforcing the politics and the policies pursued by the late imperial and colonial states.[54]

An interesting example of this can be found in the role played by the Hudson Institute, led by an intellectual product of the Rand Corporation, Herman Kahn. Sponsored by the Companhia União Fabril (CUF) with $100,000 to assess the Portuguese colony of Angola, this 'flying think tank', as Paul Dickson labelled it, visited Angola for 10 days in September 1969 in order to produce a report on the colony's possible paths forward, based on scenarios of development. Three scenarios emerged. The first was 'business as usual', which meant the replication of existing models of development. The second was the 'cut-and-run development' path, which entailed support for industries that could be removed in a scenario of forced withdrawal from the territory.

The third was an option for a large-scale development programme based on foreign investment: the favoured solution according to the Hudson Institute's experts. The promotion of large-scale oil refining and cattle ranching (involving large resettlement projects), and the damming of the Congo were the main examples. Little is known of the impact of the two-volume report produced by the Hudson Institute, but its contents clearly matched some policies of development associated with counter-insurgency measures developed by the Portuguese in wartime Angola and Mozambique. Of equal importance, they confirmed older existing plans and mechanisms of colonial development such as those envisaged by projects of white settlement – *colonatos* – or by similar schemes of rural intervention and projected transformation.[55]

The funding of social-engineering programmes that aimed to colonize and transform the Angolan and Mozambican overseas provinces was a priority. The most important example was the *colonatos*, considered to be the 'complete model of colonial development'. The models of Cela (on the Amboim plateau in Angola, 1952), Matala (in the River Cunene valley, south-east Angola, 1956) and Limpopo (Mozambique) were the mainstays of an overall imperial programme of modernization that united economic, political and socio-cultural purposes, and, soon, also military ones.[56] Articulation between the promotion of controlled industrialization (assured by a controlled agricultural revolution) and the promotion of managed colonization (*colonização dirigida*) was crucial in the imperial, political, economic and social imagination of these decades. Moreover, the *colonatos* were considered to be a solution to the problem of demographic pressure in Portugal and to the problem of low population density in Portuguese overseas provinces, replicating the forms of autarky promoted in the metropole, as Orlando Ribeiro duly noted, and reproducing the programmes of internal colonization (*colonização interna*) that aimed to transform the metropole's rural landscape. They were a form of *social imperialism* in which the promotion of labour migratory schemes to the peripheries of the pluricontinental Portugal aimed to decrease the potential for domestic, metropolitan social conflict.[57] As Adriano Moreira noted, these *colonatos* should become replicas and carriers of the *pátria* (homeland) in the rural areas of the overseas provinces.[58] They were also seen to be potential instruments in the prevention of anti-colonial movements and also of potential territorial expansion by other colonial powers (as in the case of the *colonato de Matala* in southern Angola), via the local increase of the national demographic weight and interests. Although with a longer and diverse history, the debates on the forms and purposes of ethnic colonization unsurprisingly came to the forefront of imperial political discussions during the early 1950s, being closely related to the formulation of a new imperial strategy, both in relation to the colonial policies and the foreign policy on imperial affairs.[59] These efforts would only prove visible in the 1960s with the construction of important hydroelectric dams, the consolidation of the mining industry (iron ore, manganese, mica and copper) and of several industries for the local markets, and with the growing importance of migratory movements from Portugal to Angola and Mozambique.[60]

At another level, the issue of ethnic colonization was also related to two other historically inter-related problems of the Portuguese colonial venture in Africa: native labour and 'race relations'. In the first case, the *colonatos* were seen as improvements to the traditional, long-standing forms of labour relations within the empire. Given the fact that the economic function of the *colonatos* could only rely on metropolitan labour (and mechanized crops), they supposedly marked a decisive transformation of the social and moral economy of the empire, simultaneously with the end of the *indigenato* regime on 6 September 1961, the suppression of compulsory crop growing, and of forced labour in the overseas provinces, which occurred one year later. Together, these aspects were declared to have terminated the ruling discriminatory politics and policies engineering social and economic difference. However, this was not the reality on the ground, and debates about the civilizational shortcomings of this policy soon appeared. What was promoted as progressive could be said to entail a demise of the long-standing civilizing mission of the imperial venture. In the second case, obviously related to the first one, the racial divide entailed by the creation of white settlement nuclei (frequently involving the displacement of African communities already occupying those territories) was inconsistent with the lusotropicalist propaganda and the proclaimed exceptionality in patterns of ethnic co-existence and interaction.[61] The social and economic spatial division between the colonists and the natives was seen to endanger the resonance of the new modalities of imperial legitimization: the developmental and modernizing evidence and the lusotropical rhetoric. The contemporary, political international Zeitgeist advised a careful evaluation of the impact of this type of solutions. The recognition of this inconsistency and the pragmatic evaluation of the consequences brought about by the dissemination of conflicts in the north of Angola after 1961 led to the end of the prohibition of African labourers in the *colonatos*. While contributing, even if marginally, to the development and modernization of the colonial economy, the *colonatos* certainly contributed to enhance social and economic injustice within the colonial polity. In this sense, after two decades and circa $100 million spent in large planned schemes of rural settlement, characterized by strong developmental and modernizing rationales, the economic consequences appeared to be less significant than the social and political ones.[62]

All these goals were to be programmed and managed by a series of governmental agencies at a metropolitan and local level, the 'plethora of bureaucracy' mentioned earlier, controlled by the late-colonial state. The role and purpose of the Settlement Provincial Departments (Juntas Provinciais de Povoamento), set up in 1961, the formation of the Psycho-Social Service (Serviço Psico-Social) intervention teams (a clear hearts-and-minds project comprising a social worker, a male nurse, African instructors, one assistant and a leader), the formulation of a doctrine of rural welfare – *bem estar rural* (rural well-being) – and the instrumental use given to the community development paradigm in the Portuguese empire serve as consummate examples of the importance that planning and management of the politics and policies of rural settlement acquired within the developmental and modernizing empire.[63] The Cairo Conference on Problems of Economic Development in 1962, in which the theme of development was ubiquitous, also impacted on how the Portuguese understood the winds of change and strived to counterbalance their effects. These doctrines and agencies were important instruments in this process, which had the *colonatos* as main targets, and had a clear goal: to induce rapid but strictly controlled social transformation, based on modernizing principles, while at the same time demonstrating the country's commitment to the international, developmental progressive Zeitgeist. The exemplification of modern techniques of agricultural production, farm management, home economy, hygiene, and education were pillars of their activities. In 1965, twenty teams worked in Mozambique. In one year, 1963, they allegedly made 1,240 visits to *colonatos* and other rural areas. These doctrines and agencies also exemplify how the supposedly insulated imperial authoritarian regime engaged with and appropriated evolving global developmental languages and strategies to further its own ends: change to remain.

This was evident in relation to colonial labour issues, as it was in relation to community development. The creation of a commission for studies of development plans, related to the third development plan (1964–69) marked the institutionalization of community development as a planned policy, which aimed to modernize, sustain, and legitimize the new imperial strategy, giving instrumental use to global languages such as the one formulated at the Cambridge Summer Conference on African Administration in 1948, the Ashridge Conference on Social Development in 1954, at the UN in the Social and Economic Council (also in 1954), and the Community Development Guidelines prepared in 1956 by the US International Cooperation Administration to direct its technical assistance programmes at a local village level.[64] From the outset, the main debates over the doctrine and policy of community development were marked by a dialogue with international imperial development and security idioms and repertoires.[65] First, this was clear in the debate over its political utility: that is, over how it could be assessed as a state security issue and as a tool for international assertion. As an important expert advocated in 1962, 'if we fail in the field of social action in the overseas territories, in a more or less near future, the very existence of the Portuguese state will be seriously threatened'.[66] Second, this was also perceptible in the debates over its economic rationality: that is, over how community development could be an inexpensive propeller of economic growth.[67] Both of these debates were significantly related to older debates on the political and economic usefulness of plans of native 'villagization', evolving, not without dissension, since 1941, which involved the Superior Imperial Council and the corporate chamber, both producing lengthy and revealing reports on the matter, based on the evaluation of the law being devised at the time.[68]

Already being promoted since the mid-1940s, as the native *colonato* set up in Caconda (Angola) demonstrates,[69] the new African villages were another important example of the integrated conception of a developmental plan, in which – alongside a specific military-strategic reasoning – the creation of safe areas in which nationalist, insurgent influence could be restricted – a complete modernization package was conceived, articulating economic production, medical and sanitary assistance, educational upbringing and evangelization, as well as political control and indoctrination.[70] The villages were models of economic and social development, and were also central mechanisms of an over-arching counter-insurgency policy that unfolded steadily after the beginning of the colonial wars, a period in which the entire rural resettlement paradigm became a central element in the counter-insurgency strategy, which co-existed with 'search and destroy' operations.[71] The goals of the native *colonatos* were clear: coordination of agricultural produce according to the interests of the colony; promotion of Western forms of family; regulation of forms of property (marked by the increasing allocation of land and resources to Portuguese families or institutions);

control of migration and labour mobility; and rationalization of settlement patterns. They were also declared to entail the gradual implementation of wage labour, obviously defined according to the interests of the late-colonial state and of the private companies it favoured, and the promotion of a peasant middle class. Almost all these aspects were at the forefront of the villages schemes, despite their evident political, economic, and socio-cultural differences, and their geographical variation, associated with the particularities of local colonial realities.[72]

Promoted in the 1950s as an answer to economic, demographic, and land pressures, these rural resettlement schemes were one part of a larger project of societal transformation in the imperial world, which sought to modernize the empire in the context of growing political and diplomatic pressures and, from 1961, military strains. Military and security rationales soon prevailed over strict economic considerations. In Mozambique by 1973 it was argued that around one million Africans were confined to the many types (and functions) of villages devised as important spaces for the overall planning of counter-insurgency strategies, as crucial instruments of population control and indoctrination, as loci of progress, even if no concept or policy of *mille villages* was formulated, as happened in Algeria, a constant model for the Portuguese social and military reasoning.[73] Like the white or mixed *colonatos*, which were seen as possessing an important security and defence function, the native settlement schemes were at the forefront of the overall strategy of imperial resilience. As in other colonial contexts, they were examples of the 'spatialization of the colonial state of emergency', an attempt to change to remain, which failed to meet their declared goals.[74] Alongside other political, administrative, economic, and socio-cultural mechanisms, the schemes of rural resettlement were an important element in the historical uneven constitution of the late-colonial state in the Portuguese Empire, a particular 'repressive version of the developmentalist colonial state'. They would also become central to the post-colonial African societies.[75]

Conclusion

Portuguese late colonialism was characterized by a distinctive arrangement of coercive repertoires of rule, planned developmental strategies of political, economic, and socio-cultural change, and processes of engineering socio-cultural differentiation. A partial legacy of similar phenomena that characterized the so-called Third Portuguese Empire from the start, and also a manifest component of a wider strategy of imperial preservation and resistance to the manifold winds of change, this arrangement was based on entangled policies of a repressive developmentalism, co-ordinated, not without numerous deficiencies, by the empire and the colonial states. This chapter provides several arguments in order to demonstrate this centrality, exploring (inter-related) examples such as the design of new legal and administrative frameworks – at the metropole and colonial levels – the politics and policies of imperial developmentalism and the strategies of colonial social engineering, related, but not reducible to military and security rationales.

The history of these inter-related historical processes needs to be examined in a more detailed and empirical manner. This chapter does not, and could not, aim to provide an in-depth and exhaustive approach to any of these phenomena. The actual impact of these pro-cesses in the colonies is a central problem that is not addressed properly in these pages. At the same time, the understanding of the multiple historical connections that supported the mutual constitution of these processes needs to prevail over their isolated analysis. The history of late-colonial developmentalism requires an understanding of the mili-tarization of its rationale: that is to say, the understanding of the ways in which the military and security reasoning, enhanced by the growing colonial conflicts and by the consolidation of a police state, influenced the evolution of the former. Conversely, it is useful to understand the transformations of the military and security rationales, exploring how they were influenced, for instance, by developments in idioms and rep-ertoires of (international and imperial) developmentalism. The case for an imperative dialogue and combination of disparate historiographies can be easily argued, as can the case for a similar move in respect of the integration of scales of analysis.[76] Finally, an important aspect that was mentioned at the beginning of this chapter is the importance of explor-ing the inter-imperial, international, and transnational connections and dynamics influencing the historical manifestation of the distinctive arrangement mentioned above. Serving as an effective antidote to the long-standing and still prevailing doctrines of the exceptional nature of the Portuguese colonial empire (and others) and their variegated forms of methodological nationalism, the advancement of cross-imperial comparisons – the comparative assessment of the circulation, appro-priation, and instrumental use of idioms and repertoires of imperial and colonial rules, and of politics of difference – also enables a richer understanding of the late-colonial period, enhancing as well our evalu-ation of its legacies.[77]

Notes

1. F. Cooper, *Africa since 1940: The Past of the Present*, Cambridge, Cambridge University Press, 2002, p. 62. For the debate on the existence and nature of the late-colonial state see, among others, C. Young, *African Colonial State in Comparative Perspective*, New Haven, CT, Yale University Press, 1994; B. J. Berman, 'Review: The perils of Bula Matari: Constraint and power in the colonial state', *Canadian Journal of African Studies*, 31 3, 1997, pp. 556–570 (a critique of Young's assessment); J. Darwin, 'What was the late-colonial state?', *Itinerario*, 23, 3–4, 1999, pp. 73–82; M. Newitt, 'The late colonial state in Portuguese Africa', *Itinerario*, ¾, 1999, pp. 110–22. For the evolution of the colonial state in the 'Third' Portuguese colonial empire, see M. B. Jerónimo, 'The states of empire', in L. Trindade, ed., *The Making of Modern Portugal*, Newcastle, Cambridge Scholars Publishing, 2013, pp. 65–101. For a more general and rich contribution, see J. Scott, *Seeing like a State: How Certain Schemes to Improve the Human Condition have Failed*, New Haven, CT, Yale University Press, 1988.
2. For a recent overview see the special issue edited by M. B. Jerónimo and A. C. Pinto, 'International dimensions of Portuguese late colonialism and decolonization', *Portuguese Studies*, 29, 2, 2013. A recent book expanded these approaches: M. B. Jerónimo and A. C. Pinto, eds, *Portugal e o Fim do Colonialismo: Dimensões Internacionais*, Lisbon, Edições 70, 2014.
3. For the case of international development see F. Cooper and R. Packard, eds, *International Development and the Social Sciences: Essays in the History and Politics of Knowledge*, Berkeley, CA, University of California Press, 1997; for the globalization and localization of Cold War dynamics, see the now classic O. A. Westad, *The Global Cold War: Third World Interventions and the Making of Our Times*, Cambridge, Cambridge University Press, 2005, and the collective assessment in R. J. McMahon, ed., *The Cold War in the Third World*, Oxford, Oxford University Press, 2013. For one example of the role of one international organization and late colonialism and decolonization see D. R. Maul, *Human Rights, Development and Decolonization: The International Labour Organization, 1940–70*, Basingstoke, Palgrave Macmillan, 2012.
4. The emphasis on metropolitan or metro-centric dimensions is a notorious tendency in the study of imperial and colonial formations. For instance, see A. Porter, *European Imperialism, 1860–1914*, Basingstoke, Palgrave Macmillan, 1994. For an overview of the problem in social theory and in sociological literature see D. Chernilo, *A Social Theory of the Nation State: The Political Forms of Modernity beyond Methodological Nationalism*, London, Routledge, 2007. For an example of the benefits that can result from the incorporation of international, transnational and inter-imperial connections and dynamics see M. B. Jerónimo and J. P. Monteiro, 'Internationalism and the labours of the Portuguese colonial empire (1945–1974)', *Portuguese Studies*, 29, 2, 2013, pp. 142–163.
5. Obviously, this chapter does not pretend to address all these relevant aspects and issues. Much needs to be done on what relates to their articulated manifestation and historic co-constitution.
6. See, for instance, the diverse possible understandings proposed by N. Crawford, *Argument and Change in World Politics: Ethics, Decolonization*,

Humanitarian Intervention, Cambridge, Cambridge University Press, 2002; M. Callahan, *A Sacred Trust: The League of Nations and Africa, 1929–1946,* Brighton, Sussex Academic Press, 2004; E. Manela, *The Wilsonian Moment: Self-Determination and the International Origins of Anticolonial Nationalism,* Oxford, Oxford University Press, 2007.

7. In different measures and degrees of elaboration, we may argue, of course, that all these investigative modalities were part of previous imperial and colonial repertoires of rule. We are essentially interested in analysing their mid-20th century formulations and manifestations. For the notion and the types of investigative modalities see B. S. Cohn, *Colonialism and its Forms of Knowledge: The British in India,* Princeton, NJ, Princeton University Press, 1996.

8. For an overview see C. Bonneuil, 'Development as experiment: Science and state building in late colonial and. postcolonial Africa, 1930–1970', *Osiris,* 15, 2000, pp. 258–281.

9. The importance of state traditions – especially the metropolitan one, which 'shaped the subliminal premises of statecraft by colonial state agents', is mentioned by C. Young, 'The African colonial state revisited', *Governance,* 11, 1, 1998, p. 109.

10. For the notion of politics of difference see J. Burbank and F. Cooper, *Empires in World History: Power and the Politics of Difference,* Princeton, NJ, Princeton University Press, 2010.

11. These are some of the guidelines and questions of the international project Internationalism and Empire: The Politics of Difference in the Portuguese Colonial Empire in Comparative Perspective, coordinated by Miguel Bandeira Jerónimo (2013–2015). A comparative assessment of some or all of these questions has unfortunately yet to be done.

12. F. Cooper, 'Modernizing bureaucrats', 1997, p. 64.

13. For its history see M. Hailey, *An African Survey,* Oxford, Oxford University Press, 1938, pp. xxix–xxv; J. W. Cell, *Hailey: A Study in British Imperialism, 1872–1969,* Cambridge, Cambridge University Press, 1992, p. 211; H. Tilley, *Africa as a Living Laboratory: Empire, Development, and the Problem of Scientific Knowledge, 1870–1950,* Chicago, IL, Chicago University Press, 2011, especially pp. 69–114. For the formation of scientific knowledge in Portugal related to imperial affairs, see F. Ágoas, 'Estado, universidade e ciências sociais: A introdução da sociologia na Escola Superior Colonial (1952–1972)' and C. Castelo, 'Ciência, estado e desenvolvimento no colonialismo português tardio', in M. B. Jerónimo, ed., *O Império Colonial em Questão (Sécs XIX–XX): Poderes, Saberes e Instituições,* Lisbon, Edições 70, 2012, pp. 317–347, 349–387.

14. For the circulatory regimes and the epistemic communities, see P.-Y. Saunier, 'Circulations, connexions et espaces transnationaux', *Genèses,* 57, 4, 2004, pp. 110–126; P.-Y. Saunier, 'Les régimes circulatoires du domaine social 1800–1940: Projets et ingénierie de la convergence et de la différence', *Genèses,* 71, 2, 2008, pp. 4–25; S. Kott, 'Une 'communauté épistémique' du social? Experts de l'OIT et internationalisation des politiques sociales dans l'entre-deux-guerres', *Genèses,* 71, 2, 2008, pp. 26–46.

15. There were four development plans: 1953–58; 1959–64; 1965–1967; and 1968–73. V. Pereira, 'A economia do império e os planos de fomento', in Jerónimo, ed., *O Império Colonial em Questão,* 2012, pp. 261–295.

16. For a rich example see J. P. B. Coelho, *Protected Villages and Communal Villages in the Mozambican Province of Tete (1968–1982): A History of State Resettlement Policies, Development and War*, unpublished doctoral thesis, University of Bradford, 1993.

17. For the second colonial occupation see D. A. Low and J. Lonsdale, 'Towards the new order, 1945–1963', in D. A. Low and A. Smith, eds, *History of East Africa*, vol. III, Oxford, Clarendon, 1976, p. 12.

18. For the good government see J. M. Lee, *Colonial Development and Good Government: A Study of the Ideas Expressed by the British Official Classes in Planning Decolonization 1939–1964*, Oxford, Clarendon, 1967, p. 3. For a critical appraisal of its history see V. Hewitt, 'Empire, international development and the concept of good government', in M. Duffield and V. Hewitt, eds, *Empire, Development and Colonialism: The Past in the Present*, Woodbridge, James Currey, 2013, pp. 30–44. A comparative assessment of this history has still to be done.

19. After two timid reforms in the Revision of 1945 and in the Organic Charter of the Colonial Empire in 1949.

20. See M. B. Jerónimo, 'Geografias vitais: A imaginação (geo)política do novo imperialismo europeu (1870–1920)', in Á. Rivero and J. M. Hernández, eds, *El Espacio Político*, forthcoming, D. Bell, *The Idea of Greater Britain: Empire and the Future of World Order, 1860–1900*, Princeton, NJ, Princeton University Press, 2007; G. Wilder, *The French Imperial Nation-State: Negritude and Colonial Humanism between the Two World Wars*, Chicago, IL, University of Chicago Press, 2005, pp. 24–40.

21. The New State's single-party.

22. See decree-laws 2016, 29 May 1949 and 2048, 11 June 1951. J. F. Bossa, 'Organização política das províncias ultramarinas', *Boletim Geral das Colónias*, 2356, 1945, pp. 37–71. See also V. Loff, *Estudo de Base sobre o Ordenamento e Coordenação dos Serviços e Organismos Executivos da Política Económica Nacional de Âmbito Ultramarino*, Lisbon, Centro de Estudos Políticos e Sociais, 1960; A. H. Wilensky, *Tendencias de la Legislación Ultramarina Portuguesa en África*, Braga, PAX, 1968; A. E. D. Silva, 'Salazar e a política colonial do Estado Novo: O Acto Colonial (1930–1961)', in *Salazar e o Salazarismo*, Lisbon: Dom Quixote, 1989, pp. 101–152.

23. Salazar's speech of 11 July 1947, quoted in Y. Léonard, 'O ultramar português', in F. Bethencourt and K. Chaudhuri, *História da Expansão Portuguesa*, Vol. V: *Último Império e Recentramento (1930–1998)*, Lisbon: Círculo de Leitores, 1999, p. 34.

24. M. Caetano, *Portugal e o Direito Colonial Internacional*, Lisbon, Oficinas Gráficas Casa Portuguesa, 1948, p. 203. For the French case see F. Cooper, 'Citizenship and the politics of difference in French Africa, 1946–1960', in H. Fischer-Tiné and S. Gehrmann, eds, *Empires and Boundaries: Rethinking Race, Class, and Gender in Colonial Settings*, New York, NY, Routledge, 2009, pp. 107–128.

25. For the relationship between Portugal and the UN see A. E. D. Silva, 'O litígio entre Portugal e a ONU (1960–1974)', *Análise Social*, 30, 130, 1995, pp. 5–50; F. Martins, 'A política externa do Estado Novo: O ultramar e a ONU. Uma doutrina histórico-jurídica (1955–68)', *Penélope*, 18, 1998, pp. 189–206.

26. Decree-Law 2048, 11 June 1951, Article 159. M. Caetano, 'Discurso de S. Ex.ª o ministro das colónias no acto de posse do director geral, interino, de

fomento colonial e do inspector superior de fomento colonial', *Boletim Geral das Colónias*, 236, 1945, p. 8.

27. For a synthesis see J. C. Paulo, 'Ministério das colónias/ultramar', in F. Rosas and B. de Brito, *Dicionário de História do Estado Novo*, vol. II, Lisbon, Bertrand, 1996. For the GNP see C. Silva, 'Administrando o império: o Ministério das colónias/ultramar (1930–1974)', unpublished doctoral thesis, Universidade Nova de Lisboa, 2008, pp. 70–80. For the PIDE see D. C. Mateus, *A PIDE/DGS na Guerra Colonial (1961–1974)*, Lisbon, Terramar, 2004.

28. Decree-Law 41169, 29 June 1957; Decree-Law 45259, 21 September 1963. See Silva, *Administrando o Império*, 2008, pp. 56–59.

29. See *Revisão da Lei Orgânica do Ultramar. Reunião Extraordinária do Conselho Ultramarino*, Lisbon, Academia Internacional da Cultura Portuguesa, 1988.

30. For the notion of infrastructural power of the state see M. Mann, 'The autonomous power of the state: Its origins, mechanisms and results', *European Journal of Sociology*, 25, 1984, pp. 185–213.

31. See Jerónimo, 'The states of empire', 2012, pp. 81–2; Newitt, 'The Late Colonial State', 1999, pp. 110–22. For an informative coeval appraisal see, among others, N. A. Bailey, 'Government and administration' and 'The political process and interest groups', in D. M. Abshire and M. A. Samuels, eds, *Portuguese Africa: A Handbook*, New York, NY, Praeger, pp. 133–45, 146–64.

32. For a historical comparative account of the forms and processes of integration of native elites see A. Keese, *Living with Ambiguity: Portuguese and French Colonial Administrators, Mutual Influences, and the Question of Integrating an African Elite, 1930–1963*, Stuttgart, Steiner, 2007, pp. 111–75.

33. See H. Galvão and C. Selvagem, *Império Ultramarino Português: Monografia do Império*, vol. III: *Angola*, Lisbon, Empresa Nacional de Publicidade, 1950, pp. 236, 350.

34. F. A. Fernandes, *O Posto Administrativo na Vida do Indígena*, Lisbon, Europa-América, 1953.

35. Young, 'African colonial state', 1998, pp. 105–6. For a recent overview of the debates over colonial development in Portugal see Cláudia Castelo, 'Developing "Portuguese Africa" in late colonialism: confronting discourses', in Joseph Hodge, Gerald Hodl and Martina Kopf, eds, *Developing Africa: Concepts and Practices in Twentieth Century Colonialism*, Manchester, Manchester University Press, 2014.

36. For the classic account see A. Sarraut, *La Mise en Valeur des Colonies Françaises*, Paris, Payot, 1923.

37. For the civilizing mission question see M. B. Jerónimo, *Livros Brancos, Almas Negras: A 'Missão Civilizadora' do Colonialismo Português (c.1870–1930)*, Lisbon, ICS, 2010. For lusotropicalism, see C. Castelo, *'O Modo Português de Estar no Mundo': O Luso-tropicalismo e a Ideologia Colonial Portuguesa (1933–1961)*, Oporto, Afrontamento, 1999. Freyre went to Portugal and to the Portuguese colonies in 1951–1952. As a result he published *Aventura e Rotina: Sugestões de uma Viagem a Procura das Constantes Portuguesas de Carácter e Acção*, Rio de Janeiro, José Olympio, 1953.

38. M. B. Jerónimo, 'The "civilization guild": Race and labour in the Third Portuguese Empire c.1870–1930', in F. Bethencourt and A. Pearce, eds, *Racism and Ethnic Relations in the Portuguese-Speaking World*, London, Oxford University Press/British Academy, 2012, pp. 173–99; M. B. Jerónimo and

J. P. Monteiro, 'On "the difficulties to make the natives work": The "system" of indigenous labour in the Portuguese colonial empire', in Jerónimo, ed., *O Império Colonial*, 2012, pp. 159–96.

39. J. S. Cunha, *O Sistema Português de Política Indígena (Subsídios para o seu Estudo)*, Coimbra, Coimbra Editora, 1953, pp. 6–7. For the doctrine of integration see G. Freyre, *Integração Portuguesa nos Trópicos*, Lisbon, Junta de Investigações do Ultramar, 1958; A. Moreira, *A Batalha da Esperança*, Lisbon, Panorama, 1962, p. 106; J. P. Neto, *Angola: Meio Século de Integração*, Lisboa, Instituto Superior de Ciências Sociais e Política Ultramarina, 1964. Adriano Moreira was undersecretary of state of the overseas administration from 1959, and at the overseas provinces ministry from April 1961 to December 1962. For the civilizing mission as a mechanism of engineering inequality see J. Penvenne, 'We are all Portuguese!: Challenging the political economy of assimilation, Lourenço Marques 1870–1933', in L. Vail, ed., *The Creation of Tribalism in Southern Africa*, Berkeley, CA, University of California Press, 1989, pp. 265–269; Jerónimo, *Livros Brancos*, 2010.

40. See, for example, J. H. Saraiva, *Formação do Espaço Português*, Lisbon, Sociedade de Geografia de Lisboa, 1963; A. Moreira, *Congregação Geral das Comunidades Portuguesas*, Lisbon, Sociedade de Geografia, 1964; *Problemas do Espaço Português: Curso de Extensão Universitária*, Lisbon, Junta de Investigações do Ultramar, Centro de Estudos Políticos e Sociais, 1972.

41. For a general overview see M. Murteira, 'Formação e colapso de uma economia colonial', in Bethencourt and Chaudhuri, eds, *História da Expansão*, 1999, pp. 103–130. For a synthesis of the colonial expenditures of the central government, see L. Ferreira and C. Pedra, 'Despesas coloniais do estado português 1913–1980', *Revista de História Económica e Social*, 24, 1988, pp. 89–103.

42. See, for example, S. Cunha, *O Ultramar a Nação e o 25 de Abril*, Coimbra, Atlântida, 1977, p. 146.

43. Economic Reconstitution Law, Decree-law 1914, 24 May 1935; *Great Britain. Commercial Relations and Exports. Department of Portuguese East Africa (Mozambique). Economic and Commercial Conditions in Portuguese East Africa (Mozambique)*, London, HMSO, 1938, p. 8.

44. The Colonial Development Act of 1929 and the Colonial Development and Welfare Act of 1940; Fonds d'Investissements pour le Développement Economique et Social and the Caisse Centrale de l'Outre-Mer. For the British case see F. Pedler, 'British planning and private enterprise in colonial Africa', in P. Duignan and L. H. Gann, eds, *Colonialism in Africa*, vol. 4: *The Economics of Colonialism*, Cambridge, Cambridge University Press, 1975, pp. 113–117; D. J. Morgan, *The Official History of Colonial Development*, London: Macmillan, 1980; S. Constantine, *The Making of British Colonial Development Policy*, London, Frank Cass, 1984; M. Havinden and D. Meredith, *Colonialism and Development: Britain and its Tropical Colonies, 1850–1960*, London, Routledge, 1993, pp. 199–205. For the French case see V. Thompson and R. Adloff, 'French economic policy in tropical Africa', in P. Duignan and L. H. Gann, eds, *Colonialism in Africa*, vol. 4: *The Economics of Colonialism*, pp. 127–164, *maxime*, pp. 131–133; S. Dulucq, 'Fonds d'investissement pour le développement economique et social (FIDES)', in K. Shillington, ed., *Encyclopedia of African History*, vol. 1, London: Routledge, 2004, pp. 527–528.

45. The main areas and goals of the first developmental plan were: development of agriculture; increase of hydroelectric energy; installation of iron and steel industry; development of transport and communications.
46. When compared to other colonial powers, we can argue that a considerable investment was made. Mozambique received £20 million, whereas Uganda and Tanganyika received £16 and £17 million, respectively. Even if essentially provided by the colonial treasury or via loans provided by the metropolis ($18.5 million for Angola and Mozambique), the investment made becomes especially significant when compared to the past record of colonial development. *Plano de Fomento*, Decree-law 2058, 29 December 1952; Organic Law of the Overseas Provinces, Decree-law 2066, 27 June 1953.
47. M. S. Rodrigues, 'O aproveitamento dos recursos e povoamento do Ultramar português', *Boletim Geral do Ultramar*, 336–337, 1953, p. 67.
48. See *Economic Survey* (1959), table 4–xxii and xxiv, pp. 245–246. For the evolution of the provincial budgets see F. Brandenburg, 'Development, finance, and trade', in Abshire and Samuels, eds, *Portuguese Africa*, 1969, pp. 234–236, based on Banco de Angola, *Relatório e Contas. Exercício de 1966*, Lisbon, 1967, p. 193; and Moçambique, *Boletim Mensal da Direcção Provincial dos Serviços de Estatística*, 8, 3, 1967, p. 9. On the civilization guild see Jerónimo, 'Civilization Guild', 2012.
49. Decree-law 46312, 28 April 1964 and dispatch 24 August 1965. See Banco de Angola, *Investment of Foreign Capital in Portuguese Territories*, Lisbon, 1965.
50. Decree-law 35670, 28 May 1946 (Bank of Angola); Decree-law 41957, 13 November 1959 (transforming the Fundo de Fomento Nacional into the Banco de Fomento Nacional). For a survey of its history see A. B. Nunes, C. Bastien, N. Valério, R. M. de Sousa and S. D. Costa, 'Banking in the Portuguese Colonial Empire (1864–1975)', *Working Paper 41*, Gabinete de História Económica e Social, 2010, pp. 25–27.
51. See, among others, F. Brandenburg, 'Development, Finance, and Trade', 1969, pp. 226–230; L. Rist, 'Capital and capital supply in relation to development of Africa', in E. A. G. Robinson, ed., *Economic Development for Africa South of the Sahara*, New York, NY, St Martin's Press, 1964, pp. 446–447.
52. In the metropole, the same process was under way. For instance, the Anglo-American Corporation of South Africa controlled the largest production of wolfram and General Tire and Rubber, a company from Ohio, controlled the production of tyres. Organization for Economic Co-operation and Development. *Economic Survey: Portugal*, Paris, OECD, 1966, pp. 31–35, 114–121 (for a list of US interests in Angola in the 1960s onwards), cit. p. 119; W. Minter, *Portuguese Africa and the West*, New York, NY, Monthly Review Press, 1974, pp. 31–34, 115–127 (for US business interests in Portuguese Africa).
53. W. Clarence-Smith, 'Business empires in Angola under Salazar, 1930–1961', *African Economic History*, 14, 1985, pp. 1–13.
54. For some contributions see F. Rollo, 'O Programa de Assistência Técnica: O interesse americano nas colónias Portuguesas', *Ler História*, 47, 2004, pp. 81–123; M. B. Jerónimo, 'A question of priorities: The United States of America and the Portuguese Colonial Empire (1945–1961)', paper presented at the International Seminar on Decolonization, National History Center, Washington DC, 31 July 2009. For a global appraisal of the Marshall Plan see

D. S. Chassé, 'Towards a global history of the Marshall Plan: European post-war reconstruction and the rise of development economic expertise', in C. Grabas and A. Nützenadel, eds, *Industrial Policy in Europe After 1945: Wealth, Power and Economic Development in the Cold War*, Basingstoke, Palgrave, 2014, pp. 187–212. For the US-Africa policy see the revealing report prepared by the Office of African Affairs, 'The United States in Africa south of the Sahara', 4 August 1955, *FRUS*, 1955–1957, vol. XVIII, pp. 13–22, esp. 15 [direct reference to economic interests]. Among many other references see M. Leffler, 'The United States and the strategic dimensions of the Marshall Plan', *Diplomatic History*, 12, 3, 1988, pp. 277–306. See also N. J. White, 'Reconstructing Europe through rejuvenating empire: The British, French, and Dutch experiences compared', *Past&Present*, 210, 6, 2011, pp. 211–236. For a new overall appraisal of post-war economic transformations see M. Mazower, J. Reinisch and D. Feldman, *Post-war Reconstruction in Europe: International Perspectives, 1945–1949*, Oxford, Oxford University Press, 2011.

55. The Hudson Institute was involved in many similar operations, for instance in Brazil. Hudson Institute, *Thoughts and Impressions of Angola. By Members of the Hudson Institute Intensive Aerial Survey Team*, Croton-on-Hudson, NY, Hudson Institute, 1969. See also P. Dickson, *Think Tanks*, New York, NY, Atheneum, 1972, pp. 99–103; A. Rich, *Think Tanks, Public Policy, and the Politics of Expertise*, Cambridge, Cambridge University Press, 2004, pp. 46–49; W. Minter, *Portuguese Africa*, 1974, pp. 125–127. A reference to the impact of the Hudson Institute's reports is on G. Bender, *Angola under the Portuguese: The Myth and the Reality*, London, Heinemann, 1978, pp. 189–190, fn 84.

56. For Cela see R. Ventura, 'O caso da Cela e a colonização étnica de Angola', *I Congresso dos Economistas Portugueses: Problemas das economias ultramarinas, IV Secção*, Lisbon, Instituto Nacional de Estatística/Centro de Estudos Económicos, 1955, pp. 152–190; J. Denis, *Une Colonie Agricole Européenne en Afrique Tropicale: Cela, Angola Portugais*, Brussels, Direction de L'Agriculture des Forests et de l'Élevage, 1956; C. K. Abecassis, 'Prosseguimento dos trabalhos do colonato da Cela', *Boletim Geral do Ultramar*, 426, 1960, pp. 85–126; J. V. Jordão, *Povoamento em Angola 1962–1967*, Luanda, JPPA, 1969; E. Costa, 'Os colonatos em Angola: Génese, evolução e estado actual', unpublished doctoral thesis, Instituto Superior de Agronomia, Lisbon, 2006. For Matala see W. Marques, *Problemas do Desenvolvimento Económico de Angola*, Vol. 2, Luanda, Junta de Desenvolvimento Industrial, 1965, pp. 581–582. For Limpopo see T. de Morais, 'O colonato do Limpopo', *Estudos Políticos e Sociais*, 11, 2, 1964, pp. 477–498; R. Júnior, 'Industrialização e o colonato do Limpopo', *Boletim Geral do Ultramar*, 482, 1965, pp. 282–285.

57. E. de Castro Caldas, *Modernização da Agricultura: Conferências, Palestras e Artigos (1952–59)*, Lisbon, Livraria Sá da Costa, 1960, pp. 23–5; O. Ribeiro, *A Colonização de Angola e o Seu Fracasso*, Lisbon, Imprensa Nacional, 1981, p. 182. For the thesis of social imperialism see H.-U. Wehler, 'Bismarck's imperialism, 1862–1890', *Past & Present*, 48, 1970, pp. 119–155; G. Eley, 'Defining social imperialism: Use and abuse of an idea', *Social History*, 3, 1976, pp. 265–289.

58. A. Moreira, *Política Ultramarina*, Lisbon, Junta de Investigações do Ultramar, 1961.

59. For the 1940s see V. Ferreira, *Colonização Étnica da África Portuguesa*, Lisbon, Bertand & Irmãos, 1944. For the 1950s and 1960s see the entire volume *I*

Congresso dos Economistas Portugueses: Problemas das economias ultramarinas: IV Secção, Colonização Étnica. Comunicações e Debates, Lisbon, Instituto Nacional de Estatística/Centro de Estudos Económicos, 1955; J. M. Gaspar, 'A colonização branca em Angola e Moçambique', in *Colóquios de Política Ultramarina Internacionalmente Relevante*, Lisbon, Junta de Investigações do Ultramar, 1958, pp. 31–53; and the debates in *Colóquios sobre Problemas de Povoamento*, Lisbon, Junta de Investigações do Ultramar/Centro de Estudos Políticos e Sociais, 1960.

60. For ideas regarding the problem of settlement, see Junta de Investigações do Ultramar, *Colóquios sobre Problemas de Povoamento*, Lisbon, Tipografia Minerva, 1960. For the policies of emigration to the colonial world see C. Castelo, *Passagens para África: O Povoamento de Angola e Moçambique com Naturais da Metrópole (1920–1974)*, Oporto: Afrontamento, 2007.

61. See the debate between Reis Ventura and Valdez dos Santos in *I Congresso dos Economistas Portugueses*, pp. 343–347. See also G. Bender, 'Planned rural settlements in Angola: 1900–1968', in F. W. Heimer, ed., *Social Change in Angola*, Munich, Weltforum Verlag, 1973, pp. 235–279.

62. For a careful analysis of all these issues see Bender, ibid., pp. 104–131.

63. A. C. Soares, *Política de Bem-Estar Rural em Angola*, Lisbon, Junta de Investigações do Ultramar/Centro de Estudos Políticos e Sociais, 196; Junta de Investigações do Ultramar, *Promoção Social em Moçambique*: Grupo de Trabalho de Promoção Social de Moçambique, Lisbon, Centro de Estudos de Serviço Social e de Desenvolvimento Comunitário, 1964. See also 'Education, health, and social welfare', in Abshire and Samuels, eds, *Portuguese Africa*, 1969, pp. 194–195. For Diamang, see T. Cleveland, 'Rock solid: African laborers on the diamond mines of the Companhia de Diamantes de Angola (Diamang), 1917–1975', unpublished doctoral thesis, University of Minnesota, 2008. For Cassequel, see J. Ball, ' "The colossal lie": The Sociedade Agrícola do Cassequel and Portuguese colonial labor policy in Angola, 1899–1977', unpublished doctoral thesis, University of California, Los Angeles, 2003.

64. For the labour issue see M. B. Jerónimo and J. P. Monteiro, 'O império do trabalho: Portugal, as dinâmicas do internacionalismo e os mundos coloniais', in M. B. Jerónimo and A. C. Pinto, eds, *Portugal e o Fim do Colonialismo: Dimensões Internacionais*, Lisbon: Edições 70, 2014. For the community development see, among others, A. de Sousa, 'Desenvolvimento comunitário em Africa', *Estudos Ultramarinos*, 4, 1959, pp. 7–17; A. de Sousa, 'Desenvolvimento comunitário em Angola', in *Angola: Curso de Extensão Universitária do Ano Lectivo de 1963–1964*, Lisbon, Instituto Superior de Ciências Sociais e Política Ultramarina, 1964, pp. 421–440; A. J. de P. Guerra, 'Reordenamento rural e desenvolvimento comunitário', *Trabalho: Boletim do Instituto do Trabalho, Previdência e Acção Social*, 4, 1963, pp. 83–128; F. A. S. Alberto, 'Integração dos programas de desenvolvimento comunitário nos quadros da política nacional', *Mensário Administrativo: Publicação de Assuntos de Interesse Ultramarino*, 192–197, 1963, pp. 3–14. For a general comparative appraisal see, for example, S. N. Bhattacharyya, *Community Development in Developing Countries*, Calcutta, Academic, 1972, pp. 1–3, and a balance in L. E. Holdcroft, 'The rise and fall of community development 1950–65: A critical assessment', in C. Eicher and J. Staatz, eds, *Agricultural Development in the Third World*, Baltimore, MD, Johns Hopkins University Press, 1984,

pp. 45–58. For the broader issues see F. Cooper and R. Packard, eds, *International Development and the Social Sciences: Essays in the History and Politics of Knowledge*, Berkeley, CA, University of California Press, 1997, pp. 1–43.

65. For the appropriation of international idioms of community development by the Portuguese see J. P. Neto, 'Política de desenvolvimento comunitário nas províncias portuguesas de África', *Ultramar*, 9, 1962, p. 41; A. de Sousa, 'Organização e programas de desenvolvimento comunitário', *Estudos Políticos e Sociais*, I, 3, 1963, p. 553; A. Cancelas, 'A terra e o desenvolvimento comunitário em Moçambique', unpublished Master's dissertation, Lisbon, ISCSPU, 1966, pp. 120, 126–128.

66. Neto, 'Política de Desenvolvimento', 1962, p. 57.

67. For one example of this reasoning see A. de Sousa, 'Desenvolvimento comunitário e desenvolvimento económico', *Estudos políticos e sociais*, II, 2, 1964, p. 294.

68. See 'Organização social e económica das populações indígenas' and 'Parecer sobre o decreto relativo à organização social e económica das populações indígenas', *Boletim Geral das Colónias*, 191, 1941, pp. 7–97, 98–119. See also J. C. Pereira, 'Da influência do aldeamento na melhoria da organização social e económica das populações indígenas (aspectos particulares do problema na Província da Zambézia, unpublished Master's dissertation', Lisbon ISCSPU, 1949.

69. Created in 1945–46, this native *colonato* was reinforced in 1949 with technical assistance and some machinery given by the Agricultural Central Services. From 1952 to 1966, the number of farmers increased steadily and more than 4,000 natives lived in the *colonato* and its nucleus. For the early native *colonatos* see F. Boaventura, 'Os colonatos indígenas em Angola', *Agros*, ½, 1951, pp. 44–50; M. Feio, *As Causas do Fracasso da Colonização Agrícola de Angola*, Lisbon, Ministério da Ciência e Tecnologia, Instituto de Investigação Científica Tropical, 1998, p. 30.

70. See R. F. de Freitas, *Conquista da Adesão das Populações*, Lourenço Marques, Serviços de Centralização e Coordenação de Informações, 1965; C. Bessa, 'Angola: A luta contra a subversão e a colaboração civil-militar', *Revista Militar*, 8/9, 1972, pp. 407–443. For an overview see J. P. Cann, *Counterinsurgency in Africa: The Portuguese Way of War, 1961–1974*, Solihull, Helion & Co, 2012, pp. 148–169 and Bender, *Angola under the Portuguese*, 1978.

71. See, for example, the debates in the bulletin of the *Junta de Investigações do Ultramar*, 62, 1963; the *Congresso de Povoamento e Promoção Social*, 5–9 October 1970; namely, Hermes Araújos Oliveira's participation. See his *Povoamento e Promoção Social in África*, Famalicão: Centro Gráfico de Famalicão, 1971. Oliveira was also the author of one of Portugal's most important counter-insurgency manuals. See *Subversão e Contra-subversão*, Lisbon, Instituto Superior de Ciências Sociais e Política Ultramarina, 1963; J. P. Neto, 'Movimentos subversivos de Angola: Tentativa de esboço sócio-político' in *Angola: Curso de Extensão Universitária*, Lisbon, Instituto Superior de Ciências Sociais e Política Ultramarina, 1964, pp. 343–386.

72. For the strategies of rural resettlement, see R. M. S. Ravara, *Contribuição Para uma Política de Reordenamento Rural no Ultramar*, Lisbon, Junta de Investigações do Ultramar, 1970; A. J. de P. Guerra and J. B. Veiga, *Revisão do III Plano de Fomento: Promoção Social*, Luanda, Junta Provincial de

Povoamento, 1970, pp. 113–129. See also B. Jundanian, 'Resettlement programs: Counterinsurgency in Mozambique', *Comparative Politics*, 6, 4, 1974, pp. 519–540; G. Bender, 'The limits of counterinsurgency: An African case', *Comparative Politics*, 4, 3, 1972, pp. 331–360. For geographical variations, see Bender, *Angola under the Portuguese*, 1978, pp. 159–160, 165–196. For a typology of settlement schemes in tropical Africa, see R. Chambers, *Settlement Schemes in Tropical Africa*, London, Routledge, 1969, pp. 18–22.

73. This estimate was offered by the commander-in-chief in Mozambique, General Kaúlza de Arriaga. See B. Jundanian, Ibid., p. 523. Thomas Henriksen confirms this in *Revolution and Counterrevolution: Mozambique's War of Independence, 1964–1974*, London, Greenwood, 1978, p. 155. A similar figure is advanced for Angola. See W. van der Waals, *Portugal's War in Angola 1961–1974*, Rivonia, Ashanti, 1993, pp. 200–201. For the concept of *mille villages* see M. Cornaton, *Les Camps de Regroupement de la Guerre d'Algérie*, Paris, L'Harmattan, 1998, pp. 68–74; F. Klose, *Human Rights in the Shadow of Colonial Violence: The Wars of Independence in Kenya and Algeria*, Philadelphia, University of Pennsylvania Press, 2013, pp. 168–171.

74. For a comparative assessment of similar processes see Klose, Ibid., p. 236.

75. For the historical legacies see M. L. Bowen. *The State Against the Peasantry: Rural Struggles in Colonial and Postcolonial Mozambique*, Charlottesville and London, University Press of Virginia, 2000; M. Mahoney, '*Estado Novo, Homem Novo* (New State, New Man): Colonial and anticolonial development ideologies in Mozambique, 1930–1977', in D. C. Engerman, N. Gilman, M. H. Haefele and M. E. Latham, eds, *Staging Growth: Modernization, Development, and the Global Cold War*, Amherst, MA, University of Massachusetts Press, 2003, pp. 165–198; J. P. B. Coelho, 'State resettlement policies in post-colonial rural Mozambique: The impact of the communal village programme on Tete province, 1977–1982', *Journal of Southern African Studies*, 24, 1, 1998, pp. 61–91.

76. See M. B. Jerónimo, 'A escrita plural dos impérios: Economia, geopolítica e religião na obra de Andrew Porter', in A. Porter, ed., *O Imperialismo Europeu, 1860–1914*, Lisbon, Edições 70, 2011, pp. 7–67.

77. For two recent comparative approaches see M. Shipway, *Decolonization and its Impact: A Comparative Approach to the End of the Colonial Empires*, Oxford, Blackwell, 2008; M. Thomas, B. Moore and L. J. Butler, *Crises of Empire: Decolonization and Europe's Imperial States, 1918–1975*, London, Hodder Education, 2008.

3
Commanders with or without Machine-Guns: Robert Delavignette and the Future of the French-African 'Imperial Nation State', 1956–58

Martin Shipway

> *Let's be frank, we are worried – above all we are worried by the prevailing colonial policy, we who will one day become its instruments. Our good faith is met with contradictions, immobilism and pretence. Perhaps the hope is to use our idealism in order to manoeuvre us into making a 'last stand' for colonialism.*
>
> *It would be a vain hope. For we will not do imperialism's handiwork, not even if imperialism is dressed up as 'French sovereignty', nor will we act as 'machine-gunner commanders' ['commandants mitrailleurs'] for the years of transition to come. We must put a stop to this ambiguity: we will stand by the peoples whom we wish to help in their efforts to emancipate themselves – but whom we are as yet ill-prepared to understand and to serve.*[1]

In February 1956, cadets at the *École Nationale de la France d'Outre-Mer* (ENFOM), who were being trained to run an empire that would barely outlast their first overseas posting, mounted a minor and largely unsung revolt against the system into which they were being initiated. In their self-published student paper (quoted above), the leaders of the revolt complained about the outdated curriculum, but also questioned the future of the French Union and their place within it. In particular, their editorial spoke of an 'evolution of the Overseas Territories towards a desirable autonomy' and of the 'necessary transformation of the role of the administrator, who must cede political power to Africans and

Malagasy, becoming merely a temporary economic or administrative counsellor'. This analysis was dismissed by the Director of ENFOM, Pierre Bouteille, but what no doubt irked officials was the polemical tone, and especially the inflammatory allusion to '*commandants mitrailleurs*', an untranslatable pun that denotes a cavalry officer commanding a tank from its machine-gun turret, but which irresistibly evokes a colonial officer (*commandant*) wielding a machine-gun. Though the cadets were brought before a disciplinary panel which recommended expulsion, this was rescinded by the newly appointed minister of overseas France in Guy Mollet's Socialist-led government, Gaston Defferre, following the intervention of a number of African *députés* in the National Assembly, including the future presidents of Senegal and Guinea, Léopold Sédar Senghor and Ahmed Sékou Touré.[2] It would in any case be difficult to imagine Defferre courting the scandal that would have resulted from the expulsions when he was poised to embark on major reformist legislation, in the shape of the June 1956 Loi-Cadre (Framework Law) that would bear his name.[3]

It is perhaps not so surprising that a group of highly articulate, well-educated, if essentially unformed, young men, who read the news, had followed the proceedings of the 1955 Bandung Conference (which, they complained, was absent from the curriculum), and who fraternized with African students in student halls, should have taken a view on the future course of France's imminent peaceful or 'successful' decolonization in sub-Saharan Africa.[4] The ENFOM rebels were not exactly convincing as revolutionaries, having already risen to the top of the fiercely competitive entrance scheme for one of France's *grandes écoles*, the training academies of France's administrative, political, and business elites. Once the threat of expulsion was lifted, they had little to fear in their future careers. Even without an empire to run, graduation from ENFOM served to incorporate them into the higher echelons of the state in an increasingly technocratic French Republic where, alongside so-called *énarques* (graduates of the then recently founded but already prestigious Ecole Nationale de l'Administration (ENA), whose curriculum and ethos were in part inspired by those of ENFOM), they enjoyed high-flying careers in the prefectural or diplomatic *corps*, or in other ministries, particularly those for Culture and for Cooperation.[5]

However, a subtle but bold claim has been made for the cadets by Pierre Vérin, remembering his own role as one of the rebellious cadets (and subsequently a distinguished academic ethnographer), that they had '*defined* [...] the lines of what would become the future of a peaceful decolonization'.[6] As he suggests, although the institutions of the French

Union were in any case set to evolve rapidly along reformist lines, thanks to the impending Loi-Cadre, the cadets had given an undertaking that, in their future capacity as administrators, they would not 'drag their feet', and would play their part in that evolution. Conversely, by refusing to 'do imperialism's handiwork',[7] Vérin argues, they were setting limits to their future action, and hence defining the scope of future colonial policy.

This claim is essentially unprovable in specific terms, and it has about it more than a hint of post-colonial 'wisdom after the event'. Nonetheless, it is worth taking seriously, if only for the light which may be shed on a still under-examined enigma of the period of decolonization, and of French decolonization in particular, namely the workings of the French 'official mind' in the face of the impending end of empire. The specific focus for this chapter is on a man who was well known to the rebellious ENFOM cadets, Governor-General Robert Delavignette (1897–1976), a distinguished exemplar of French officialdom, and one of a very select band of 'intellectuals' of the French colonial establishment. By the mid-1950s, Delavignette was approaching the end of a long career stretching back to the 1920s, and thus embracing much of the lifespan of the post-conquest French African 'imperial nation-state'. By the time of his students' revolt, he had withdrawn from front-line colonial administration to a chair at ENFOM, to writing, and to continued membership of the French colonial establishment, but, as it turned out, not yet to inactivity and certainly not to docility.

The counter-claim to that made on behalf of the ENFOM rebels is twofold. First, for all their youthful radicalism, the rebels were to some considerable extent reflecting the teaching they were receiving at ENFOM; indeed, filtered only very slightly, the paragraphs quoted at the outset might almost be a paraphrase of Delavignette's writings and teaching. Delavignette's lecture notes on the history and constitutional development of the French Union have been preserved in his private papers, and, although no reference has so far turned up to Bandung, it is clear that, *pace* the editorialists of *Le Bleu d'Outre-Mer*, Delavignette's teaching was up-to-the-minute: his lecture on Ghana delivered in 1956 was updated by hand in 1957 to reflect the coming of independence, and delivered again in 1958.[8] Though the subject matter was no doubt predominantly 'dry', it was enlivened by the tall, white-haired, stentorian and affectionately respected Delavignette (*'le grand Bob'*), whom his students recall 'rambling on' about *Eurafrique*.[9] But his influence is detectable in the idea of 'peoples whom we wish to help [...] but whom we are as yet ill-prepared to understand and to serve'. This may be read as a distillation of twenty or more years of colonial reformist thinking, collected under the banner of 'colonial humanism'. In particular, the figure of the *commandant*, without machine-gun and transmuted into a 'temporary economic or administrative counsellor', is clearly recognizable as an updated version of the *broussard*, or *commandant de cercle* (the French equivalent of the British District Officer), the solitary, heroic *homme à tout faire* (another trope which the cadets semi-plagiarized) who had been at the centre of Delavignette's vision since the 1930s.

Secondly, and perhaps more importantly, it is claimed that, whatever Delavignette's influence may have been on the ENFOM cadets, it was returned with interest. This is not to suggest that we can trace direct influence exerted by the rebels on Delavignette, but certainly Delavignette's respectful understanding of the young men in his charge, profound awareness of the responsibility that was being placed on their shoulders – and of the limits of that responsibility – are crucial to an understanding of Delavignette's role in the episode to which we turn in the latter part of this chapter. This relates to Delavignette's membership of the Commission for the Safeguard of Human Rights (hereafter Commission de Sauvegarde) appointed by the Mollet Government to investigate allegations of abuse in Algeria, and from which Delavignette was to resign spectacularly in September 1957.

Before turning to Delavignette's brief moment in the spotlight of late-colonial controversy, we must first consider how to approach his career and his impact. How should we read Robert Delavignette in the 1950s; and indeed, why should we study him at all?

Reading Delavignette across time and space

Delavignette is a pivotal figure in our understanding of the French late-colonial establishment, not least because he found himself, through the biographical contingencies of a long and influential career, at the intersection of two historical axes. In one dimension, he represented a kind of institutional memory in French colonial thinking going back to the 1920s, which he sought to update for the rapidly changing environment of the post-war period. But in another dimension, he was able to bring his influence to bear on a broad front, operating across an unofficial and largely unspoken partition which separated off Algeria from the 'rest' of France's overseas territories, and in particular from the sub-Saharan African territories in which he was a specialist. Without the role he created for himself in this latter dimension, Delavignette might simply be dismissed as a 'throwback' from an earlier phase of French colonialism. But, conversely, it was the insights he derived from his career as a colonial practitioner, and the authority it conferred, which allowed him to act momentarily and perhaps unexpectedly as the official conscience of France in Algeria.

Delavignette's *cursus honorum* as colonial official, field officer, senior administrator, as well as publicist, theorist, teacher, and writer, would be sufficient to maintain an interest in a distinguished 'proconsul'. Born in Burgundy, the son of a sawmill owner, and mobilized in 1916 as an artillery officer, Delavignette was a colonial administrator from the early 1920s, serving as a *commandant de cercle* in the French West African territories of Niger and Haute-Volta (Burkina Faso today). By 1930, through ill-health and family circumstances, Delavignette had retreated, almost for good, from active service in the field to a desk job in Paris, and to writing. He was Marius Moutet's *chef de cabinet* at the ministry of colonies in Léon Blum's Popular Front Government when, in 1937, he was appointed as director of ENFOM. He held this post throughout the Occupation, when he helped ENFOM cadets evade conscription into the Service du Travail Obligatoire (Compulsory Labour Service); this, and his discreet encouragement of cadets engaging in the Resistance, exempted him from administrative *épuration* in 1944–45, with the advocacy of his stepson, Jean Mairey, then Commissioner for the Republic in Dijon, and subsequently an outspoken official critic of policing in Algeria.[10] Delavignette's name is third in the list of eminent ethnographer-administrators who directed ENFOM from the 1920s, succeeding Maurice Delafosse and Georges Hardy, and preceding Paul Mus.[11] After ENFOM, he served as high commissioner in Cameroun (1946–47), where he acted to stabilize the territory following the unrest amongst the small but fractious settler community, before becoming director of political affairs at the ministry of overseas France (1947–51). In this latter role, he succeeded the slightly younger and more outspoken Henri Laurentie; work remains to be done on Delavignette's impact on policy in this period, not only in Africa, but also in Indochina through the period of implementation of the 'Bao Dai solution'.[12]

Véronique Dimier has made the case for Delavignette as theorist of an emerging 'science' of colonial administration, placing him as one of a select Anglo-French band of colonial specialists in the inter-war period.[13] It was to a newly created chair in colonial administration that Delavignette was appointed when he returned to teach at ENFOM. Though it was not intended as a personal chair, it was certainly created in his image and to his specification, and he would be the sole incumbent. In 1967, following his retirement in 1963, he was the subject of a respectful special issue of the *Revue française d'Histoire d'Outre-Mer*, with contributions from Léopold Senghor (then president of Senegal), his former boss Marius Moutet (who died before the volume appeared), various former colleagues and pupils, and from Delavignette himself; and in 2001, he was accorded the posthumous academic recognition of a colloquium, which surveyed his career, his political writings, and literary output.[14] This colloquium built on the work of William Cohen, who placed Delavignette at the centre of his pioneering study of ENFOM and of the *corps colonial*; Delavignette belonged quite properly in Gann and Duignan's 1978 collection of *African Proconsuls*, again with Cohen's advocacy.[15]

The core of Delavignette's thinking and action derived from his association with the school of thought that has come to be known as 'colonial humanism'; the term was not used by its practitioners, but was first generalized by Raoul Girardet in his 1972 study *L'Idée coloniale en France de 1871 à 1962*.[16] Colonial humanism was 'the interwar [colonial] reform movement, its underlying political rationality, and the corresponding form of government that developed in AOF after World War I';[17] the movement is chiefly associated with the idea of promoting the welfare of colonial populations, with a view to increasing their economic productivity and more generally easing their path to modernity. Gary Wilder places this movement's doctrine at the heart of his argument concerning the necessary contradiction, or 'antinomy', lying deep within French colonial doctrine, and indeed underpinning a broader national and Republican narrative, which held in permanent tension the French Republic's claims to universalism, on the one hand, and French imperialism's insistence on an inevitably racialized and hierarchized particularism on the other.[18] This antinomic tension helps explain why French colonial government could be 'simultaneously rationalizing and racializing, modernizing and primitivizing, universalizing and particularizing'.[19] Not least, it resolves the recurrent, and deeply sterile, debate between the supposedly antithetical French doctrines of association and assimilation, which for Wilder can be seen as 'one-sided reifications of a doubled colonial rationality within which both tendencies remained interconnected'.[20] A further concept of Wilder is of critical importance to what follows. This is what he terms the 'analytic of failure' within which French colonial doctrine has tended to be discussed, which measures its (lack of) achievements according to an implied paradigm of 'rhetoric versus reality', presupposing a 'narrative of progress against which reformers' failure and success may be easily evaluated'.[21] According to this framework, colonial humanism failed either because its practitioners were well-intentioned idealists whose 'dream' was prevented from becoming 'effective reality' because of administrative paralysis;[22] or because it was only ever a dissimulating ideology designed to mask colonialism's true nature.

Bypassing the 'analytic of failure' allows us to consider Delavignette's contribution to the colonial reform movement on its own terms, but it also eases our passage forwards with him into the 1950s: after all, if Delavignette 'failed', then he did so over a very sustained period. Three recurring themes are particularly associated with Delavignette, which he elaborated in a variety of genres and publications, often lyrically: he was, as Wilder puts it, 'the movement's sentimentalist'.[23] The first of these themes is an evocation of an imagined Franco-African fusion, which readily overlapped with the parallel theme of a trans-imperial Greater France (*'la plus grande France'*), but which was driven by a deep sense of respect and affection for African culture and the way of life he encountered – and, as an administrator, delved into and reordered – in the villages of the Sahel. This theme first found expression in the official pamphlet he wrote on AOF (*Afrique Occidentale Française*, French West Africa) for the Great Colonial Exposition of 1931 – that great celebration and indeed sacralization of a utopian Greater France. It was developed further and more personally in his novel *Paysans Noirs*, published pseudonymously in 1931, the fictionalized account of a year in the life of a colonial administrator in the African bush, which Girardet describes as 'a sort of African *Georgics*, the attentive and affectionate chronicle of the works and days of African villages'.[24] Further, in his travel-memoir *Soudan-Paris-Bourgogne* (1935), he recounted a journey to the French Soudan (Mali) and back, to a Paris, in 1934, apparently on the brink of civil war, reflecting on how his own identity had been shaped by both the Soudan and Paris, as well as by his provincial origins in Burgundy; he urged his readers to 'create in thought, not only a European France but an African France'.[25]

The second theme revolved around Delavignette's ideal of colonial command embodied in the archetypal 'broussard' (man of the bush), the protagonist of *Paysans Noirs*, but also at the centre of Delavignette's manifesto-cum-teaching manual from the end of the decade, *Les vrais Chefs de l'empire*.[26] These themes are intertwined with each other, and in turn with a third theme, which is Delavignette's insistence on the essential modernity of colonial administration. In the opening chapter of *Les vrais Chefs*, for example, Delavignette argued that the apparently undifferentiated daily tasks of the *broussard* reflected the modernity of the colonial enterprise in which he was engaged:

The first time I was able to step back and see the colony in perspective, that is, on my first leave, I found it was not easy to explain what I had been doing. If I told French people in Europe of all the things I had to do in the same job and even on the same day, they did not understand that all these made up one job, and that in going from the courts to a road-making project, from road-making to a census, from a census to agriculture – from one task to another, I was not changing my job; or else they thought: This colony is only a black man's country and does not require a highly developed government if one man can do everything. They did not recognize the revolution in administrative method which this meant, or the new world it had produced. They did not suspect that the colony was no longer a strange and alien realm but an integral part of the modern world with a vigorous native life.[27]

Here, surely, is one of the sources for the ENFOM rebels' trope of the imperial 'homme à tout faire'. Writing in 1939 when he was already director of ENFOM, he was self-consciously instructing a future cohort of would-be *broussards*. In its first edition, *Les vrais Chefs* was censored by the Vichy regime (for reasons that remain obscure – it was hardly subversive), and republished, largely unchanged but with a more progressive title, *Service Africain*, in 1946.[28] So, too, the figure of the *broussard* straddled the Second World War, was central to Delavignette's resumed teaching at ENFOM, and resurfaced in his largely unmediated response to African decolonization, and to the Algerian endgame, published in 1962 as *L'Afrique noire et son destin*. By 1968, the *broussard* had transmuted into the post-colonial (or neo-colonial) figure of the *coopérant* engaged in development projects that had barely changed in nature and purpose since the 1920s.[29] As we will see, this theme also conditioned Delavignette's response to the Algerian conflict.

Delavignette's involvement in Algerian affairs started only after he had stepped down from the ministry of overseas France. Algeria's status as an 'external province' of France dictated an institutional divide, sometimes referred to as a 'cloison étanche' (sealed partition) which could be measured not only in terms of ministerial responsibility – Algeria was governed from the ministry of the interior rather than from foreign affairs (as was the case for Tunisia and Morocco) or from overseas France – but also at a deeper level, extending for example to elite formation: despite Delavignette's efforts, Algerian officials were trained not at ENFOM but at the National Foundation for Political Sciences (Sciences Po), followed (from around 1950) by ENA.[30] But it was also a symbolic divide, determined by geographical proximity to France and by the substantial presence of settlers, and which would steadily deepen as the war in Algeria lengthened and intensified. Even before joining Mollet's Commission de Sauvegarde, Delavignette had already crossed this invisible boundary in 1955, the first full year of the war, when, as a member of the Economic Council (Conseil Economique, a constitutionally enshrined consultative assembly of the French Fourth Republic), he had prepared a ground-breaking report on 'The social and economic situation of Algeria' which, not least, opened the way to the kind of development reforms introduced in de Gaulle's 1958 'Constantine Plan'.[31] No doubt the reasons why Delavignette was selected for membership of the Commission de Sauvegarde included the evidence the report provided of his attachment to a French Algeria. A year later, in April 1956, he put his name to the declaration creating the Union for the Salvation and Renewal of French Algeria (USRAF), the brainchild of Jacques Soustelle, until early 1956 the Governor-General of Algeria, with whom Delavignette had come into contact during the compiling of the report. However, Delavignette quickly distanced himself from the Union once he realised the uses to which it was intended by Soustelle, as a means of mobilising support for French settlers in Algeria.[32]

Delavignette and the Commission de Sauvegarde

As we turn to the short-lived and largely forgotten Commission de Sauvegarde, it is as if we have switched narratives from the intellectual history of French colonialism to the *histoire événementielle* of the war in Algeria, and to the thick of its central, burning issue circa 1957, that is, the debate surrounding French abuse and torture of detainees at the time of the Battle of Algiers. Here, failure was more immediate and tangible: as Raphaëlle Branche comments, amongst former activists against the war, the Commission de Sauvegarde warrants a shrug of the shoulders, having served merely to 'deflect the indignation that was starting to be expressed'; while former soldiers struggle to remember it at all.[33] Though Robert Delavignette's resignation from the Commission created a stir in September 1957, all the more so when he leaked the Commission's general report to *Le Monde* a month later, its impact was soon eclipsed (and has remained so ever since), not least by the publication in February 1958 – followed almost immediately by its seizure – of Henri Alleg's *La Question*, relating the Communist journalist Alleg's own detention and torture. As if to underscore the Commission's uselessness, its investigations in Algiers coincided with Alleg's arrest in June 1957, as well as with the detention and 'disappearance' (which we now know to have been his murder, ordered by General Paul Aussaresses) of Alleg's fellow Communist, the 25-year-old mathematician Maurice Audin.[34] Delavignette joined a select band of senior official 'whistle-blowers', as well as legions of junior, typically anonymous, dissidents, protesters, conscientious objectors, and rebels, and the more celebrated canon of journalists, intellectuals, and activists. Indeed, the Commission was established by Guy Mollet in April 1957 precisely to counter the impact of a number of high-profile protests, notably that of General Jacques Pâris de Bollardière who, having requested to be relieved of his command in Algeria in January 1957, publicly denounced torture in the pages of *L'Express* and was sentenced to 60 days' military detention for his pains, also in April 1957. Pierre Vidal-Naquet, in the updated edition of his invaluable collection of documents *La Raison d'État*, salutes Delavignette as one of three 'traitors' (the speech-marks are Vidal-Naquet's) who in 1961 provided him with the documents which gave substance to the original edition; the others were Delavignette's stepson Jean Mairey, author of three highly critical reports on the police in Algeria, and Paul Teitgen, secretary-general responsible for the police at the Algiers prefecture from August 1956 to September 1957, who provided critical evidence to the Commission.[35] The point of departure for what follows, however, is Vidal-Naquet's further, somewhat drily understated, comment on Delavignette that 'he was not an anti-colonialist on principle, but he had a sense of the State to the highest degree'.[36] As will be argued, that 'sense of the State' may be understood as embracing the distilled lessons of Delavignette's colonial humanism.

The Commission de Sauvegarde never fully escaped from the taint of its ambiguous origins, nor from the constraints that were placed on its actions from the outset. Stirred into action by General de Bollardière's *démarche*, but also by the controversy surrounding the alleged 'suicide' while in detention of the Algerian lawyer Ali Boumendjel, Guy Mollet announced the creation of the Commission on 5 April 1957 in a communiqué which opened with a tribute to the '700,000 men' of the French Army whose efforts in Algeria were restoring 'peace and Franco-Muslim friendship, when some would wish to present them as so many torturers'; and which credited the ministers for Algeria and defence, and the secretary of state for the armed forces (Robert Lacoste, Maurice Bourgès-Maunoury, Max Lejeune) with the idea for the Commission, when they had in fact opposed it. The Commission was to investigate, as they arose, cases of 'individual failures' in respect of 'this policy of a France attached to the safeguard of human rights'; and was charged with establishing 'not only the truth or otherwise of reported cases, but also the calumnious and systematically exaggerated nature of any information'.[37] It was perhaps to be expected that a group of twelve members of the 'great and the good' would include a preponderance of conservatives likely to respond positively to the government's line of reasoning.[38] No doubt Delavignette's credentials recommended him as just such a person. However, the Commission split between those who, like Delavignette, believed that their task was to 'know the truth whatever the cost and to insist on respect for human rights whatever the cost', and others who saw the primary mission as defending France (and the Army) against 'a violent and deceitful campaign on the part of all its enemies'.[39] Delavignette was the only commissioner with colonial experience, but also, apparently, the only one with a developed sense of what it meant to inspect an institution, and in particular the independence this required: Delavignette alone refused to be formally 'received' by the minister-resident Robert Lacoste for this reason. The Commission's work was in any case hampered by its limited resources and lack of an independent budget; while in Algeria, the commissioners were in effect the guests of the Army and the civil administration. The more visible work of the Commission, in part for this reason, took the form of carefully staged 'set piece' visits, in particular the five-day tour in May 1957 undertaken by General Zeller and Professor Richet (of the Académie de Médecine), escorted and assisted by the Army.[40] Pressure of time obliged commissioners to rely on their own contacts in Algeria, and to base their work substantially on written documentation: this was the case, for example, for the only report other than Delavignette's to be made available to Vidal-Naquet, that of the chairman Maître Garçon.[41]

For all of these reasons, Delavignette's report stands somewhat apart from the rest of the Commission's work, and also for the fact that, while the Battle of Algiers almost inevitably dominated the horizon over the summer of 1957, Delavignette's investigation took him away from Algiers to Oran, and took as its focus the rural guerrilla war which had continued unabated in the *bled*. No doubt part of the merit of the report lies in the fact that, notwithstanding its subsequent publication, it was written confidentially and may therefore be taken as the unselfconscious voice of the French 'official mind'. Nonetheless, Delavignette was too much the writer not to set the scene with a brief evocation of daily life (do we infer life *for Europeans*?) in an Algeria torn between 'a state of war which has nothing in common with classic warfare, and the normal activity of work which is not the norm of peacetime', insisting also on the 'atrocity of terrorism fomented by our enemies'.[42] Though the report touches also on the question of torture, its main focus is on a quite distinct case of abuse, or rather, two separate but similar cases, where Algerian detainees had been held overnight, in the absence of suitable facilities, in disused wine vats. In the first incident, at Ain-el-Isser in March 1957, after a number of suspects had been held for one night unharmed, 101 'suspects' had been placed in four vats, each about 3 metres by 3.5 metres by 3 metres, for a second night; the following morning, 17 were found dead in one vat, 24 in another, asphyxiated by sulphur dioxide fumes (though the vats had reportedly not been used since 1942). Quite apart from the use of the vats in the first place (the British popular press inevitably evoked the 'black hole of Calcutta'), and the fact that the prisoners' desperate knocking and cries for help had apparently gone unheard (presumably as no guard was kept), what shocked Delavignette was what happened next: the junior officer in charge, Lieutenant Curutchet, had the 41 bodies driven off and dumped some 50 kilometres off in the *bled*. In the second incident, a month later at Mercier-Lacombe, 120 kilometres away from the original incident, 23 'suspects, having displayed an arrogant attitude' (as the military report had it) were similarly detained overnight, and all 23 were found dead the following morning. Delavignette had studied these cases before coming to Algeria, but learned of a third case the day before leaving, which occurred on 27 June 1957, in which a further 21 detainees died under similar conditions.[43]

Delavignette's analysis of these incidents takes him substantively beyond the remit of the Commission, which was to investigate individual cases. Rather, as he argued: 'Algeria's situation is a global one, all the elements of which are indissociable from each other. For the purposes of analysis we may separate them, in order to study them. But in reality they constitute a whole.' He was at pains to point out that the Army had behaved properly in disciplining the men involved, and in bringing them to justice: two officers were arraigned for 'involuntary homicide', though in fact, subsequent to Delavignette's investigation, Lieutenant Curutchet's case was never concluded, and no sentence was ever passed.[44] However, he draws attention to three problematic aspects of the two cases. The first concerned the youth of the officers responsible, all in their twenties, Curutchet the oldest at 26 years old. As Delavignette commented, France was engaged in 'a very special war' for which the military academies could not as yet provide any training (though strategies of counter-insurgency were of course being developed in Algeria and elsewhere), and yet it was on these young panicked officers that responsibility fell. Secondly, he criticized the Army's laxity in reporting the first incident: the 'note de service' circulated on 18 April 1957 forbade the use of wine vats for housing 'all categories of personnel: troops, suspects or prisoners', but drew attention only to the 'ignorance of the most elementary rules of hygiene', without mentioning the 41 dead. Thirdly, he pointed to the disposal of the bodies as evidence of the 'global situation' in Algeria: why had Curutchet's first instinct been to remove the evidence of his mistake, who had helped him in providing the vehicles for the job, and who had provided moral cover for his actions? Delavignette also pointed to the worrying absence of any reaction from the local inhabitants or their representatives, only one of whom had come forward to enquire after two of his relatives amongst the deceased. As he commented: 'This silence does not preclude the psychoses of either indifference or terror. [...] Protest? What would be the point?'[45]

The remainder of Delavignette's report extended his analysis and broadened its scope, first considering two aspects of what he termed 'counter-terrorism', the first of which consisted in the proliferation of settler groups which were being established in Algiers and elsewhere at this time, parallel to, but independent of, the 'legal' forces of order and administration, and which were to be such a characteristic feature of the latter stages of the war in Algeria, including the 'events' of May 1958. Secondly, he condemned the illegal methods of counter-terrorism spreading through the Army and administration which, 'in the name of efficiency, [display] contempt for human life': the bullet in the back of 'escaping' prisoners in the infamous 'corvées de bois', torture, disappearances outside the provisions of special powers. Here too it was his 'sense of the State' which guided his analysis: 'a hypocritical state of siege reigns in Algeria, [which] rots with gangrene the relations between the military and civil powers and deepens the gulf between Europeans and Muslims'.[46]

In a short final section, Delavignette picked up a more positive theme with an enthusiasm that might cynically be seen as the triumph of hope over experience: 'After I had breathed in so many miasmas [...], the SAS brought a gust of pure air'. If Curutchet and his hapless comrades appear almost as the mirror-image of Delavignette's future *broussards* at ENFOM, then the men of the *Sections Administratives Spécialisées* (SAS) were the Algerian version of the real thing, at least in terms of Delavignette's ideal. These were the military specialist units deployed to administer to the welfare needs of local populations, though this happened typically within the context of the 'centres de regroupement' where, as Vidal-Naquet points out, the reality was typically far grimmer, and the role of the SAS more compromised, than Delavignette allowed (or knew about), whatever the good intentions of the SAS officers themselves.[47] Delavignette promised a separate report on the work of the SAS, but in the circumstances this never materialized. However, the second chapter in his 1962 publication, *L'Afrique Noire française et son destin*,[48] in a return to the lyricism of an earlier style, recounts his visit to an SAS outpost during his 1957 visit, and draws explicit parallels between the social welfare role of the SAS, established after 1954 to tackle the 'plague of under-administration', and the need for more far-reaching reforms, in ways which recall his 1955 social and economic report on Algeria. These same parallels also surface in the concluding remarks of his 1957 report:

> In the confusion of powers which results from a hypocritical state of siege, neither agrarian reform nor municipal reform can start to grow, much less bear fruit. I repeat, the admirable work of the SAS will be undone by the lies which barely disguise the rotting away of the State in other areas.

It is high time to improve the global situation in Algeria. Very little time remains.[49]

Conclusion

In conclusion, we return to an earlier question: Why read Delavignette? Writing in 1968, Delavignette himself showed a keen awareness of being on the wrong side of the 'page' that France had turned in 1962, with the independence of Algeria:

> On the side of the ex-colonizer, in this case French, the effect of decolonization has been to reawaken the myth of the scapegoat. Accused of the sin of colonialism, the scapegoat is hounded from the city by a metropolitan sensibility which purges itself through its belief that decolonization is easier than colonization. The best scape-goat is an innocent, in the sense of a simpleton. It is the official or the settler, even the missionary, who believed in his work overseas, who carried it out without thinking that colonization was evil, and that he was the perpetrator of that evil. What a relief for the metro-pole to be able to declare its own innocence, having uncovered the guilty party! He is condemned while everyone forgets who sent him to Africa in the first place![50]

Certainly, there is much in Delavignette's writing that is out of step not only with modern post-colonial sensibilities, but already even in the late 1950s with an increasingly unanswerable anti-colonialism. In 1957 and perhaps still in 1962, Delavignette remained an unapologetic 'colonialist' whose no doubt sincerely humanist position was sustained by a certain degree of self-delusion, if not wilful misinformation, notably in his view, expressed in the conclusion to his 1957 report, that '80% of Muslims [...] maintain confidence in justice, in France and in a new French Algeria'.[51] On the face of it, Delavignette's awkward reformism would seem to offer a good example of what Martin Thomas and Andrew Thompson have recently characterized as: 'a problem of cognitive dissonance, a failure to recognise that the internationalisation of colonial problems [...] made the local containment of colonial problems impossible to achieve'.[52]

Two broad reasons may nonetheless be adduced why it may still be considered worthwhile to spend time with Delavignette, and more generally with the French 'official mind' in the period of late colonialism and decolonization. The first, in this specific case, is that Delavignette's actions, like those of other official whistleblowers such as Bollardière, Teitgen, Rocard et al., and notwithstanding the fact that many of them sought to act confidentially within French officials circles, give the lie to any notion of a monolithic 'French late-colonial state' seeking to protect and maintain itself 'envers et contre tout'. In Delavignette's case, this is not simply because he serves as a kind of 'alibi' for French officials, proving that they were 'not all bad', but because there is arguably intrinsic merit in his highly critical analysis of French action in Algeria, viewed through the long lens of his accumulated experience and guided by his moral probity.

Secondly, and finally, French colonial officials, particularly those of a liberal or 'humanist' disposition such as Delavignette, may well have suffered from 'cognitive dissonance' in the later 1950s, as they sought to sustain their belief in a continuing French imperial nation state, despite the gathering pace of an international movement towards decolonization.[53] But this is surely the starting point for any analysis, rather its conclusion. The recent study of decolonization has quite rightly focused on the agency of the colonized, and Thomas and Thompson have highlighted the important and exciting ways in which the historiographical focus is shifting to the study of decolonization's international aspects, and in particular of transnational actors and networks. There is a danger in this, however, arising from a simple reversal of perspectives, collapsing the depth of the late-colonial state to concentrate simply on its surface. Taking our cue from Gary Wilder, rather than simply 're-enacting' the struggles of decolonization, we must surely 'work through' late colonialism and the workings of the late-colonial state, including the very real moral and intellectual challenges which confronted the French 'official mind'.[54] In particular, just as Wilder locates the colonial humanism of the inter-war period in a structural antinomy between the contradictory principles of republicanism and imperialism, so for the late-colonial period we might tentatively identify an emerging antinomy between the competing demands of late-colonial rationality, as represented by Delavignette, on the one hand, and 'futile intransigence gradually abandoned', as identified by Thomas and Thompson, on the other.[55] Or, to put it another way, and to leave the last word with the ENFOM rebels of 1956, between the 'necessary transformation of the role of the administrator' and 'imperialism [...] dressed up as "French sovereignty"'.

Notes

1 *Le Bleu d'Outre-Mer*, February 1956, quoted by Pierre Vérin, 'Révolte et antici-pation à l'Ecole Nationale de la France d'Outre-Mer', in Bernard Mouralis and Anne Pirious, eds, *Robert Delavignette savant et politique (1897–1976)*, Paris, Karthala, 2003, pp. 165–172, quoted pp.170–171. All translations from the French by the author, unless otherwise indicated.

2. Pierre Vérin, 'Révolte et anticipation', p.172.

3. See Martin Shipway, 'Gaston Defferre's Loi-Cadre and its application 1956–57: The last chance for a French African "empire-state"?', in Tony Chafer and Alexander Keese, eds, *The Year of African Independence: Francophone Africa 1960*, Manchester, Manchester University Press, 2013, pp. 15–29.

4. Tony Chafer, *The End of Empire in French West Africa: France's Successful Decolonization?*, Oxford, Berg, 1992.

5. Danièle Lamarque, 'La formation des administrateurs: de l'ENFOM à l'ENA', in Mouralis and Pirious, *Robert Delavignette*, pp. 149–164.

6. Vérin, 'Révolte et anticipation', p.172. Emphasis added.

7. Ibid., This translates *'nous ne serons pas les «hommes à tout faire» de l'impérialisme'*: literally, 'we will not be imperialism's "men to do everything"'.

8. Archives Nationales d'Outre-Mer (ANOM), Aix-en-Provence, 19AP (Papiers Delavignette), 15–199.

9. Vérin, 'Révolte et anticipation'.

10. Pierre Vidal-Naquet, ed., *La Raison d'État: Textes publiés par le Comité Audin*, Paris, Minuit, 1962, reed. La Découverte, 2002, and see below.

11. On Delafosse and Hardy, Raoul Girardet, *L'Idée coloniale en France de 1871 à 1962*, Paris, La Table Ronde, 1972, p. 476. On the directorship of the emi-nent Vietnam specialist, Paul Mus (1947–50), David Chandler, 'Paul Mus, 1902–1969: Esquisse d'une biographie', in David Chandler and Christopher Goscha, eds, *Paul Mus (1902–1969): L'espace d'un regard*, Paris, Les Indes Savantes, 2006, pp. 34–38.

12. On Laurentie, Martin Shipway, 'Thinking like an empire: Governor Henri Laurentie and postwar plans for the late colonial French "Empire-State" ', in Martin Thomas, ed., *The French Colonial Mind*, vol.1, *Mental Maps of Empire and Colonial Encounters*, Lincoln NE and London, University of Nebraska Press, 2011, pp. 219–250; on Delavignette's role as directeur des AP, see Alexander Keese, *Living with Ambiguity: Integrating an African Elite in French and Portuguese Africa, 1930–61*, Stuttgart, Franz Steiner, 2007, passim and e.g. pp. 193–194.

13. Véronique Dimier, *Le gouvernement des colonies, regards croisés franco-britanniques*, Brussels, Editions de l'Université de Bruxelles, 2004; Véronique Dimier, 'Robert Delavignette: un politologue?', in Mouralis and Pirious, eds, *Robert Delavignette*, pp. 61–72.

14. *Revue française d'Histoire d'Outre-Mer*, vol. 14, 1967; Mouralis and Pirious, *Robert Delavignette*.

15. Cohen, *Rulers of Empire*; William B. Cohen, 'Robert Delavignette', in L.H. Gann and Peter Duignan, *African Proconsuls: European Governors in Africa*, Stanford, CA, Hoover Institution, 1978; see also William B. Cohen, ed., *Robert Delavignette on the French Empire: Selected Writings*, Chicago and London, University of Chicago Press, 1977.

16. Girardet, *L'Idée coloniale*, p. 272ff.

17. Gary Wilder, *The French Imperial Nation-State: Negritude and Colonial Humanism between the Two World Wars*, Chicago, University of Chicago Press, 2005, pp. 76ff and passim.

18. Ibid., pp. 10–12.

19. Ibid., p. 80.

20. Ibid., p. 81.

21. Ibid., p. 321, note to p. 77.

22. Ibid., p. 77, quoting Girardet, *L'Idée coloniale*, p. 272.

23. Ibid., pp. 58–59.

24. Robert Delavignette, *Paysans Noirs*, Paris: Payot, 1931; Girardet, *L'Idée coloniale*, p. 233.

25. Robert Delavignette, *Soudan-Paris-Bourgogne*, Paris, Grasset, 1935, quoted in Wilder, op.cit., 36.

26. Delavignette, *Les vrais Chefs de l'Empire*, Paris, Gallimard, 1939.

27. From the English translation, see following note, p.8.

28. Robert Delavignette, *Service africain*, Paris, Gallimard, 1946; translated as *Freedom and Authority in French West Africa*, London, Oxford University Press, 1950, re-ed. Frank Cass, 1968.

29. Robert Delavignette, *L'Afrique noire et son destin*, Paris, Gallimard, 1962; *Du bon usage de la décolonisation*, Paris, Casterman, 1968.

30. Lamarque, 'La formation des administrateurs'.

31. Journal Officiel de la République Française (JORF), Avis et Rapports du Conseil Economique, Séance du 28 juin 1955, 'Situation sociale et économique de l'Algérie', 5 July 1955; on the Constantine Plan, Daniel Lefeuvre, *Chère Algérie: La France et sa colonie, 1930–1962*, and see Martin Shipway, 'The Wind of Change and the Tides of History: de Gaulle, Macmillan and the beginnings of the French decolonising endgame', in Larry Butler and Sarah Stockwell, eds, *The Wind of Change: Harold Macmillan and British Decolonisation*, Basingstoke, Palgrave, 2013, pp. 180–194.

32. Ibid., p. 177.

33. Raphaëlle Branche, 'La commission de sauvegarde pendant la guerre d'Algérie: Chronique d'un échec annoncé', *Vingtième Siècle*, no 61 (January–March 1999), pp. 14–29, cited p. 14, quoting Pierre Vidal Naquet, *La Torture dans la République*, Paris, Minuit, 1972.

34. Ibid., pp. 23–24, 26–29; Henri Alleg, *La Question*, Paris, Minuit, 1958; and see Alexis Berchadsky, *La question d'Henri Alleg: Un livre-événement, dans la France en guerre d'Algérie*, Paris, Larousse, 1996.

35. Vidal-Naquet, *La Raison d'État*, pp. 3–4; and for Mairey's and Teitgen's contributions, see pp. 80–100, 104–113, 194–210.
36. Ibid., p. 3: '[...] il n'était pas un anticolonialiste de principe, mais il avait au plus haut degré le sens de l'État.'
37. Vidal-Naquet, *Raison d'État*, pp. 138–139.
38. Alongside Delavignette, the membership of the Commission comprised: four lawyers (including the chairman, Maître Maurice Garçon, a Paris advocate), two senior medical practitioners, one university rector, the president of the French Red Cross (a former ambassador, André François-Poncet), one former prefect, the president of the French Union of Veterans and Deportees, and the military governor of Paris, General André Zeller (who would later be one of the 'clique of retired generals' who led the *putsch* of April 1961, for which he served five years of a fifteen-year sentence): Branche, 'La Commission de Sauvegarde', pp. 17–18n.
39. Delavignette and Professor de Vernejoul, quoted by Branche, 'La Commission de Sauvegarde', p. 18.
40. When Zeller and Richet asked to inspect a detention centre (*centre de tri*), they were taken by Colonel Roger Trinquier to El Biar, but, as Trinquier revealed much later (at his trial), the visit only took place after Henri Alleg and Maurice Audin had been hastily transferred to another site: Vidal-Naquet, *Raison d'État*, p. 140. Trinquier was one of the principal theorists of 'revolutionary warfare'; see his *La Guerre moderne*, Paris, La Table ronde, 1961.
41. Vidal-Naquet, *Raison d'État*, pp. 141–175, quoted p. 141.
42. 'Rapport de Mission en Algérie de Monsieur le Gouverneur-Général Robert Delavignette', in Vidal-Naquet, *Raison d'État*, pp. 179–192.
43. Ibid., pp. 180–83, 186. Sulphur dioxide (SO2), highly toxic in its gaseous state, is a normal additive in wine production. On the British press, see Branche, 'La Commission de Sauvegarde', p. 27.
44. Vidal-Naquet, *Raison d'État*, pp. 182–3. Curutchet finished 'his' war by deserting to the *Organisation Armée Secrète* (OAS) in 1961): Vidal-Naquet quotes Lt Curutchet's letter of explanation *in extenso*; his reasons for deserting include his 'certainty in being historically right', pp. 183–184n.
45. Ibid., pp. 185–187.
46. Ibid., pp.187–189.
47. Ibid., p. 190n., and see the report compiled by a young (and, in the 1962 edition, anonymous) Michel Rocard, pp. 219–242.
48. Op.cit., pp. 31–35.
49. 'Rapport de Mission', loc.cit., p. 192.
50. Delavignette, *Du bon usage de la décolonisation*, p. 25.
51. Loc.cit.
52. Martin Thomas and Andrew Thompson, 'Empire and Globalisation: From "High Imperialism" to Decolonisation', *The International History Review*, 36, 1, 2014, pp. 1–29, cited p. 17.
53. Delavignette's own analysis is pertinent here, whether in his lectures or in the cogent and perceptive history of French Africa he published as early as 1962, in *L'Afrique Noire française*, op.cit.
54. Wilder, *The French Imperial Nation-State*, p. 8.
55. Loc. cit.

Part II
Comparing Endgames: The *Modi Operandi* of Decolonization

4

Imperial Endings and Small States: Disorderly Decolonization for the Netherlands, Belgium, and Portugal

Crawford Young

In the age of European imperial expansion that opened at the close of the 15th century and lasted for more than four centuries, three of the smallest countries emerged with some of the largest colonial domains.[1] Portugal and the Netherlands pioneered the construction of far-flung sea-borne mercantile empires in the 16th and 17th centuries. By the 20th century, the original maritime imperial expansion had evolved into large African territorial conquests and scattered Asian enclaves for Portugal, and for the Netherlands the vast archipelago colony that became Indonesia, sprawling 3,600 miles from east to west, as well as much smaller Caribbean holdings. Belgium, through the extraordinary skill of King Leopold II in the predatory diplomacy of African partition, acquired by inheritance from its monarch a large part of central Africa. All three countries came to attach great value to their imperial domains, and entered the era of decolonization determined to retain them into an indefinite future.

In part, their tenacious resistance to decolonization merely performed a territorial possessiveness that is inherent to states; a particular domain once inscribed as a sovereign possession is rarely voluntarily abandoned. Only military defeat, external imposition or irresistible challenge by a subject population can annul territorial possessiveness. In the three cases at hand, a key difference with larger colonial powers was the delay in drawing the inevitable inferences from these factors overriding the reproduction of overseas sovereignty.

In all three instances, the end of empire came suddenly and unexpectedly, although by strikingly different routes. The process was disorderly, accompanied during and after the transition by protracted violence and international crisis. In different ways, the troubled course of decolonization escaped the control of the colonizer, who far too long resisted the implacable logic of global trends and events. Belated searches by the imperial centres for a redefined partnership offering forms of autonomy within a residual imperial sovereignty failed, and independence was initially accompanied by rupture.

Each in its own fashion, the three small imperial centres had come to view their overseas empires as critical to their national well-being or even identity. The vast scale of their overseas holdings dwarfed the modest dimensions of the metropole, multiplying the significance of the three states as international actors. Embedded but deceptive public ideologies clothed the colonial mission with apparent success and moral worth that persisted until an unexpected collapse. Thus, the loss of empire was traumatic and associated with a national crisis. Their small size made them singularly vulnerable to external pressures, while their nationalist adversaries found growing external support as a changing international normative discourse grew increasingly hostile to colonial rule. In this chapter I seek to identify the key dynamics in the end of empire for the Netherlands, Belgium, and Portugal, focusing on Indonesia, Congo, and the mainland Portuguese African territories. I offer a brief summary of the colonial practice and road to decolonization in these three cases, as well as the aftermath in the successor states and at home.

The Dutch mercantile role in Asia dates from 1595, and was formalized with the charter of the United East India Company (VOC) in 1602. The Dutch transformed their mercantile domain into a fully fledged despotic colonial state only after 1816, largely based on the exploitation of Java throughout the 19th century. By 1831, a system of high land taxation and obligatory crops, the 'cultivation system', was generating sufficient revenue to meet colonial administrative expenses and export a surplus to contribute to the Netherlands' metropolitan budget. Between 1831 and 1850, colonial proceeds provided 19 per cent of the Dutch budget, and 32 per cent between 1851 and 1860. This revenue windfall embedded within the Dutch national psyche a presumption that the East Indies holdings were an indispensable resource for the Netherlands.[2]

The cultivation system was modified after 1870, replaced by a 'liberal system', with large parcels of land passing into the hands of European planters in league with village headmen: in 1904 the state land tax still captured 23 per cent of peasant cash income.[3] After 1900 an 'ethical system' came to the fore, for the first time incorporating into policy a vision of the welfare of the subject, with expanded educational opportunity and medical services. The new doctrine was especially successful in persuading the Dutch public it was 'unselfish rule in interest of the colonized'.[4] The exploitative nature of colonial subjugation remained, and the economic crisis of the 1930s resulted in a reversion to more despotic practices.

Until the latter part of the 19th century, effective Dutch occupation was mostly limited to Java, the Moluccas, and some of the Sumatran north coast. The completion of colonial conquest extended into the 1920s, with the final subjugation of Papua. Though the colonial budget no longer generated a surplus transferable to the Netherlands, Indonesia was a crucial source of foreign exchange and national wealth: in 1938, Indies investment return represented 15 per cent of Dutch national income, and its dollar earnings were critical to covering foreign exchange deficits.[5]

Nationalism became a social force in the early 20th century, taking form around a precocious naturalization of a concept of Indonesia. Strikingly, the new political leadership, although in large part ethnic Javanese steeped in a richly elaborated aristocratic historical culture, chose the larger Indonesia idiom as the frame for challenging colonial rule. They also made the crucial choice to foster the coastal trading language of the region, Malay, as a national language, reframed as Indonesian.

Indonesian national organizations emerged by 1908, at first moderate, but by the 1920s including more radical Islamic, communist, and nationalist streams. A large communist uprising in 1926–27 shook the colonial establishment, and from the 1920s coping with nationalism became a major Dutch preoccupation, oscillating between management and repression. The three most visible nationalist leaders – Sukarno, Mohammed Hatta, and Sutan Sjahrir – were all imprisoned through most of the 1930s. A 1936 Indonesia advisory council petition for autonomy within a dual kingdom was firmly rejected. The penultimate governor-general declared in 1933 that Dutch rule was indispensable for another 300 years. The Indies, writes Frances Gouda:

> served as a tangible reminder of an era when the 17th-century Dutch republic had performed a starring role in the world-wide coliseum of politics and commerce [...]. Only the continued possession of the colonies could assuage the oversensitivity of a 'small nation with a great past' and verify its claim to be a mouse that still roared.[6]

The destruction of Dutch colonial rule came from without, not from within. The fateful transformative event was the Japanese invasion in

January 1942. The isolated Dutch Indies establishment had few means to resist the invasion, and surrendered two months later. Although at the local level the Japanese maintained the indirect rule structures of village administration, they liquidated the superstructure of alien authority. Their primary aim was access to critical raw materials for the war effort, above all oil and rubber. The ruthlessness of their rule and the hardships occasioned by the occupation antagonized many, without triggering much nostalgia for Dutch rule. A December 1942 promise from exiled Queen Wilhelmina for a post-war partnership under the Dutch crown had little Indonesian resonance. The Japanese trained military forces that would subsequently form the core of an Indonesian independent army and offered a collaborative role to the leading Indonesian nationalist figures, an invitation accepted by Sukarno and Hatta.

By 1944, as the tides of war ran heavily against Japan, Indonesian nationalists found the Japanese occupation receptive to pleas for support for independence. On 17 July 1945, Japan promised independence, and Sukarno and his allies began to make preparations. Three days after the 14 August Emperor Hirohito surrender broadcast, in a very brief and laconic statement, Sukarno declared Indonesia a sovereign republic.

Sukarno and Hatta quickly formed a government and adopted a constitution. They won support in most of Java and much of Sumatra, but some of the outer islands were reluctant to accept their authority. The Dutch, however, clung to dreams of full restoration. The East Indies were a vital economic resource for a Netherlands economy crippled by the German occupation and war effort; the wartime prime minister declared that 'distinguished economists of every school of thought' had concluded that 'if the bonds that attach the Netherlands to the Indies are severed there will be a permanent reduction in the national income of the Netherlands which will lead to the country's pauperization'.[7] Their determination on reconquest was reinforced by the conviction that Sukarno and Hatta were untrustworthy Japanese collaborators and unacceptable partners, whose popular support was shallow.

However, Dutch capacities were not at the measure of their ambitions. The Dutch Army had been disbanded by the Germans, and only a small number escaped to the United Kingdom, while some elements of the colonial constabulary had fled to Australia. Meanwhile, the United Kingdom was assigned the task of receiving the surrender of Japanese forces in Indonesia, as well as freeing the 170,000 interned Dutch and Eurasians. Most of the British forces were Indian, which precluded their use to restore Dutch authority, a task that could begin only when the first Dutch troops landed in late 1945. But illusions of early reconquest soon foundered on the discovery that the Republic of Indonesia, despite internal tensions, was already too well established to be easily overcome. In core areas of the archipelago, the republic enjoyed strong support, especially in Java, Madura, and much of Sumatra. In the outer islands, however, a number of indigenous rulers were reticent regarding the republic. Some groups in eastern Indonesia had experienced intense Christian mission activity, and had relatively large elites who harboured apprehensions about the religious intentions of the Muslim majority (90 per cent).

Strong international pressure for negotiations quickly built up. A compromise truce, the Linggajati Accord, was signed in November 1946, reluctantly by both sides, confirming republic authority only in Java, Sumatra, and Madura. The Dutch plan was to assemble elsewhere under their umbrella an assemblage of outer-island territories. A federated United State of Indonesia was promised by January 1949: the republic would be one of the federated states, with Queen Wilhelmina as titular head of a Netherlands-Indonesia union of sovereign states. The accord won the requisite two-thirds approval in the Dutch parliament only after adding clauses asserting ultimate Dutch political and economic authority, and pledging self-determination for any region wishing to stay out of the federation.[8] However, each side distrusted the other, and hoped for a more complete victory.

The Dutch launched two major military offensives, in July 1947 and December 1948. On both occasions intense international pressure compelled their suspension, even after substantial success. The second offensive, with 150,000 troops, not only reconquered key Java centres and the Sumatra plantations, but also captured Sukarno and most other Indonesian leaders. However, Indonesian forces now numbered more than 300,000, with a capacity for guerrilla resistance in the countryside to which the Dutch had no answer.

The republic faced its own major challenges, beginning with on-going conflicts within the leadership. Among the Muslim organizations there was restiveness concerning the refusal of Sukarno to declare Indonesia an Islamic state, and his insistence on religious neutrality. More radical Islamic groups revolted in west Java in March 1948. The resulting Darul Islam insurgency was contained after serious fighting, but skirmishing spread to the outer islands and dragged on until 1962.

An even larger insurrection broke out in central Java in August 1948, led by the Communist Party of Indonesia (Partai Komunis Indonesia, PKI). Although decimated by its crushing defeat in 1926–27, the PKI regained momentum after the war. The PKI insurgency was defeated by November 1948, but only after a number of pitched battles and thousands of casualties. The communist uprising was critical in inscribing a Cold War transcript on unfolding Indonesian events, particularly for the United States.[9] The success of the republic in subduing the PKI revolt led the US to see new merit in the Indonesian regime as a barrier to communist expansion, and added urgency to reaching a definitive settlement regarding independence.

Confronted with an American threat to suspend Marshall Plan assistance unless a final agreement on Indonesian independence were reached, the Netherlands finally abandoned its dream of colonial restoration. A final accord was signed in November 1949, providing for full acknowledgment of Indonesian sovereignty over the entire archipelago save Papua by the following month as a united federation, with the Queen only as symbolic head of a Netherlands-Indonesia association. Dutch resistance now focused on the status of West New Guinea (Papua). Parliamentary assent was contingent on it remaining under Dutch administration, pending eventual self-determination. An ultimate compromise provided for a one-year interim period, followed by negotiations on its future status. Indonesia thus won formal independence in January 1950. The ultimate culmination of the Indonesian revolution then followed on 17 August 1950, five years after the original declaration of independence, with the federal structure of the 1949 accord abandoned, the symbolic linkage with the Dutch monarchy dissolved, and Indonesia reconfigured as a unitary republic.[10]

There remained the unfinished business of Papua, termed 'West Irian' by Indonesian nationalists, which assumed towering symbolic importance on both sides. For Indonesia, assuming the full dimensions of colonial territoriality was manifest destiny. For the Dutch, Papuans were an entirely different population stock in terms of culture, religion, and language. Further, an illusion held sway that the territory could serve as sanctuary for relocation of the Eurasian population and even new Dutch settlers. By 1957, the continued deadlock over its status helped provoke Indonesian nationalization of all Dutch enterprises without compensation, and the expulsion of the remaining Dutch and Eurasian population once numbering 250,000, erasing what remained of the three centuries of Dutch presence. In turn, these punitive measures fortified Dutch determination to guarantee the Papuan population a choice other than incorporation into Indonesia. However, in the face of continued international support for the Indonesian claims to complete the territoriality of the former Dutch East Indies, and small-scale military invasions by Indonesian forces, the Netherlands reluctantly agreed in 1962 to a brief UN interregnum, which led to incorporation into Indonesia. But to this day the culturally distinct Papua remains a restive and reluctant subject of Indonesia, whose hold is reinforced by substantial immigration from core areas of the republic.

The end of empire in the East Indies was a severe trauma for the Netherlands, well captured by Arend Lijphart:

> The agonies of the decolonization process are well exemplified by the painful and reluctant withdrawal of the Netherlands from its colonies [...]. Holland acted with an intense emotional commitment, manifested in pathological feelings of self-righteousness, resentment, and pseudo-moral convictions. These emotions started to decrease in intensity in the late 1950s, but protracted and ultimately unsuccessful resistance to decolonization still left the country internally divided, frustrated, and humiliated.[11]

Curiously, the remarkably consensual domestic politics managed through the first two post-war decades by consociational practice, well conceptualized by Lijphart, helped the Netherlands recover from the war years and achieve new levels of prosperity at home, but proved ill-equipped to oversee decolonization.[12] A key aspect of consociationalism was the amicable agreement to disagree and postponement of difficult decisions, a fatal flaw in decolonization politics.

Ironically, our second case of small state turbulent decolonization, Belgium, was itself an earlier instance of painful territorial loss by the Netherlands. Belgium was created in 1830 through a successful revolt of the Dutch southern provinces, and recognized by the Netherlands only in 1839 after the failure of an effort at military reconquest in 1831. The successful secession created a new binational country lacking a national narrative and clear identity. Upon this uncertain social base a unitary state with French as its primary language was erected.

In 1865, Leopold II ascended the throne, convinced his country required the bracing invigoration of colonial territories. The example of the East Indies under the cultivation system was at hand. A British lawyer, appropriately named J. W. B. Money, extolled the profits generated by the Dutch state in a work closely read by Leopold, entitled *Java, or How to Manage a Colony*.[13] The Belgian political and economic elites did not share his imperial appetites: Belgium lacked the naval and military power to nurture such ambitions. Leopold, however, was undeterred. With explorer Henry Morton Stanley as his prime agent, a zone of influence was stitched together in the Congo basin, based on a host of treaties with local rulers. In a remarkable diplomatic tour de force, Leopold managed to secure, at the Congress of Berlin in 1885, international blessing for his claim to personal sovereignty over nearly one million square miles of central Africa, with the pledge to guarantee free trade and impose no customs, while also combating slavery and fostering Christian mission activity. Thus was born the mistitled Congo Free State.

To finance his vast proprietary domains, and achieve the 'effective occupation' that the Berlin Congress reconfirmed as requisite for secure colonial title, Leopold had to find a revenue flow, at the time usually based on import customs collections he had promised to avoid. Instead the Leopoldian state was funded by forced deliveries of wild rubber, imposition of a state ivory monopoly, and renting sovereignty to several major chartered companies, the whole underwritten by ruthless brutality and innumerable atrocities. By the 1890s, revenues were beginning to flow, and by 1900 the Congo Free State was by far the most profitable colony in Africa, with Leopold extracting a profit estimated by Belgian historian Jules Marchal at $1.1 billion in contemporary dollars.[14]

Belgium and Leopold II became, by 1903, the target of an international campaign against the grotesque abuses of the Congo Free State, led by the United Kingdom and a number of humanitarian organizations. To parry the external pressures, in 1908, a year before Leopold's death, Belgium formally assumed sovereignty over the Congo. The first imperative for Belgium was to regularize and reform colonial administration, bringing its practices more closely into line with what by the standards of the time was 'normal' colonial exploitation.

The stain of Leopoldian atrocities was largely removed. In the decades that followed, Belgium fashioned a remarkably dense, coercive and thorough paternalistic superstructure of hegemony. Over time the embarrassing Congo Free State by metamorphosis became an extraordinary beneficent achievement of the king bequeathed to the country, and its growing prosperity a token of Belgian national identity. By the later 1950s, European personnel in the administration numbered 10,000. When one adds the 6,000 European missionaries, and the mines and plantations that blanketed the territory, the infrastructure of domination was imposing.[15]

During the Second World War, with Belgium under German occupation, the colonial administration under its ablest proconsul, Pierre Ryckmans, was essentially independent, only loosely under the oversight of the exile government in London (itself of contested legitimacy).[16] The London regime depended entirely on the Belgian Congo for funding. The colonial administration placed intense pressure upon the subject population to redouble production of strategic minerals and other commodities for the Allied war effort. Post-war Belgium acknowledged a 'war debt' owing to the colony, which influenced policy debate on improving the welfare of the colonial subject.

The first post-war decade was a golden age for the Belgian colony, which now basked in an image of success. The foreign exchange earnings of colonial exports were a crucial resource for post-war Belgian recovery. The commodity price boom that continued almost until independence brought a remarkable expansion of colonial revenues. In the period from 1939 to 1950, state revenues increased elevenfold, then again tripled in the final colonial decade.[17] The fiscal bonanza made possible major state investment in social infrastructure – notably education and health – that earlier was largely delegated to the missions. In 1955, King Baudouin made a triumphant royal tour of the colony, its image for the Belgian public and many others serving as a model of paternal governance still intact. Before an enthusiastic crowd of 70,000 in the colonial capital, Baudouin declared that 'Belgium and Congo form a single nation'.[18]

Although there was some subdued conversation in colonial circles about the eventual destiny of the Belgian Congo and the participation of the African subject in its governance, the dominant assumption until the mid-1950s was that some form of reformed linkage to Belgium was permanent. Any change in status was presumed to lie in so remote a future that no immediate preparatory steps were required. The main grievance of the emergent elite at the time was the pervasive racism they encountered, and obstacles to their social promotion on an equal basis with Europeans, which was addressed by a 1952 decree providing 'immatriculation' to a handful that survived a humiliating administrative test of their mastery of the cultural codes of the colonizer.

Mesmerized by the success image of the colony, until the mid-1950s Belgian officials felt relatively little pressure from the international system, domestic opinion or the Congolese subject still in thrall to colonial mythology. Nationalist hero Patrice Lumumba himself, in a posthumously published manuscript written in 1955, expressed admiration for the grandiose achievement of Leopold II in constructing the Congo, and endorsed the project of a Belgo-Congolese union as its fulfilment.[19] Only the future will tell, he then wrote, when the Congo has reached 'the more advanced degree of civilization and the required political maturity' to advance to self-government.[20]

Fissures began to appear in the colonial monolith by 1956. The powerful Catholic Church defected in 1956 when a conclave of bishops in the Congo declared their support for Congolese emancipation. Inflamed social issues over school finance then agitating metropolitan Belgium found their way into the Congo. An unusual socialist–liberal coalition took power in 1954, determined to introduce a state school system into the colony to compete with the Catholic schools. Growing Flemish–French tensions in Belgium also spilled into the Congo. The accelerating evolution of decolonization elsewhere in Africa, and the potential costs of combating it, became daily more evident.

Notwithstanding these changes, a summons in 1955 by a Belgian professor, A. A. J. Van Bilsen, to develop a 30-year plan for emancipation provoked a wave of indignation. The brevity of his timetable shocked the Belgian public, and he endured a torrent of abuse. In mid-1956, the public call for emancipation (in effect a codeword for independence) also came from the Congolese side. By 1958, political language across a broad spectrum evolved to frame the core demand as swift independence.

But the Belgian commitment to controlled gradualism remained intact. With a minority government under the Social Christian Party (Parti Social Chrétien, PSC) coming to power in 1958, a working group composed entirely of Belgians was designated to design an institutional blueprint for achieving a Belgo-Congolese union of separate states. The illusion remained that an apolitical programme for cautious construction of a Congolese polity could be unilaterally fashioned by Brussels. In the event, the working group report in late 1958 was overtaken by events by the time of its issue. The most distinguished chronicler of Belgian decolonization, Benoît Verhaegen, captured one crucial flaw: its conception and mode of work 'were commanded by the preoccupation with resolving a metropolitan political problem: to find a formula [...] that satisfied and convinced the Belgian political parties', propelled to the fore by the weak position of a Social Christian minority government holding power, and the PSC–Liberal coalition that followed in late 1958.[21]

Formation of political parties became legal in 1958, and they soon multiplied, mostly based in the six provincial capitals. Politicization of the populace proceeded rapidly, especially in the cities. The critical decolonization trigger, however, came in January 1959 when Leopoldville (now Kinshasa) exploded in days of mass rioting. Although the mass eruption was unplanned and leaderless, its sheer scale was unprecedented, as was the incapacity of the security forces to quickly subdue it. Cautious gradualism was upended, and from this point forward Belgium lost the capacity to control the process and timetable. Later that year the Belgian administration realized its administrative control of the lower Congo and some other areas was fast weakening in the face of nationalist mobilization. But even still, Brussels presumed a transitional timetable of 15 years.

The Leopoldville riots introduced a profound disjuncture, shattering colonial complacency. Only a week after the riots, King Baudouin, still imbued with a sense of a special royal role in the colony his grandfather had created, seized the initiative of making the first formal pledge of independence, 'without undue delay or ill-considered precipitation'.[22] An accompanying government declaration pledged negotiation with Congolese leaders. All restrictions on political activity were finally lifted and political parties that had begun to form in 1958 proliferated rapidly. By the end of 1959, however, only a handful had any presence outside the provincial capitals. The administration still counted on its capacity to influence rural voters in alliance with chiefs and moderate Congolese elites. By this time the Belgian colonial minister, Auguste de Schrijver, had indicated a likely 1960 date for independence, though with an expectation that the key sovereign domains of foreign affairs, defence, and finance would still remain under Belgian tutelage.[23]

However, the need for a formula for negotiating a way forward became increasingly urgent. The multiplying array of parties, mostly with ethnic clienteles, competed in the aggressiveness of their discourse. A unique formula to break the deadlock was proposed: a round-table conference, mainly composed of more than a dozen leading Congolese political parties and the Belgian government joined by the three leading domestic parties, including the opposition socialists.

To the surprise of the Belgian side, when the round table convened in January 1960, the Congolese participants formed a united front around the demand for immediate independence. After acceding to Congolese proposals for a 30 June 1960 date, Belgian hopes for some reserved powers for at least two years vanished when a socialist opposition participant supported the Congolese insistence that independence be total. Also abandoned not long after was the hope the Belgian monarch would be head of state, and that European residents could vote: the 'Eurafrican' dream finally dissolved. The Congolese themselves were taken by surprise at Belgian acceptance of their maximal demands. In the wake of the round-table conference the two most important Congolese leaders, Patrice Lumumba and Joseph Kasavubu, were mandated by their colleagues to undertake a confidential mission to seek a delay in independence, with the formation of a provisional government instead. Belgium, however, insisted there be no turning back: the round table had mandated 30 June, and all energies must now turn to succeeding in what became known as the *pari congolais* (Congolese gamble): the high-stakes gamble that a full transition could take place after the transfer of formal power.[24]

With its demands satisfied, the nationalist parties turned their attention to political organization. The first national elections were scheduled for May, and the rural areas mostly remained to be organized. A brief moment of relative good will ensued, while the details of power transfer were settled. A provisional constitution was elaborated, closely adhering to the Belgian model that few Congolese contested. The major issue was the demand for a federal structure from parties representing Katanga and the lower Congo. A mainly unitary state strongly backed by Belgium and most Congo parties prevailed. The colonial administration was scrupulous in the organization of the May 1960 national and provincial elections to create the representative structures of the new state. Although dismayed at the electoral outcome, which saw its most aggressive tormenter, Lumumba, emerge as the primary victor, in the end the Belgian managers of the transition accepted the electoral verdict, and brokered an arrangement that installed Lumumba as prime minister, and an early voice of independence, Bakongo Alliance (Alliance des Bakongo, ABAKO) leader Joseph Kasavubu, as president.

The stage was thus set for the high-risk gamble of immediate independence. Belgium still held some apparent trump cards. Especially important was the overwhelming dominance of Europeans in the core armature of the state, the administration and Army. Of the 4,642 positions in the top three grades in the civil service, only three were held by Congolese – all recent appointees.[25] Congolese had only begun to acquire the university diplomas requisite for such posts: the academic secondary schooling (except for seminaries) necessary for university admission became available only in the 1950s. The 1,000 officers in the army were exclusively European. Thus, the essence of the *pari congolais* was an exceptional form of decolonization in which the transfer of real power would occur well after independence, once an accelerated programme of training qualified personnel had been completed. In retrospect, the hope of a harmonious collaboration between an entirely Congolese political sector of ministers and parliamentarians and a wholly European operative armature of the state appears forlorn at best. The racism that saturated the colonial encounter, the accumulated frustrations of the subject and the climate of mutual mistrust and uncertainty surrounding the sudden surge to independence all ensured the instability of the formula.

But by the time the settlement acceding to the maximal demands of Congolese nationalists was reached, Belgium had few options. The rapidity of the spread of nationalist protest, and loss of administrative control in important regions, raised the spectre of ungovernability. The colonial Army warned of the limits to its capacity to guarantee security. Most important, the long shadow of the Algerian war and the costs and limits of military repression of the nationalist challenge hung heavily over the Belgians – as did their recollection of the fate of their Dutch neighbours in the efforts at military reconquest in the East Indies: pummelled into submission by international protest and American threats to suspend Marshall Plan aid.

As independence day dawned on 30 June 1960, deep uncertainties hung about the celebrations. Among Africans, soaring expectations of immediate rewards encouraged by extravagant promises of the electoral campaign mingled with vague apprehensions of an uncharted future. For Europeans, the aggressive tone of nationalist rhetoric intensified insecurities. The Belgian administration had blocked currency conversion, foreclosing the exit option for many settlers. The contradictory sentiments found reflection in the independence ceremonies. After King Baudouin delivered a paternalistic encomium to the grandiose achievement of Leopold II and the civilizing accomplishments of the colonial state, Prime Minister Lumumba seized the microphone for an unannounced and fiery recitation of African sufferings under the colonial yoke.

In the event, the decolonization settlement unravelled after only five days. Its architecture collapsed when its presumed strongest pillar, the Army, dissolved in mutiny against its Belgian officer corps. On 11 July, the richest province and source of half of the government's revenue, Katanga, declared its secession. European personnel remained to ensure its functioning. Thus, the fledgling Congo government found its elemental means of rule eviscerated: its administrative superstructure, its means of coercion and its sources of revenue. Overnight, the Congo became the epicentre of a global emergency, with the Cold War as template. The *pari congolais* became the Congo crisis.

By 10 July, Belgian troops had intervened to protect the European population. To Congolese indignation, they also shielded the Katanga secession. On 14 July the United Nations Security Council authorized a peace-keeping operation with both military and civilian components. Both the United States and Soviet Union activated their intelligence resources to support factions congenial to their respective interests. The new Congolese government, despite the frantic activity of its leaders, Kasavubu and Lumumba, was largely incapacitated. One of Lumumba's ministers offered an eloquent summary: 'Though we sat so comfortably in our sumptuous official cars, driven by uniformed military chauffeurs, and looked as though we were ruling this large and beautiful country, we were in fact ruling nothing and a prey to whatever might happen'.[26]

The collapse of the decolonization settlement became complete in early September, when President Kasavubu, with American, Belgian, and UN connivance, ousted Lumumba on debatable constitutional grounds. In the constitutional void that followed, de facto UN and international tutelage prevailed. The nadir was reached in January 1961, when the imprisoned Lumumba was transferred to Katanga with external complicity and assassinated. Although a modicum of legitimacy was restored with parliamentary confirmation of a new government in August 1961 and reunification of the country by UN military action to crush the Katanga secession in January 1963, the costs to both Congo and Belgium of a failed decolonization were high.

The fiasco of Congo decolonization was a profound shock and humiliation. The obsessive conviction of Leopold II that Belgium needed a vision of its identity to elevate its ambitions beyond a circumscribed identity as a small and inconsequential European state proved to have some validity. By the post-war period, the success image of the Congo was a critical source of national pride. Also, the colonial vocation was a potent unifying factor. Congo administration operated exclusively in French, and francophones were most numerous in the corporate sector, dominated by three giant holding companies. Flemish priests, however, constituted the great majority of the huge mission establishment; the Catholic Church had powerful influence over colonial policy, and the colonial ministers mostly came from the Catholic party. Until the late 1950s, the three major parties shared similar views on the colonial endeavour. Although lay orientations were strong and freemasons numerous among the colonial administrative and corporate hierarchies, until then anti-clericalism was seen as a sentiment appropriate only to Europeans: Catholic loyalty for the subject was a healthy source of discipline. The rise of Flemish nationalism intensified after the Second World War, but spilled into the Congo only at the very end with a belated and unsuccessful effort to promote bilingualism.

The loss of the unifying colonial vocation, and the humiliating circumstances of its demise, helped set in motion processes of decomposition that continue to this day. Following independence, linguistic divisions intensified and Flemish demands for a federal state grew louder. In 1961, the Belgian government conceded that the unitary state was doomed, and the federal principle was adopted in 1963. Soon after, the three major parties – socialist, Christian-democratic, and liberal – that had always bridged the language divide fractured into linguistic components, and chauvinistic ethnic movements appeared on the extremes. The formation of governments became increasingly protracted and painful, and the search for institutions incorporating the conflicting ambitions of Flanders, Wallonia, and a mainly franco-phone Brussels geographically situated in Flemish territory presented an unending challenge.[27] The permanence of a Belgian state can no longer be assumed. Separation is now openly mooted, and a Flemish party advocating eventual breakup was the major winner in 2010 elections. The intractable dilemmas posed by the future of Brussels are perhaps the greatest impediment.[28] The gradual erosion of affective ties that defined a Belgian national sensibility was perhaps inevitable, but at a minimum was accelerated and intensified by the trauma of decolonization.[29]

Portuguese Africa came to a comparably disorderly end by a different avenue: protracted insurgencies met by intransigent resistance, followed by the radical disjuncture of regime change in Portugal via military intervention. The unexpected coup in 1974 that ousted the regime of António Salazar and Marcelo Caetano ended an autocracy dating from 1926. Nearly 500 years of Portuguese presence came to an abrupt and unplanned end in circumstances that left in its wake nearly 30 years of bitter civil war in its most important colony, Angola.

Some distinctive attributes of the Portuguese colonial project deserve note. Empire evolved in three distinct phases: the age of discoveries in the 15th and 16th centuries, a maritime venture, with scattered footholds in Asia, Africa, and the Americas; a Brazil-centred, very profitable land-based imperium flourishing in the 17th and 18th centuries; then, as Brazil became independent in 1822, shedding its last monarch from the Portuguese royal house of Braganza in 1889, the plunge into the partition of Africa from its earlier coastal enclaves. From its beginnings, Portuguese imperial doctrine gradually developed a notion of a globalized Lusitanian polity that periodically received new stress. An 1822 constitution revived this notion, treating imperial possessions as overseas provinces. Free persons were declared Portuguese citizens.[30] Although subsequently more orthodox colonial terminology sharply distinguishing the three mainland African holdings oscillated with the global Portugal mythology in constitutional terminology, the mystique of an intercontinental polity proved a durable component in the

Portuguese self-concept of nationhood. With the birth of the dictatorship in 1926, and especially the elaboration of a reformulated national ideology by the New State in 1932–33, the vision of a greater Portugal was reinvigorated.

Also distinctive to the Lusitanian empire was the central role of the slave trade in its Atlantic development.[31] Angola was a major source, the island outposts of São Tomé and Cape Verde were way-stations and plantations, and Brazil the insatiable market. The slave trade was a mainstay of the colonial economy well into the 19th century, nominally abolished in 1836, but not finally ended until 1870. From this encounter emerged strongly Creolized populations in São Tomé and Cape Verde, and especially in Angola, where an Afro-Portuguese intermediary population expanded the slave trading networks progressively inland. Subsequently, the Cape Verdeans and Afro-Portuguese played a crucial role in an eventual institutionalized colonial administration, sometimes holding top posts. In the revolt against colonial occupation, the mestizo populace was to play a crucial role.

By the 19th century, the days of imperial glory and a leading role in the age of discoveries were long over. Portugal was a relatively poor and weak European country, shorn of its most profitable Brazilian colony, lacking the state capacity and capital of its colonial competitors. With the loss of Brazil complete by 1889, Portuguese elites feared that, without the bulwark of empire, the country risked absorption into Spain.[32] Though Portugal maintained vaguely defined sovereign claims extending far inward from its coastal bases in Angola and Mozambique, its actual rule was far more circumscribed. The European presence in Portuguese Africa was limited until 1900: fewer than 10,000 in Angola at that time and even fewer elsewhere – many of them deported convicts.

The intensifying scramble for Africa in the last quarter of the 19th century forced the Portuguese hand, with validation of its territorial claims now contingent on effective occupation. However, the full conquest of the hinterlands in Portuguese Guinea, Angola, and Mozambique was completed only in the 1920s.[33] The African subject became sharply demarcated as a 'native' distinct from the 'civilized' population of Europeans and mestizos, subjected to taxation and systematic recourse to forced labour by a harsh administration.

The struggles with European rivals over colonial territorial demarcation redefined Portuguese nationalism, placing, in the words of Clarence-Smith, 'colonialism firmly at the centre of nationalist discourse for nearly a century, and engendered the idea that every portion of national territory was sacred'.[34] The humiliation of the 1890 British ultimatum compelling abandonment of the Portuguese project of annexing the African territories lying between Angola and Mozambique remained seared in the national memory for decades. Salazar's New State resurrected and reanimated the classic doctrine of a global, multiracial Lusitanian polity, borrowing the concept of lusotropicalism from Brazilian intellectual Gilberto Freyre. Future ruler Marcello Caetano (1968–1974) in 1936 invoked 'the supreme flower of the Portuguese language, the symbol of the moral unity of the empire whose discovery and conquest it sings in imperishable terms'. As the wars for independence broke out in the African territories in 1961, Salazar defiantly insisted that 'We will not sell, we will not cede, we will not surrender, we will not share [...] the smallest item of our sovereignty'.[35]

The authoritarian character of the Portuguese state as the first hints of decolonization appeared is yet another distinguishing feature. Democratic parliamentary institutions for other major colonial occupants gave an entirely different dynamic to the end of empire. While the pressures for African independence became tangible by 1950 elsewhere, Portugal moved to tighten its hold. In 1951, the empire was once again defined as a global polity, with the African (and Asian) territories renamed 'overseas provinces'.[36] All African subjects were decreed citizens in 1961, a status that in the authoritarian corporatism of Salazar's New State brought few political rights, with little change in daily realities on the ground. Furthermore, there were no inconvenient implications of an overseas majority in representative institutions.

Ironically, only in the last two colonial decades did the African territories, especially Angola and Mozambique, begin to prosper economically. Salazar abandoned the closed imperial system and allowed a flow of foreign capital. In Angola, the European population, still only 44,000 in 1940, rose to 335,000 by the end of the colonial era, with 200,000 in Mozambique.[37] Oil production began in Angola in the late 1950s, diamond and coffee production soared. In Mozambique, cotton prices were at historic highs for much of this period, and South Africa paid a gold bounty for each Mozambican worker recruited for the mines.

Although the circumscribed educational opportunities restricted the size of African elites, by the post-war years a significant mestizo intelligentsia existed. Especially in Angola, Protestant mission education supplied future nationalist leadership. By the 1950s, currents of anti-colonial nationalist doctrine elsewhere stirred aspirations in the Portuguese territories. The autocratic cast to the Portuguese state inhibited its open expression, but unrest percolated in small discussion groups, especially in the colonial capitals. Only the clandestine far-Left offered comradeship, and their ideological currents – radical social-ist and Marxist-Leninist – flowed into emergent nationalist thought. Its revolutionary and multi-racial cast attracted many mestizos and Indians, as well as some radical whites. As they watched other African territories win independence, their frustration grew: the Portuguese dic-tatorship permitted no open challenge to colonial rule.

Left with no alternative, armed liberation emerged in Angola in 1961, Guinea-Bissau in 1963, and Mozambique in 1964. The offshore isola-tion of the island colonies, Cape Verde and São Tomé, precluded revolt, though Cape Verdean intellectuals, led by Amílcar Cabral, played a leading role in the Guinea-Bissau insurrection. Portugal responded only with military force and reforms aimed at full integration of the overseas provinces. By the early 1970s, the Portuguese had deployed 340,000 troops in the African territories, two-thirds of them African. A bitter array of guerrilla wars endured for thirteen years.

Although intellectuals supplied the top leadership, the circumstances of protracted guerrilla war compelled a very different strategy of nation-alist mobilization. Portuguese security forces could maintain a firm grip on the major cities, and could count on the loyalty of many customary rulers. Success in guerrilla struggle rested upon a capacity to persuade rural populations to join in a risky combat, the costs of which they would bear. In Guinea-Bissau, where Portuguese colonial occupation was weakest, by the late 1960s insurgents had mostly confined the security forces to urban garrisons, and had created extensive 'liber-ated zones' providing some basic services. The Mozambique liberation movement, the Mozambique Liberation Front (Frente de Libertação de Moçambique, FRELIMO), was increasingly unified and effective, even-tually winning control of much of the north. In Angola, the struggle was hampered by sharply divided insurgents, with three movements competing for the liberation terrain. Portuguese occupation was densest here, and the insurgency at an impasse when the 1974 coup suddenly transformed the situation.[38]

As time went by, although the warfare was of low intensity, Portugal tested the limits of the possible for a small state to resist the 'end of empire' currents now flowing so powerfully in world politics. On the European front, Portugal had long neutralized Western pressures in support of staged decolonization through its charter membership in the North Atlantic Treaty Organization (NATO) from 1949. However, the silence of the international community when the Indian army seized Goa and the other Portuguese enclaves by military force in 1961 was a shock. There was a brief moment of American overtures to the nationalist forces in 1961 when President John Kennedy took office, deeply resented by Salazar, then again in 1966 with a proposal for negotiations with the nationalists for an eight–ten-year transition, followed by an internationally supervised referendum offering the choice of independence, a Portuguese commonwealth, or an integrated Lusophone state.[39] However, Lisbon skilfully utilized the strategic value of its Azores bases to deflect American pressure for change. This shield had no value in the UN and other international forums, where Portugal increasingly became a target. Colonial warfare and autocratic governance also barred the door to entry into the European Community.

The deepening isolation of Portugal took its toll. But the imperial will also rotted from within as the wars became interminable. The Army relied on conscript soldiers, with service obligations extending to four years. Tens of thousands emigrated to France to escape the draft. The rank and file in Africa grew demoralized as the fighting continued with no end in sight. Over time, their disaffection seeped into the officer corps, setting the stage for the April 1974 military coup that destroyed the New State.

An important straw in the wind was the February 1974 publication of *Portugal and the Future* by General António Spínola, erstwhile governor of Guinea-Bissau, calling for an extended transition followed by a multi-option referendum whose preferred outcome would be a federation of the overseas territories, with Portugal retaining the sovereign powers of foreign affairs, defence, and finance. Caetano, who replaced Salazar in 1968, had seen the text and not blocked its publication.[40] Although some coup leaders imagined new and different overseas links might be retained, such an outcome held no appeal for the guerrilla movements.

Portugal itself was soon consumed by ideological cleavage within the Armed Forces Movement and society at large. A transition to democracy was promised for Portugal and this absorbed metropolitan energies in the period that followed. The final phase of decolonization took place under a succession of provisional regimes, with a progressive radicalization of the revolution into mid-1975.

Meanwhile, the new junta found its hand immediately forced in Guinea-Bissau, which had already declared independence in 1973 and was on the verge of winning admission to the UN. Though the first post-coup leader, Spínola, still hoped for some federal formula, the Portuguese garrison in Bissau mutinied and refused to continue fighting. The African Party for the Independence of Guinea and Cape Verde (Partido Africano da Independência da Guiné e Cabo Verde, PAIGC) rejected any negotiation except over a ceasefire and transfer of power, finally conceded in September 1974.

By this time, a new law had acknowledged the right of the colonies to independence. In Mozambique, FRELIMO ascendancy was well established, though resisted by many European and some Indian settlers, and with some transitional frictions, independence followed in June 1975. Cape Verde and São Tomé, while not having experienced any guerrilla action, had dominant nationalist movements that could inherit sovereignty the same year, though in the latter case the leadership had lived abroad for many years.[41]

Angola, however, was a different story, with post-colonial disaster awaiting. The three competing movements – the Angolan Liberation Movement (Movimento para a Libertação de Angola, MPLA), the National Front for the Liberation of Angola (Frente Nacional para a Libertação de Angola, FNLA) and the Union for the Total Independence of Angola (União para Independência Total de Angola, UNITA) – each had zones of ethno-regional support. Their rivalry was complicated by the instant importation of the Cold War; each movement had external allies and patrons (Soviet Union and Cuba for MPLA; Congo-Kinshasa and the United States for FNLA; and Zambia and South Africa for UNITA). The swiftly weakening Portuguese administration sought to broker a transitional coalition regime, as did the Organization of African Unity (OAU). However, these efforts foundered on the deep mutual distrust of the movements. Arms began to flow in from outside sponsors, followed by external combatants and operatives (Cuban, Soviet, American, South African, Congolese), and by March 1975 civil war broke out in Luanda. On 11 November 1975, in a forlorn end to African empire, the last Portuguese governor simply announced he was turning power over to 'the Angolan people', boarded a waiting ship and sailed away.

Portugal reimagined itself as a nation following the inglorious end of its African vocation.[42] The revolutionary tides of radical socialist and communist inspiration peaked in mid-1975, and soon ebbed. However, they left their strong imprint on the new constitution, with various clauses of Marxist inspiration, and an accompanying wave of nationalizations. These measures were, in the years following, gradually eroded or erased. The new role as a small but loyal member of the European Union fits its scale: imperial grandeur is relegated to the museums, with its traces visible in the mestizo and African minorities in Portuguese cities, who perhaps had once been empire loyalists. A massive statue to Prince Henry the Navigator erected by Salazar stands in Lisbon to evoke the age of discoveries, but young generations seem to have little nostalgia for the lost colonial splendour.

The comparative scrutiny of these three cases of outsized empires under the sovereignty of small, relatively weak states suggests several concluding observations. Riding with the tides of the times and adjusting to a changing international normative order seemed beyond the steering capacity of these polities. Empire, even though reluctantly assumed by Belgium, tends to find inscription in the inner recesses of national identity. The colonies are a transformative elixir dissolving the constraints of smallness in a world dominated by the large and powerful. The official mind, as well as the public at large, is mesmerized by the self-justifying promotional information diffused by colonial information offices. In the post-war era, the rapidly changing international environment for empire, textured by the Cold War and the rise of an anti-imperial third world, subjected all remaining colonizers to substantial pressures. Up until the Second World War, colonial holdings were a wholly legitimate form of rule in dominant international society, subject only to ethical limits on the scope of coercion. Professions of benevolent intent towards the subject populace, unless flagrantly contradicted, sufficed to meet the external legitimation imperative.

After the war, the international normative order evolved swiftly. The two superpowers, by different doctrinal pathways, were inimical to the perpetuation of colonial empires. So were the multiplying numbers of new states in Asia and the Middle East, joined by the formerly quiescent Latin American republics in an anti-imperial bloc. The doctrine of self-determination entered international jurisprudence in the First World War peace settlement but was only applicable to European claimants issuing from the demise of the multi-national Austro-Hungarian, Russian and Ottoman Empires. After the Second World War, the right to self-determination became extended to colonial territories (though not ethnic segments thereof).

States abandon their inherent territorial possessiveness only under duress. In 1945 the largest colonizers, France and the United Kingdom, were far from accepting an early end to empire. Both, however, after a number of false steps and through ad hoc adaptations in the end – and notwithstanding decolonization fiascos in Palestine, Vietnam, and Algeria – found a pathway to negotiated and brokered power transfer that left initially functioning new states (even if only briefly) in the wake of transition. They both found mechanisms for cordial postcolonial ties with many former colonies, through the Commonwealth for the United Kingdom, and what became *françafrique* in the French case. The policy framework provided by dominion status in the empire provided a framework for negotiated, staged transition from colonial subject to Commonwealth partner that in most former British African territories proved serviceable, a template not available to the cases under review.

For our three small states, though once loss of empire seemed inevitable each sought some formula for organic post-colonial ties, none succeeded. Indeed, aborted decolonization in all three cases led to rupture of relationships. The Dutch lost all their Indonesian holdings, as well as residence rights for their citizens. In all three cases, the disorderly circumstances surrounding decolonization led to the massive exodus of large settler populations, many abandoning possessions and property: more than 500,000 Portuguese and more than 200,000 Dutch citizens.[43] Though over time Belgium became a significant external partner for Congo-Kinshasa, the relationship remains ambivalent and marked by episodes of tension. Large Belgian capital has long withdrawn from its once huge colonial holdings. Portugal is only a moderate player in postcolonial Lusophone Africa, although the animosities of the liberation wars have long subsided.

Autocratic and multi-party parliamentary regimes appeared unsuited to consensual decolonization. Dictatorships perhaps remained locked in intransigence, perhaps through fear that compromise with anti-colonial nationalists would puncture their mystique of omnipotence. The other authoritarian African colonizer, Franco's Spain, was unable to negotiate power transfer in Western Sahara, and finally simply abandoned the territory to Moroccan occupation. In both the Netherlands and Belgium, the capacity of negotiators to find common ground with nationalist challengers was constrained by the constant threat to parliamentary majorities.

Decolonization almost invariably is a traumatic moment for the withdrawing occupant. The wars in Vietnam and Algeria delegitimized and finally destroyed the Fourth Republic in France, while a military mutiny almost overturned the Fifth in 1961. The 1956 Suez crisis, a requiem for an older version of imperial assumptions, ended the career of Prime Minister Sir Anthony Eden. But the trauma is even greater for the small state condemned to a diminished role in the world through loss of empire. Especially for Belgium and Portugal, the loss of colonies triggered a far-reaching reconfiguration of the national self. Belgium has experienced a creeping federalization and mutual disengagement between its component Flemish and Francophone communities. Portugal redefined itself as a small state with an identity tied to Europe. The therapy of time only slowly eases the pain and humiliation of disorderly disengagement of the small state from its colonial empire.

Notes

1. An earlier version of this chapter appeared in W. M. Louis, ed., *Resurgent Adventures in Britannia*, London, I.B. Tauris, 2011.
2. C. Fasseur, R. E. Elson and A. Kraal, *The Politics of Colonial Exploitation: Java, the Dutch, and the Cultivation System*, New York, NY, Southeast Asia Program Publications, Cornell University Press, 1992.
3. M. C. Ricklefs, *A History of Modern Indonesia, c. 1300 to the Present*, Bloomington, IN, Indiana University Press, 1981, p. 119.
4. F. Gouda, *Dutch Culture Overseas: Colonial Practice in the Netherlands Indies, 1900–1942*, Amsterdam, Amsterdam University Press, 1995, p. 24.
5. C. L. M. Penders, *The New Guinea Debacle: Dutch Decolonization and Indonesia, 1945–1962*, Leiden, KITLV, 2002.
6. Gouda, *Dutch Culture Overseas*, p. 23.
7. R. J. McMahon, *Colonialism and the Cold War: The United States and the Struggle for Indonesia, 1945–49*, Ithaca, NY, Cornell University Press, 1981, p. 40.
8. Penders, *West New Guinea Debacle*, pp. 31–33.
9. On American policy during Indonesian decolonization, see F. Gouda, *American Visions of the Netherlands East Indies/Indonesia: US Foreign Policy and Indonesian Nationalism, 1920–1949*, Amsterdam, Amsterdam University Press, 2002.
10. In unraveling this tormented and protracted decolonization from 1945 to 1950, I found especially helpful T. Friend, *Indonesian Destinies*, Cambridge, MA, Harvard University Press, 2003, and Ricklefs, *A History of Modern Indonesia*.
11. A. Lijphart, *The Trauma of Decolonization: The Dutch and West New Guinea*, New Haven, CT, Yale University Press, 1966, p. 285.
12. A. Lijphart, *The Politics of Accommodation: Pluralism and Democracy in the Netherlands*, 2d ed., Berkeley, CA, University of California Press, 1975. A limit to consociationalism in decolonization was its frequent tendency to overcome contentious issues by postponing decisions. See R. B. Andeweg and G. A. Irwin, *Governance and Politics of the Netherlands*, New York, NY, Palgrave Macmillan, 2002, p. 30. See also H. Daalder and G. A. Irwin, *Politics in the Netherlands: How Much Change?*, London, Frank Cass, 1998.
13. C. Young, *The African Colonial State in Comparative Perspective*, New Haven, CT, Yale University Press, 1994, p. 84.
14. A. Hochschild, *King Leopold's Ghost: A Story of Greed, Terror and Heroism in Colonial Africa*, Boston, MA, Houghton Mifflin, 1998, p. 277.
15. C. Young, *Politics in the Congo*, Princeton, NJ, Princeton University Press, 1965, pp. 10–32.
16. E. Witte, J. Craeybeckx and A. Meynen, *Political History of Belgium from 1830 Onwards*, Antwerp, VUB, 2000, pp. 135–163.
17. Young, *African Colonial State*, p. 213.
18. P. de Vos, *La decolonization: Les événements du Congo de 1959 à 1967*, Brussels, ABC, 1975, p. 24. This volume contains a summary of the debates among a number of key participants in decolonization on Belgian radio.
19. P. Lumumba, *Le Congo, terre d'avenir, est-il menacé*, Brussels, Office de Publicité, 1961.

20. Cited in J. Stengers, 'Precipitous decolonization: The case of the Belgian Congo', in P. Gifford and W. R. Louis, eds, *The Transfer of Power in Africa: Decolonization, 1940–1960*, New Haven, CT, Yale University Press, 1982, p. 314.
21. B. Verhaegen, *L'ABAKO et l'indépendance du Congo: Dix ans du nationalisme kongo*, Paris, L'Harmattan, 2003, p. 161.
22. De Vos, *La decolonization*, p. 33.
23. De Vos, *La decolonization*, p. 61.
24. A report whispered at the time, but confirmed decades later by a participant, J.-M. Bomboko, 'Vers l'indépendance: Perceptions congolaises', in C. Braekman, ed., *Congo 1960: Échec d'une decolonization*, Brussels, GRIP, 2010, p. 81.
25. Young, *Politics in the Congo*, p. 402.
26. T. Kanza, *Conflict in the Congo*, Harmondsworth, Penguin, 1972, p. 32.
27. In the words of a recent study of Belgian politics, the contemporary narrative of Belgium is 'one of a country that does not believe in itself', plagued by distrust among the elite. K. Deschouwer, *The Politics of Belgium: Governing a Divided Society*, New York, NY, Palgrave Macmillan, 2009, p. 242.
28. *Le Monde*, 27 April 2010, headlines its report, 'L'idée séparatiste fait son chemin'.
29. For a moving account by a scholar with decades of intimate contact with various segments of the Belgian elite, see R. Fox, *In the Belgian Chateau: The Spirit and Culture of a Society in the Age of Change*, Chicago, IL, Ivan R. Dee, 1994. She concludes that the reality of Belgium as a nation and societal community was disappearing into the past, its breakup a topic of serious discussion (p. 311). Guy Vanthemsche in an exhaustive inquiry into the impact of the colony on Belgium concludes that for a half-century a cult of the Congo had been at the core of Belgian nationalism: 'the loss of the Congo reduced the possibilities for the Walloons and Flemish to imagine a Belgian nation and must be considered among the factors leading to decentralization and regionalism in Belgium after 1960', in *La Belgique et le Congo: L'impact de la colonie sur la metropole*, Brussels, Editions le Cri, 2010, p. 89.
30. J. Duffy, *Portuguese Africa*, Cambridge, MA, Harvard University Press, 1959, p. 75.
31. See especially the thorough account by J. C. Miller, *Way of Death: Merchant Capitalism and the Atlantic Slave Trade*, Madison, WI, University of Wisconsin Press, 1988.
32. V. Alexandre, 'The colonial empire', in A. C. Pinto, ed., *Modern Portugal*, Palo Alto, CA, Society for the Promotion of Science and Scholarship, 1998, pp. 41–59.
33. G. Clarence-Smith, *The Third Portuguese Empire, 1825–1975: A Study of Economic Imperialism*, Manchester, Manchester University Press, 1975; J. B. Forest, *Lineages of State Fragility: Rural Civil Society in Guinea-Bissau*, Athens, OH, Ohio University Press, 2003.
34. Clarence-Smith, *Third Portuguese Empire*, p. 83.
35. B. Davidson, 'Portuguese-speaking Africa', in M. Crowder, ed., *Cambridge History of Africa*, vol. 8, *c. 1940–1975*, Cambridge, Cambridge University Press, 1984, p. 760.

36. Norrie MacQueen, in his invaluable study of Portuguese decolonization, indicates that this constitutional change was also undertaken to facilitate United Nations membership. See *The Decolonization of Portuguese Africa: Metropolitan Revolution and the Dissolution of Empire*, London, Longman, 1997, p. 11.

37. Clarence-Smith, *Third Portuguese Empire*, p. 213.

38. Among many sources, let me note: P. Chabal, *A History of Postcolonial Lusophone Africa*, Bloomington, IN, Indiana University Press, 2002; A. Isaacman and B. Isaacman, *Mozambique: From Colonialism to Revolution, 1900–1982*, Boulder, CO, Westview, 1983; R. Pelissier, *La colonie du mintaure: Nationalismes et révolte en Angola (1928–1961)*, Montaments, Pelissier, 1978.

39. MacQueen, *Decolonization of Portuguese Africa*, pp. 53–54.

40. Ibid., pp. 73–74.

41. G. Seibert, 'São Tomé y Principe', in Cabral, *Postcolonial Lusophone Africa*, pp. 261–315.

42. Useful sources on contemporary Portugal include Pinto, *Modern Portugal*; K. Maxwell and M. H. Haltzel, eds,, *Portugal: Ancient Country, Young Democracy*, Washington, DC, Wilson Center, 1990; L. S. Graham and D. L. Wheeler, *In Search of Modern Portugal: The Revolution and Its Consequences*, Madison, WI, University of Wisconsin Press, 1983.

43. Penders, *West New Guinea Debacle*, p. 271; D. Higgs, ed., *Portuguese Overseas Migration in Global Perspective*, Toronto, Multicultural History Society of Ontario, 1990, pp. 1–3.

5
Myths of Decolonization: Britain, France, and Portugal Compared

Bruno Cardoso Reis

This chapter considers the construction of the notion of decolonization in the context of national political cultures. It seeks to explore the question: What was the role of cultural prejudices and preferences in the end of the three biggest European colonial empires in Africa? Answers will be provided by tracing the impact of some explicit and recurrent cultural prejudices at the level of senior decision makers and officials in comparing British, French, and Portuguese decolonization.

It is not possible to show unequivocally here the decisive role of political culture in decolonization. My aim is simply to present arguments and evidence from some relevant sources that it did play an important role in both setting the pace and helping define the shape of decolonization.

Why decolonization myths matter

Decolonization is understood in this text as primarily the formal end of colonial empires through 'the surrender of political sovereignty over the peoples of Africa and Asia and the emergence of independent nation-states'.[1] The end of formal empires as proud political and cultural constructs is one of the cornerstones of contemporary international politics resulting in around 200 states recognized by the United Nations (UN). Yet there was no complete military collapse of these colonial powers comparable to other cases of imperial demise (Ancient Rome, Tsarist Russia). The Second World War seriously weakened Western colonial empires in some parts of Asia, but this was not true in sub-Saharan Africa. Colonial powers in Africa still had some choice, some ability to resist and shape decolonization according to core preferences and prejudices. This is where I believe that taking political culture seriously is indispensable.

Myth is defined for the purposes of my analysis as a widely shared 'traditional story of ostensibly historical events that serves to unfold part of the world view of a people or explain a practice, belief'. A 'popular belief or tradition [...] *especially*: one embodying the ideals and institutions of a society or segment of society'. This is Barthe's definition in his seminal book *Mythologies* that significantly provides as an example of the importance of myths in late modernity a cover of *Paris-Match* with a young black soldier saluting the French flag. He interprets this as an affirmation of the myth of France as a 'great empire' in which 'all' 'without colour discrimination' 'served her faithfully'.[2] The importance of myths of empire has also been explored in the field of international relations but with a focus on imperial expansion.[3] Surely it is equally worth exploring the myths of the end of empire, the myths of decolonization.

There has been some reference to potential myths of decolonization in key works on British or Portuguese decolonization. For instance, John Darwin made a strong case against romantic delusions of a well-planned British decolonization. The imperial legacy was artfully repackaged as the great work of nation building, but this could not disguise the growing fragility of British global power leading to frequent crises and unexpected accelerations of decolonization.[4] Norrie Macqueen has argued that the notion of the Portuguese coup of April 1974 organized by the Armed Forces Movement (Movimento das Forças Armadas, MFA) as a fourth liberation movement aimed at decolonization was a convenient façade covering the loss of colonies by the military by turning them into liberators overseas as well as at home.[5]

But while these mythical narratives may not be good guides for objective analysis, they are important social constructions with real impact, and require careful study. A book that illustrates the importance of this process of cultural construction is the pioneering work on the French 'invention of decolonization' by Todd Shepard; another is a recent collective volume on the 'French colonial mind'.[6]

The last Portuguese (overseas) territories co-ordination minister argues that it took more than a decade of wars in Africa for 'the greater power of realities over convictions' regarding overseas Portuguese territories to prevail, leading to decolonization.[7] This is surely a powerful indication that it is both wrong to ignore the real, potentially even deadly, power of political culture, and to argue its influence has no limits.

Approach and research questions

D. K. Fieldhouse is right in pointing out that 'the history of imperialism is distinct from that of particular imperial possessions'.[8] Even if we were to concur with Ronald Robinson that 'British and French imperialism are as different as chalk from cheese', we would still need comparative studies to better understand how and why.[9] The addition of a third case – Portugal – offers the added value of making it more difficult to argue in terms of simplistic dichotomies. These are also the three largest colonial empires in Africa, even if Portugal is often quickly dismissed as a marginal oddity. And while the comparative analysis of the history of decolonization has been present for some time, it is still indispensable to fully comprehend such an international phenomenon as decolonization.[10]

The second main element of my analytical approach is a focus on culture, in particular political and strategic culture. But is this not too fuzzy and undetermined to be of use in rigorous analysis? This has been debated in depth in the field of international relations, with advocates of a culturalist approach to international politics arguing convincingly that norms condition what is deemed acceptable in a given community/organization and often have a demonstrable impact in terms of perceptions, discourse, and behaviour.[11] The so-called constructivist school has emerged around the importance of culture understood as norms, that is collective expectations about proper behaviour for a given identity. Even if it accepts that 'the presence of norms does not dictate compliance. Any new or emergent norm must compete with existing, perhaps countervailing, ones'.[12] The notions of Greater France or Portugal are prime examples of a social definition of identity seriously constraining what is deemed do-able and acceptable in terms of political culture. The triumph of the new international norm of decolonization therefore required the difficult task of reconstructing national identity.

The key questions derived from this approach are: In what way have cultural preferences affected decisions on decolonization? Was this seen as a menace to the basic identity, the constitutional norms of a certain polity? How was this overcome or accommodated?

Britain: from liberal colonial power to centre of the Commonwealth?

Pragmatism is often emphasized as the cornerstone of Britain's approach to decolonization. Based on a massive collection of documentation,

Ronald Hyam concludes that from the Second World War on, 'pragmatic tactics operated over a broad spectrum of colonial problems'. John Darwin argues that 'British governments, or certainly their advisors in the Foreign Office, prided themselves on their pragmatism'.[13] This might seem as incompatible with the importance of cultural factors. In fact we see this proud pragmatism as an affirmation of a strong cultural preference. Furthermore, even if taken at face value and as an unproblematic affirmation of a preference for a more instrumental approach to reality, it does not automatically guarantee success in achieving an unbiased, coldly realistic vision of the actors and actions about which to be pragmatic. For instance, it does not guarantee an unprejudiced attitude towards colonized peoples, their elites and their ability for self-rule. Nor does it automatically dictate any less of a wish for (pragmatically) insisting on as much (pragmatic) metropolitan imperial control throughout the process as possible. It did not preclude British elites from showing some political blindness in an initial absolute refusal of decolonization, because of the alleged (pragmatic) strategic necessity for bases in the Suez, Cyprus, Aden or even Kenya and Rhodesia with its white settlers.[14] Pragmatism is, in other words, less linear than it might seem, but it was certainly a strong preference in British political culture and one that did have some impact.

The most obvious evidence of this British pragmatism came with the official reviews of costs and benefits of overseas territories. These reflected an attitude after the Second World War of cutting adrift from dependencies that were net losers, like Burma and Palestine, while keeping those 'possessions which remained bankable assets'.[15] Malaya was the paradigmatic example of a dollar-earner exporter of commodities essential for the sterling area that should – pragmatically – be kept under colonial control as long as possible and carefully entrusted to friendly elites.

The most cited – and one of the most systematic – of these reviews was ordered by Prime Minister Harold Macmillan in 1957. Perhaps less obviously important for decolonization, but arguably even more decisive, were the strategic defence reviews under Conservative defence secretary Duncan Sandys, also in 1957, and Labour defence secretary Denis Healey in 1965. The interesting point is that these wider reviews of colonial costs and benefits were relatively inconclusive – another illustration that pragmatism does not necessarily provide unequivocal answers for complex political questions. But the defence reviews were very conclusive regarding the colonial policy implications of deep defence cuts. The defence White Paper of 1957 states: 'It is [...] in the true interest of defence that the claims of military expenditure should be considered in conjunction with the need to maintain the country's financial and economic strength'.[16] One key implication of these defence reviews was that there should be no major overseas counter-insurgency campaigns in the future.[17] The decisions to get out even more quickly of central and eastern Africa, after the Nyasaland Emergency of 1959, or not to engage more in the campaign in South Arabia (Aden) and eventually to withdraw from all British bases east of the Suez were the logical conclusion of this. As Healey made clear when discussing the implications of the 1965 defence cuts: 'there were two military tasks that we could not undertake in the future', one of those being 'large-scale long-term counterinsurgency operations'.[18] The British approach to decolonization therefore changed from being (in the late-1940s and early-1950s) one of pragmatically balancing between places to stay and fight and places to leave, to one (from the end of the 1950s) in which the need to avoid any more conflicts to stop or slow decolonization became increasingly paramount.

Two further points should be underlined. The first is that even if not always offering an obvious answer, this pragmatic attitude was not seen as anti-patriotic anathema as was the case for a long time in discussions of French and Portuguese decolonization. The reactions to the arguments of the leading French public intellectual Raymond Aron are paradigmatic, with him being widely attacked, including by senior political figures, for selling the national honour and ignoring the moral duty of France when he argued precisely for a policy review of French engagement in Algeria and Africa in light of 'economic pragmatism'.[19]

The second is that pragmatism does not eliminate culture. Not only can it be seen as in itself an expression of a cultural preference, but it cannot work independently from perceptions of reality that are often biased by cultural prejudices. This is best illustrated by the fact that this British pragmatism was comforted by what proved to be a largely illusory myth of decolonization; that pro-British, or at least pragmatic, moderate forces would prevail in former colonies, and that as independent countries they would consequently continue to turn to Britain for experienced guidance.[20]

The central importance in British decolonization policy of a Whig narrative of deliberate gradual development of the dependent territories into self-governing dominions and then independent members of the Commonwealth is clear from the start. Creech Jones – the colonial secretary in the post-1945 Labour Government that initiated the process of decolonization – stated unequivocally in a widely distributed report that 'the central purpose of British colonial policy is simple. It is to guide the colonial territories to responsible self-government within the Commonwealth'. This vision may well be criticized as self-serving, paternalistic; representative of a grand plan that was never really implemented. Though to be fair, in the same document it is pragmatically recognized that 'though the policy is clear enough, the problems to be overcome in carrying it out are numerous and complex'.[21] Yet regardless of these problems, the central British myth of decolonization was still relevant.

A 1946 guideline for propaganda signed by Herbert Morrison for the Central Office of Information and the British Council global network stated that 'Britain is the centre of a world-wide association of free peoples', the British Commonwealth makes it a 'world power' with the credibility and the will to approach the various 'problems presented by the administration of backward tropical territories which comprised the greater part of the colonial empire' in terms that were 'both liberal and dynamic'.[22] Naturally, in a significant sign of the importance of historical change in cultural sensibility, today the notion of backward tropical territories would not be seen as liberal or pragmatic, but rather as strongly prejudiced. This gives evidence of a crucial point I wish to underline here: even during decolonization, and because of cultural prejudices shaping it, there was no notion of real as opposed to formal equality between colonizers and colonized.

The myth of British decolonization presents an ideal image of the latter as: first, the continuation of the glorious history of gradual constitutional development of the British peoples; second, the affirmation of the liberal character of British colonialism, the appropriate kind for a political community that identified deeply with liberalism as well as with pragmatism; third, not a rebuttal but a culmination of the civilizing mission of the British among primitive natives; and fourth, not undermining but enhancing its global great power status. This may not be very helpful as a guide to the concrete difficulties of setting actual policy in all its details, but it is certainly very revealing about the kind of mainstream cultural preferences according to which senior British officials and decision makers perceived and tried to shape decolonization.

The fact that two major aspects of British identity could be used to facilitate the acceptance of decolonization's appropriateness certainly made it easier. One was its linkage with a long liberal heritage. The other was the composite nature of the British polity uniting in shared allegiance to the Crown varied and varying institutional entities, starting with the United Kingdom itself and extending to the dominions. David

Cannadine's approach to empire as a historical construct closely linked to British national identity is particularly fruitful, especially his insight into the impact of decolonization as happening not just overseas but also in Britain. This chapter hopes to contribute to the effort to grapple with that process of reconstruction of the British identity during decolonization by comparing it with other cases.[23]

The acceptance of decolonization was also made easier by a great degree of cultural commonality between the UK and the US – enthusiastically 'discovered' by British elites after 1945. This tended to make British elites slightly more comfortable with a pressure for decolonization coming from the US. The reverse was true in the case of France and Portugal, which had very strong reservations about a process seen as the result of self-serving Anglo-Saxon powers sticking together bound by a common culture.[24]

France: from republican empire to *francophonie*?

There is a strong preference in mainstream French culture for rationality understood in terms of a uniformity of approach commonly referred to as Cartesianism. This has visible effects from the orthogonal landscape design of public parks to the way diplomatic negotiations are conducted with what is often perceived by others as rigidness and arrogance.[25] De Gaulle, the dominant political figure in French politics during the most crucial stage of decolonization, is often perceived abroad as an example of this. Yet he was himself aware of this as a potential problem, at least in others, complaining about the French mind 'age-old allurements of the a priori, the absolute and the dogmatic'.[26]

Girardet in his seminal study of French colonial ideology describes well the impact of this trend in the 'ever present centralizing and unitary mentality' that made any significant devolution within the so-called French Union, created after 1946, very difficult to accept in principle and implement in practice.[27] This French determination to impose a similar Cartesian approach to its relations to its overseas territories did not exclude change. But it did shape a particular kind of change; for instance, the response to the new challenge posed by the independence of Guinea Conakry in 1958. Change should logically be led by Paris, should ensure by a formal treaty and informal networks a strong linkage with and publicly expressed gratitude to France, and result in a similar status for all large French territories in continental Africa.

But how could the French be so rational and apparently – with hindsight and taking decolonization as a given – pursue such an irrational policy? Arguably, this was the case especially of French Algeria, formally a (special) part of the metropole itself. This made any attempt at rational cost/benefit analysis very difficult to accept as appropriate. The repeated violent reactions – from military *pronunciamentos* to assassination attempts – against decolonization of Algeria, targeting first the Fourth Republic and then President de Gaulle, throughout the late 1950s and early 1960s, prove the real importance of this kind of cultural taboo for policymakers who want to survive, literally, not just politically. It was no accident that Aron referred to the heroism of letting-go (*l'héroisme de l'abandon*) being required to pursue decolonization, particularly of Algeria, in the context of French political culture of this period.[28]

The strong mainstream consensus in France – from the Left to the Right, with the exception of the Communist Party and some left-wing Catholics, but only after 1956 – concerning the need to honour the constitutional norm that France extended from Dunkirk to Tamanrasset did not result, however, in a strong French government during this crucial period. The emphasis on a unitary republic can therefore be seen as reflecting a long-term cultural preference for centralization, but also a form of over-compensation for the very real fragmentation in French politics. Not only was the French party system very fragmented, but basic constitutional norms of the Fourth Republic – dating from 1946 – were not supported by two of its strongest parties: the Communists and the Gaullists. The idea of the 'weakness of the [political] institutions', in fact, gained increasing popularity as an explanation for the ills of France. This made the governing elite all the more anxious to rally support around the flag by appealing to the ideal of republican imperialism.[29]

Regardless of or despite calculations, the degree to which political leaders or intellectuals were also permeable to the power of these cultural norms that were closely linked with the social construction of national identity should not be underestimated. The very influential editor of *Nouvel Observateur*, Jean Daniel, states that in the mid-1950s all the political elite, but also all the intellectual elite, saw Algeria as 'irreversibly French' regardless of the criticism they might have of its mismanagement. And he went further by saying that 'it is difficult to make people understand' nowadays that 'French Algeria' was then 'something so natural' that it was 'audacious to discuss and blasphemous to question'.[30] This was demonstrated through the massive parliamentary majority that voted for the granting of special powers to the government in 1956 to deal with the Algerian insurgency.[31] These are clear markers of strong mainstream cultural norms – requiring unquestioning acceptance of certain assumptions, certain taboos that are then difficult to understand for people in other contexts. This is also evidence of how they could become major obstacles to decolonization. The Algerian War (1954–62) can be seen as a paradigmatic example of how 'war is an extension of culture, as well as politics'.[32] The relation with the rest of overseas France was not as legally pre-determined as with the so-called Algerian departments. But the great ideals of the French republic were still seen as the best chance for the liberation of the native population by better integration into a great fraternal French Union, the core myth that made this republican empire fit with French self-perception. These more idealistic assumptions were reinforced by the strong conviction that the greatness of France depended on Greater France overseas, and so did its security. The very recent trauma of the German occupation during the Second World War, and the role of the colonies and the colonial Army in reviving French fortunes by rallying to the Free France of de Gaulle, only reinforced this. In a speech in 1944 in Brazzaville, de Gaulle had promised progress for the colonies. But after 1945, he emphasized, and his followers devoutly echoed, the notion that for France 'to lose the French Union would be a downgrade in status that might cost us our independence. To keep it, to give it vigour, is to remain great and consequently free'.[33] It took the cumulative erosion caused by the successive wars of decolonization in Indochina (1946–54) and Algeria (1954–62), and growing international isolation, to eventually force de Gaulle and a majority of Frenchmen to do some painful rethinking.

In the meantime, however, decolonization had been made more difficult because the war in Algeria gave an increasingly strong role to the French Army, which traditionally saw itself as the guardian of empire. This allowed the military to add its own veto to that of multiple political actors, blocking any major change and creating even more of an impasse.[34] The return of de Gaulle to power was the ultimate proof of this, being the direct result of the military *pronunciamento* of 13 May 1958 – even if the end result would be the exact opposite of the wishes of those colonial officers who promoted it. The French Empire 'offered a field of glory for the fighting services [...] it is this part played by the French army in Africa [...] which explains the attitude of certain "colonels" of the present time, and their implacable hostility to the prospect of "decolonization"'.[35] For colonial officers, the survival of their corporate identity, the meaning of their life of service overseas, was at stake.

One of the most influential of these colonial officers, Colonel Trinquier, chose for his memoirs the title *Le Temps Perdu* – his life defending Greater France had been wasted. He had, after all, been a major actor in developing French counter-insurgency in Indochina and Algeria, had advocated the use of brutal interrogation – torture – to defeat the National Liberation Front (Front de Libération Nationale, FLN) network in Algeria. He had been a major player behind the May 1958 *pronunciamento* that led to the fall of the Fourth Republic, a fact duly acknowledged by Trinquier's appointment as the third-highest ranking figure in the Algiers committee of public safety. This provides context for a revealing *tête-à-tête* with de Gaulle. The new French president made a point of visiting the remote sector to which Trinquier had been transferred after all officers had been ordered out of politics. De Gaulle told Trinquier: 'You people must not press me!' Trinquier replied that, surely, he 'did not reproach the army for its passion for Algeria'. De Gaulle curtly replied: 'Every passion has its limits!'[36] This is revealing of the kind of high emotional attachment to goals that are highly valued culturally.

Reason and therefore decolonization had to prevail over strongly entrenched cultural preferences. To do this de Gaulle would need to legitimise his Fifth Republic centred on a 'Clausewitzian presidency' with total control over all key strategic decisions.[37]

General de Gaulle may have been emotionally torn between the present rational need to turn the page on the glorious past of the French Empire, but he was also uniquely equipped with charisma and cultural sensibility to make this as acceptable as possible in the context of French political culture. What de Gaulle believed was required was a reconstruction of French national identity and a reframing of its links with former colonies, but also the reconstruction of the French Republic so as to make the state stronger, to overcome the difficult problems not only of imposing decolonization but also of rebuilding post-colonial French status in the world.

De Gaulle decided upon the strategic necessity of abandoning Algeria, not because of a sudden conversion to the goodness of emancipation, or the equality of the colonized. In fact he described the task of decolonization as a 'cruel trial', but it was necessary to 'disengage from the costs, no longer countered by benefits, of our empire'.[38] There was also a wider global normative calculation in his choice, as he put it to a close confidant, to recover French prestige 'we cannot have the entire world against us'.[39] This only shows that de Gaulle's cultural preferences and assumptions, and his difficulty in overcoming them, were not fundamentally different from those of his adversaries.

President de Gaulle also moved towards decolonization, however, because in his understanding of French identity it would be absurd to try to retain sovereignty by integrating fully all Algerians as citizens of France, as required after the collapse of the international legitimacy of the standard of civilization that had solved the contradictions of having a republican empire. It would simply be unimaginable, in his strongly culturalist, if not racialist, vision of France, to eventually have an 'Arab in the Elysée' as French president.[40]

Another key concern for de Gaulle was to avoid any impression of a new traumatic and humiliating defeat, to be able to say: 'there will be no Dien Bien Phu. The army will withdraw victorious' from Algeria.[41] As for decolonization more broadly, he explicitly stated that it was essential to grant independence voluntarily not 'by a defeat inflicted by the colonized on the colonizers'.[42] The success of the Challe Plan In Algeria and the defeat of an uprising in the Cameroons provided him with that in 1959–60. De Gaulle also needed a political victory. He turned the October 1958 referendum into a choice for him, for the new constitution of the Fifth Republic, but also in the overseas territories into a choice for France. Vote 'Yes for France' as his propaganda posters put it. His victory meant he could present his decision for decolonization in 1959–60 as not being imposed by Algerians or other Africans, but as wisely given by France, despite the continued political allegiance of the population of their overseas territories. Even if this has a strong dimension of myth – because it is unclear how representative the vote was or how long this would last – it still performed an important symbolic role. It was indeed especially important for the acceptance of decolonization in terms of French political culture for de Gaulle to be able to plausibly argue, as he did, that France was 'leading the people of overseas France into self-rule and at the same time building between them and us close co-operation'. The French manifest destiny as a universal civilizing power would not be lost, because 'the progress, the friendship, the attitudes, the interests' that had resulted from French 'vocation of influence and expansion would make them privileged partners' of France.[43]

Once the decision by de Gaulle was made to accelerate towards decolonization it was naturally carried out according to a Cartesian logic. If a few wanted to go – namely in 1959, the leaders of Madagascar and Mali – then all had to go. This imposition of a French approach is best illustrated by the fact that the presidents of the Ivory Coast and Gabon had to be more or less pressed into independence, even if most pro-French African leaders were showing a growing desire for a more prestigious international status. The norm of union with France without independence could be logically replaced by a new norm of close co-operation with independence for all major French territories in the African continent.[44]

This turned out to be not just culturally adequate, but also really significant with the emergence of a French sphere of influence in most of its African colonies, with formal summits of *francophonie* and frequent state visits being complemented by close support for African ruling elites by French intelligence and military force if need be.[45] For all the weaknesses and normative criticism that can be made of this neo-colonial French way of decolonization, for all the bad press it has had in English, the fact remains that France was the most successful case of the three in obtaining, at least for a while, the stated aims of this *Gaulliste* decolonization. Not bad for a Gaullist France so often accused of delusions of grandeur, and powerful evidence that to see culture and power, myth and reality as fundamentally opposite is simply wrong.[46]

The decolonization of French sub-Saharan Africa was made to conform to French political culture. A French preference for Cartesian uniformity led to a rapid uniform granting of independence to all the major French colonies in continental Africa.

This created some difficulties for Britain, which suddenly could no longer keep on planning for a more conditioned and slower decolonization in certain areas of central and eastern Africa and claim that it was the great liberal colonial power. Not when even France, soon to be followed by Belgium – that had long provided a useful contrast for British diplomats – was granting it all and granting it fast. Whitehall still claimed it was not going to be pressed; in fact it suddenly had to accelerate its pace if it wanted to keep its myth of decolonization alive and avoid alienating African elites. Portugal would, of course, be in even greater difficulties.

Most crucial of all, this Cartesian shaping of French decolonization, granting independence to all its African colonies in 1960, not only made the 'year of Africa' at the UN possible; it was also vital in creating the very concept of decolonization that only then entered common usage.

Portugal: from Republican imperialism to fraternal liberation

Portuguese imperial policy under Salazar, who ruled the country from 1928–68, has been portrayed as paradigmatic of lack of realism, of a fundamental disconnect between foreign policy and international systemic imperatives of realpolitik. It would therefore seem to provide the ideal case to show the potentially overwhelming influence of cultural political constructs in determining foreign policy against any rational calculation of interest. And yet, as we just argued, a linear concept of the decolonization of Africa was far from clear until at least 1959–60.

Still, when in 1963 George Ball, a US undersecretary of state, was sent by President Kennedy as a personal envoy to try to convince Salazar to be more realistic and adopt a policy of gradual decolonization, he reported to Washington that he had failed, because Portugal was ruled not by one dictator but 'by a triumvirate consisting of Vasco da Gama, Prince Henry the Navigator and Salazar'.[47] Ball was right in pointing to the importance of a deep-rooted colonial nationalism in Portuguese political culture. But this was neither exclusive of the New State regime, nor did it mean Salazar was totally lost in the past and unaware of the dynamics of the modern world or the potential costs of his choice.

There is evidence that this manifest colonial mission was deeply rooted and widespread in Portuguese political culture for most of the 20th century. It was not simply something forced by Salazar's authoritarian regime. Salazar claimed that 'this union [with the overseas territories] gives us an indispensable optimism and sense of greatness';[48] while General Norton de Matos – supported by all the groups opposing Salazar as their presidential candidate in 1949 – in his electoral manifesto went as far as to state: 'the Nation is one [...] the development of the colonies must therefore be properly called national development, because there is no such thing as colonial policy, there is only national policy'.[49] Almeida Santos, an influential figures of a new generation of political leaders opposing the New State regime, who would himself eventually play an important role in the decolonization process, in 1974–75 as the last (overseas) territories co-ordination minister, did not hesitate to confess his conviction that in 1961, when Salazar reacted by sending massive numbers of troops against the first major nationalist uprising in Angola, 'he [Salazar] had with him the majority of the people, including some of his most prestigious political adversaries'.[50]

This very strong and widespread political prejudice in favour of a Greater Portugal was formalized into Portuguese constitutional law by the Colonial Act of 1930, which stated in Article 2 that: 'it is part of the organic essence of the Portuguese nation to pursue the historic mission of holding and colonizing overseas territories, and civilizing their native populations'; and that all territories under Portuguese sovereignty were part of a unitary Portuguese Republic.[51] In 1951 the empire was replaced by the even more integrationist concept of Overseas Provinces, formally part of a single multi-racial and pluri-continental single Portuguese state.

The Portuguese military was particularly immersed in this political culture that saw the empire as part of a glorious legacy going back to the golden age of the discoveries. Officers – who would later became critical of colonialism and who played crucial roles in the post-1974 decolonization process – recognize that initially they too saw 'their' counter-insurgency as the continuation of the epic of the *africanistas*, officers who became part of the national pantheon of heroes because of their role in occupying Angola, Mozambique, and Guinea. This was even more the case, of course, among the militant nationalists who volunteered to fight in Africa. For them, Portuguese Africa and the whole empire overseas was 'a myth, a principle, and as with all myths [...] untouchable, indisputable'.[52] Any wavering in this respect, moreover, by an authoritarian regime that had as its official motto 'Everything for the Nation' would have potentially disastrous political costs, as would be shown by the reactions to the feeble attempts of Salazar's successor Marcelo Caetano to change something in the Portuguese politico-administrative framework overseas.[53]

Does this mean that Portugal was so blinded by cultural prejudices that it refused to see decolonization coming its way? In part the answer is yes. And yet Salazar always prided himself of being a realpolitiker, as is made clear by his reaction to American attempts to make him see the world as Washington did. After an attempt at regime change resulted in a failed *pronunciamento* by senior military commanders in April 1961, Salazar complained to a close confidant that he did not mind so much the politically logical attempt 'to get rid of me', what 'irritates me is the fact they are treating me as a fool', that is as someone whose political differences with Washington could only be the result of his failure to understand global politics.

Salazar could credibly claim that he did not ignore the strong global trend towards decolonization, or the risks in resisting it, but he still wanted to fight it for reasons that had to do with culturally shaped preferences as well as a certain perception of realpolitik. Indeed, in 1957 – anticipating Macmillan's famous speech, and probably reflecting knowledge of Eisenhower's second inaugural address, and most certainly his analysis of the implications of the Suez Franco-British debacle – Salazar publicly stated that 'one of the winds that dominate the world is anti-colonialism'.[54] What he probably did not expect was for the wind to gain so much speed so quickly. Portugal was partly deceived by the confidential information it was receiving from quadri-partite consultations with Belgium, Britain, and France, during which it was far from clear that speedy decolonization of all of Africa was on the cards until as late as 1959, namely for the territories bordering Angola and Mozambique. To a certain degree, Salazar was therefore most likely somewhat surprised by the sudden and generalized nature of French and then Belgian decolonization in Africa.

Salazar's conclusions even then remained different from the ones extracted by Macmillan or even de Gaulle. He would not seek to appease this new political wave by giving in to it. The Portuguese dictator believed he had to resist this wind of change at all costs because it was contrary to his notion of Portuguese identity as a great country whose manifest destiny it was to be present overseas.

Salazar knew this was a risky option for a relatively weak country like Portugal. In a private conversation with one of his confidants, who questioned him about the state of national defence, Salazar simply replied: 'in the case of Portugal [...] it is a permanent miracle!' But in his view, the very existence of Portugal as a truly independent state of some importance in the world was at stake. Salazar's vision of international politics took into account power politics but also what can perhaps best be characterized as a notion of balance of wills, where strong convictions and firmness in defence of a certain vision had a major role as a power multiplier. Salazar argued in November 1951 that while no state was ever 'entirely free', it was possible to resist foreign pressure if: first, there was a clear political vision; second, the latter was pursued relentlessly by a strong government with solid public support.[55]

Two major questions remain. Would a different regime have acted differently and decolonized earlier? What happened to these cultural preferences that led to a collapse of the commitment to a Greater Portugal alongside the collapse of the New State in 1974?

The first question is impossible to answer definitively, inevitably requiring speculative counter-factuals. But this comparative approach allows us to point out that France had a democratic regime but with a very similar political culture to that of Portugal in terms of the importance of a republican empire and of a profoundly colonial nationalism. Therefore a democratic regime in Portugal in the 1950s or 1960s would plausibly not have been less nationalistic than that of France. On the other hand, it is probably true that a democratic regime in Portugal would have been more open to outside pressure than the one led by Salazar – as the French Fourth Republic indeed was, but then this was a major factor in its downfall in 1958. It is worth bearing in mind that the only realistic option of a fall of the New State during this period was the failed military pronunciamento of April 1961, which had been preceded by informal conversations between the military leaders involved in the attempt to force some kind of regime change and the US Embassy. During the talks, these possible future leaders of Portugal asked for, and apparently obtained, informal US support for a prolonged period of transition ending in self-determination, but not necessarily independence. The most that can be said is that it would be mistaken to take as a given that, in light of Portuguese political culture, decolonization could have been pursued with ease by a different of Portuguese regime.

What had changed then, in the run-up to 1974? There were short-term triggers, like the global crisis of 1973, which hit Portugal particularly hard; and the replacement of Salazar by a less charismatic successor, Marcelo Caetano. Caetano, even if he had more doubts than Salazar about the possibility of full integration and of successful resistance, still felt very much bound by the taboo that the fatherland could not be questioned. Therefore, in his eyes, any changes in Portuguese Africa would have had to be contained within a vague 'progressive autonomy'. Perhaps he would have liked to go further, perhaps not. He avowedly 'belonged to a generation to whom overseas [territories] had become the focus of national hopes [...] the Republic was from the beginning a dogmatic defender of the overseas heritage'. For him independence, certainly in the short to medium term, was simply unthinkable: 'Portuguese public opinion would be nauseated to see the butchers [i.e. the nationalist insurgents] rewarded'. He went on to ask rhetorically: '[H]ow could we give up [to] a few dozen adventurers all these people, the work we had accomplished?'[56]

The Portuguese population had also changed. Demographic growth had led to an increasingly young population that was more and more integrated into Western Europe because of better education, economic migration, and the flow of migrants and tourists from Europe every summer; because, among the elites, of membership of NATO and the European Free Trade Association (EFTA). The urgency of a rethink evidently came from the protracted and seemingly endless nature of the war to which all this younger population were exposed as conscripts. This was even more the case for the reduced cadre of professional officers, whose colonial patriotism was brutally tried by the experience of often three two-year tours of combat duty in Africa in the span of a decade. This was made more urgent given the possibility of serious military problems from 1973 onwards, at least in Guinea, where a number of military outposts on the borders were on the verge of becoming a Portuguese Dien Bien Phu. Last but not least, the close identification of the war and the empire with an increasingly discredited authoritarian regime ended up increasingly discrediting by association the tradition of nationalist imperialism.

What is amazing, in light of this context, is not that the will to fight against decolonization of many military officers collapsed in April 1974.

Rather, it is the fact that strong cultural attachments to this idea of a Greater Portugal kept the struggle going for more than a decade, and that, indeed, some of the leading officers in the April 1974 coup, not least its first formal leader General Spínola, still tried to retain some kind of close federal connection with at least Angola. In the book that helped ignite the revolution and promote Spínola to head the new transitional junta – *Portugal e o Futuro* (Portugal and the Future) – he argued for a Lusitanian federation. More importantly, he argued this should be achieved by 'gradual evolution' to permit the 'development in political consciousness of all populations' – that is, of whatever colour – as a way towards 'self-determination' that would preserve 'harmonious and permanent unity'.[57] The points of contact with other myths of decolonization are obvious.

Major crises like a war or a revolution – or, in the case of Portugal, both – are typically necessary to allow a major revision of deeply rooted cultural norms and identity. They allowed the unthinkable decolonization to become conceivable. Yet decolonization still required some kind of cultural myth-making to make it more acceptable. As one of the most politically committed officers in the MFA, Major Melo Antunes later acknowledged, the suppression of a reference to independence or even self-determination in the coup manifesto – that he wrote for the most part – was due to the fact that 'despite all the cares in terms of semantics' this was still 'an extremely delicate subject'.[58]

Even in defeat, when forced by circumstances on the ground in Africa and politically in Portugal to move faster towards independence than he had hoped, Spínola still tried to save his honour and the myth of decolonization he was attempting to create by affirming that this was just another way to achieve what had always been his ultimate vision. This was why Spínola claimed the Law of July 1974 corresponded to his aims of self-determination going back to his time as governor of Portuguese Guinea. Another way of doing this was to identify the former Portuguese regime as their common oppressor, and point to independence as shared liberation. The Portuguese military conspirators, the MFA, who openly took over from Spínola after September 1974, quickly came to frame themselves as the fourth armed liberation movement, closely identifying with the nationalist anti-colonial movements in Angola, Mozambique, and Guinea, as brothers-in-arms, all victims of the oppression, the violence, and the war imposed by the former Portuguese regime.

National liberation in Portugal – democratization – was increasingly seen as logically implying decolonization, that is national liberation for its African territories. This may well be largely a myth and a cover for many military officers who wanted to stop fighting. But even if this was the case, the question remains: Why did this myth become necessary? Why not simply state the obvious interest in stopping the conflict? In my view, the answer is that Portugal also required some variant of the myth of decolonization for it to be acceptable as the appropriate and honourable thing to do, not as simply being forced by military exhaustion – and this was indeed not necessarily the case in all theatres. And here again we are caught in the traps of political culture; if the regime, and more broadly Portuguese nationalism, had for so long presented the overseas territories as one *Ultramar*, then conversely they had to decolonize them as one, even areas like East Timor where, initially at least, it is unclear this was what locals wished.

Decolonization was perceived and portrayed not as a sacrifice of a close Lusotropical connection with former colonies, but rather as the creation of new and better bonds, of a new fraternal community based not only on shared language and culture, which would not be lost, but also shared oppression and liberation. We should not dismiss out of hand myths' power of attraction even for their own creators, or their real political impact. Melo Antunes was the major military figure in the MFA articulating this programme of rapid decolonization, and also for years after the 1974 coup an influential figure as a presidential advisor working towards closer relations with the former Portuguese colonies. Some of his even more revolutionary comrades went on to sacrifice their military careers for their – more or less recent, but sincere – radical political convictions, sometimes in exile in the former colonies.

The Portuguese case certainly seems to show that, even in the face of major, international systemic pressure and international normative ruptures, to change cultural preferences that are deeply rooted in domestic political traditions requires not only time and major crises and/or losing a war, but also some effort at reframing identity by cultural myth-making.

Conclusion: myths of decolonization and their study

The main common element of the myths of decolonization in these three cases was that decolonization should not be equated with defeat, decline, or a definitive loss of a traditional overseas connection. From this common aspect derive specific constructions of decolonization according to different political cultures. In the case of Britain, there was the Whig version of the history of decolonization as a great liberal design pragmatically administered resulting in the Commonwealth. In the case of France, there was the ideal of a republican empire giving way to a French Union and then *la francophonie*. The union of French-speaking countries could be presented plausibly as being wisely transformed by de Gaulle's Fifth Republic into a *francophonie* united by a shared language and a shared culture, with Paris still its undisputed centre. In the case of Portugal, the notion of a single pluri-continental country was replaced by the notion of a fraternal partnership based on mutual liberation by armed movements. This transformed the Portuguese officers involved in the 25 April coup into liberators both overseas and at home, using the complete change in governing elites and the turn to the Left in Portugal to give credence to a narrative of a common struggle against an authoritarian regime, oppressive in Europe and in Africa, eventually leading to a new community of equals. The Commonwealth, *la francophonie*, and eventually the Community of Portuguese-Speaking Countries (Comunidade dos Países de Língua Portuguesa, CPLP) can be seen, in part, as a formal manifestation of this cultural construction of decolonization.

The main argument of this text is that these three colonial powers linked their colonial empires closely to national identity. Britain, France, and Portugal were very much proud imperial nations, at least at the level of mainstream views. Even if the degree of imperialist conviction is hard to judge exactly, few will dispute that generic anti-colonialism – as different from specific criticisms of particular colonial practices – was significantly very much a minority view well into the 20th century. This close association in British, French, and Portuguese political culture between imperialism and nationalism became a major obstacle to decolonization. Decolonization, therefore, only became acceptable once a new cultural construct, a myth, was built around it. This had to be a credible story, but it evidently does not have to be the whole story. It still performed the crucial task of reconciling decolonization with a partially reconstructed national identity. Historians have for some time been carefully deconstructing, based on archival work, these myths of decolonization. This is a very important task, but it is insufficient: it is also necessary to take these myths seriously and analyse them in depth. Another key point is that the very word 'decolonization' was very much a cultural construction that only spread rapidly from France from 1959 onwards. This is of course an area of research to be pursued further, not just by comparing colonizing powers, but also by looking at the mutual re-constitutions of national identities of former colonizers and the former colonized. This can best be done through a comparative approach, as a way of analysing cultural specificities without falling into essentialist or organic notions of culture.

Notes

My research for this text was financed by a post-doctoral fellowship by FCT funds from 6th EU Framework programme. I would like to thank the organizers of this volume and all those at a seminar at Brown University where this paper was first presented for their comments and suggestions.

1. J. Darwin, *Britain and Decolonization: The Retreat from Empire in the Post-Cold War World*, London, MacMillan, 1988, p. 6.
2. R. Barthes, *Mythologies*, Paris, Seuil, 1957, p. 189.
3. J. Snyder, *Myths of Empire: Domestic Politics and International Ambition*, Ithaca, NY, Cornell University Press, 1991.
4. J. Darwin, *The Empire Project: The Rise and Fall of the British World-System, 1830–1970*, Cambridge, Cambridge University Press, 2009, pp. 612–614, 634–635.
5. N. MacQueen, *The Decolonization of Portuguese Africa: Metropolitan Revolution and the Dissolution of Empire*, London, Longman, 1997, pp. 80–84.
6. T. Shepard, *The Invention of Decolonization: The Algerian War and the Remaking of France*, Ithaca, NY, Cornell University Press, 2006; M. Thomas, 'Introduction: Mapping the French colonial mind', in M. Thomas, ed., *The French Colonial Mind*, vol. 1., Lincoln, NE, Nebraska University Press, 2011, Loc. 25.
7. MacQueen, *Metropolitan Revolution*, 1997, p. 92.
8. D. K. Fieldhouse, *The Colonial Empires*, 2nd ed., London, Macmillan, 1982, p. ix.
9. R. Robinson, *French colonialism 1871–1914: Myths and Realities*, London, Pall Mall, 1966, p. vii.
10. P. Gifford and W. R. Louis, eds, *The Transfer of Power in Africa: Decolonization in Africa 1940–1960*, New Haven, CT, Yale University Press, 1982; R. F. Holland, 'Review of Ronald Hyman, Britain's declining Empire [...]', *Journal of Imperial and Commonwealth Studies*, 36, 1, 2008, pp. 135–137.
11. T. Terriff, '"Innovate or die": Organizational culture and the origins of maneuver warfare in the US Marine Corps', *Journal of Strategic Studies*, 29, 3, 2006, p. 479.
12. R. L. Jepperson, A. Wendt and P. J. Katzenstein, 'Norms, identity, and culture in national security', in P. J. Katzenstein, ed., *The Culture of National Security: Norms and Identity in World Politics*, New York, NY, Columbia University Press, 1996, pp. 54, 56. See also T. Farrell, 'Constructivist security studies: Portrait of a research programme', *International Studies Review*, 4, 1, 2002, pp. 49–72.
13. R. Hyam, *The Labour Government and the End of Empire 1945–1951*. vol 1. *High Policy and Administration*, London, HMSO, 1992, *British Documents on the End of Empire*, series A, vol. 2, p. xxix; J. Darwin, *The End of the British Empire: The Historical Debate*, Oxford, Blackwell, 1991, p. 115.

14. See J. Darwin, *The Empire Project: The Rise and Fall of the British World-System 1830–1970*, Cambridge, Cambridge University Press, 2009, pp. 615 ff.

15. R. F. Holland, 'The imperial factor in British strategies from Attlee to Macmillan', *Journal of Imperial and Commonwealth History*, 12, 1, 1984, p. 169.

16. Ministry of Defence, *Defence: Outline of Future Policy*, London, HMSO, 1957 (Sandys' White Paper).

17. Holland, 'The imperial factor', 1984, p. 179; R. Hyam and W. R. Louis, *The Conservative Government and the End of Empire 1957–1964*, vol. 1, *High Policy, Political and Constitutional Change*, London, TSO, 2000, p. xlii.

18. NA, CAB 130/213 MISC 17/8 Defence Policy Record Meeting 10 Downing Street, 13 November 1965.

19. R. Girardet, *L'idee coloniale en France de 1871 a 1962*, Paris, Table Ronde, 1972, pp. 329–332, 345–346; R. Aron, *Le spectateur engage: entretiens avec Jean-Louis Missika et Dominique Wolton*, Paris, Fallois, 2004. pp. 259 ff.

20. P. Brendon, *The Decline and Fall of the British Empire 1781–1997*, London, Vintage, pp. 516 ff.

21. CO 875/25 circular memorandum 28, 'Notes on British colonial policy', March 1949, Doc 71, *The Labour Government and the End of Empire 1945–1951*, vol. 1, *High Policy and Administration*, 'Introduction', London, HMSO, 1992, 'British documents on the end of empire', series A, vol. 2, p. 327.

22. Doc. 68 CAB 124/1007, 62, 17 August 1946, 'Projection of Britain overseas', BDED, pp. 308–309.

23. D. Cannadine, *Ornamentalism: How the British Saw their Empire*, London, Penguin, 2002, p. xvii passim.

24. D. Reynolds, *From World War to Cold War: Churchill, Roosevelt, and the International History of the 1940s*, Cambridge: Cambridge University Press, 2006, pp. 309–330; J. Kent, *The Internationalisation of Colonialism: Britain, France and Black Africa*, Oxford, Clarendon, 1992, pp. 154–155, 186.

25. C. Cogan, *French Negotiating Behavior*, Washington, DC, USIP, 2003.

26. C. de Gaulle, *The Edge of the Sword*, London, Faber & Faber, 1960, p. 94.

27. Girardet, *L'idée coloniale*, 1972, pp. 300–301.

28. Aron, *Le Spectateur Engagé*, 2004, p. 267 passim.

29. M. Agulhon, *La République: De Jules Ferry à François Mitterrand – 1880 à nos jours*, Paris, Hachette, 1990, p. 373.

30. F. Malye and B. Stora, *François Mitterrand et la guerre d'Algérie*, Paris, Calmann-Lévy, 2010, pp. 57–58.

31. M. Thomas, *Algeria: France's Undeclared War*, Oxford, Oxford University Press, 2012, pp. 2284–2297.

32. K. Booth, *Strategy and Ethnocentrism*, New York, NY, Holmes and Maier, 1979, p. 64.

33. De Gaulle speech of 15 May 1947 cited in Girardet, *L'idée colonial*, 2009, p. 287.

34. H. Spruyt, *Ending Empire: Contested Sovereignty and Territorial Partition*, Ithaca, NY, Cornell University Press, 2005, p. 265 passim.

35. R. Aron, *Imperialism and Colonialism*, Leeds, The University of Leeds, 1959, p. 6.

36. R. Trinquier, *Le Temps Perdu*, Paris, Albin Michel, 1978, pp. 357, 365.

37. S. Cohen, *La Défaite des Généraux: Le Pouvoir Politique et l'Armée sous la Ve République*, Paris, Fayard, 1994, p. 48.

38. C. de Gaulle, *Mémoirs d'Espoir: Le renouveau 1958–1962*, Paris, Plon, 1970, pp. 41–42.
39. Peyrefitte, *C'Était*, pp. 88–89.
40. Ibid., p. 56. This is a collection of table talk between de Gaulle and a close confidant.
41. De Gaulle to Ély, 8 November 1960. See M. Faivre, *Le Général Paul Ély et la politique de défense (1956–1961)*, Paris, Economica, 1998, p. 83.
42. De Gaulle, *Le renouveau*, Paris, p. 43.
43. Ibid., p. 43.
44. J. Foccart, *Foccart parle: Entretiens avec Philippe Gaillard*, vol. 1, Paris, Fayard/ Jeune Afrique, 1995, pp. 194–195, 223.
45. J.-P. Bat, *Le Syndrome Foccart: Politique Francaise En Afrique, 1959 à nos Jours*, Paris, Gallimard, 2012.
46. For a carefully nuanced analysis of de Gaulle's policy of grandeur, see S. Hoffmann, *The Diplomats 1939–1979*, Princeton, NY, Princeton University Press, 1994, pp. 228–254; see also M. Vaïsse, *La puissance ou l'influence? La France dans le monde depuis 1958*, Paris, Fayard, 2009.
47. G. Ball, *The Past has Another Pattern*, New York, NY, Norton, 1982, p. 277.
48. V. Alexandre, 'A África no imaginário português, séculos XIX–XX', *Penélope*, 15, 1995, p. 62.
49. A. Santos, *Quase Memórias do Colonialismo e Descolonização*, vol. 1, Cruz Quebrada, Casa das Letras, 2006, p. 16.
50. Santos, *Quase Memórias*, 2006, p. 16. For an example of this among the most distinguished adversaries of Salazar see C. Leal, *O Colonialismo dos Anticolonialistas*, Lisbon, Autor, 1961.
51. C. Castelo, *'O Modo Português de Estar no Mundo': O luso-tropicalismo e a ideologia colonial portuguesa (1933–1961)*, Oporto, Afrontamento, 1998, p. 46.
52. J. N. Pinto, *Jogos Africanos*, Lisbon, A Esfera dos Livros, 2008, pp. 16–17 passim.
53. Castelo, *O Modo Português*, 1998, pp. 50, 57.
54. A. de O. Salazar, 'A atmosfera mundial e os problemas nacionais', *Discursos e Nota Políticas*, vol. 5: *1951–1958*, Coimbra, Coimbra Editora, 1958, pp. 414–444.
55. Salazar, 'Independência Nacional – Suas Condições', *Discursos*, vol. 5, Coimbra, pp. 63, 66–67.
56. M Caetano, *Depoimento*, Rio de Janeiro, Record, 1974, pp. 17, 33–34.
57. Macqueen, *Metropolitan Revolution*, 1997, pp. 67, 80, 92.
58. M. M. Cruzeiro, *Melo Antunes: O Sonhador Pragmático*, Lisbon, Notícias, 2005, p. 70.

6
Exporting Britishness: Decolonization in Africa, the British State and Its Clients

Sarah Stockwell

The end of the European empires represents by any standards an extraordinary process of global transformation and state formation.[1] In the British case this centred on the creation of parliamentary democracies on the Westminster model. State building and the transition to independence also entailed disentangling colonial institutions from the British imperial system and the development in the colonies of the apparatus associated with modern independent nation states: or to put it another way, the 'decolonization' of a whole raft of institutions from colonial civil services and armies to financial institutions. On the efficient and sound operation of the administrative apparatus of the ex-colonial state and its military, financial, as well as judicial, instruments, rested the success of wider British strategic and economic interests. Yet the process of what is perhaps best conceptualized as 'institutional devolution and transition' rather than 'decolonization of the colonial state' (for reasons to be discussed below) has remained largely below the radar in general accounts of British decolonization, which focus rather on developments leading to constitutional independence and the dynamics behind imperial decline. Instead, discussion of institutional devolution and transition has mostly taken the form of case studies dealing with discrete regions or sectors. Policing and defence have received most attention, but in these instances and in relation to other sectors too, many studies appeared before the relevant archival sources were open to researchers.[2] Although some sectors are now beginning to receive more attention,[3] there remain considerable lacunae in our understanding of the transformation of colonial institutions, and while democratization, governance, development, and militarism have been central to the conceptual apparatus of political scientists discussing the developing world as a whole, what work there is on these themes by historians of decolonization remains fragmented both by region and sector. By bringing the different historiographies into dialogue this chapter hopes to illuminate broad synergies and perhaps generate new questions and conceptualizations, with key features emerging with clarity and force once brought together.

Specifically, this chapter will argue that this process of decolonization and transition in diverse aspects of institution building in Africa saw the British entrench British training and personnel. While such transfers of expertise are intrinsic to programmes of aid and technical assistance, in these cases they also reflected British determination to perpetuate British influence, traditions, and models. The idea of substituting 'influence' for control – a transition from formal to informal empire – is an established trope of the historiography of British decolonization.[4] But rather than simply reproduce this, this chapter has three specific objectives.

First, and as already indicated, it seeks to bring empirical analysis across different sectors of institution building into the frame for this discussion of influence. The account that follows makes reference to a series of institutions, including bureaucracies, armies, banks and currencies. There are other areas that might well merit consideration in the same way, but nevertheless the wide-ranging brief of this chapter makes it possible to establish that there was a pervasive use of a *language of influence* as a range of British actors sought to imagine their role within a new post-colonial order. It demonstrates how the British pursuit of influence originated and developed in more than one place. This in turn reflects how within the imperial system power was not simply concentrated within the state but rather diffused across a range of British institutions and actors, some of which lay on the borders of the state or beyond. These institutions had become to varying degrees stake-holders in a British imperial project and formed the context for countless individual careers. Each possessed a 'corporate mission' which required reconfiguring for a post-colonial world; conversely, each had relevant expertise which they now sought to deploy to model successor institutions in emergent states along British lines.

Secondly, this chapter seeks to refine our understandings of how 'influence' was constituted: not simply through the exercise of financial or geopolitical muscle, but also through more subtle – and perhaps in some cases less instrumental and conscious ways – such as the attempt to inculcate ethos, which could be understood in terms of the promotion of best practice and good governance, but which nonetheless rested on assumptions about the intrinsic superiority and desirability of a 'British way'. We might argue that in this respect the British approach was distinctive within parameters which were broadly but not fully comparable to those of the French in francophone Africa. By emphasizing these elements of the British approach, the argument to be presented here elaborates upon that advanced in my more localized study some years ago of the inculcation of British traditions in creating a Ghanaian central bank,[5] and builds on recent research on policing and intelligence, as well as constitution writing at the end of empire.[6] Through analysis of British training and other initiatives designed to entrench British expertise across different sectors in new African states at independence, this chapter also aims to contribute to emerging literatures on international educational and technical aid to decolonized states[7] and on the transfer of colonial knowledge at the end of empire.[8]

Finally, this chapter seeks to show how the processes by which the apparatus of the old imperial and colonial state was localized or dismantled as new national institutions were constructed was not simply one of attrition for domestic British institutions. Instead, it could present new opportunities for organizations that lay on the boundaries of the domestic state and civil society and which operated on a commercial basis. Such opportunities were not confined to anglophone African states, but might also be sought within other emergent states where, as in the case of Portugal, the outgoing colonial power was not sufficiently strong to exploit them itself. This point is illustrated in this chapter by reference to one institution's interest in Mozambique.

The late colonial state

Any analysis of Britain's management of institutional devolution and transition in colonial Africa must focus on the 1950s and 1960s. Until then much of the essential apparatus of the colonial state continued to be either an extension of that of the imperial state or dominated in its upper echelons by Britons – even when its costs were largely met by the colonial territory concerned. British imperial rhetoric emphasized the importance of laying sound foundations for the attainment of what, in 1943, had been declared to be the long-term goal of Britain's imperial mission: the gradual advancement of British colonies 'along the road to self-government within the framework of the British Empire'.[9] After the war, the Labour Government took tentative steps towards the realization of this goal, convening a conference of Britain's African governors in 1947 to discuss the various constitutional stages through which Britain's African colonies would travel to attain self-government. But for all that these initiatives differentiated the British from other European colonial powers in Africa, and arguably reflected a more liberal turn in British policy, other wartime and post-war priorities eclipsed longer-term development. Indeed, while the south Asian transfers of power were taking place, remaining parts of the colonial empire assumed enhanced importance to Britain and were bound more tightly into the British system through the retention of wartime controls and structures. For example, the War Office maintained the control of African colonial armies it had assumed with the outbreak of war. Wartime exchange controls, which had transformed the loosely knit sterling bloc into the highly regulated sterling area, were also retained as Britain sought to profit from the dollar-trading activities of its colonies.

Insofar as Britain did anything to prepare the colonies for self-government its efforts focused upon colonial economic and social development, until the early 1950s regarded across the British political spectrum as the essential prerequisite for colonial political progress. But, like the ambition to maximize colonial-dollar earnings, this in practice extended the British colonial presence, necessitating a post-war influx of British recruits to the Colonial Service.

Underlying this comparatively leisurely approach were what in hindsight were to prove greatly unrealistic projections of the timetable for transition to colonial self-government. When Britain's African governors met in conference in 1947, the Colonial Office advised that it would not be much less than 'a generation' before even the Gold Coast (Ghana),[10] widely perceived to be the most politically advanced of Britain's African colonies, achieved internal self-government; while elsewhere the 'process is likely to be considerably slower'.[11]

Little British consideration was consequently given to the future organization of colonial bureaucracies and institutions until at least the late 1940s, and little progress made with the indigenization of even the lower ranks of African bureaucracies and of the officer class of African armed forces. New initiatives in relation to higher education, crucial to the building of the local state apparatus, took time to bear fruit. Evidence from the Gold Coast provides one illustration of the slow rate of localization: in 1948, only 98 of 1,300–1,400 senior appointments in the country's administration were African.[12] Elsewhere the record of Africanization was even worse.

By the late 1940s, and even more so the early 1950s, as Britain lurched from colonial crisis to crisis, colonial politicization and unrest were proving official forecasts of the likely rate of constitutional change hopelessly conservative. Riots in the Gold Coast in 1948 initiated a process of constitutional change that led to Ghana becoming the first full British African colony to attain internal self-government in 1954 and independence in 1957. Nigeria followed hot on its heels and Sierra Leone shortly after. With the emergence of anti-colonial nationalist organizations came demands for greater Africanization and for the creation of new national institutions.[13] Britain's east and central African colonies initially lagged behind: the former advanced rapidly to independence only after 1960 and the latter were incorporated in a federation from 1953, entailing the transfer of administrations and institutions: first to the new federal government, and only later – with the dissolution of the federation – to new independent governments. As we shall see, in British Africa it was to be in relation to the Gold Coast and Nigeria that localization and indigenization were consequently first discussed (and it is these examples to which most reference is made in this chapter).

Even then, aspects of the British system encouraged imperial inertia or caution. Devolution was inherently difficult in relation to institutions that still served a critical role in Britain's management of an orderly decolonization process.[14] Indeed, while the Gold Coast riots led British officials to make sweeping constitutional changes that in turn unleashed new pressures for reform of the administration, banking and the Army, the shock the disturbances delivered to the imperial system, together with the onset of the Malayan emergency and the Cold War, simultaneously prompted an overhaul of imperial intelligence that, in this area at least, resulted in more rather than less imperial machinery.[15]

In some sectors of the British establishment there was also less immediate awareness of, and sensitivity to, growing colonial politicization than in the Colonial Office. Complacency abounded. On the eve of Ghanaian independence, the vice-chief imperial general staff saw a case for transferring military control quickly while, as he put it, 'the reins were still fully in our hands'; nevertheless, since he believed the existing system worked perfectly, he thought best to leave well alone.[16] So long as the Gold Coast was in receipt of British military aid the War Office assumed it would accept some measure of British control,[17] provoking a Colonial Office reminder that after constitutional independence the Gold Coast government would be under no 'enforceable obligation' to collaborate with the UK. The British military establishment betrayed a similar lack of political awareness in relation to the creation of east African national armies from the region's King's African Rifles (KAR). Parsons argues that Britain's military commanders were 'almost entirely caught off guard' by Macmillan's 1960 'wind of change' speech; and, even after that, they continued to overestimate the time remaining to them in which to effect the establishment of national forces.[18]

Localization and devolution were also complicated by the differing rates of political advance across the colonies. The strongly territorial element to the British system – in contrast to the more centralized arrangements favoured by the French – rendered the creation of distinct national institutions relatively straightforward. We can see this in relation to the creation of new national armies. In west Africa the federal arrangements of the region's Royal West African Frontier Force were ended in 1956 with the transformation of different colonial units into four independent forces. Financial responsibility for these forces, which since 1939 had largely rested with the British government, also now passed to local administrations.[19] Control of the different east African battalions of the KAR similarly passed to the governments concerned, although initially through British persuasion under a unified east African command. At independence these battalions became the new national armies of Tanganyika, Uganda, and Kenya. The transition in central Africa was complicated by the creation of the federation, whose Central African Command had in 1954 been given control of the Nyasaland battalion of the KAR and of the Northern Rhodesian Regiment. However, in 1964 these too were transferred from federal command to form respectively the Malawi Rifles and the national army of Zambia. [20]

Even so, disentangling regional and federal institutions entailed separate negotiations with governors whose colonies were at different stages of political and economic development. Territorial and regional dynamics produced what in retrospect seem almost ridiculously divergent tendencies. For example, the creation of new central banks could occur in advance of or at independence, as was the case in the Gold Coast and Nigeria where nationalist pressure to establish state banks arose in the later 1940s and central banks opened in the late 1950s. In other places it occurred after. Central banks were not established in Tanzania until 1965 and in Uganda and Kenya before 1966 following the break-up of the East African Currency Board. In central Africa the process initially entailed the creation of federal organizations: the Bank of Rhodesia and Nyasaland was formed from the Currency Board of Rhodesia and Nyasaland in 1956.

Many of these new 'national' bureaucracies, banks, and armies were initially independent in little but name. They not only continued to be organized along British lines, but in their early stages remained under British direction, albeit now reporting to new African ministers and their governments. Although the end of empire saw the return of many thousands of expatriates, some stayed on working in advisory capacities to the new independent governments or continued to occupy posts within the administrations. Others were newly recruited for overseas roles. The fledgling armies of anglophone Africa provide a particularly striking illustration. All initially operated under the command of British officers seconded from the British Army;[21] and British cadet and specialist military schools and staff colleges were used at independence by all African Commonwealth countries.[22] Turning to the establishment of new national and central banks in former colonies, a similar picture prevails. Here, too, British advisers and expatriate personnel served key roles. Simultaneously, many local entrants to overseas public administration, the armed services, and banking travelled to Britain to attend training courses. Those courses, funded by the British state, became a key element in Britain's provision of technical co-operation to developing especially Commonwealth nations, from 1961 given an institutional home within Whitehall in the new Department of Technical Co-operation.[23]

Decolonizing the colonial state?

Historical analysis of cross-sectoral British approaches towards localization and devolution in Africa provides compelling evidence of British ambitions to model institutions along British lines and to generate influence via technical education and the diaspora of advisers and personnel. This was justified by reference to a paternalistic British mission in bequeathing to the colonies sound institutions likely to ensure future stability.[24] Behind this rhetoric of 'good governance' it is impossible to disentangle Britain's own strategic interests in a Cold War context and investment in the future stability of the Commonwealth, as well as what we might see as the more abstract notions of British prestige, from disinterested motives of concern for the future well-being of its former colonies.

Nevertheless, the British not only sought as a distinct objective to secure continuing adherence to a British system, including most obviously via British-Commonwealth defence and financial co-operation (both beyond the scope of this chapter), but were also active across different sectors in seeking to ensure the perpetuation of British models and continued employment of British personnel. As already indicated, what is particularly striking is the way in which a discourse of influence was deployed across different sectors. Moreover, as we will see, some British institutions that inhabited a state-sponsored, but none-theless semi-commercial, position, such as the Royal Mint, also found themselves fostering the maintenance of British styles and expertise in the newly independent countries; in these instances, however, this approach could also reflect more a hard-nosed commercial impulse than a cultural or strategic imperative. This chapter will now explore through more specific examples how these processes manifested them-selves in the dynamics of, and languages deployed in, particular sectors.

We begin with the case of colonial bureaucracies. By the early 1950s constitutional change had provided new momentum for indigeniza-tion at least in British west Africa, with several commissions established to consider future arrangements for public administration in the Gold Coast and Nigeria.[25] As the speed with which the two colonies were progressing to independence became apparent, officials turned to con-sidering the future of those expatriates then working in the colonies as members of the service, and, specifically, how to encourage these officers to stay on after independence by providing some mechanism to protect their employment and pension rights.[26] This was an objective shared by the new African governments that were conscious of the damag-ing effects of an exodus of expatriate personnel when comparatively few Africans had yet reached senior administrative positions. Extensive discussions through the 1950s as to how continuity of personnel might best be achieved resulted in the service being restyled as Her Majesty's Oversea (from 1956, Overseas) Civil Service (HMOCS) (1954), incor-porating a number of safeguards to protect expatriate careers; and the creation within HMOCS specifically for Nigeria (where the difficulties of retaining British officers were proving most acute) of a Special List A (1956) and Special List B (1958) of officers who would be in the service of the British government but seconded to the Nigerian government. Initial plans to extend these arrangements to other colonies did not come to pass; but, in the Overseas Aid Act (1961) the British government assumed new responsibilities for officers recruited to overseas public service. Further changes laid the foundation for Britain's technical aid programme by shifting the employment model to one in which British-based officers would be seconded on short-term contract terms only.[27]

Because much of the archival source material relating to these initia-tives focuses on the difficulties – amidst growing disquiet about career security – of recruiting and retaining expatriate personnel, it may contribute to a sense that Britain's governmental actions were driven primarily by its obligations to former colonies and to British members of the service.[28] A. H. M. Kirk-Greene, noting how opposition from the Treasury had to be overcome before provision sufficiently attractive to persuade British officers to remain in overseas public service could be agreed, justifiably presents these objectives as key themes around which he weaves his authoritative analysis of the changes made to the service in the 1950s.[29] In these discussions there is less evidence of overt British ambition to exercise control via influence than in the case of other institutions discussed in this chapter, but the underlying premise of all the discussions was of the inherent desirability of continuity of practice and personnel.

Perhaps more striking, however, were the ways in which, as the numbers of local recruits appointed to senior posts in overseas public administration gradually increased, the Colonial Office sought to induct them into its established training regime in Britain, delivered at the Universities of Oxford, Cambridge, and London. This was seen as a valuable way of promoting understanding between Britain and its colonies as they approached independence and as 'one of the most potent means of ensuring continuance of the British tradition and British ideals in administration in the Colonies'.[30] Over the next few years this consideration was repeatedly emphasized as the Colonial Office in conjunction with representatives of the three universities sought to adapt the existing training courses to the changing political environment.[31] In this matter the views of colonial officials corresponded to those of academics in Oxford, Cambridge, and London. The universities' enhanced role in a new training regime introduced in 1946, together with new funds available for colonial research under Colonial Development and Welfare legislation, had opened new opportunities for their subject areas within the universities. Academics working within these areas had been quick to capitalize on these openings and were now correspondingly reluctant to forego them. Indeed the survival of the training courses following a review conducted in 1953 owed much to the Universities' staunch defence of their role and of the value of the existing training regime, although this was now concentrated at Oxford and Cambridge.[32]

The decision to encourage local bureaucrats to attend training in Britain initiated a situation which would eventually result in courses devised for *British* Colonial Administrative Service probationers taught at the universities of Oxford and Cambridge evolving into training programmes tailored to *local* entrants to public administration in independent countries, mostly within the British Commonwealth, funded initially by the Colonial Office, and subsequently by the Department of Technical Co-operation and its successor the Ministry of Overseas

Development (ODM). Initially, the number of local entrants was small. However, the widespread constitutional change which followed as the 'wind of change' swept through east and central Africa transformed the situation. In March 1960 the first comprehensive review of the process of localization in Britain's colonies gave greater impetus to building local civil services.[33] The profile of those attending the Oxbridge training courses changed dramatically as the number of local recruits increased – albeit that these still constituted only a tiny proportion of those eventually appointed locally to senior positions within overseas public services. By the academic year 1963–64 all students at both institutions were from overseas.[34] New overseas institutes of public administration to provide training locally were also established in which former British colonial officers played leading roles.[35]

This transition was not without its difficulties. In the short term the changing profile of recruits to the British training courses necessitated changes to curricula and to modes of delivery and assessment. Changes of name were also introduced to render the courses and associated institutes more palatable to overseas governments, like that of newly independent Ghana, which the Colonial Office learned was becoming 'rather suspicious of offers from the UK to nominate people for what are in effect the same courses which they attended in the bad old days of colonial servitude'.[36] Numbers also fluctuated, and there was on-going uncertainty – sometimes to an almost paralyzing extent – over the future of state funding. In the later 1960s and the 1970s, as new centres for development studies at other British universities emerged, challenging Oxbridge's role,[37] government development funding became increasingly dispersed among a wider variety of institutions. Oxford ceased to deliver its existing courses in 1969, although it retained a role in overseas training, and at Cambridge the eventual withdrawal of funding led to the collapse of the course as it existed in 1981 and to fundamental reorganization in the related area of studies. Yet, in the new environment of the late 1950s – in which 'colonial' became an ever more toxic brand – the value of association between Britain and its former colonies at a professional and institutional level – including via the universities – rather than at that of the state, was increasingly recognized and the years after Britain's African colonies attained constitutional independence were in many respects ones of remarkable continuity in relation to the universities' role in training for overseas administration.

The same goal of maintaining British influence and traditions through a diaspora of personnel and the provision of training is equally evident in relation to defence and finance. Anthony Clayton has argued that for Britain, 'independence [in Africa] meant military independence'. As Clayton observes, Britain did not leave permanent garrisons in its former colonies and nor in the immediate post-colonial era did it inter-vene militarily to any significant extent in the politics of its former col-onies (although its role in support of the federal forces in the Nigerian Civil War 1967–70 constitutes one exception). Analysis of British discus-sion of the future of colonial armed forces nevertheless shows that this proposition that 'while Britain was willing to offer newly-independent African states training aid she never sought a monopoly position' falls somewhat short of the reality of the imperial state's ambitions to maintain anglophone traditions and influence.[38] The contrast with the French approach, which entailed the retention of military bases in former colonies and negotiated agreements with francophone states permitting future French military intervention,[39] should not distract from acknowledging the determination of British purpose.

When it came to colonial armed forces, discussions about the future were wide-ranging and involved a blueprint for reform across the empire, set out in 1955 by General Sir Gerald Templer in a report com-missioned by a Cabinet ministerial committee on security in the colo-nies.[40] Templer advised that the UK should proceed rapidly with the localization of the forces 'as soon as ever is practicable' since 'the longer their future owners have to run them in under our supervision, the less mess are they likely to make of them in the end'.[41] His prescription reflected also a conviction that in the new world of nuclear weaponry the role of the colonial armed forces would be confined largely to the maintenance of internal security as opposed to defence;[42] and a desire within the defence establishment to reduce their costs by transferring them to local governments.[43] While the issue was receiving broad consideration at a senior level, political change in west Africa and the Gold Coast in particular had already forced discussion of the future of the region's Royal West African Frontier Force (RWAFF). The first con-sideration of Africanization of the officer corps had taken place in the late 1930s and the first west African officer was appointed in 1942.[44] But in the late 1940s the rate of Africanization was still very slow and further measures were introduced to accelerate the process. Places were reserved at Sandhurst specifically for African students, and serving non-commissioned officers (NCOs) and warrant officers were also eligible for short-service commissions once they had successfully completed a short course at the British officer cadet schools at either Mons or Eaton Hall. In 1953 a local officer training course was inaugurated at Teshie in the Gold Coast, followed later by the establishment of army cadet training units attached to various west African educational institutions.[45] Two conferences attended by representatives of the west African governments were held on the west African forces in 1949 and 1953; by the time of the second, in Lagos, the achievement of partial self-government in the Gold Coast rendered the issue pressing and the conference agreed to the establishment of territorial forces.[46] Serious consideration first began to be given to the issue within the Colonial Office the following year.[47] It is worth considering these discussions in some detail as they provide further, and explicit, statements of British objectives.

Officials at the Colonial Office believed, like Templer, that the best way forward was for Britain to proceed quickly with the transformation of the Gold Coast Regiment of the RWAFF into a new national army, with a view to shaping the process and securing future co-operation with the UK, anglophone west Africa and the Commonwealth. John Bennett, who had recently returned from secondment to the Imperial Defence College course to take control of the Colonial Office's Defence and General Department, argued that in the case of the Gold Coast, influence would stand Britain in better stead than a formal defence agreement. In his words, 'the passage of time shows that cooperation within the Commonwealth depends more on political realities than on formal agreements'. Indeed, the experience of Ceylon showed that formal defence agreements could backfire: Britain's agreement with Ceylon had been the 'peg' on which the Soviet Union had objected to the newly independent country's admission to the UN. Britain should 'rely on political cooperation fortified by a strong professional link with the Gold Coast armed forces'.[48] The British priority was hence to enable the governor to discuss matters as soon as possible with his African ministers so that he might – in one official's revealing words – 'lead them in the direction of choosing of their own free will to collaborate in some mutually agreed manner'.[49]

The absence of British bases in the Gold Coast rendered the case more straightforward than in some other locations, and very different in nature to that of south-east Asia, as well as Nigeria, where defence agreements were signed. Even so, the case articulated in relation to the colony was of wider geographical application. The case of the old Indian Army showed, the Colonial Office thought, how British traditions were not only 'unquestionably a stabilising factor', but also provided a 'ready-made professional link' to Britain. This 'had not been without its influence on cooperation with the rest of the Commonwealth despite the neutralism of Indian foreign policy'.[50] To this end a continued British role in training and command was essential. Britain had taken what was referred to in one draft document – whose title, 'Retention of British influence in Colonial and Commonwealth Forces' is worth noting – as the 'risk' of granting independence before sufficient time had passed to enable the creation of a 'qualified and reliable corps of officers'. The role of volunteer British army officers and also NCOs in building up local forces after the transfers of political power was hence crucial, ideally under the command of British officers owing allegiance to the local government. Equally important was that Britain should supply arms and equipment, as well as training for the up-coming African officer class.[51]

The management of the process in the case of Ghana might appear a textbook example. British army officer Major General A. G. V. Paley was appointed first general officer commanding the Ghanaian Army, a post he held from 1957 until the end of 1959, when he was succeeded by another British officer. He was a useful source of intelligence, penning regular secret and personal letters to Templer as well as to the chief of the imperial general staff, Field Marshal Sir Francis Festing. [52] His role was not always easy: on one occasion he tendered his resignation to the Ghanaian premier, Kwame Nkrumah, prompting Templer to emphasize to him 'the very great value we attach to the retention of British influence in the armies of the New Commonwealth', advising that this was an important factor in the stability of these countries. Duly chastened, Paley promised in future to act with more caution.[53]

In securing a strong expatriate role in the new armies as well as in other areas, the imperial state was assisted by the obvious need that new African nations had for external expertise and aid, especially in east and central Africa, where Africanization had been most limited. In central Africa the first Zambian did not receive a commission until 1964, the same year that local military training facilities were opened in the region.[54] In east Africa there had been some patchy attempts from London to encourage Africanization of the officer corps, but senior British officers here had obstructed African promotion.[55] Further, no local military training facilities were established in east Africa until 1958.[56] Parsons argues that the problem was most acute in the case of Tanganyika, which of the three east African territories progressed most quickly to independence. At that point only six of the 58 officers in the Tanganyikan force were African. That Julius Nyerere was prepared to accept a continued British role reflected the territory's economic weaknesses and dependence on external aid.[57] In other cases, however, the continuation of a British role served local political interests: for the federal government of Nigeria the initial retention of British officers was important from an internal security perspective.

Paley's experience in Ghana nevertheless illustrates the difficulties of keeping a grip on local discussions and initiatives. These could prevent British officials from easily securing the influence they sought. Other external influences also threatened to supplant the British, especially where Britain itself lacked the requisite resources sought by the emergent nations. For example, in the late 1950s problems were encountered in securing sufficient vacancies for African officer cadets at both Sandhurst and Mons.[58] This led to some Ghanaians and Nigerians going for training to Pakistan – only a 'short step to elsewhere' as Sir Lashmer (Bolo) Whistler, the last colonel commandant of the RWAFF, noted[59] – and increasingly to other destinations including Canada, Australia, India, and the United States.

Another case where we see clear evidence of the pursuit of influence through the creation of institutions modelled on British lines is the colonies' secession from the existing regional colonial currency boards and the establishment in their place of new central banks with currency-issuing functions. British authorities initially tried to resist calls for banks with currency-issuing functions, but when it became apparent that anything short of full central banks would not satisfy local opinion, they aimed to exercise as much oversight over the new institutions as possible. This is hardly surprising, but it is worth emphasizing just how self-consciously, and with what determination, the Bank of England in particular set about meeting this objective.

Steering the new monetary authorities 'into the right channels' entailed directing African aspirations along lines that were also acceptable to Britain, by instilling what one referred to as 'a "sterling tradition"'.[60] The role of British personnel was crucial and officials at the Bank of England and in Whitehall aimed to ensure that British advisers – or if there were insufficient British candidates, experts from countries they deemed to follow British orthodoxy – oversaw the creation of, and filled senior posts at, the new institutions.

Such was anticipated to be the demand for bank staff that in 1956 senior bank personnel drew up tables detailing where and when it was expected such requirements would arise within the colonial empire. They also set in motion new ways of bringing mid-career high-fliers within the bank up to speed on the requirements of developing economies so that as and when requests for their staff to be sent abroad arose, there would be an adequate supply of suitable candidates. This development was driven in part by the governor of the Bank of England, who proposed that the Bank find some way of providing 'some appropriate experience' to those identified for potential future overseas postings.[61]

Despite these preparations, the Bank sometimes struggled to find suitable candidates, not least as demand peaked in the mid-1960s, probably earlier than the bank had anticipated as the pace of colonial political change outstripped initial conservative estimates. Demand declined thereafter, but rose once again in the mid-1970s in line with a second wave of transfers of power in Britain's remaining colonial possessions. In all, between 1955 and 1978 the Bank appointed six men as deputy-governors, eight as governors and others to various other posts within foreign central banks, principally in African countries.[62]

The traffic of banking personnel did not run only one way. The inauguration at the Bank of England of a new biannual Commonwealth Central Banking Course in 1957 provided further opportunity for the induction of key local figures into British and Commonwealth banking ideology as well as an introduction to British City institutions. The Bank regularly welcomed visitors on an ad hoc basis already, but the course originated in 1956 when it was suggested that 'a more positive approach' was required for the Commonwealth, especially in view of the likely development of new central banks in British colonies and what was perceived to be 'a complete absence of [local] adequately-trained personnel'. Participation was initially confined to Commonwealth member states or British colonies and was by invitation only.[63] Representatives participated in a course lasting some weeks while resident in London. Former participants were invited back to future courses and, with further colonies entering into the central banking field, numbers rose steadily over the years. A handful of countries declined to attend, but even so, by 1967 the bank was not only refusing requests to attend from non-Commonwealth states that had learned of the course, but, in one illustration of the huge number of new states created by British decolonization, was considering demolishing an internal wall at the bank in Threadneedle Street in order to expand the capacity of the lecture room.[64] The course not only survived reappraisals in the late 1960s and early 1970s but continued until 1989, when the Bank embarked upon a new educational venture with the establishment of its Centre for Central Banking in 1990 (which appears to have been directed at the states of another collapsing empire, being focused on eastern Europe). Through these years the Bank's Commonwealth connections continued to be regarded as a valuable means of generating 'goodwill and understanding' even as the importance of the Commonwealth dwindled and Britain entered the EEC.[65] Hence, although a handful of representatives from EEC states participated in the course from 1973, the core attendees remained those from Commonwealth countries, including South

Africa, which despite its departure from the Commonwealth in 1961 continued in the sterling area.

Undertaken as a form of 'education and propaganda', the course aimed 'to attract visits from good men' and 'to have them with us when they are young and receptive'.[66] One obvious interpretation of the dynamics behind this and other initiatives concerns the interests of the sterling area, and the desire by successive British governments to encourage new states to continue to maintain a high percentage of sterling backing for their currencies – thereby supporting sterling's continued role as an international currency. Bank of England officials hoped the inauguration of the central banking course would enable them not only to 'preach' the sterling area 'gospel', but let members 'see the advantages in practice'.[67] But the significance of the sterling area became progressively less important in the decolonization era. By the 1960s successive changes – beginning with the restoration of sterling convertibility in 1958 and followed by devaluation in 1967 – were eroding its continued existence. Even before then, a recent authoritative account argues, British governments had 'at best, an ambiguous commitment to sterling as an international currency', which they perceived as a source of weakness rather than strength to the British economy.[68]

Beyond concern to do with the sterling area, there was a broader set of considerations that lay behind the Bank's eagerness to exercise influence over the new institutions, including promoting the financial services of the City,[69] and the future financial stability of new states. Further, the Bank aimed at the promotion of 'close and good central bank relations',[70] an objective that must be seen in the context of the Bank's key role in the inter-war years in the development (including in the Commonwealth) of international central banking,[71] at that stage still a relatively recent phenomenon. Creating a community of professional central bankers corresponded to the Bank's own interests; but it also reflected a sense of responsibility to help nurture new financial institutions. By the late 1960s, when the composition of the central banking course had become – in one official's words – 'increasingly negroid', staff perceived a lowering of intellectual standards.[72] Perhaps in part because of such racial and cultural prejudices, the Bank's education and propaganda reflected an innate confidence that British institutions and personnel could and should shape overseas developments.

By the late 1960s the Bank estimated that at least 50 per cent of the alumni of the central banking course had gone on to attain senior positions in their own banks. While it is impossible to properly evaluate the precise significance that should be attached to this diaspora of bank personnel and alumni in both encouraging good banking practice (as it was conceived by British authorities) and the more self-interested goal of adherence to British practice and sterling, senior personnel at the Bank believed the central banking course had at least generated new friendships and contacts and shown 'at first hand the financial services the City has to offer'.[73]

It is nevertheless worth pointing out that in relation to banking, too, the British authorities sometimes struggled to retain the initiative, even before the transfers of power had occurred. They only discovered that the African minister of finance from the Gold Coast was holding discussions with various banks while on a visit to London when he failed to keep an engagement at a cocktail party.[74] In Nigeria, Britain was wrong-footed by the International Bank for Reconstruction and Development (World Bank, IBRD) when in 1953 it made a proposal in favour of the establishment there of a central bank in Nigeria, although the Bank of England subsequently succeeded in steering it in the 'right' direction. The difficulties of exercising influence were even greater after independence. For example, despite the best efforts of Bank of England adviser J. B. Loynes, who remained a member of the East African Currency Board which initially continued in operation after the transfers of power, Britain was unable to persuade the three east African countries to retain a common currency to be issued by a regional central bank. In Tanzania, where Loynes failed to maintain any effective role, new banking statutes, drafted by American lawyers of the International Monetary Fund (IMF), were, he feared, 'a nasty prospect'.[75]

If we turn to the creation of new national currencies we see a different dimension of efforts to maintain British traditions. The Royal Mint, which had produced old colonial currencies as well as supplying other imperial as well as foreign coinage,[76] inhabited a state-sponsored but nonetheless semi-commercial position. It too found itself fostering the maintenance of British styles and expertise; however, in this instance this approach reflected as much commercial as cultural or strategic imperatives.

Faced with impending constitutional decolonization and the establishment of central banks in former colonies, the Mint was anxious to retain its overseas business. Not only had this helped the Mint maintain capacity while domestic demand fluctuated, and hence helped keep the production of coin overall relatively cheap, but the retention, and indeed expansion, of the Mint's overseas business was crucial to a planned redevelopment of the Mint itself. Indeed, in one recent year (1952), overseas production had accounted for as much as 90 per cent of the Mint's production. Of all overseas business, that relating to the colonial empire was acknowledged by the Mint as 'by far the most important'.[77] It went all out to secure the custom of the emergent nations, badgering the Colonial Office and Treasury to intercede on its behalf, while also stressing that only the Mint could deliver coins bearing the authorised image of the Queen.[78]

The Gold Coast became the target of a determined Mint campaign. The chief clerk visited the colony in November 1955, the Mint stressing the importance of the visit from the 'economic no less than the political point of view'.[79] Concerns that the Mint might lose out to other producers of coin, notably the Pakistan Mint, which it was feared were also trying to secure the contract for the Gold Coast coinage,[80] indicate that in this case, too, the British sometimes found it hard to control developments. In seeing off potential competition, the Mint was obliged to offer highly competitive rates and the production of some of the west African coins had to be outsourced to the Birmingham Mint and Imperial Chemical Industries (ICI).[81]

In retrospect it seems that the outcome for the Mint could hardly have been in doubt. While the Mint worried at points that officials in Whitehall were not doing as much as they might to argue their case, it was nevertheless able to draw on a range of contacts within Whitehall, in colonial administrations and through the Crown Agents, as well as at the Bank of England, that competitors could not. In this respect the growing diaspora of Bank of England officials acting first in an advisory capacity in the development of new banking institutions and secondly as governors to the new institutions must have been of particular importance. A visit to the Mint was also included on the programme at the Bank of England's central banking course until 1969 when the Mint's impending move to Cardiff rendered this impractical.[82] While fearful that there would be 'severe competition' for the contract for the new coinage for Sierra Leone, advance notice of developments in relation to central banking via the Colonial Office ensured the Mint had the edge. Sticking its neck out, it commissioned an artist to produce a selection of possible designs in advance of any formal request to do so; these were then sent to Sierra Leone where they won favour and seem to have helped the Mint secure the contract.[83] Obtaining the first commissions was presumably also especially useful: thereafter the Bank could cite its role as coin supplier when addressing other colonies approaching independence and newly independent countries. It could also show examples of the coins already produced. The order for 240 million coins for Ghana, received in 1957, was followed by one for Nigeria for 1,000 million coins, the largest single order the Mint had ever received.[84] In the 1960s it went on to supply coins to the three former British territories in east Africa, and to Malawi and Zambia after the break-up of the Central African Federation. The Mint was also tasked with striking commemorative medals to be issued at the independence of some former colonies, including Ghana, Nigeria, and Sierra Leone: a transaction that seems to capture all the ambiguities of the transition to independence by former British colonies.

New banks, armies, and bureaucracies were emblems of nationhood: and coins, medals, as well as stamps, fascinating sites of political and cultural negotiation. On the country's independence medal, Nkrumah's Government opted for a statement of cultural decolonization, showing Nkrumah in national as opposed to Western dress; but in a further direction that speaks to the absorption of Western racial ideas, they nonetheless objected to the Mint's first attempt to capture Nkrumah's image on the grounds that it made him appear 'more negroid' than they thought was in fact the case.[85] Producing a satisfactory image of Malawian leader Hastings Banda was similarly fraught, amidst concerns that the first attempt gave 'an impression of harshness' which his Government was keen to avoid.[86]

Britain and the decolonization of Lusophone Africa

The case of the Mint just considered clearly takes us into a world where decolonization was as much a commercial as a constitutional experience, and shows that it was not only purely private commercial organizations that had to adapt to new political situations, which in turn forged equally new commercial environments. Other British institutions could well be brought within this frame of analysis, including postal and philatelic services. The Crown Agents, which procured supplies for the colonies, and also handled currency orders at the Royal Mint as well as those for munitions and military hardware, provide another prime example of institutional adaptation, as David Sunderland's account of their changing fortunes demonstrates.[87]

Further, shifting our focus from British Africa to other regions shows how some of the attitudes that underlay the pursuit of influence were apparent in relation to British understandings of the prospects and opportunities presented by the decolonization of other European empires. We can see this in relation to Mozambique, through a consideration of British commentators' analyses of Portuguese decolonization.

In Mozambique not only did Portugal's own circumstances militate against it acting as a neo-colonial power, but the speed with which the handover from Portugal to the Mozambique Liberation Front (Frente de Libertação de Moçambique, Frelimo) was effected after April 1974 left issues unresolved. These included the fact that no attempt had been made to retain experienced Portuguese administrators or professionals, and that the future of the Mozambican units of the colonial army was undecided.[88] Watching developments unfold, British observers, convinced that Portugal would be unable to offer much to its former colonies, foresaw problems – not least in relation to two of the areas discussed in this chapter: the establishment of a new central bank, to be formed from the country's branch of the Banco Nacional Ultramarino under the terms of the September 1974 Lusaka Agreement to transfer power; and the issue of a new currency.

Conscious of the country's economic problems and anticipating the Portuguese would 'wash their hands' as far as banking was concerned, with the result there would be no metropolitan experts remaining to handle the affairs of the new bank, British commentators were pessimistic about the country's economic future.[89] Given this perceived failure of the Portuguese state to exercise its own influence over its departing colony, officials at the Bank of England were keen that guidance be sought 'before', as one wrote, 'the sharks descend':[90] the IMF was approached to fill the vacuum (though in the event it transpired that Portugal had already requested an IMF mission should visit the colony).[91]

But the failure of Portuguese influence also provided an opportunity for a further extension of British interests and the benefits of British expertise beyond its own empire. 'There should be plenty of scope for other countries', as one officer at the British consulate general in Mozambique commented. He advised that prospects in the commercial sector were problematic, presumably in view of a likely programme of nationalization, but that Britain should do what it could to secure government contracts. The production of Mozambican currency offered one such opportunity, with the Portuguese deemed 'technically incapable' of producing the currency by a representative of British note manufacturer De La Rue.[92] De La Rue duly secured the note contract, while a 1975 coin issue was produced secretly by the Royal Mint in 1974. This particular intervention ended mysteriously.[93] But the Portuguese example nevertheless suggests that the British interest in post-colonial influence provided a perspective on other decolonizations that highlighted not just geopolitical dangers but commercial opportunities that could see the extension of British influence overseas.

Conclusions

This chapter has adopted a cross-sectoral approach to analysis of the decolonization of the colonial state, bringing into dialogue discussion of institutions that are generally accorded quite separate treatment by historians influenced by different methodologies and traditions. Doing so reveals the extent to which the British state and its clients demonstrated common purpose: a desire to spread British models, traditions, and influence. These ambitions emanated from different considerations and from different quarters of the British establishment, albeit that in the 1950s and early 1960s they were generally channelled through the Colonial Office, while the Crown Agents, through their procurement and financial roles, provided another connecting thread. The Colonial Office and the Commonwealth Relations Office, like other interested departments such as the Treasury and the War Office, had a vested interest in ensuring post-colonial stability. So too did the Bank of England. On the success of former British colonies hung not only the wider security objectives of upholding Western interests in the Cold War era, but also the more specific ones of military and financial stability within the Commonwealth and sterling area. In this context it is worth emphasizing how some of the British institutions discussed here generally aimed not to promote generic Western values but rather British influence and British procedures, reflecting a belief in British models as best practice. The commercial institutions within the public sector also had a natural interest in self-preservation and the maintenance or, where possible, extension of, their existing operations. What may appear – and indeed to some extent were – quite different goals, namely the pursuit of influence by the British state and of commercial gain by institutions occupying a semi-state position, were nevertheless inextricably linked. The Mint and similar organizations were key vehicles in the spread of Britishness, here used to refer to the export of British models and expertise; they were also potential beneficiaries of the British presence embedded in the institutions of the new nation states, which inevitably inclined to do business with those with whom they were culturally familiar.

As an earlier reference to France suggests, there was common ground between British and French ambitions to exercise influence, albeit that the French may appear to have done so with more long-term commitment and success. But there may also be features of the British approach that are quite distinct. Although it is hard to generalize across the different regions of the British Empire even within an African context,[94] there was nevertheless a particular inclination to eschew formal mechanisms of post-colonial influence in favour of more informal means. This may speak to a weaker commitment to a post-colonial role than was the case with France; a desire to shed rather than increase costs, and a greater reluctance to become ensnared in potentially troublesome post-colonial political contexts. But it also derived from a recognition that influence loosely exercised might be more compatible with prevailing anti-colonial sentiment, whether in the former colonies, at home, or in the wider world.

Underlying this chapter's discussion is the proposition – in itself hardly novel, and the basis for 'neo-colonial' style critiques as well as more recently those associated with post-colonial studies – that the transfers of power did not necessarily result in the cessation of colonialism in all its other guises, whether economic, cultural, or military. That this was the case was the inevitable consequence of the asymmetric relationship between imperial metropole and colony, with the former not only ambitious to exercise influence, but also in a strong position from which to do so. The colonies, at least initially, had little choice but to accept. Focused primarily on the attainment of constitutional independence, and without reservoirs of local skilled personnel or technical expertise, African politicians were willing to enter independence with British personnel at the helm of emergent national institutions.

However, although the idea that constitutional independence did not bring full decolonization is intrinsic to the argument presented in this chapter, it is important to remember that the transfers of power awarded the new governments of anglophone Africa ultimate authority over their bureaucracies, banks, and armies. Within certain practical and financial constraints, new governments could and did seek aid on a multi-lateral basis, diversify their reserves away from sterling,[95] and secure arms and military assistance from other sources, although discussion of all these falls beyond the scope of this chapter. In a situation in which other nations were increasingly important players in anglophone Africa, Britain's own economic weaknesses sometimes prevented it from being fully able to realize its ambition of influence in all areas. British advisers and personnel only remained in former colonies with the consent of new African governments. African governments were quick to cast off these British experts when popular opposition arose or it became inconvenient to retain them.

The degree to which new institutions were British-led hence declined rapidly in some sectors as new African governments encountered popular resistance to the continued expatriate role, or found the British presence restrictive.[96] With other nations from West and East offering generous packages of technical aid and donating educational scholarships for study in their countries as they too jockeyed for influence,[97] anglophone African states were able to source arms and training on a more multi-lateral basis. While some aligned with the West, others pursued alternative allegiances. In succeeding years as the British became caught up in the interplay between local political struggles and those of the Cold War, their ability to interject British training and supplies waxed and waned. Equally, and as indicated earlier, it is difficult to assess the outcomes of bringing overseas students from former colonies to train in Britain, especially as these constituted only a small fraction of the total number of local entrants to new armies, bureaucracies, and banks. Nor was it impossible that studying or training in Britain might not undermine the very objectives the British sought to achieve, especially where some overseas students encountered racism, not only within institutions but in the wider British community.

Yet, this does not render the British pursuit of influence discussed in this chapter ultimately insignificant. British institutions continued to exercise a significant role in some areas, and, even where this was not the case, colonial structures and practices survived long after the departure of expatriate personnel. Further, some British institutions that have hitherto attracted little scholarly attention from historians of empire enjoyed considerable success in securing their interests within former colonies. A semi-commercial state institution such as the Mint was well placed to achieve its goals. It had technical expertise unavailable in the new colonies, and the interlocking web of institutions and expatriates – of which it constituted one part – only assisted its case. The Mint's role supplying currency was also less visible than, for example, British soldiers seconded to head new African armies. Domestic British institutions – also 'clients' of the imperial state – which had over time assumed important imperial dimensions, have retained roles or commercial interests, often significant, in former colonies. The Mint is today the world's leading export Mint,[98] with some 15 per cent of the world market, supplying 100 issuing authorities around the world.[99]

Even where British practices were supplanted by other models, it is hoped that this chapter brings into sharp perspective not only British ambitions to exercise influence, but also how these were born of an innate confidence in British traditions and models. Initially, at least, their African clients bought into this worldview, generally accepting British advice and expertise in the creation of institutions based on British models (albeit that it sometimes suited their own specific political interests). From this perspective the unequal features of the new world order and a continued strong British presence in the emergent countries did not rest upon imperialist capitalist conspiracies. Instead, like the adoption (if not survival) of Westminster-style parliamentary democracies and the influence of Western development discourse,[100] they reflected a continuing, and powerful, if in some sectors short-lived, British intellectual and technical hegemony in the colonies.

Notes

1. I would like to thank Arthur Burns, David Killingray, Ashley Jackson, and Christopher Brain for reading a draft of this chapter; any mistakes remain of course my own. Earlier versions of it were presented at the King's College London–Georgetown Forum 2011 and in Lisbon in 2011, and I am grateful to participants, especially Richard Drayton, for helpful comments and questions. I am also grateful to the Bank of England Archive, the Syndics of Cambridge University Library for permission to quote from papers in the Archives of Cambridge University, and to the Keeper of University Archives, University of Oxford and to the Trustees of the Liddell Hart Centre for Military Archives, for assistance and access to their collections.

2. Many very perceptive: e.g. on the military, see R. Luckham, *The Nigerian Military: A Sociological Analysis of Authority and Revolt 1960–1967*, Cambridge, Cambridge University Press, 1971; D. Austin and R. Luckham, *Politicians and Soldiers in Ghana, 1966–1972*, London, Cass, 1975; N. J. Miners, *The Nigerian Army, 1956–1966*, London, Methuen, 1971; A. Clayton, 'The military relations between Great Britain and Commonwealth countries, with particular reference to the African Commonwealth Countries', in W. H. Morris-Jones and G. Fischer, eds, *Decolonisation and After: The British and French Experience*, London, Cass, 1980, pp. 193–223; C. A. Crocker, 'The military transfer of power in Africa: A comparative study of change in the British and French systems of order', unpublished doctoral thesis, Johns, Hopkins University, 1969. J. M. Lee, *African Armies and Civil Order*, London, Chatto and Windus, 1969 was allowed to consult but not reference government papers. Y. Bangura, *Britain and Commonwealth Africa: The Politics of Economic Relations, 1951–75*, Manchester, Manchester University Press, 1983, was also published before most of the relevant archival sources were open to researchers, but is similarly perceptive. For more recent work on defence, policing, and intelligence see: T. Parsons, *The African Rank-and-File: Social Implications of Colonial Military Service in the King's African Rifles, 1902–1964*, Westport, CT, Praeger, 1999; T. Parsons, *The 1964 Army Mutinies and the Making of Modern East Africa*, Portsmouth, NH, Heinemann, 2003; D. Percox, 'Internal security and decolonization in Kenya, 1956–1963', *Journal of Imperial and Commonwealth History*, 29, 1, 2004, pp. 92–116; G. Sinclair, *At the End of the Line: Colonial Policing and the Imperial Endgame, 1945–1980*, Manchester, Manchester University Press, 2006; P. Murphy, 'Creating a Commonwealth intelligence culture: The view from Central Africa, 1945–1965', *Intelligence and National Security*, 17, 3, 2002, pp. 131–162; Calder Walton, *Empire of Secrets. British Intelligence, the Cold War and the Twilight of Empire*, London, William Collins, 2012.

3. For one pioneering study, see E. Feingold, 'Decolonising justice: A history of the High Court of Tanganyika, c. 1920–1971', unpublished doctoral thesis, University of Oxford, 2011; and also in relation to colonial currencies (an area discussed in this chapter) the 'Money in Africa' project based at the British Museum and led by Catherine Eagleton.

4. Among many, see W. R. Louis and R. Robinson, 'The imperialism of decolonization', *Journal of Imperial and Commonwealth History*, 22, 3, 1994, pp. 462–511.

5. S. Stockwell, 'Instilling the "sterling tradition": Decolonization and the creation of a central bank in Ghana', *Journal of Imperial and Commonwealth History*, 26, 2, 1998, pp. 100–119; On banking, see also C. U. Uche, 'Bank of England vs the IBRD: Did the Nigerian colony deserve a central bank?', *Explorations in Economic History*, 34, 1997, pp. 220–241. C. Schenk, 'The origins of a central bank in Malaya and the transition to independence, 1954–1959', *Journal of Imperial and Commonwealth History*, 21, 2, 1993, pp. 409–431.

6. Sinclair, *At the End of the Line*, pp. 59–60, Chapter 3, contends that the British government sought to generate a sense of Britishness within the Colonial Police Service by facilitating a transition (largely frustrated) from military-style policing to a British civilian model during the last years of empire. Particularly relevant too is Murphy's analysis of how the British intelligence services sought to maintain influence over colonies approaching independence through British or British-trained intelligence personnel: Murphy, 'Creating a Commonwealth Intelligence Culture', 145–151. On constitutions, see Harshan Kumarasingham, *A Political Legacy of the British Empire. Power and the Parliamentary System in Post-Colonial India and Sri Lanka*, London, I.B, Tauris, 2013.

7. C. Unger, 'The United States, decolonization, and the education of Third World elites', in J. Dülffer and M. Fey, eds, *Elites and Decolonization in the Twentieth Century*, Basingstoke, Palgrave Macmillan, 2011, pp. 241–261.

8. For example, J. Hodge and B. Bennett, *Knowledge and Networks of Science across the British Empire, 1800–1970*, Basingstoke, Palgrave Macmillan, 2011; J. Hodge, *Triumph of the Expert: Agrarian Doctrines of Development*, Athens, OH, Ohio University Press, 2007.

9. Secretary of State for the Colonies Oliver Stanley, *House of Commons Debates*, 391, 13 July 1943, col. 48.

10. British names will be used when referring to colonies before independence.

11. TNA, CO 847/36/1, no 9, A.G.C. no 2, Report of the Committee on the Conference of African Governors', 22 May 1947, appendix III, para. 2.

12. *Report of the Commission of Enquiry into the Disturbances in the Gold Coast, 1948*, chairman, Aitken Watson, London, 1948, paras. 124–127.

13. For example, in relation to banks, see Stockwell, 'Sterling Tradition', 1998; Bangura, *Britain and Commonwealth Africa*, 1983, pp. 50–53.

14. For example, D. Anderson and D. Killingray, 'An orderly retreat? Policing the end of empire', in D. Anderson and D. Killingray, eds, *Policing and Decolonisation: Politics, Nationalism and the Police, 1917–1965*, Manchester, Manchester University Press, 1992, p. 9; Sinclair, *At the End of the Line*; D. Percox, 'Internal security and decolonization in Kenya, 1956–1963', *Journal of Imperial and Commonwealth History*, 29, 1, 2001, pp. 92–116.

15. R. Rathbone, 'Police intelligence in Ghana in the late 1940s and 1950s', *Journal of Imperial and Commonwealth History*, 21, 3, 1993, pp. 107–128. Walton, *Empire of Secrets. British Intelligence, the Cold War and the Twilight of Empire*, e.g. pp. 214–215.
16. TNA, CO 968/475, no 5, Lt-Gen. Harold Redman to W. Gorrell Barnes (CO), 1 September 1954.
17. Ibid., CO minutes on no 5, 9 September 1954 and 17 September 1954; no 33, Carstairs to Redman, 4 March 1955.
18. Parsons, *The 1964 Mutinies*, 2003, pp. 60–90.
19. In the Gambia, however, it was subsequently decided the colony could not afford a separate military establishment and the government opted instead to rely on the police to fulfil the country's security needs. D. Killingray, *The British Military Presence in West Africa*, Oxford Development Records Project, Report 3, 1983, p. 39.
20. Parsons, *The 1964 Mutinies*, 2003, pp. 46, 52–63; Parsons, *The African Rank-and-File*, 1999, pp. 40–46. The UK government also reassumed operational control of the East African forces, at some cost to the British Treasury in late 1959.
21. Details in the case of the armed forces derived from the country entries in J. Keegan, *World Armies*, London, Macmillan, 1979; Clayton, *Military Relations*, 1980, pp. 193–223.
22. A. Clayton, 'Foreign intervention in Africa', in S. Baynham, ed., *Military Power and Politics in Black Africa*, London, Croom Helm, 1986, pp. 223–224.
23. PP 1960–1, Cmd, 1308, 'Technical Assistance from the UK for Overseas Development' (March 1961).
24. See e.g. the language used in: TNA, WO 216/913, 'Draft. Top secret. Retention of British influence in colonial and Commonwealth Forces', 1958; CO 1017/233, A. E. Benson, governor of Nigeria to Sir Thomas Lloyd (CO), 27 July 1953; CO 1025/42, no 29, 'Gold Coast currency and banking', CO notes for a meeting with the Treasury and Bank of England, 1 September 1955.
25. *Report of the Commission of Enquiry on the Civil Services of West Africa, 1945–6* (Chairman, Sir Walter Harragin), Col. 209; *Report of the Commission on the Civil Service in the Gold Coast 1951* (Chairman, Lidbury); and on Nigeria, *Report of the Commission Appointed by His Excellency the Governor to make Recommendations about the Recruitment and Training of Nigerians for Senior Posts in the Government Service of Nigeria* (Chairman, Sir Hugh Foot) (Lagos, 1948); *Federal Government of Nigeria. The Nigerianization of the Civil Service: A Review of Policy and Machinery* (Lagos, 1953).
26. Richard Rathbone, 'The Colonial Service and the Transfer of Power in Ghana', in John Smith ed., *Administering Empire. The British Colonial Service in Retrospect* (London: University of London Press, 1999), 149–166, see esp. 155–6; Martin Lynn, 'Nigerian Complications: the Colonial Office, the Colonial Service and the 1953 Crisis in Nigeria', in *ibid.*, 181–205.
27. A.H. M. Kirk-Greene, On Crown Service. A History of H.M. Colonial and Overseas Civil Sevices, 1837–1997 (London: I. B. Tauris, 1999), pp. 62–73.
28. See e.g. papers in CO 1017/233.
29. Kirk-Greene, *On Crown Service*, pp. 62–73.
30. Cambridge University Archives [CUA], Archives of the Course on Development, GBR/0265/CDEV/11/1, The Standing Joint Committee on

Colonial Service Training CST (51) 1, Note by the Colonial Office, circulated prior to meeting, 25 January 1951.

31. See e.g. CUA, Papers of the University General Board, GB 760/939, Extract from Lord Munster's Opening Address to the 1953 Conference to consider Colonial Service Training, 14–17 September 1953.

32. The details of this lie beyond the scope of this chapter, but it is a theme I am exploring in other work.

33. *Report on the Public Services Conference*, Colonial no 347.

34. CUA, CDEV 2/22, Annual Report, Overseas Studies Committee, 1963–64 (20 July 1964); Oxford University Archives, UR 6/Col 4/file 13, Col 798, 'The future of the Overseas Service courses A and B at Oxford University'.

35. See Rhodes House Library Oxford, MSS. Brit. Emp. S. 478, Boxes 1–5.

36. CUL, CDEV 2/5, CCS, Minutes, 28 April 1958.

37. CUA, CDEV/2/23, OSC 397, 'Overseas Studies Committee. Director's report for the year 1979–1980', 22 October 1980.

38. Clayton, 'Foreign intervention', 1986, pp. 203–258, esp. 222. For Britain's extensive military connections to Africa in recent decades, see A. Jackson, 'British–African defence and security connections', *Defence Studies*, 6, 3, 2006, pp. 351–376.

39. Lee, *African Armies*, 1969, pp. 10, 14.

40. TNA, CAB 129/76, CP (55) 89, 'Cabinet security in the Colonies', 5 July 1955, incorporating 'Report on colonial security' by Templer, 23 April 1955. See Cab C (58) 92, 1 May 1958, 'Security in the colonies', note by the Lord Chancellor dated 30 April 1958. Much of this report was dedicated to security issues: for an introduction to this aspect, see R. Cormac, 'Organizing intelligence: An introduction to the 1955 report on colonial security', *Intelligence and National Security*, 25, 6, 2010, pp. 800–822.

41. TNA, Cab C (58) 92, 'Report by the Committee on Security in the colonies', section 7, 'The problem of handover', para 17.

42. Ibid., para. 23.

43. Parsons, *The 1964 Mutinies*, 2003, p. 42.

44. D. Killingray, *Fighting for Britain: African Soldiers and the Second World War*, Woodbridge, James Currey, 2010, pp. 85–87.

45. Lee, *African Armies*, 1969, p. 38; Killingray, *British Military Presence*, 1983, pp. 39, 63; Miners, *The Nigerian Army*, 1971, pp. 33–39, 48–50.

46. *Report of the West African Forces Conference, Lagos 20–24 April 1953*, Col. No 304, HMSO, London, 1954, paras 9–14.

47. Although publication of the 1953 conference conclusions had been delayed by negotiations over officers' pay TNA, CO 968/475, minute by J. Bennett (CO), 7 July 1954.

48. TNA, CO 968/475, memo by John Bennett on the defence implications of the Gold Coast's transition to independence, 5 July 1954, see esp. section C, para 4 and section D, para.7.

49. Ibid., no 33, Carstairs to Lt-Gen. Harold Redman, 4 March 1955.

50. Ibid., no 6, W. draft letter from W. H. Gorrell Barnes to Governor Charles Arden-Clarke, 22 September 1954 (this was omitted from the final copy sent).

51. TNA, WO 216/913, 'Draft. Top secret. Retention of British influence in colonial and Commonwealth forces' (1958); see also earlier documents, such as CO 968/475, memo by John Bennett on the defence implications of the Gold

Coast's transition to independence, 5 July 1954. For the importance attached to this in east Africa, see Parsons, *The 1964 Mutinies*, 2003, pp. 63–64.

52. TNA, WO 216/913, no 40A, Maj. Gen. V. Paley to General Sir F. Festing, 7 March 1959.
53. Ibid., no 23A, Templer to Paley, 20 June 1958; 24B, Paley to Templer, 25 June 1958.
54. Lee, *African Armies*, 1969, pp. 39–42.
55. Through the creation of new African governors' commissions (inferior to the Queen's commissions given to British officers). Parsons, *The 1964 Mutinies*, 2003, pp. 50–52.
56. Lee, *African Armies*, 1969, pp. 39–42.
57. Parsons, *The 1964 Mutinies*, 2003, pp. 67–68.
58. TNA, WO 216/913, no 28B, Paley to Templer, 14 July 1958.
59. Ibid., no 36A: Paley to Festing, 17 Dec. 1958; General Sir Lashmer Whistler to Festing 23 February 1959.
60. As discussed in Stockwell, 'Sterling Tradition', 1998.
61. Archive of the Bank of England BoE OV 21/25, 'Probable calls on the Bank for personnel', 28 June 1956; notes by Governor of Bank of England, 7 August 1956 and 14 August 1956 on 'Colonies: Bank of England assistance to monetary authorities', memo. by J. B. Loynes, 27 April 1956.
62. F. Capie, *The Bank of England 1950s to 1979*, Cambridge, Cambridge University Press, 2010, pp. 336–338, citing Eric Haslan, *Central Banks in the Making: the Role of the Bank of England 1948–1974* (BoE, 1979, private circulation).
63. BoE, OV 21/26, 'Commonwealth Central Banking School', memo. 1 October 1956, G. M. Watson.
64. BoE, OV 21/26, annotation on 'Tanzania: Bank of England course', 28 October 1966
65. BoE, OV 21/26, 'The Commonwealth etc., Central Banking Course', memo by R. P. Fenton, 4 November 1971.
66. Ibid., 'Commonwealth Central Banking Summer School', memo. 1 October 1956, G. M. Watson.
67. Ibid.
68. C. Schenk, *The Decline of Sterling: Managing the Retreat of an International Currency, 1945–1992*, Cambridge, Cambridge University Press, 2010, pp. 31, 94.
69. BoE, OV 21/26, 'Review' [of the CW Central Banking Course], draft, 11 March 1970.
70. *Ibid.*
71. P.L. Cottrell, 'The Bank in its international setting', in Richard Roberts and David Kynaston eds, *The Bank of England. Money, Power and Influence, 1694–1994*, Oxford, Clarendon Press, 1995, pp. 83–139; David Kynaston, 'The Bank and the Government', in Richard Roberts and David Kynaston eds, *The Bank of England. Money, Power and Influence, 1694–1994*, Oxford, Clarendon Press, 1995, pp.19–55.
72. BoE, OV 21/26, memo on the central banking course by J. L[oynes], 20 September 1968.
73. BoE, OV 21/26, 'Review' [of the CW Central Banking Course], draft, 11 March 1970.
74. BoE, OV 69/3, no.38B: minute of a telephone call from the CO, 18 November 1954.

75. BoE. OV 7/87, esp. no 132, J. B. Loynes to H. J. Hinchey, East African Common Services Organization, 6 May 1965.
76. G.P. Dyer and P.P. Gaspar, 'Reform, the New Technology and Tower Hill 1700–1966' in C.E. Challis ed., *A New History of the Royal Mint* (Cambridge: Cambridge University Press, 1992), 398–606.
77. TNA, MINT 20/2563, Sir Lionel Thompson to A. N. Galsworthy (CO), 11 July 1955; Sir Lionel Thompson to Sir Herbert Brittain (T), 11 July 1955 (copy); Sir Lionel Thompson to A. N. Galsworthy, 27 July 1955, enclosing note on the services of the Royal Mint.
78. Except Canada, Australia and South Africa: ibid.
79. TNA, MINT 20/2563: see Sir L. Thompson to T. J. Bligh (T) 21 October 1955; 'Gold Coast Currency' report produced by Stride following his visit to the Gold Coast, 22 November 1955; T. M. Kodwo Mercer (Gold Coast minister) to Sir L. Thompson, 29 December 1955.
80. Ibid., 'Note', 30 September 1955 by the Deputy Master of the Mint.
81. TNA, MINT 20/2802 and MINT 20/2775, esp. H. G. Stride (RM) to W. F. Brazener (The Mint Birmingham), 3 March 1958.
82. BoE, OV 21/26, 'Future Central Banking Courses'. 14 July 1969, by R. P. Edgley.
83. TNA MINT 20/3067, various correspondence, but esp. Mint to M. S. Mustapha (Minister of Finance, Sierra Leone), 27 April 1962; A. J. Dowling (Mint) to M. G. Rizzello (artist), 15 February 1963.
84. Dyer and Gaspar, 'The new technology', 1992, pp. 594–595.
85. TNA, MINT 20/2633, Captain Everard (Gold Coast Independence Day Celebrations Officer) to Sir L. Thompson, 25 September 1956 and 3 November 1956.
86. TNA, MINT 20/3101, H [?] Robertson (Secretary to Treasury, Nyasaland) to A. J. Dowling (RM), 6 June 1964.
87. David Sunderland, *Managing the British Empire. The Crown Agents 1833–1914* (Woodbridge: Boydell, 2004).
88. M. Newitt, 'Mozambique' in P. Chabal, D. Birmingham, J. Forrest and M. Newitt, eds, *A History of Postcolonial Lusophone Africa*, London, Hurst, 2002, p. 194.
89. BoE. OV 62/34, no 125, 'New Currency for Mozambique' by A. L Free-Gore (British consulate general, Lourenço Marques) referring to visit by Mr Napier of De La Rue.
90. Ibid., no 128, minute on response from British Department of Trade and Industry to above, 7 November 1974.
91. Correspondence on Ibid.
92. Ibid., no 112, S. F. St Duncan to A. B. Moore, 2 October 1974; no 125, 'New Currency for Mozambique' by A. L Free-Gore referring to visit by Mr Napier of De La Rue.
93. It appears the currency was never circulated.
94. For example, British approaches to post-colonial defence relations in west Africa need to be understood in terms of weaker British interest in the region than was the case in east Africa, regarded as of more strategic significance.
95. Bangura, *Britain and Commonwealth Africa*, pp. 97–114.

96. For example, by 1961 the Nigerian government had rejected the defence agreement signed at independence, and the Ghanaian government dismissed Paley's successor, General H. T. Alexander, after the Ghanaian Army's part in the UN mission to the Congo threw into sharp relief the potential conflicts and humiliation of continued reliance on expatriate expertise for a country which sought wider pan-African leadership. See King's College London, Liddell Hart Military Archive, papers of General H. T. Alexander.

97. Notably Israel, the Soviet Union, and Czechoslovakia (see e.g. in the Ugandan case, Omara-Otunnu, *Politics and the Military*, 1987, pp. 66, 95–97, and the US (e.g. as discussed by D. Branch, Kenya: *Between Hope and Despair*, 1963–2011, New Haven, CT, Yale University Press, 2011, p. 38, 69. On US philanthropic organizations in the Third World see, most recently Unger, 'Education of third world elites', 2011.

98. From April 1975 the Royal Mint Trading Fund; and, since January 2010, the Royal Mint Limited, a commercial organization free to sell its products in global markets, but wholly owned by HM Treasury.

99. *The Royal Mint Trading Group Fund Annual Report and Accounts 2009–10*, London, The Stationery Office, 2010, pp. 12, 22. Its profits are continuing to grow. For example, overseas sales rose greatly in recent years from £55,229,000 in the financial year 2005–06 to £110,046,000 in 2009–10.

100. See Hodge, *Triumph of the Expert*, 2007.

7
Acceptable Levels? The Use and Threat of Violence in Central Africa, 1953–64

Philip Murphy

Monographs by Caroline Elkins and David Anderson on British policy in the campaign against the Mau Mau insurgency in Kenya, both published in 2005, served to focus scholarly attention on the role of extreme force in sustaining colonial rule, and to puncture the commonly held notion that the transfer of power in the British Empire was a largely peaceful process.[1] They have been followed by more recent studies that have shed light on some of the darker corners of British policy in Kenya.[2] The idea that there was a brutal and largely hidden history of British decolonization received a powerful boost in 2011 by the revelation that the British government had withheld thousands of files on late-colonial policy relating not only to Kenya but to scores of other British territories. These so-called migrated archives were generated by the local colonial administrations and removed to the UK at independence, where they were secretly stored, latterly at offices in Hanslope Park, Buckinghamshire.[3] The British government admitted to their existence during a case brought against it in the High Court in London by a group of elderly former Mau Mau detainees who were claiming they had been brutally treated while in custody.[4] The year 2011 also saw the publication of a number of high-profile historical studies that served as a further reminder the British Empire was sustained by the ruthless deployment of violence, and that its end was accompanied by vicious counter-insurgency campaigns in Palestine, Malaya, Kenya, and Cyprus.[5] Research of this kind is likely to receive a further boost from the phased release from 2012 of the Hanslope Park files.

This renewed focus on the use of repression by the late-colonial state has tended to exacerbate an older tendency to make a distinction between violent and peaceful instances of decolonization. This, in turn, has tended to obscure the extent to which the implicit threat of violence suffused the negotiations surrounding many apparently peaceful transfers of power. This chapter attempts to explore that phenomenon in the case of the central African territories of Northern Rhodesia (Zambia), Southern Rhodesia (Zimbabwe) and Nyasaland (Malawi) which, at least before 1965, appeared to have been spared the worst excesses witnessed in some other British territories.

The history of these three territories during the twenty years after the end of the Second World War formed the theme of the central Africa volume in the British Documents on the End of Empire project (BDEEP).[6] The turning point and the natural dividing line for the two parts of the volume was the Nyasaland Emergency of 1959. In terms of the numbers arrested and killed, this was a relatively minor incident compared with the Mau Mau campaign in Kenya or the Algerian civil war. Around 1,320 were arrested, including the leader of the Nyasaland African Congress, Dr Hastings Banda, and around 50 killed. Yet it dealt a fatal blow to confidence in the federation, not least because of the highly critical report of the commission of enquiry into the affair, which was chaired by Lord Devlin.[7]

Why did this limited outbreak of violence have such an impact on the history of central Africa? An answer of sorts can be extrapolated from an otherwise unremarkable letter written in March 1960 by the prime minister of Southern Rhodesia, Sir Edgar Whitehead, to the British secretary of state for Commonwealth relations, Lord Home. Whitehead complained about a collapse of confidence in his country, which had led to a downturn in the economy. He blamed this on deteriorating political conditions in the region, telling Home:

> Events in Nyasaland last year, the farce of the Southworth Commission, the beginning of apparent anarchy in the Katanga, the renewal of Panga attacks in Kenya and the irresponsible utterances of the Labour Party in Britain have all had a depressing effect on a people who have not had to fire a shot to maintain law and order since 1896.[8]

This letter was not included in the BDEEP collection – its contents are largely replicated in documents that can be found elsewhere in the volume. In many ways, however, this passage exemplifies the troubled politics not merely of post-war central Africa, but of other settler-dominated regimes.

At one level, Whitehead's letter to Home was merely another example of the horse-trading that was an all too familiar part of the winding down of the Central African Federation. By the beginning of 1960, the recently appointed colonial secretary, Iain Macleod, was pushing for the release of Banda and his involvement in constitutional talks. Whitehead saw this as an opportunity to promote a policy he had been arguing for since shortly after the British Conservative Party was returned to power in the October 1959 general election – the granting of greater autonomy to the settlers of Southern Rhodesia by removing the remaining reserved powers of the country's constitution. These reservations broadly stipulated that Southern Rhodesian legislation that was either deemed discriminatory against Africans or which sought to amend the 1930 Land Apportionment Act required the approval of the British secretary of state. Whitehead made clear to London that his ultimate aim was to achieve for Southern Rhodesia 'full self-government within the framework of the federal constitution' before the federal review talks began in 1960.[9] In February 1960, both Whitehead and the prime minister of the Central African Federation, Sir Roy Welensky, suggested to London that their objections to Banda's release and involvement in constitutional talks might be assuaged if the reserved powers were surrendered. As the cabinet secretary, Sir Norman Brook, noted with dismay, this would effectively mean augmenting the political rights of Africans in one territory by taking them away in another.[10] Nevertheless, that is effectively what the British government did by surrendering the reserved powers in the 1961 Southern Rhodesian constitution. There is a myth, adumbrated by Ian Smith and his Rhodesian Front colleagues, and maintained by some of their contemporary apologists, that Southern Rhodesia was pushed into a unilateral declaration of independence (UDI) in 1965 by a British government determined to foist an African nationalist government on the country.[11] It would be more true to say that in the interests of ensuring a smooth transition to majority rule in Northern Rhodesia and Nyasaland, and a peaceful dissolution of the Central African Federation, London was culpable in allowing a further entrenchment of settler power in Southern Rhodesia in the early 1960s, and in allowing settler leaders to believe self-government might be within their grasp.

Yet Whitehead's 'more-in-sorrow-than-in-anger' reference to violence in the region having had a 'depressing effect on a people who have not had to fire a shot to maintain law and order since 1896' carried with it a far more fundamental message, one that lay at the heart of the unspoken contract between settler regimes and London. It was this:

> You may not approve of or understand everything we do here. You may see what you perceive to be instances of injustice. But ultimately

we will maintain peace, and spare you the costs and dangers of inter-vention. And on that basis, we know you will do nothing to curb our powers or privileges.

London's reaction to the politics of the region up to the end of 1958 more than bore this out. Whitehall knew that the hostility of Africans towards the Central African Federation, which had been present at its birth in 1953, showed little sign of abating. It knew that rather than seeking to win Africans over with political concessions, the federation's European leaders appeared far more concerned to press ahead with their plans to turn the region into a white dominion. It was also well aware of Southern Rhodesia's brand of de facto apartheid, and of its leaders' failure to deliver, or even to promise, meaningful political advance to the country's African majority. Yet all this remained academic so long as settler leaders could guarantee to maintain order. There might be concerns, but so long as there was peace there was no problem as such.

Under such circumstances, even fairly limited instances of violence such as occurred in Nyasaland in the early months of 1959, and in Southern Rhodesia in October–November 1960, could have a profound impact on metropolitan perceptions of the legitimacy of a settler regime. When one studies the reactions of the British Conservative Party to the development of the Central African Federation, it is particu-larly striking what a shock the Nyasaland Emergency delivered to the debate in the UK. Before the emergency, even progressives within the party on colonial issues, while prepared to admit the Federation's flaws, were generally happy to support their party's line that it was here for good. In the wake of the emergency, there was general consensus across the party (not withstanding later Left–Right splits over the Federation's future), that there needed to be a change of policy.[12] This sense of disil-lusionment went to the very top of the party. Only two days after the declaration of the Emergency, Harold Macmillan recorded in his diary that federation had proved a political failure since African opposition had rendered it unacceptable.[13]

The settler leaders of Southern Rhodesia were, in a sense, luckier. In the period up to the declaration of UDI in November 1965, the situ-ation within the country was relatively peaceful, with protest nipped ruthlessly in the bud. Whitehead's tactic in February 1960 of portraying Southern Rhodesia as a small island of tranquillity surrounded by a sea of instability remained a fruitful one in subsequent years as the Congo descended into anarchy and as other recently independent African countries proved unstable. Events in east Africa in January 1964 gave a considerable boost to the Southern Rhodesian case. A coup in the newly independent state of Zanzibar overthrew the sultan, and British troops were called in to suppress a rising in Tanganyika and an army revolt in Uganda. When the Southern Rhodesian prime minister, Winston Field, met Sir Alec Douglas-Home (by then prime minister, having renounced his peerage) and Commonwealth secretary Duncan Sandys for talks in London at the end of that month, he argued that the avoidance of a premature handover of power to Africans 'was all the more important in the light of events in East Africa'.[14] Indeed, Sandys himself subsequently expressed his conviction that these events meant it would be 'wrong morally' and 'indefensible' for the British government to press Southern Rhodesia to introduce significant African advance.[15] Even Labour ministers after the British general election in October 1964 were highly susceptible to this line of reasoning when they contemplated the feasibility and morality of overthrowing the Rhodesian Front Government.[16]

What is striking, however, is the reaction of the British government when, in October–November 1960, it seemed possible major violence might sweep Southern Rhodesia. Before that point, and indeed in the years thereafter, London was keen to point to Southern Rhodesia's long history of self-government as a means of explaining why it could not intervene in the territory's affairs. When, however, rioting broke out in the township of Harare on 8 October and spread to other areas, Southern Rhodesia's much vaunted autonomy was quickly forgotten in Whitehall. A month later, Macmillan suggested to Sandys that the government should 'consider the possibility of facing a complete breakdown of law and order' in Southern Rhodesia. He added: 'We could not send in our troops and put them under local command. We might have to take control. It might be that we should need to send in a strong man to take charge, rather as in Malaya'.[17] Sandys replied that this scenario was already being considered and that 'if the situation did break down we would probably need to send a politician as well as a general to take charge'.

One of the great counter-factuals of the history of central Africa is what would have happened had African nationalists in Southern Africa resorted to a sustained campaign of violence in 1960. Would the British government have intervened and, if so, would they have restructured Southern Rhodesian politics – as they did in Kenya – to undermine white settler power? And had they done so, might that have averted a unilateral declaration of independence by the settlers? Is the moral, in short, that African nationalists were not violent enough, early enough when that violence might have had a real impact?

If an essential part of the compact between London and the settler regimes of central Africa was that the former would maintain peace, there was another side of that coin: namely that the settlers themselves might, if their demands were not met, engage in some kind of Boston Tea Party-style revolt, leading to violence and disorder. This kind of threat – what one British official described as 'government by blackmail' – was a major motivating factor behind the establishment of the Central African Federation, which was in the late-1940s and early-1950s the least settler leaders were prepared to accept in the pursuit of their longer-term goal of amalgamating of the two Rhodesias.[18] The industrial muscle of European mineworkers on the Copperbelt and the economic influence of Southern Rhodesia over its two British administered northern neighbours gave the settlers a leverage that went well beyond the power of their arguments. As early as June 1943, an official brief for the secretary of state for the colonies, Oliver Stanley, predicted that a negative response from the British government to calls for the amalgamation of Northern and Southern Rhodesia 'would cause intense disappointment and dissatisfaction among the European population of the two territories' and might lead some Europeans, particularly those on the Copperbelt, 'to take the law into their own hands'.[19] An official from the Colonial Office visiting central Africa in February 1949 warned that if the British government did not prove sympathetic to the latest settler plans for federation, Southern Rhodesia might actively 'apply economic pressure on Northern Rhodesia and Nyasaland primarily by increasing chrome output and reducing the number of railway wagons available for the transport of copper'. Threats of this kind of economic disruption – which in itself had the potential to bring violence in its wake – and of a Boston Tea Party-style revolt continued after the Federation was created and became a regular means by which settler leaders attempted to intimidate the British government.

This constant underlying threat – that the central African settlers might attempt to achieve their objectives by economic blackmail, or even the use of force – helps explain why London undertook the risky business of including Nyasaland in the Federation, against the explicit advice of Nyasaland's governor, Sir Geoffrey Colby. As the negotiations leading to federation gained momentum, Colby's warnings to London became ever more insistent. At the end of November 1951, shortly after the Conservatives took office, he told the Colonial Office, 'I feel very strongly that we should take the initiative and pull out'.[20] These warnings culminated in March 1952 in an explicit recommendation to the secretary of state 'that Nyasaland should not be included in any Central

African Federation and that consideration of its participation should be postponed indefinitely'.[21] He warned that the African congresses of the two northern territories were working closely together to oppose federation and enjoyed the backing of communist organizations. With threats of strikes and civil disobedience emanating from these quarters, and the Nyasaland police lacking the capacity to deal with major unrest, there was a risk of 'very serious trouble'. In normal circumstances, such a clear warning from a governor that a policy being pursued by the British government might lead to serious unrest would have given London serious pause for thought. Yet Colby's objections were quietly brushed aside. In simple terms, the British government believed it was the settlers of central Africa rather than the Africans who posed the greater potential threat to British interests in the region, and that it was they who should be appeased while African objections to federation should be ridden out. This lesson – that the British would ultimately side with those capable of inflicting the greater disruptive force – was not lost on African leaders.

The sense within the Colonial Office that the principal threat to its authority in central Africa came not from Africans but from European settler leaders, did not significantly decline with the establishment of the Central African Federation. In June 1956, the Colonial and Commonwealth Relations offices were asked by the recently convened committee on counter-subversion in the colonial territories to draw up a paper on the Federation. One official from the Colonial Office objected to the emphasis placed on the challenge from African nationalism in an early draft of this document. He noted:

> The most likely source of unrest in the federation at the present moment is the attempt now being made by the federal government itself to jockey HMG [Her Majesty's Government] into taking steps to give it some kind of early 'Dominion status'. The governors of both Northern territories fear that *any* action of this nature is liable to produce the most profound and violent reactions among the Africans of the Northern Territories.[22]

Evidence that these fears were not misplaced came in the autumn of 1956, when in a particularly inflammatory speech by the prime minister of the Federation, Lord Malvern, he raised the prospect of a Boston Tea Party if full independence were not granted to it. Considering Britain's likely response to any such action, officials at the Colonial Office agreed with the assessment of Arthur Benson, governor of Northern Rhodesia, that it was 'inconceivable that any British government would ever send British troops to fight against British people (white) in Africa; the corollary being that HMG must gain their political aims in Central Africa by political means'.[23] This remained, in effect, the British government's position throughout the period under consideration, and owed as much to racial solidarity as it did to logistical considerations. When the issue was again discussed in September 1958, fears were expressed within the Colonial Office – no doubt with Algeria in mind – that 'There would be a real risk that British troops would not obey when pitted against e.g. the European mineworkers on the Copperbelt'.[24] Indeed, civil servants themselves viewed with distaste 'the possibility of our having to take arms against our countrymen in Central Africa'.[25]

The closest Britain came to armed intervention against the central African settlers came in February 1961, when there seemed a real threat that the federal government might respond to the breakdown of constitutional talks over Northern Rhodesia by staging some sort of coup. Detailed plans were drawn up for armed intervention, and transport aircraft in Kenya were placed on a state of high alert.[26] Yet the British were able to contemplate this prospect in part because under the circumstances of the time the distinction between the reinforcement and the invasion of the Rhodesias was far from clear. Having stared into the abyss on this occasion, and having been persuaded by military chiefs that any intervention was likely to result in the deaths of white civilians, British politicians were never prepared seriously to contemplate this again. When Ian Smith declared UDI in 1965, an invasion was not regarded by the British government as a serious alternative.

There were, needless to say, far fewer, qualms in Whitehall about using violence against Africans. Again, deep-seated racial attitudes came into play. The habit of associating Africa and Africans with savagery and anarchy was deep-seated in Western societies.[27] It was certainly present at the very highest levels of the British administration. Considering the final version of the Devlin Report, shortly before its publication, the cabinet secretary, Sir Northern Brook, took issue with the commission's criticism of the Nyasaland government's policy that every crowd should be dispersed, if necessary by shooting. Brook commented, 'Even in a highly civilised community, the preservation of law and order rests on the respect for authority. The need to enforce that respect is infinitely greater in places like Nyasaland where a handful of white men are controlling hordes of primitive people'.[28] That unreconstructed views of Africa and its peoples should have lingered on in Whitehall for many decades after the end of the Second World War should hardly come as a surprise; yet it is rather jolting to witness Britain's most senior civil servant using this kind of Ryder Haggard imagery as late as 1959.

The fact that African nationalism in the region was largely characterized by non-violence did little to assuage these attitudes. Indeed, the ghost of Mau Mau haunted the minds of British officials and politicians dealing with central Africa, and the idea that movements either akin to Mau Mau or directly inspired by it might be taking root formed a fairly regular part of the intelligence reports that found their way to London. In August 1957, for example, the acting governor of Northern Rhodesia passed London a recent intelligence report on the Action Group of the Northern Rhodesian African National Congress (ANC), claiming it was being 'developed into a near terrorist organisation, which if not checked may well lead to conditions developing in Northern Rhodesia on much the same lines as they did in Kenya which led up to the Mau Mau emergency in that country'.[29]

Defending the declaration of the Nyasaland Emergency in the Commons on 3 March 1959, both the colonial secretary, Alan Lennox-Boyd, and his under-secretary, Julian Amery, notoriously reached for the imagery of Mau Mau to justify the Nyasaland government's actions. Lennox-Boyd claimed action had been required to prevent a massacre that was being planned by Congress. Amery spoke even more chillingly of a potential bloodbath, claiming there might have been 'a massacre of Africans, Asians and Europeans on a Kenyan scale'.[30] Yet if the two ministers were playing up this angle in an attempt to avert criticism from the Opposition that the emergency had been declared in response to pressure from the federal government, Amery did not conjure the reference to Kenya out of thin air. The most detailed intelligence on the putative Nyasaland African Congress plan to assassinate Europeans and collaborators in the event of Banda's arrest came from a Nyasaland Special Branch report of 13 February. It reported that a secret meeting of Congress on 25 January had decided on 'a widespread campaign of assassination of government officials, murder of European men, women and children and wholesale sabotage'.[31] It incorporated the account of an informer which suggested the programme of violence would be activated by one of two developments: either Banda's arrest, or his rejection of new constitutional proposals. In the event of the former development, a committee of four would take over the direction of Congress, and would fix a day – 'R Day' – on which a programme of mass sabotage and murder would be carried out. Having set out these details, it presented evidence suggesting that 'at least one person from Kenya had advised Dr Banda and, in fact, the plan above bears a strong resemblance to the original Mau Mau plan'.[32]

When the authorities did act in Nyasaland in 1959, it was with a lack of restraint reminiscent of the campaign against Mau Mau in Kenya, albeit for a far shorter period and with far fewer fatalities. This was a point Lord Devlin picked up on in his report, although as Brian Simpson noted, Devlin removed some of his most relevant comments on this matter from the final draft of the document.[33] In one of these passages, which does not appear in the final version, the report says:

> In Nyasaland we found that, perhaps under the strain of the emergency, there was at every level of the administration an indifference to and misuse of the law. By misuse of the law we mean that the emergency regulations were treated solely as a source of power to be exploited and added to if necessary and not as setting any limits to what the government could do.[34]

Devlin's implied criticisms of this lack of restraint were focused principally at the colonial administration in Nyasaland. Yet it could be argued that one of the problems arose from the fact the British government itself did not act as an effective agent of restraint, and that one reason for this was that the notion of 'a handful of white men [...] controlling hordes of primitive people' was powerfully alive in the minds of so many of the politicians and officials responsible for African police.

One disturbing feature of the lack of restraint concerned Operation Instructions (No. 2/59) drawn up by the Nyasaland government for the conduct of the emergency. These specified that the security forces should engage in 'tough punitive action in areas where lawlessness and acts of violence are perpetrated or planned'.[35] In the pursuit of this objective, 'swift and offensive retribution must be meted out to convince that lawlessness does not pay'. In the published version of its report, and even more forcefully in earlier drafts, the Devlin Commission implicitly blamed the plan for having granted excessive latitude to the security forces, with the result that 'there was a great deal of aggressive and bullying behaviour'. What is not mentioned in the Devlin report is that Armitage sent a copy of the operation plan to the Colonial Office on 10 March. London did not, apparently, question the terms of the plan and the reference to 'tough punitive action'. Indeed, three days before, the Colonial Office had approved a further expansion of the Nyasaland government's ability to use violence against protesters. On 4 March, Armitage had asked London to confirm that it would not be acceptable for aircraft to fire on rioters, and had been told that indeed it would not be. Yet three days later he asked for this to be reconsidered, and requested that where troops on the ground had exhausted all effective means of resistance they should be able to call on machine-gun fire from the air. The colonial secretary, Alan Lennox-Boyd, recommended to Macmillan that this should be allowed under limited circumstances. Macmillan agreed, but insisted on inserting the following paragraph in London's instructions to Armitage:

> In a situation where aircraft fire may have to be used as a last resort in the circumstances envisaged above, it would be proper to make some preliminary dummy runs of a menacing kind which might frighten and disperse the mob without actually opening fire and inflicting casualties. It might even be possible to open fire, in the first instance, in such a way as not to cause casualties, as for example, in the old days troops 'fired over the heads of the mob'.[36]

This remarkably flippant attitude to a potentially lethal escalation in the use of force says much about the lack of restraint coming from the very top of the chain of command.

Perhaps the main consideration that did encourage Whitehall to apply a restraining hand, both in the Nyasaland Emergency and other instances, was the fear that any abuses might be taken up by the press and in Parliament. As I have argued in a recent article with Dr Joanna Lewis, there was a symbiotic relationship between Parliament and the press over colonial affairs: parliamentary questions about particular incidents – probably the most important means by which British ministers were called to account over their conduct of colonial affairs – were frequently inspired by press reports.[37] The rare occasions when London questioned Armitage's conduct of the Nyasaland Emergency, for example the use of corporal punishment against youths, were usually the result of a press report leading to a hostile parliamentary question. Indeed, in authorizing the use of aircraft fire against rioters, Lennox-Boyd's main concern had been that this might cause 'casualties in the surrounding African crowd, including possibly deaths of women and children' leading to 'a wave of African reaction throughout our territories, with repercussions in Parliament and internationally'.[38]

In situations where press and parliamentary scrutiny were not likely to be a factor, one gets the occasional chilling sense of how cheap African life could sometimes appear from the perspective of London. A striking example is that of UK policy towards the Belgian Congo. On 13 January 1959, in the immediate wake of serious rioting, King

Baudouin of Belgium promised independence for the Congo at some unspecified point in the future. A year later, a conference was held to agree the terms of independence, the date of which was set for the end of June. Elections to the provincial and national assemblies were held in May. Patrice Lumumba's National Congolese Movement (Mouvement National Congolais, MNC) emerged as the largest party in the national House of Representatives, although it lacked an overall majority. The Democratic Republic of the Congo was born on 30 June 1960. Joseph Kasavubu, founder of the pioneering nationalist movement the Bakongo Alliance (Alliance des Bakongo, ABAKO) became the country's first president, and Lumumba its prime minister.

Lumumba was increasingly viewed in London and Washington as a dangerous communist fellow-traveller who needed to be neutralized. In September 1960, with considerable covert US encouragement, Colonel Joseph Mobutu staged a coup. He attempted to arrest Lumumba, but was prevented from doing so by UN troops. Later in the month, the British Foreign Office official, H. F. T. Smith (later to become head of the British security service) coolly considered the means by which the impasse could be broken. He envisaged two possible solution:

> The first is the simple one of ensuring Lumumba's removal from the scene by killing him. This should in fact solve the problem since, as far as we can tell, Lumumba is not the leader of a movement within which there are potential successors of his quality and influence.[39]

Smith's second solution was to transfer more constitutional powers to the Congolese president. He breezily concluded: 'Of these two possibilities, my preference (though it might be expressed as a wish rather than a proposal) would be for Lumumba to be removed from the scene altogether, because I fear that as long as he is about, his power to do damage can only be slightly modified'.

What is so striking about this is not just the author's casual discussion of the assassination of a democratically elected politician, but the fact no attempt seems to have been made to withhold the document. It was released to the national archives in 1991 under the standard 30-year rule, despite the fact that it rather undermines repeated British denials that assassination is or ever has been used as an instrument of policy. It is difficult to think that the vetting teams at the Foreign Office would have allowed the release of a document from the 1960s in which one of its officials calmly contemplated the assassination of a European politician or, more generally, a white one.

From 1959 onwards, British policy began to move towards an acceptance of the need to bring African nationalist leaders into the bargaining process, but that innate suspicion of African politicians in the minds of British politicians far from disappeared. Iain Macleod, appointed colonial secretary in October 1959, whose famous calculation of the 'lesser risk' persuaded him of the need to make an imaginative approach to nationalist leaders in Northern Rhodesia and Nyasaland, remained, along with most of his senior colleagues, remarkably hawkish in his attitude towards Lumumba in the Congo. Indeed one sometimes feels that the murderous hostility towards Lumumba was a form of displacement therapy for British politicians and officials who had meekly to accept the wind of change elsewhere in Africa.

Macleod faced formidable obstacles in attempting to change the course of British policy in Africa. As we have seen, the threat of a settler Boston Tea Party had far from abated, and during the tense negotiations over the Northern Rhodesian constitution in February 1961 the threat became so great that the British grew closer than they ever had before or would do since to contemplating an armed invasion of central Africa. Macleod faced opposition in Cabinet to concessions to nationalist leaders that might wreck the federation, and he had a distinctly fair-weather friend in the prime minister, Harold Macmillan. Under the circumstances, he found himself in the slightly bizarre position of having to highlight the potential for violence of Kenneth Kuanda's hitherto largely non-violent political movement the United National Independence Party (UNIP) as a means of justifying bringing Kaunda into the bargaining process.

This tactic is clear in a letter Macleod wrote to Macmillan in March 1960 describing his first meeting with Kaunda in Lusaka. Macleod claimed:

> [...] I told Kaunda in forcible terms that I wasn't impressed by demonstrations and that I won't deal with violence in any form, that if he wanted to show himself a true leader he must first show that he could control his own followers and I invited him to go out to the very large crowd that was gathering at the gates of Government House to tell them to go away and to make a speech advocating non-violence and finally to call off demonstrations. To my considerable surprise he did this. The crowd dispersed without a murmur, he later made a speech advocating non-violence and there was not a single banner or placard in sight when I left next day. All this was in fact rather impressive and showed some control, if he wishes to exercise it, over the party.[40]

The message was extremely clear – here was a movement with considerable potential to create unrest and violence, but with a leader who could
contain that violence if kept on side. To do so, however, it would be necessary to offer concessions. Macleod reinforced this message when record-
ing a meeting with Kaunda at the Colonial Office in May 1960. Although
the sentiments themselves are largely attributed to Kaunda, Macleod
himself was clearly eager to commit them to paper. Macleod recalled that:

> Kaunda put forward the familiar thesis that the ordinary African
> thought that independence in the Congo had only been achieved
> because of violence and that the Nyasaland talks had been secured
> because of violence [...]. Kaunda said that he would try to put over as
> far as he could a policy of non-violence and also to explain, as I had
> explained to him why there could not be immediate constitutional
> advance. But he added that he might well be committing political
> suicide in doing this. For myself I am sure there is some truth in
> this when one looks at the other leaders of the UNIP in Northern
> Rhodesia. He added that it would make a great deal of difference if
> some undertaking could be given that after the federal review there
> would be some sort of discussions.[41]

The argument that by making an imaginative concession the British
government would pre-empt violence and ensure African nationalism
developed on 'moderate' lines was at the heart of Macleod's hard-fought
battle to secure a major increase in African political representation in
the Northern Rhodesia constitution of February 1961. In June, Welensky
succeeded in forcing the British government into a partial retreat on
the Northern Rhodesian constitution. In August, UNIP responded by
launching a campaign of violence and disorder. In a sense, this simply
reinforced in concrete terms the argument Macleod had been making
to his colleagues since his first visit to central Africa the year before. In
considering whether to respond by reopening talks about the Northern
Rhodesian constitution with a view to shifting the balance of advantage back in favour of the Africans, the minister of state at the Colonial
Office, Lord Perth, acknowledged that such concessions would tend to
demonstrate 'violence pays'. Yet in setting down the pros and cons of
reopening talks, he made clear that he did not see this as an overriding
factor. He described the considerations as follows:

> The main 'cons' are that any change would be a concession to vio-
> lence; is not wanted by the unintimidated African; and would be

going back on our agreement with Welensky who would be bound bitterly to oppose such change. The 'pros' are that the changes would ensure a period of peaceful constitutional progress rather than continuing the possibility of serious unrest; should avoid loss of African goodwill and perhaps that of the world as it is hard to show that the present hurdle is not deliberately set higher for Africans than Europeans; and that they are limited and in practice should not affect the election.[42]

The Colonial Office duly concluded that the balance of advantage lay in reopening talks. Indeed, in a sense, this strategic outbreak of violence had served the interests of the Colonial Office, in allowing it to tear up the agreement reached in June over the Northern Rhodesian constitution, and to return to something like Macleod's original conception of the constitution. It was vital, however, that Kaunda should be able to turn off the violence in order to achieve the 'period of peaceful constitutional progress' that would justify the granting of concessions.

In his own subsequent writings, which stressed his party's reliance on Gandhian principles of non-violence, Kaunda conceded this strategy existed against a background of the threat of both settler and African nationalist violence and disruption. He recalled a meeting in 1958 with Benson, the governor of Northern Rhodesia, at which Kaunda and his then colleague Harry Nkumbula set out their demand for the end of the Federation. According to Kaunda, Benson:

> heard us out and then said to me, 'Mr Kaunda, don't you realize the whites would paralyse government if we accepted your demands?' I replied, 'Are you saying, Your Excellency, that for our demands to be met, *we* have got to be in a position to paralyse government?' He did not answer.[43]

In a fascinating passage, Kaunda acknowledged that his policy of non-violence drew much of its strength from the threat that violence might result from the failure to respond to peaceful demands. He argued:

> While the party was following instructions and avoiding violent confrontation I was shrugged aside as irrelevant; when widespread violence became a real possibility, I was suddenly seen as a rational alternative to the so-called 'men of violence'[...]. I suspect that Gandhi and his *satyagraha* policy became much more attractive to the British government when Nehru's National Congress began

rioting in the streets. It is the stars and the dark night again – the play and counter-play of violence and non-violence. Just as the stars do not stop shining when the night has gone, so non-violence has its own validity quite apart from violence. Nonetheless, it is not wise for the pacifist to be too self-righteous about the 'men of violence' – their very existence often guarantees his effectiveness.[44]

In the period leading up to full independence, it remained crucial that the nationalist leaders in the northern territories should be able to keep violence to an 'acceptable level', so as not to encourage press or parliamentary opposition in the UK to the final transfer of power. In July 1963, concerns that Hastings Banda, by then firmly established as elected prime minister of Nyasaland, might not be doing so, prompted K. J. Neale of the Central Africa Office to pen a remarkably cynical minute spelling out what 'acceptable levels' were. He noted:

As far as I know there has been little press or parliamentary interest in the N Rhodesia situation although the security record there, including political violence against Europeans, has been very considerably worse than in Nyasaland over the past two years and might well deteriorate further. The fact is that although there are some serious underlying tendencies in the Nyasaland situation (common to all Africa) recent incidents have been comparatively trivial and blown up in order to discredit Dr Banda. In my view the Nyasaland record in law and order over recent years – and currently – compares favourably with that of any other territory in Bantu Africa at comparable stages of constitutional development and it is worth bearing this in mind when dealing with this subject. It is no use expecting a highly sophisticated concept of national behaviour to appear overnight in the rapidly advancing African territories where the political froth is running down the side of the glass. But Nyasaland, unlike Kenya, Congo and N Rhodesia has avoided killing Europeans, and for that we should be thankful to Dr Banda.[45]

There are disturbing reminders here of the British government's more recent policy towards Robert Mugabe's Zimbabwe. The contrast between the Thatcher Government's apparent wish to downplay the massacre of the regime's Ndebele opponents in Matabeleland in 1983–86, and the indignant protests of subsequent British administrations over the invasion of white farms, suggests that keeping violence at 'acceptable levels' continues to involve avoiding harming Europeans.[46]

What can we conclude from these various reflections on the use and threat of violence in central Africa? The British government promised that the creation of the Central African Federation would herald a new era of racial partnership in the region. What it actually did was to enhance white settler power, in a fairly naked surrender to threats of disruption from the settler community. As the European leaders of the Federation set about entrenching that power still further, ministers in London seemed oblivious. What mattered was that their chosen collaborators could maintain the appearance of order and stability.

In order to compete for power, African nationalism had therefore not merely to shatter that illusion of stability, but to convince London that it potentially had as great an ability as the settlers, if not greater, to challenge British interests in the region. Ultimately, the Southern Rhodesian nationalist movements failed in both respects before 1965. These threats would resurface periodically whenever settler leaders felt London was not responding to its concerns. Far from offering concessions to the African majority, settler leaders sought to entrench their influence still further. The British government recognized this, but chose to tolerate it, so long as the federal and Southern Rhodesian administrators proved themselves effective allies – which is to say so long as they maintained what appeared to the outside world to be political stability.

Under such circumstances, Britain effectively created conditions in which any group competing for power had to demonstrate it had the capacity to disrupt the illusion of peace and normality projected by the settler-dominated regimes. As the case of Nyasaland in 1959 demonstrated, African nationalists had to face the prospect that any challenge to this established order would be met by force, the brutality of which was exacerbated by British perceptions of the 'savage' African. Paradoxically, however, by 1960, when the British government was beginning to contemplate significant advances in African representation, there was virtual complicity between nationalist leaders and British ministers to exaggerate the threat of nationalist violence in order to offset the influence of white settlers over UK policy. Even under relatively peaceful circumstances, then, the threat of violence was a significant factor in the choreography of end of empire.

Notes

1. D. Anderson, *Histories of the Hanged: Britain's Dirty War in Kenya and the End of Empire*, London, Weidenfeld and Nicolson, 2005; C. Elkins, *Britain's Gulag: The Brutal End of Empire in Kenya*, London, Jonathan Cape, 2005.

2. See e.g. H. Bennett, 'The British army and controlling barbarisation during the Kenya emergency', in G. Kassimeris, ed., *The Warrior's Dishonour: Barbarity, Morality and Torture in Modern Warfare*, Aldershot, Ashgate, 2006, pp. 59–80; D. Branch, *Defeating Mau Mau, Creating Kenya: Counterinsurgency, Civil War and Decolonization*, Cambridge, Cambridge University Press, 2009.

3. For an account of the treatment of the records of British colonial administrations on independence, which provides a useful background to the Hanslope Park case, see M. Banton, 'Destroy? "Migrate"? Conceal? British strategies for the disposal of sensitive records of colonial administrations at independence', *The Journal of Imperial and Commonwealth History*, 40, 2, 2012, pp. 323–337.

4. For three fascinating accounts of the trial ('Ndiku Mutua and others v the Foreign and Commonwealth Office') by the historians who advised the claimants' legal teams, see D. Anderson, 'Mau Mau in the High Court and the "lost" British Empire archives: Colonial conspiracy or bureaucratic bungle?', *The Journal of Imperial and Commonwealth History*, 39, 5, 2011, pp. 699–716; H. Bennett, 'Soldiers in the court room: The British Army's part in the Kenya Emergency under the legal spotlight', *The Journal of Imperial and Commonwealth History*, 39, 5, 2011, pp. 717–730; and C. Elkins, 'Alchemy of evidence: Mau Mau, the British Empire and the High Court of justice', *The Journal of Imperial and Commonwealth History*, 39, 5, 2011, pp. 731–748. For a full transcript of Mr Justice McCombe's judgment in favour of the claimants on 21 July 2011, see www.judiciary.gov.uk/Resources/JCO/Documents/Judgments/mutua-v-ors-judgment.pdf, accessed 26 June 2012.

5. R. Gott, *Britain's Empire: Resistance, Repression and Revolt*, London, Verso, 2011; B. Grob-Fitzgibbon, *Imperial Endgame: Britain's Dirty Wars and the End of Empire*, London, Palgrave, 2011; D. French, *The British Way in Counter-Insurgency, 1945–1967*, Oxford, Oxford University Press, 2011.

6. P. Murphy, *British Documents on the End of Empire: Central Africa*, Parts I & II, London, The Stationery Office, 2005.

7. See P. Murphy, 'A police state? The Nyasaland Emergency and colonial intelligence', *Journal of Southern African Studies*, 36, 4, 2010, pp. 765–780.

8. The National Archives, Kew (hereafter TNA) DO 35/7559, Whitehead to Home, 16 March 1959.

9. TNA, DO 35/7558, Whitehead to Home, 22 October 1959.

10. TNA, PREM 11/3075, Brook to Macmillan, 10 February 1960.

11. The classic exposition of this myth is in Smith's own memoir. See I. Smith, *The Great Betrayal*, London, John Blake, 1997.

12. P. Murphy, *Party Politics and Decolonization: The Conservative Party and British Colonial Policy in Tropical Africa, 1951–1964*, Oxford, Oxford University Press, 1995, pp. 73–74.

13. Entry for 5 March 1959, P. Catterall, *The Macmillan Diaries: Prime Minister and After, 1957–66*, London, Macmillan, 2011, p. 203.

14. Murphy, *Central Africa*, Part II, 2005, pp. 399–401.

15. Ibid., pp. 402–403.

16. P. Murphy, ' "An intricate and distasteful subject": British planning for the use of force against the European settlers of Central Africa, 1952–1965', *English Historical Review*, CXXI, 492, 2006, pp. 773–774.

17. TNA, PREM 11/3949, 'Record of a conversation at Admiralty House on Wednesday, 9 November 1960'.
18. P. Murphy, ' "Government by blackmail": The origins of the Central African Federation reconsidered', in M. Lynn, ed., *Retreat or Revival: The British Empire in the 1950s*, London, Palgrave, pp. 53–76.
19. TNA, DO 35/1390, 'Future policy in Central Africa', Colonial Office memorandum for Oliver Stanley, June 1943.
20. C. Baker, *Development Governor: A Biography of Sir Geoffrey Colby*, London, British Academic Press, 1994, p. 290.
21. Murphy, *Central Africa*, Part I, 2005, p. 197.
22. TNA, CO 1035/119, Minute by Morgan, 6 July 1956.
23. D. Goldsworthy, *British Documents on the End of Empire*, series A, vol. 3: *The Conservative Government and the End of Empire 1951–1957*, part II, London, The Stationery Office, 1994, pp. 307–310.
24. Murphy, *Central Africa*, Part I, 2005, pp. 423–426.
25. Ibid., p. 426.
26. Murphy, 'An intricate and distasteful subject', 2006, pp. 755–763.
27. See e.g. J. N. Pieterse, *White on Black: Images of Africa and Blacks in Western Popular Culture*, London, Yale University Press, 1992.
28. TNA, PREM 11/2783, Minute by Brook, 20 July 1959.
29. Murphy, *Central Africa*, Part I, 2005, pp. 375–377.
30. *House of Commons Debates (Hansard)*, vol. 601, cols 290 and 337, 3 March 1959.
31. *Nyasaland: State of Emergency*, Cmnd 707, March 1959, paragraph 25.
32. TNA, CO 1035/143, 'The emergency conference of the Nyasaland African Congress held at Blantyre on the 24/25 January 1959', 13 February 1959.
33. B. Simpson, 'The Devlin Commission 1959: Colonialism, emergencies and the rule of law', *Oxford Journal of Legal Studies*, 22, 1, 2002, pp. 17–52.
34. Ibid., p. 37.
35. Murphy, *Central Africa*, Part II, 2005, pp. 29–34.
36. Ibid., p. 28.
37. P. Murphy and J. Lewis, '"The old pals' protection society?" The Colonial Office and the British press on the eve of decolonisation', in C. Kaul, ed., *Media and the British Empire*, London, Palgrave, 2006, pp. 55–69.
38. Murphy, *Central Africa*, Part II, 2005, pp. 27–28.
39. Ibid., pp. 167–169.
40. Ibid., pp. 129–130.
41. Ibid., pp. 141–142.
42. Ibid., pp. 253–255.
43. C. M. Morris, ed., *Kaunda on Violence*, London, Collins, 1980, p. 50.
44. Ibid., p. 53.
45. Murphy, *Central Africa*, part II, 2005, p. 384.
46. For a trenchant discussion of reactions to the massacres, including that of the Thatcher Government, see I. Phimister, 'The making and meaning of the massacres in Matabeleland', *Development Dialogue*, 50, 2008, pp. 197–212.

Part III
Confronting Internationals: The (Geo)Politics of Decolonization

8
Inside the Parliament of Man: Enuga Reddy and the Decolonization of the United Nations

Ryan Irwin

This chapter explores the decolonization of the United Nations (UN) in the late 20th century. It considers two interlocking riddles: first, was third-world nationalism – defined as the movement that crystallized at the UN General Assembly at the height of post-war decolonization – distinct from the non-governmental movements that allegedly remade the global community during the 1970s? Second, did trends within the Afro-Asian world influence the human rights revolution that became so ubiquitous after 1970?

Numerous historians have offered answers in recent years. Roland Burke, Frederick Cooper, Jan Eckel, Mary Ann Heiss, Akira Iriye, Paul Gordon Lauren, Erez Manela, Mark Mazower, Michael Morgan, Samuel Moyn, Glenda Sluga, and Jay Winter, among others, have advanced arguments about decolonization's relationship to rights discourses in the 20th century. For some, decolonization gave life to the human rights project and laid the foundation for the transnational social movements of the post-1960s era. For others, the rights movement emerged as a minimalist alternative to the grand designs associated with state planning in the global South. For others still, both decolonization and human rights were Gramscian chimeras that disguised the growth of Western hegemony during the late-20th century.[1]

This chapter's approach grows from a simple historiographical observation: scholarship on human rights and decolonization has focused almost exclusively on large structures and intellectual abstractions. Few historians have looked at how specific individuals shaped – and were shaped by – the networks that linked post-colonial politics to human rights movements. This chapter attempts to fill a void by looking at the life and times of a seemingly unimportant UN bureaucrat: Enuga

Reddy. At first glance, Reddy was merely one of hundreds of low-level functionaries who worked at the UN during the Cold War. His 35-year career unfolded mostly in the crevices of world politics and it ended relatively quietly in early 1985. 'I do not think of myself as great or not great', Reddy commented in response to a question about this legacy. 'If I had to choose, I would choose the latter'.[2]

Refuting Reddy's self-assessment is not my goal. The argument here is merely that Reddy's life sheds useful light on the questions posed above. As a UN employee, he had a front row seat at the General Assembly's transformation during the 1950s and 1960s, when African and Asian nationalists stepped onto the world stage and set themselves to the task of remaking the organization's raison d'être. During this tumultuous period, Reddy worked at the UN Apartheid Committee, collaborating closely with nationalist diplomats as they combated racism in southern Africa. Moving to the UN Secretariat's Unit on Apartheid in 1966, Reddy spent much of the 1970s quietly recasting the anti-apartheid struggle in the language of human rights and striving to expand the role of non-governmental organizations within the UN.

Reddy was never a main actor in the dramas he lived through. Looking at this period through his eyes merely provides a window to consider how individuals and political causes influenced the intellectual movements of the late 20th century. His efforts provide insight into the way bureaucrats experimented with the meaning and form of anti-racist and anti-colonial politics during the Cold War. Reddy's activities also shed light on historiographical debates about how and when decolonization changed the UN. Finally, Reddy's life illuminates the strange relationship between political strategy and the phraseology of rights in the years after African independence. This chapter examines several moments in Reddy's long career; moments that not only set his professional trajectory at the UN, but also reveal much about decolonization's contorted relationship with human rights, broadly defined.

Reddy's path from India to the UN was unexpected. He came from wealth. His father was a manager in a mica-exporting company north of Madras (now Chennai), in the small village of Gudur, and Reddy's family resided comfortably at the interface of the British colonial world and the Indian subcontinent. Mica prices were high throughout the depression of the 1930s, and Reddy was insulated from many of the hardships that accompanied the final stages of British imperial rule. Although he understood that 'times were bad [... his] attention was on [his] studies'.[3] Always the youngest of his classmates, Reddy learned English and Telugu before he turned four and he enrolled in the fifth grade at age seven. 'I come from a well-knit family', he later explained.[4] A supporter of Mahatmas Gandhi, Reddy's mother had given away 'all her jewellery [...] in 1933 during [Gandhi's] tour to collect funds for the uplift of the Harijans (untouchables)', and his father served as the president of the Indian National Congress in Gudur during the pre-war years, spending three months in jail for *satyagraha* in 1941. Both parents saw education as the stepping-stone of independence.[5]

Reddy attended Madras Christian College (MCC) during the early 1940s. Even then, the city was one of India's most populous urban centres, and while MCC was a Scottish missionary school with roots in colonial history, its campus was alive with the fervour of Indian nationalism during the Second World War. 'It was an intensely political period', Reddy recalled. 'My grades suffered because of strikes, meetings etc. While my father was prepared to go to jail he discouraged me from getting into trouble by more active involvement'.[6] The writings of 'Gandhi and [Jawaharlal] Nehru were everywhere in those days', inspiring middle-class Indians to imagine a social order without the British Raj.[7] As a student, Reddy gravitated towards a particular brand of socialism. He believed in Gandhi's vision of *swaraj* – especially the notion that true self-rule required self-transformation – but found special inspiration in Nehru's expositions on economic development, scientific growth, and state-led planning. 'India had to build [...] the future lay in the city not the village', he reflected.[8] Independence necessitated technological advancement, and true legitimacy flowed from the government's ability to distribute 'food, clothing, housing, education and sanitation' to India's people.[9]

With this in mind, Reddy left home in 1946 to attain a degree in engineering from the University of Illinois in the United States. It was a portentous decision, born from his passions and his family's growing anxiety about India's political instability. Reddy initially believed he would return to India after a few years, but his plans began to change when he arrived in New York. Having missed the start of the spring term, he enrolled instead at New York University, and then entered a public administration programme at Columbia University. His interest in engineering and government planning slowly gave way to an obsession with international relations. 'Western politicians and academics were denouncing nationalism as a menace' in those days, and Reddy fell in with a cosmopolitan niche of students who rejected the paternalism they perceived around them in higher education. 'For us in India (and in other colonial countries) nationalism meant striving for national freedom from colonial domination and exploitation by other countries', he explained. 'For them nationalism was the cause of conflicts in Europe. Their definition suited the imperialists.' For Reddy, this disjuncture was institutionalized inside and outside the classroom:

> My first professor on international relations [...] explained imperialism by drawing a diagram on the black board to show that it is like water flowing from a higher level to a lower level – from an advanced country to a poorer country. Those were the days when students learned the theory that people in temperate climates were superior to those in warmer climates. All that could have been offensive if I did not have a sense of humour.[10]

Reddy's commitment to anti-racism deepened within this milieu and as he completed his course work he began to think seriously about life as a permanent expatriate. His reasoning was partly personal – he fell in love with a Turkish student at Columbia in 1948, and neither he nor his future wife wanted to return to India against the backdrop of the sectarian and religious violence engulfing that country during the late 1940s. Professional considerations also weighed on Reddy's mind. With the creation of the UN three years earlier, New York had become the epicentre of international politics. The UN – which reflected several distinct internationalisms – provided a forum to express new views about racism's past and imperialism's future.[11] At the 1946 General Assembly meeting, for instance, Vijaya Lakshmi Pandit, India's first delegate to the organization, had shocked the West by collecting enough votes to lodge an official complaint about South Africa's discrimination against people of Indian descent, a resolution that purposefully cast racism as incompatible with membership in the post-war international community. The UN was a place where diplomats like Pandit, as well as individuals such as Reddy, could seemingly challenge the intellectual norms of the time.[12]

Nine months before his wedding in 1950, Reddy attained an entry-level position at the UN Secretariat. 'I used to say, "I had to forget all I was taught at the university and think with my blood"'.[13] His ideas tended to fit with the mainstream of mid-century Indian internationalism. Like Nehru, Reddy felt that world federalism and decolonization went hand in hand. 'The world, in spite of its rivalries and hatreds and inner conflicts, moves inevitably towards closer cooperation and the building up of a world commonwealth', Nehru had argued in 1946. 'It is for this one world that free India will work, a world in which there is the free cooperation of free peoples, and no class or group exploits another.'[14] Political life flowed through the UN, in other words. It was a mind-set with wide appeal during the late 1940s. Two sides of a common conceptual coin, sovereignty and interdependence were the imagined panaceas for capitalist greed and colonial racism – and the supposed prerequisites of real social change and shared economic prosperity.[15]

It was not by accident that India's first post-war diplomatic initiative was a complaint against South Africa. Apartheid, which began to crystallize as a coherent political ideology in the inter-war years, posited that territorial autonomy and economic development required neither racial equality nor international co-operation. According to apartheid's architects, South African whites could provide each ethnic group in South Africa with autonomous control of land and financial resources to achieve development on their own terms, making apartheid an agent of – rather than an abomination against – decolonization. Race equality, according to Afrikaner planners, was merely a misguided ruse that violated the Biblical lessons of Babel. This argument was rife with problems, most obviously its inability to explain the white community's continued exploitation of non-white workers, but such contradictions did not prevent apartheid's theorists from garnering support in many pan-European circles during the early Cold War. At stake was a fundamentally different assessment of racial equality's relationship to decolonization. Expert planning was essential still, but white paternalism now stood as the prerequisite of economic freedom and self-government.

Reddy was already invested in the fight against South African racism when he relocated to New York. In 1943, his cousin had given him three pamphlets about life in Durban. Written by Yusuf Dadoo, Peter Abrahams and Bill Andrews, the documents explained the plight of Indians in Johannesburg and detailed the hardships facing South Africa's mine workers. Initially, Reddy's 'sympathies were with the Indians in South Africa', but he took cues from Indian nationalists at the UN. 'Nehru and others always believed that we [had] to join with Africans, not only in South Africa but all over Africa', he explained.[16] In 1946, Reddy had joined the Council on African Affairs (CAA), a volunteer organization created in 1937 to spread information about Africa, and he began to make regular sojourns to the group's library on 26th Street to read newspapers from the Union, specifically *The Guardian* and *The Bantu World*. When members of the African National Congress (ANC) visited New York in November 1946 to protest against apartheid at the UN, Reddy participated in a picket line at South Africa's consulate and attended a meeting at Harlem's Abyssinian Church, where

ANC members spoke with Indian diplomats Vijaya Lakshmi Pandit and V. K. Krishna Menon. 'I was not interested in the Cold War and other things', Reddy reflected. Such affairs were 'relatively minor, in a sense'. He and the diplomats he idolized 'felt very strongly [...] and took it up, the question of South Africa [...] and tried to get support from other countries, and, in fact, build up support in the public'.[17]

Reddy's new co-workers did not share his passion. The 'atmosphere was oppressive' at the UN in those days, Reddy recalled. 'Most of the UN officials were from a few Western countries – the United States, Britain, Canada and France,' and a 'substantial number of them had been working for the US Office of War Information and other agencies'. As the Korean War escalated, McCarthyism swept through the organization and many of Reddy's like-minded colleagues found themselves cast out of the parliament of man for ideological reasons. Reddy worked initially for a research unit that gathered information about the Middle East and Africa, giving him an opportunity to read African papers on 'company time'. His co-workers included a Greek diplomat, a Canadian Jew, an Egyptian diplomat and two American secretaries – and they bickered constantly about the place of racial equality in the UN. When India and twelve other states asked the 1952 General Assembly to consider 'race conflict resulting from apartheid, the Greek head of the section called me in for a chat', Reddy remembered. For nearly an hour, his superior lectured him about the UN Charter's scope and meaning, lamenting India's interference in South Africa's domestic problems. '[W]hen the UN Charter was signed, India was not there', Reddy responded. The 'real India was not there, and we had an attitude, a different attitude towards the charter than some of the Western countries – it was a psychological thing.' Apartheid was simply incompatible with decolonization. He didn't like that at all, and within a week Reddy had been moved to a new unit. 'Supposedly', Reddy scoffed retrospectively, the UN 'staff [was to] be objective, neutral and all that sort of thing'.[18]

Reddy plodded along for a decade, writing research papers on varied topics as he learned the ins and outs of the secretariat's byzantine bureaucracy. 'I survived in this oppressive atmosphere', he explained later, 'because of my faith that the situation would change, at least partially when more Asian and African nations [became] independent'.[19] The situation indeed altered in 1960, as second-wave or African decolonization remade the membership of the UN General Assembly. At first, Reddy stayed cautiously on the sidelines: his interactions with the UN's newest delegates and diplomats limited to casual exchanges in the building's cafeteria. 'They were not [...] rich [enough] to go to the more expensive restaurants [in New York], so I would meet them' and talk about 'current events, politics, and decolonization'. Within twelve months, however, professional doors began to open. As a result of diplomatic manoeuvring at the 1961 General Assembly, the UN's newest members successfully established a committee – to be directed by African and Asian countries – to hasten full decolonization throughout the global South, which gave way in 1962 to a similar committee that monitored and confronted the problem of apartheid in South Africa. Reddy was tapped to be secretary to this latter group, an opportunity he embraced with relish. 'Rightly or wrongly, I had a feeling that I [had] not [done] enough' up until that point, he reflected. 'India's freedom' was meant to be 'the beginning of the end of colonialism [... but] I had not made enough sacrifice for India's freedom'. Now it seemed possible 'to compensate by doing what I could for the rest of the colonies'.[20]

Working for the Apartheid Committee was like a breath of fresh air. 'We all thought alike', Reddy said. 'We were all against apartheid and so on', and without American, British, or French representatives, the group 'didn't have the Western problem', making it 'easier to work together very closely'.[21] Historians are beginning to understand the implications of this moment. The UN's original 51 members had hailed exclusively from Europe, the Americas, and parts of the British Commonwealth, and the political order they forged together at Bretton Woods, Dumbarton Oaks and San Francisco in 1944–45 had been designed to buttress – not erode – pan-European legitimacy.[22] However, as Reddy's experience highlights, the meaning of the UN's founding documents was not static. As Reddy moved into his new office in early 1962, the decolonization drama was reaching a turning point. In the same moment that the UN created new committees to promote anti-apartheid activism, the General Assembly elected U Thant – from newly independent Burma – as its fourth secretary-general, and announced that the UN's next decade would be dedicated to the development needs of the global South. 'There were still 51 white states' at the UN, an observer explained crassly, 'but the Afro-Asians now totalled 53', signalling that an organization invented by Europeans to be a bulwark against another great power conflagration was now being reinvented in the spirit of pluralism and anti-colonialism.[23]

Reddy drove none of these events, but worked nonetheless in the eye of the storm. The anti-racism agenda, the centrepiece of which was the fight against apartheid, helped focus the diverse impulses underlying the UN's political transformation.[24] South Africa 'is a museum piece in our time, a hangover from the dark past of mankind, a relic of an age which everywhere else is dead or dying', an African diplomat argued in 1962. 'This is Africa's age – the dawn of her fulfilment, the moment when she must fulfil her destiny' by winning the 'fight for noble values and worthy ends, and not for lands and the enslavement of man'.[25] The centrepiece of this movement was showing that '[c]olonialism and racism' – cast as mutually constitutive problems – '[were] the source of *all* the troubles which afflict[ed] mankind' in modern times. Apartheid, by framing itself as a benign reformulation of the decolonization experience, constituted an existential threat to this campaign.[26] It had to be both delegitimized and destroyed, and as Reddy's compatriots plotted a course forward they embraced a two-part strategy that worked to isolate Pretoria within the UN and push the Security Council towards sanctions that would end white rule in Africa.

There were two theoretical pathways to UN sanctions. First, support could be built for action through the General Assembly. While Article 2 (7) of the Charter explicitly forbade the organization from 'interven[ing] in matters which are essentially within the domestic jurisdiction of any state', Article 14 gave the assembly the ability to recommend measures for the peaceful adjustment of any situation that threatened the 'general welfare or friendly relations between nations'. If the UN's new members could convince enough countries to endorse a resolution that cast apartheid as a clear threat to international peace and security, Article 2 (7) would be moot and the Security Council would be permitted to take action under the provisions of Chapter VII, which outlined the Council's role in dealing with member-state aggression.[27] So long as the General Assembly resolution framed apartheid as a 'clear threat to international peace and security', the argument could be made that South African issues were transnational in nature and required an international solution.

Alternatively, nationalist diplomats could focus their efforts on the South African government's tentative legal claims in territory of South West Africa. By 1960, the International Court of Justice (ICJ) had already issued a series of advisory opinions that condemned the Union of South Africa's refusal to place its First World War era mandate under the recently expanded UN trusteeship programme. Further action would require a formal, contentious ICJ case and a binding judgment at The Hague. If the Court ruled against the Union, the Security Council would be obliged to take action under Article 94 of the UN Charter, which outlined the its role in enforcing the Court's decisions. In this scenario, not only were sanctions possible, but post-colonial nationalists could also argue for a UN intervention in South West Africa if Pretoria refused to accept the Court's authority.

Throughout the early- and mid-1960s, Reddy served faithfully as the bureaucratic page of this diplomatic fight. When a friend expressed unease about his growing boldness, Reddy's response was unequivocal: the 'UN belongs to us [now] – we constitute most of the world'.[28] Reddy's *Reminiscences* detail the many initiatives he spearheaded on behalf of his superiors. Aware that he would 'face disciplinary action in the secretariat' if his 'personal correspondence became known', he nonetheless threw himself into the contest, drafting resolutions and writing speeches for his superiors while he composed reports about the suffering of non-white people in South Africa. '[B]inding sanctions require[d] action by the Security Council', but the secretariat had the ability to act independently on several fronts, and Reddy used what he called his 'inside knowledge' to help isolate South Africa at the UN, regularly publishing reports about political prisoners and government suppression of domestic activism. He also built support discreetly for a special trust fund – organized by Christian activists in London but supported by donations from UN member-nations – that funnelled money to the lawyers and families of South African political prisoners. 'I was prepared to take risks', and do things that were 'improper for civil servants who were supposed to be "neutral"'.[29]

Most notably, Reddy bent the UN's rules regarding non-governmental organizations (NGOs). Although Article 77 gave the UN's Economic and Social Council permission to consult non-state groups in special circumstances, only 'Western university-types' were allowed to present opinions in New York during the 1940s and 1950s because 'strict procedures' policed the 'nature and scope' of consultative work. NGOs participated in the UN as economic consultants and social experts, but rarely had access to political debates. By developing contacts with NGOs and friendships with UN delegations, Reddy made himself into an interlocutor, quietly removing procedural hurdles that blocked anti-colonial activism at the UN while lining up writers, politicians, singers, and students to present 'expert' testimony to the Special Committee against Apartheid. 'I led [the way] in encouraging such participation', he later argued, making it possible for 'the Special Committee on Decolonization, the UN Council for Namibia and the Special Political Committee of the General Assembly' – all of which were formed in the early 1960s – to adopt similar approaches in subsequent years. His aim was to remake the UN's relationship with NGOs: 'I wanted to set an important precedent [...] the NGOs and individuals were not to be treated as "petitioners" but as [equal] participants'.[30]

The Apartheid Committee gave him unusual leeway in this effort. Unlike most special committees, the group lacked Western representatives – its membership included five African states, three Asian countries, two Latin American nations, and one East European state – which provided Reddy with freedom to bend the rules. He knew precisely what he was doing: if invitations and reports were done in the 'secretariat's name, I would have to be "objective" and give the views of the oppressed people as well as that of the South African government'.[31] But the Apartheid Committee reported to the General Assembly directly, giving Reddy a shield to mask the nature of his personal involvement. International politics worked in his favour as well. 'Apartheid had become a bad word after the Sharpeville Massacre', Reddy said, referring to Pretoria's widely condemned and highly publicized 1960 attempt to suppress African nationalist upheaval in South Africa, which resulted in the death of 69 black activists. Neither Washington nor Moscow 'wanted to seem to be for apartheid' because both superpowers hoped to incorporate the decolonized world into the anti-communist and anti-capitalist coalitions, respectively. Consequently, while European representatives grumbled frequently about the methods of the Apartheid Committee, few publicly challenged the objectives of Reddy and his compatriots.[32]

Initially peripheral to the diplomatic chess match that surrounded the sanctions effort, Reddy's quiet efforts grew more important after 1966. Ironically, his prominence grew because of the setbacks of his superiors. African and Asian diplomats successfully cast apartheid as a 'clear threat to international peace and security' in the mid-1960s – marshalling support for resolutions in 1964–65 that explicitly announced that 'action under Chapter VII of the charter [was] essential in order to solve the problem of apartheid'. However, the Security Council refused to accept the logic that undergirded Afro-Asian demands: the General Assembly, the argument went, was not designed to dictate when and where the UN applied economic sanctions. When Africa's legal team lost the South West Africa case at the ICJ in 1966 – eliminating the possibility of action through Article 94 – most observers agreed that Pretoria had weathered the storm of third world nationalism.[33] Secretary-General U Thant wrote:

[T]he winds of change have swept right across the continent of Africa from west to east and from north to central Africa but they seem to have come up against a stony wall running somewhere across the southern part of the African continent. Not only have the winds produced no change beneficial to the non-white people living in this part of Africa but the attitude of the white minority groups that have settled in these areas seems to have hardened and the attainment of self-determination of the non-white inhabitants of these regions indefinitely deferred.[34]

When UN delegates began to reconsider their strategy against apartheid in 1966 and 1967 – gathering together for a pair of workshops in Brasilia, Brazil, and Kitwe, Zambia – Reddy participated vigorously in the discussions. In his mind, 'calling for sanctions as the *only* solution – putting all [our] eggs in one basket – was not wise as we had reached a deadlock'. It was time to adopt a wider 'range of actions – some of which [could] be approved by the General Assembly where we had a large majority'.[35] Reddy pushed his superiors to invite numerous liberation groups, solidarity organizations, labour unions, writers, and politicians to the seminars – essentially the individuals who had testified at his behest to the Apartheid Committee in earlier years. The future, Reddy argued, belonged to these NGOs. Although the United States, the United Kingdom, and France would not accept sanctions through the Security Council, 'their democratic traditions' made it possible for non-state activists to lobby against apartheid domestically. Even if the great powers resisted such activism, they 'would find it difficult to take any action to restrict these groups', giving the anti-apartheid struggle new life.[36]

The Brasilia and Kitwe proposals incorporated some of Reddy's ideas and foreshadowed trends that came into focus during the 1970s. On the one hand, participants called for the creation of an official UN office to document examples of South Africa's 'crimes against humanity', and requested more funds for refugee assistance. They also asked for additional donations to the UN trust fund that Reddy had helped create a few years earlier, and protested against the treatment of political prisoners in South Africa.[37] On the other hand, the rhetoric attached to these pronouncements moved in a new direction. The gathering's press releases and published reports linked domestic upheaval in Africa explicitly to the policies of discrimination in southern Africa. The 'forces of apartheid' – with Pretoria 'playing the primary role' – were no longer content simply to oppress black South Africans: they were now engaged 'in a deliberate and calculated attempt' to undermine 'the rightful and lawful governments of independent Africa' through 'psychological warfare, espionage activities and sabotage'. Insulated from UN sanctions, South Africa had allegedly gone on the offensive.[38]

This mind-set formed the cornerstone of the vision that emerged from the Brasilia and Kitwe meetings. Although some UN delegates had drifted towards anti-American views after the US takeover of the Vietnam War, delegates generally appreciated that the US, with its unique influence over the United Kingdom and France, and distinctly anti-colonial national narrative, was an essential ally in the fight against South Africa. However, the discussions and presentations at Brasilia and Kitwe offered a different explanation of Washington's relationship to South Africa. An 'unholy alliance' had formed from the 'Cape to Katanga', claimed one pre-distributed paper, supported by a 'giant economic complex' that originated from the US. Economic sanctions were still 'the most appropriate peaceful measures under the UN Charter', but it was 'unrealistic to ignore the fact that the main trading partners of southern Africa' were simply 'unwilling to implement these measures'.[39]

Such sentiment pointed towards an important sea-change. Disillusioned by the limits of their influence at the General Assembly, UN delegates increasingly embraced a vision of the organization that was more in line with Reddy's thinking. In fact the only original 'action' proposal of the Brasilia and Kitwe gatherings focused on information and non-state activism, rooted in the burgeoning conclusion that the UN was best utilized to 'counteract the massive and misleading propaganda campaign' of South Africa and encourage 'NGOs to play a more effective role in opposition to racism and colonialism'.[40] Although neither premise was wholly novel, the meetings effectively formalized the primacy of such tactics over the fight for sanctions and elevated what had been means in the anti-apartheid contest to an end in its own right. The UN would not liberate South African blacks, but it could help legitimize the activities of people and groups that opposed apartheid. The UN's principal importance, in short, came from its ability to enhance the moral legitimacy of non-governmental activists.[41]

Observers recognized the significance of this shift. As the UN Secretariat centralized anti-apartheid information activities in 1967 – a move mandated by the Brasilia and Kitwe meetings and orchestrated by Reddy under the auspices of the new 'special unit on apartheid' – permanent members of the Security Council reflected on the porous boundary between knowledge production and anti-apartheid activism at the UN. In response to the unit's first pamphlet in 1967, a British official commented that while the document was 'an up-dating of similar studies' that had been 'circulated by the special committee on apartheid' in the early 1960s, the 'new format' clearly sought to 'promote publicity through the UN sales network'. The 'evils of apartheid' were as important as giving 'maximum publicity to Western investment in South Africa'. He continued, 'We could of course protest that apartheid is a human rights question and that foreign trade does not determine the political systems within a country, but we would find the UN impervious to this argument'.[42] In Washington, officials worried about the precedent of using UN money to link Western economic interests and white racism in southern Africa.[43] Although the push for sanctions had ground to a halt, the resulting initiatives were making South African racism into a flashpoint in a larger, integrated fight against neo-colonial power in the world.

Not everyone in the secretariat supported Reddy's ideas. G. L. Obhrai, for instance, who also hailed from India, bristled at the creation of the new special unit on apartheid. 'The question seems to me to boil down to this: is the Office of Public Information henceforth to be permitted, indeed required, to function, not merely as a purveyor of objective and factual information about the aims and activities of the UN, but also as a public-relations agency actively engaged in the actual promotion of those activities and the attainment of those aims?' He continued, 'Are we to remain an Office of Information or become an agency for political action?' Quoting former UN Secretary-General Dag Hammarskjold, Obhrai answered his own question:

> The UN should not indulge in propaganda – *for itself or any of the positions taken within the organization*. Thus, public information activities are information activities in the true sense of the word, not a selling operation in any kind of disguise. One sometimes hears it said that there is nothing wrong in making propaganda for something that is good. This argument seems to me to be a very dangerous one, as everyone resorting to propaganda certainly feels that he is serving a good purpose, whatever his aims may be.[44]

Reddy outmanoeuvred his critics. When facing Anglo-American officials, he argued that the unit's emphasis on economic investment simply reflected the on-going discussion among UN member-states. His section was a 'dumping ground for resolutions on any aspect of apartheid'.[45] To bureaucrats like Obhrai, he responded that his proposals were unexceptional. The office of public information was being asked to 'intensify information on the work of the UN organs on apartheid,' but it was not 'undertak[ing] any research or initiat[ing] any "propaganda"', he explained in a memorandum in September 1967. 'The effectiveness of the information would depend mainly on the work of the committee.'[46] Reddy later admitted that his efforts were probably 'improper for a civil servant who was supposed to be "neutral"', but it did not matter.[47] With support from Secretary-General U Thant, anti-apartheid publications proliferated at the UN after 1967, and the special unit on apartheid, despite its relatively modest budget and small staff, took an increasingly important role in articulating and advancing anti-apartheid criticism in the international arena. Capable of linking official committee reports at the General Assembly with papers by the UN Educational, Scientific and Cultural Organization (UNESCO), the International Labour Organization (ILO), and other expert organizations, Reddy's unit helped institutionalize a uniquely activist portrait of the problems in southern Africa.

Reddy saw himself as an innovator. He explained his mind-set in his private correspondence. Because 'the African group [had] ceased to be a dynamic force' after the 1966 ICJ judgment, it was essential to diversify the struggle and reach out to new groups interested in the future of South Africa. 'To keep the issue alive', he explained, 'all organizations' needed 'to engage in great activity at their *own* level and according to their *own* policies'. Some efforts 'may be purely humanitarian. Others may be pacifist or limited to specific aspects, etc. Action at any level is useful. It is only by involvement that people will learn and take the next step'.[48] Reddy hoped to expand the fight against racism by emphasizing individual human rights. His group published reports on topics like education, law, and prison conditions in South Africa, and intentionally built an audience of 'larger groups in the world' with interests in 'humanitarian and human rights' questions. This effort, far from 'diverting the issue,' offered a way 'out of the impasse' at the General Assembly.[49] The UN would provide information on South Africa, encoding apartheid as a global crisis with broad moral implications, and non-state activists and organizations would take autonomous action in their own local environments.

The seeds of this shift towards non-governmental anti-apartheid activism were woven into discussions dating from 1946. Different NGOs had long journeyed to New York for moral support and political leverage in the fight against South African racism.[50] However, a turning point, especially in the debate over South Africa, came in the late 1960s, as bureaucrats like Reddy carved out a new place for NGOs at the UN.[51] The UN Year of Human Rights, 1968, saw South Africa's policies framed as morally unjust because apartheid disregarded liberties inherent to all humans, such as life, security, freedom of assembly, freedom of movement, and equality under law.[52] These linkages, reified by the

UN Office of Publication as it published 'millions of pamphlets in over 60 languages' that year, became the centrepiece of anti-apartheid discourse at the UN in the years to come.[53] Apartheid was illegitimate not simply because it defied the inevitability of decolonization, but because it embodied a worldview that was out of step with the 'shared values of all peoples' in the world community.[54]

What do Reddy's experiences tell us about decolonization's relationship to the wider human rights revolution of the late 20th century? While it is dangerous for an essay on one person's experiences to universalize its findings, Reddy's early life followed an interesting trajectory. Politicized by India's freedom struggle, he gravitated towards the UN for the same reason other nationalists gravitated to the organization in the early post-war years – the UN appeared to support decolonization. Like many mid-century nationalists, he rallied against apartheid because it focused deeper frustrations with racial paternalism. Reddy found the trope of human rights somewhat late and for admittedly opportunistic reasons. Was third-world nationalism distinct from non-governmental activism? Yes, absolutely. Reddy's experience underscores the distinction, and his invocation of human rights – which only grew during the 1970s and early 1980s – came organically from setbacks at the General Assembly.

But does this mean that the common Afro-Asian movement existed in an entirely different conceptual milieu from the human rights revolution of the late 20th century? This is a harder question. In real time, neither Reddy nor his many compatriots dwelled excessively on the meaning of the semantic shift charted here. Today, in fact, most chroniclers of the anti-apartheid story – Reddy included – embrace narrative tropes as Whiggish as any of the histories of Western progress they railed against in the mid-20th century. It would be easy to chalk this tendency up to the flaws of memory, but the truth is more complex. For both third-world nationalists and human rights activists, apartheid was a powerful 'other' – a rallying point that not only sharpened pre-existing assumptions, but also helped define what politicians, intellectuals, and activists thought they believed. To this day, Reddy rejects deceptively the suggestion his views altered from the 1940s to the 1980s. 'Perhaps I lost some of my youthful naïveté', but 'I have always been an Indian nationalist and I've always opposed racial discrimination' – an answer that obscures Reddy's own jagged path to the present. His story compels a third question: Is it possible to define a 'right' – national, human, or other – without something to juxtapose that right against?

The Afro-Asian and human rights struggles did not so much exist in separate milieus as alternative historical moments. Reddy is interesting, in part, because he straddled these moments. He entered the UN at a time when the organization was dominated by pan-European interests and ideas. From his vantage point on the sidelines of history, he watched as the drama of decolonization remade the UN during the late 1950s and early 1960s, and worked diligently to delegitimize apartheid and champion the third-world political project. When decolonization's contradictions began to come into focus, Reddy reached out nimbly to NGOs and, in the process, quietly reimagined both the boundaries of the UN and the nature of international society. He was not one of the 'great men' of the 20th century. But Reddy's life sheds useful light on the individuals and relationships that gave form to the political and intellectual movements of our times.

Notes

1. See R. Burke, *Decolonization and the Evolution of International Human Rights*, Philadelphia, PA, University of Pennsylvania Press, 2010; F. Cooper, *Colonialism in Question: Theory, Knowledge, History*, Berkeley, CA, University of California Press, 2005; A Iriye, *Global Community: The Role of International Organizations in the Making of the Contemporary World*, Berkeley, CA, University of California Press, 2002; P. G. Lauren, *Power and Prejudice: The Politics and Diplomacy of Racial Discrimination*, New York, NY, Westview Press, 1988; F. Logevall and A. Preston, eds, *Nixon in the World: American Foreign Relations, 1969–1977*, New York, NY, Oxford University Press, 2008; E. Manela, *The Wilsonian Moment: Self-Determination and the International Origins of Anticolonial Nationalism*, New York, Oxford University Press, 2007; M. Mazower, *No Enchanted Palace: The End of Empire and the Ideological Origins of the United Nations*, Princeton, NJ, Princeton University Press, 2009; S. Moyn, *The Last Utopia: Human Rights in History*, Cambridge, MA, Harvard University Press, 2010; N. Ferguson, C. Maier, E. Manela and D. Sargent, eds, *The Shock of the Global: The 1970s in Perspective*, Cambridge, MA, Harvard University Press, 2009.
2. Correspondence with Reddy, 15 July 2012.
3. Correspondence with Reddy, 3 September 2008.
4. Correspondence with Reddy, 15 July 2012.
5. Correspondence with Reddy, 20 April 2008; E. Reddy, *Reminiscences of The International Campaign Against Apartheid – With Special Reference to the United Nations*, 8–10, unpublished manuscript.
6. Correspondence with Reddy, 15 July 2012.
7. Correspondence with Reddy, 20 April 2008.
8. Correspondence with Reddy, 5 June 2008.
9. Ibid., For further reflections on Indian nationalism, see M. Gandhi, *Hind Swaraj and Other Writings*, Cambridge, Cambridge University Press, 2009; J. Nehru, *The Discovery of India*, New York, NY, Oxford University Press, 2004; J. Nehru, *Glimpses of World History*, New York, NY, Oxford University Press, 2004, as well as the voluminous secondary literature on this topic.

10. Correspondence with Reddy, 13 January 2009.
11. Interview with Reddy, 3 September 2008.
12. For a useful primer, see E. Luard, *A History of the United Nations*, Vol. 1: *The Years of Western Domination, 1945–1955*, London, Palgrave, 1982; Vol. 2: *The Age of Decolonization, 1955–1965*, London, Palgrave, 1989.
13. Correspondence with Reddy, 13 January 2009.
14. J. Nehru, *India's Foreign Policy: Selected Speeches, September 1946–April 1961*, Delhi, Ministry of Information and Broadcasting, 1961, p. 2.
15. For an introduction, see M. Bhagavan, *The Peacemakers: India and the Quest for One World*, New York, NY, HarperCollins, 2012, and I. Abraham, 'Migration and citizenship in Asian international relations and state formation', in S. S. Tan and A. Acharya, eds, *Bandung Revisited: The Legacy of the 1955 Asian African Conference for International Order*, Singapore, NUS Press, 2008, as well as M. Goswami, *Producing India: From Colonial Economy to National Space*, Chicago, IL, University of Chicago Press, 2004. For a survey of Jawaharlal Nehru's thinking, see J. Brown, *Nehru: A Political Life*, New Haven, CT, Yale University Press, 2003, and S. Gopal, *Jawaharlal Nehru: A Biography*, Vols. 1–3, Cambridge, MA, Harvard University Press, 1976–1984.
16. Correspondence with Reddy, 5 June 2008.
17. Ibid.
18. Correspondence with Reddy, 13 January 2009.
19. Correspondence with Reddy, 20 April 2008.
20. Ibid.
21. Interview with Reddy, 3 September 2008.
22. For an interesting reflection about this period, see Mazower, *No Enchanted Palace*, 2009, as well as D. Bosco, *Five to Rule Them All: The UN Security Council and the Making of the Modern World*, New York, NY, Oxford University Press, 2009; P. Kennedy, *Parliament of Man: The Past, Present, and Future of the United Nations*, New York, NY, Vintage, 2007; S. Schlesinger, *Act of Creation: The Founding of the United Nations*, New York, NY, Westview, 2004.
23. H. Tinker, *Race, Conflict, and the International Order*, London, Macmillan, 1977, pp. 100, 132.
24. G. Sluga, 'The transformation of international organization', in Ferguson et al., eds, *Shock of the Global: The 1970s in Perspective*, Cambridge, MA, Harvard University Press, 2010.
25. Propaganda by Anti-Apartheid Movement, 3 June 1962, BTS 14/11, vol. 4 (sub-files), Archives of the South African Ministry of Foreign Affairs, South Africa.
26. Nkrumah, cited in F. Wilcox, *UN and the Nonaligned Nations*, New York, NY, Foreign Policy Association, 1962, p. 34.
27. *Yearbook of the United Nations*, New York, NY, United Nations, 1961, pp. 108–115.
28. Correspondence with Reddy, 13 January 2009.
29. Correspondence with Reddy, 13 January 2009.
30. Ibid.; see also Reddy, *United Nations, NGOs, and Anti-Apartheid Campaign*, unpublished manuscript.
31. Reddy, *Reminiscences of The International Campaign Against Apartheid*, 16.
32. Correspondence with Reddy, 13 January 2009.
33. For lengthy consider of these issues, see R. M. Irwin, *Gordian Knot: Apartheid and the Unmaking of the Liberal World Order*, New York, NY, Oxford University

Press, 2012. This section of the chapter overlaps with *Gordian Knot*, pp. 144–146.

34. Statement by the secretary-general to the seminar, 25 July 1967, International Seminar on Apartheid, Racial Discrimination and Colonialism in Southern Africa, series 0196, box 12, file 6, United Nations Record Office (UNRO).
35. Reddy, *Reminisces*, 45–46.
36. Ibid. 57.
37. Conclusions and Recommendations of the Seminar, 4 August 1967, International Seminar on Apartheid, Racial Discrimination and Colonialism in Southern Africa, series 0196, box 12, file 6, UNRO.
38. Final Declaration of the Seminar, 4 August 1967, International Seminar on Apartheid, Racial Discrimination and Colonialism in Southern Africa, series 0196, box 12, file 6, UNRO.
39. A Marof, 'The crisis in Southern Africa with special reference to South Africa and measures to be taken by the international community', 4 August 1967, International Seminar on Apartheid, Racial Discrimination and Colonialism in Southern Africa, series 0196, box 12, file 6, UNRO.
40. Report of the International Seminary on Apartheid, Racial Discrimination and Colonialism in Southern Africa held in Kitwe, Zambia, 25 July–4 August 1967, series 0196, box 12, file 6, UNRO.
41. C. Legum, 'The future of apartheid', 4 August 1967, International Seminar on Apartheid, Racial Discrimination and Colonialism in Southern Africa, series 0196, box 12, file 6, UNRO.
42. New York to London, 23 May 1967, FCO 25/706, NA.
43. Report on the Kitwe Seminar on July 25–August 4, 1967, RG 59 General Records of the Department of State, Bureau of African Affairs, POL3–6, NARA.
44. G.L. Obhrai to J. Rolz-Bennett, 9 August 1967, series 0196, box 12, file 6, UNRO, emphasis in original.
45. New York to London, 24 May 1967, FCO 25/706, United Kingdom National Archives (UKNA).
46. Reddy to Narasimhan, 14 September 1967, series 0196, box 12, file 6, UNRO.
47. Personal Correspondence with Reddy, 10 January 2009.
48. Reddy to Tambo, 3 June 1968, Oliver Tambo: Correspondence, E. S. Reddy Collection, Yale University Manuscripts and Archives (YUMA), emphasis added.
49. Ibid.
50. For excellent overviews of early non-governmental anti-apartheid activism, see C. Anderson, 'International conscience, the Cold War, and apartheid: The NAACP's alliance with the Reverend Michael Scott for South West Africa's liberation, 1946–1952', *Journal of World History*, 19, 3, 2008, pp. 297–326; L. V. Baldwin, *Toward the Beloved Community: Martin Luther King, Jr., and South Africa*, Cleveland, OH, Pilgrim, 1995; D. Culverson, *Contesting Apartheid: US Activism, 1960–1987*, New York, NY, Westview, 1999; J. Love, *The US Anti-Apartheid Movement: Local Activism in Global Politics*, Westport, CT, Greenwood, 1985; R. K. Massie, *Loosing the Bonds: The United States and South Africa in the Apartheid Years*, New York, NY, Nan A. Talese, Doubleday, 1997; B. Magubane, *The Ties that Bind: African-American Consciousness of Africa*, Trenton, NJ, Africa World Press, 1987; W. Minter, *King Soloman's Mines*

Revisited: Western Interests and the Burdened History of South Africa, New York, NY, Basic Books, 1986; F. N. Nesbitt, *Race for Sanctions: African Americans against Apartheid, 1946–1994*, Bloomington, IN, Indiana University Press, 2004; G. W. Shepard, *Anti-Apartheid: Transnational Conflict and Western Policy in the Liberation of South Africa*, New York, NY, Greenwood, 1977; and E. Morgan, 'Into the struggle: Confronting apartheid in the United States and South Africa, 1964–1990', unpublished doctoral thesis, Colorado State University, 2009. For broader scholarship on non-governmental activism, Anderson, *Eyes off the Prize: The United Nations and the African American Struggle for Human Rights, 1944–1955*, New York, NY, Cambridge University Press, 2003; T. Borstelmann, *The Cold War and the Color Line: American Race Relations in the Global Arena*, Cambridge, MA, Harvard University Press, 2001; M. L. Dudziak, *Cold War Civil Rights: Race and the Image of American Democracy*, Princeton, NJ, Princeton University Press, 2000; P. M. von Eschen, *Race against Empire: Black Americans and Anti-colonialism, 1937–1957*, Ithaca, NY, Cornell University Press, 1997; G. Horne, *Black and Red: W. E. B. Du Bois and the Afro-American Response to the Cold War, 1944–1963*, New York, NY, State University of New York Press, 1985; B. G. Plummer, *Rising Wind: Black Americans and US Foreign Affairs, 1935–1960*, Chapel Hill, NC, University of North Carolina Press, 1996.

51. For description of this shift, see P. G. Lauren, *The Evolution of International Human Rights: Visions Seen*, Philadelphia, PA, University of Pennsylvania Press, 2003, pp. 233–247.

52. Ibid., p. 246. For introduction to scholarship on human rights, see S. Power, *A Problem from Hell: America and the Age of Genocide*, New York, NY, Basic Books, 2002; M. A. Glendon, *A World Made New: Eleanor Roosevelt and the Universal Declaration of Human Rights*, New York, NY, Random House, 2002; J. Laber, *The Courage of Strangers: Coming of Age with the Human Rights Movement*, New York, NY, Public Affairs, 2005, as well as forthcoming work by Sarah Snyder.

53. *Yearbook of the United Nations*, New York, NY, United Nations, 1968, 536. For instance, when the General Assembly called on the Security Council to expel South Africa from the United Nations in 1974, this request was cast in the language of human rights rather than of post-colonial nationalism. Although the Security Council did not take action, the Assembly nonetheless voted to rescind the republic's credentials. South Africa was unable to participate in General Assembly debates until 1994.

54. Report on the International Human Rights Conference, 22 April–13 May 1968, series 0196, box 12, file 1, UNRO.

9
Lumumba and the 1960 Congo Crisis: Cold War and the Neo-Colonialism of Belgian Decolonization

John Kent

The Belgians had made little effort after The Second World War to prepare their African territory for a future as a self-governing state. Nor had they provided resources, as the French and British did, to assist their colony stand on its own two feet as a participant in the international economy under different political arrangements. The end of colonial rule in the Congo was always unlikely to fit into the traditional Western liberal model of decolonization whatever effort was made by academics. The Congo was a special case with deep colonial roots in the past and enormous implications for the future. The role of the United Nations (UN) was fundamentally altered by the Congo, along with US foreign policy, as turmoil affected politics in Brussels and London as well as a number of important non-governmental actors and African politicians in the Congo. There was also the murder and suspicious deaths of key protagonists Patrice Lumumba and Dag Hammarskjöld. All in all, there was a lot to cover up or distract attention from in the Congo, with the Cold War conflict centring temporarily on the emerging independent states in black Africa.

The inconvenient fact for liberal models of decolonization in the Cold War was that Western policy did not look attractive in the particular and often unique circumstances of the Congo. It was not the vastness of the country and its variety of African ethnic groups that made the Congo so different, but its economic history, located in the Congo Free State of Leopold II. These early experiences before and during the transition to Belgian colonial rule in 1908 provided it with the unique institutions, economic governance, and white-settler attitudes under European rule that made it so different and unsuitable for a smooth transition to African independence.

The first key difference was in the linkages between the Belgian colonial state and the mining companies in Katanga. King Leopold's Free State provided some continuity between the old form of exploitation that had attracted so much international criticism and its modified form (development) that used the Congo's resources under a new guise. 'Responsible' European enterprises would provide capital and take over some concessionary rights while Leopold's old companies could be connected institutionally to the colonial state. In 1900 the Special Committee of Katanga (Comité Spécial du Katanga, CSK) was created as the holding company providing the concessions and incorporating the state as a majority shareholder along with King Leopold's Company of Katanga (Compagnie du Katanga, CK). The latter had important concessions in Katanga from its establishment in 1891 to fend off the expansion of the British South Africa Company. The further need for capital and legitimization was provided by the Société Générale de Belgique (SGB) and the creation of a new operating company in 1906 by combining King Leopold's company with the resources of the British concessionary company Tanganyika Concessions. The latter company had a significant shareholding – 50 per cent in the new operating company, the Mining Union of Upper Katanga (Union Minière du Haut Katanga, UMHK) until the Depression when it sold all but 14 per cent of its UMHK holdings while retaining seats on the UMHK board for three British Conservative politicians and 20 per cent of voting rights. The other half of UMHK shares were held by the SGB. The final element in the state-private enterprise linkage over operating and concessionary dividends was the Congo portfolio. This was made up of a mix of para-state institutions, public utility companies, and shares and bonds issued as securities for exploitation rights owned, and was managed by the Belgian government in Brussels. Its earnings in 1959 were BEF1 billion francs.

The British company Tanganyika Concessions was able to receive significant payments from the extraction of resources in the form of concessionary payments and shares and had holdings in the CSK. These arrangements, going back to Leopold, involved British and Belgian operating, concessionary, and holding companies also having shares in other companies along with the Belgian colonial state. They were still in place in 1960. Thus, the issue of how to disentangle or give up and possibly surrender the earnings they had produced over more than 50 years was bound to be abnormally problematic when compared to other colonies where economic and financial issues were much simpler. Tanganyika Concessions shareholders still received large payments from concessions granted under Leopold.

Whether or not the Belgian colonial administration prepared the path to transferring political power with a view to maintaining economic control of the existing system through an independent neo-colonial state was initially not entirely clear. The role of private companies was not obviously and directly linked to the plans to transfer power as they first emerged in 1958 under the guise of internal autonomy – although they eventually became so. The initial Belgian government proposal was that a Congo state with internal autonomy should first prepare for its own independence before deciding on the form it should take. The Belgian colony was still largely devoid of African administrators or an educated elite who could fill a governmental role. Unfortunately, the riots that occurred in January 1959 convinced the Belgians that independence should be proclaimed as the goal of colonial policy,[1] and in October 1959 Auguste de Schrijver stipulated a maximum of four years before independence.[2] In that short timescale some Belgians, notably those with right-wing views, attached priority to making sure the affairs of highly profitable European capital could remain largely in Belgian hands. Others were attracted by the more liberal ideas of independence whatever the economic importance of the colony for the Belgian state or companies operating within it.

The Belgian Congo's foreign exchange earnings were covering the metropolitan country's deficit, which thus added to the colony's importance for shareholders in UMHK and its Katangan copper production. In Katanga, dominated as it was by highly reactionary settlers, there was also increasing concern about the implications of independence. Some members of the colonial government were equally ill-disposed towards the idea of independence if it involved severing completely all economic and political ties to Brussels. The key point about any election prior to independence was that it should not make this more likely.

At all events a determination that any liberal moves to transfer power would not involve significant costs for the colonial state in equipping the Congo for an independent role was clear. What the Belgians did prepare for, in the wake of a large flight of capital, was passing any colonial public debts to the independent state while not immediately passing on the lucrative investments held in tandem with private companies. Although private Belgian investment in the colony amounted to $3.5 billion, public borrowing, especially that for the belated and inadequate improvements of services, were financed by borrowing in foreign bond markets. The first payments on the loans would be due shortly after independence and were expected to absorb 23 per cent of ordinary Congo budget expenditures. Thus, the newly created state would inherit power and debt with independence at the end of June 1960. The gap between revenue and expenditure produced by the colonial legacy would require an International Bank of Reconstruction and Development loan of $180 million to bridge.[3] If that were not bad enough, the transfer of the economic rights of the colonial state, with their linkage to private companies in the CSK and the Congo portfolio in particular, was not going to take place. Six days before independence the CSK was dissolved and an agreement was reached to transfer two-thirds of its assets to the Congo portfolio and one-third to the CK. None of its assets would be transferred to the new government of the independent state. Of the six managing directors of the CSK, four were appointed by the Belgian government and two were on the board of the CK. The portfolio would continue to be managed in Brussels.[4]

The May 1960 elections would normally have been the liberal precursor to transferring power to significant African collaborators. They had taken place under the Belgian fundamental law (*loi fondamentale*) which requires a *formateur* to determine what government could be established. Whether or not it had been intended that the difficulties of establishing 'national' political parties, as opposed to the politicization of localized ethnic groupings, would guarantee opportunities to divide and still effectively rule such a vast and ethnically diverse state as the Congo, no party won an overall majority. The largest party, and therefore the one whose leader was most likely to form a government, was the National Congolese Movement (Mouvement National Congolais, MNC), led by a radical left-wing demagogue, Patrice Lumumba. The minister in the Congo, Ganshof van der Meersch, was given the task on behalf of Belgium's King Baudouin of appointing a *formateur*, but he was determined to try and avoid a Lumumba Government. As the largest party had won only 36 of 137 seats, Van der Meersch chose to attempt to establish a government of national unity, and some two weeks after the election finally and reluctantly appointed Lumumba as merely *informateur* of such a government.

Whatever the Belgian concerns about Lumumba's potential economic or political policies, or the role of British and Belgian private companies in wanting their arrangements with the colonial state to continue relatively unaffected, this did not end the Belgian efforts to prevent Lumumba acceding to power. When Lumumba made clear that a government of national unity was not possible, Van der Meersch had to fall back on the idea of an anti-Lumumba government that would exclude the leader of the largest political party produced by the parliamentary elections.

Van der Meersch therefore turned to Joseph Kasavubu, a Lumumba rival from the Bakongo people, and a strong supporter of a federal rather than a centralized state. On 21 June Kasavubu was able to report that he could form a government without any elected members of the MNC. What he failed to explain was that members from three parties would not serve if Lumumba were not in the government and Lumumba would not serve unless he formed his own government.[5] In this stalemate, Kasavubu hoped to put his government before the elected assembly, but Lumumba's supporters successfully ensured Kasavubu's nomination for president of the National Assembly was decisively defeated by the pro-Lumumba candidate.

Thus, Lumumba, through democracy, but after this rather ill-tempered process, eventually emerged with the prize of *formateur* to produce his own government. By now, however, there were other balls in play to stop Lumumba. The Americans were already aware that the African tribal political leader Moishe Tshombe, and his party Confederation of Katanga Tribal Associations (Confédération des associations tribales du Katanga, CONAKAT) from the mineral-rich Katanga, were planning the secession of that province as advocated by settler groups, which the Eisenhower Administration was trying to discourage.[6] And there was another possibility of Katanga joining the Central African Federation under Roy Welensky, also at the instigation of Belgian settlers, which would unite the copper-producing regions of Northern Rhodesia with Katanga.[7] The US State Department indicated that 'if this particular province were to separate from the rest of the Congo with European support, it might prevent the depreciation of mining investments in this region, which might be a desirable objective from our point of view'.[8]

European investors in British and Belgian enterprises in the Congo and some members of the Belgian governments in Leopoldville and Brussels were soon to make the same argument.

The impact and meaning of the machinations were noted by the British consul Ian Scott, who became Britain's first ambassador and was critical of Belgian colonial policy. Scott believed the Belgian efforts to prevent Lumumba becoming prime minister were influential in Lumumba's reactions to King Baudouin's speech at the independence-day celebrations in Leopoldville. In what was clearly a provocative speech by Baudouin, Scott recounted how the latter, as part of the independence celebrations, had praised King Leopold's achievements in the Congo, despite the horror and resentment they had provoked at the time. The great work by the Belgians since then was also referred to by the Baudouin in a long list of their alleged benefits to the Congo.

Whatever their truth or falsity, it was clearly not an appropriate time or place to draw attention to them. Lumumba responded by emphasizing (accurately) the racial discrimination practised by the Belgian colonial regime and the settlers supporting it, which almost caused Baudouin to walk out.[9]

There now began a co-ordinated Belgian effort to smear Lumumba, to which the new prime minister soon contributed by alluding to some personal indiscretions and excessive demands on trips to the US. By 19 July the US ambassador, Clare Timberlake, was telling Ian Scott that Lumumba was 'mad', a fact Scott explicitly contradicted in his dispatch to the Foreign Office.[10] Indeed, the day after the independence ceremony, the newly elected Congo leader made a special radio broadcast emphasizing his commitment to the activities of Belgian capitalist enterprises. Nevertheless, perhaps because this could be deemed too little too late, the efforts by Belgium to undermine the new government and discredit Lumumba now had to be stepped up. As with many Cold War situations, the actual situation arising from the threat to the Western way of life's socio-economic status quo presented by radical non-communist left-wing ideas had to be presented under the guise of a communist threat and, if possible, the expansionist goals of the Soviet state, however unrelated to reality.

An important opportunity to begin this arose almost immediately, following a mutiny of the old Force Publique on the night of 5–6 July 1960. The causes of that mutiny were ironically reported differently to the US State Department than they were to the British Foreign Office, with the Americans tending to accept the gloss put on them by the Belgians. The fact that Scott had previously been highly critical of the colonial regime may have encouraged him to look more deeply into the events at the camp at Thysville, some 100 miles from Leopoldville. Scott believed the mutiny had three causes, the first of which was Bangala resentment at Lumumba not giving their ethnic political leader a key governmental role. Second, resentment was exacerbated by having to do extra independence-day duties without adequate financial reward. Then there was the general African dislike of being told by the Belgian officer commanding, General Janssens, that things were not going to change with the achievement of independence, particularly as democracy did not apply to the Congolese Army. As a result of the soldiers at Thysville refusing to serve under Belgian officers, soldiers at Camp Leopold II in Leopoldville also mutinied and Lumumba failed to calm them.[11]

The first indication that something broader was afoot than the mutinies and the settler groups in Katanga's efforts to undermine the new state, was when the Belgian foreign minister suggested to the British ambassador to Brussels that the colonial powers (not exclusively, as the Belgians were no longer a colonial power) should institutionalize meetings on the territories they were responsible for. An odd statement given that Patrice Lumumba and the MNC had just been elected as those responsible for the Congo. Wigny's argument had been provoked by the Congo mutiny, which he was trying to portray as a communist plot. The implication was that a new left-wing government was susceptible to such phenomena unless it could rely on responsible elements for much needed assistance.[12]

Meanwhile, in the Congo, Lumumba decided to immediately announce that all soldiers were being promoted one grade, and his radio message also promised action would be taken against the Belgian officers he deemed responsible for the unrest. By the evening of 7 July, 'refugees' from Thysville began arriving in Leopoldville with stories of rape and pillage by the mutinous soldiers. Lumumba had already met the US ambassador to discuss a bilateral aid agreement, promising to intervene personally if problems were encountered. He did the same thing with the Thysville mutiny by travelling there with Kasavubu early the following day to try and reach agreement with the soldiers, which he duly did. Meanwhile, to add to the communist plot idea floated by the Belgian foreign minister, there was some reality reflected in the atrocities perpetuated against the white population in several parts of the Congo. Scott's report on them on 19 July noted that not a single Belgian was seriously hurt in Leopoldville, despite the exodus of American women and children over the river to Brazzaville. The deaths that occurred over the whole of the country were fewer than twenty, and he pointedly noted the Belgian response 'allegedly to save civilization'. It appeared to Scott that the objective of the Belgians was to drive Belgian civilians to leave, which was absurd unless the objective was to make it more difficult for the Congo to recover from the disturbances.[13]

The day after Lumumba's and President Joseph Kasavubu's Thysville meeting came an indication that this was the case when, after a call for order to the people of the Congo by Radio Leopoldville, the Belgian government announced it was sending 1,200 additional troops to the Congo, which according to Madeleine Kalb was acceptable to Lumumba and Kasavubu if they were limited to 'the protection of persons and property'.[14] These would reinforce the 16,000 troops already in the bases at Kitona and Kamina because of a recent, but as yet unratified, treaty between Belgium and the Congo government. It was the disturbances in Kasai that were now causing most concern to Lumumba.

The same day, the US ambassador expressed doubt about the reliability of the Force Publique and instability resulting from the disparity in certain sectors of the economy between white and black wages. Timberlake thus successfully persuaded Lumumba to approach the UN about assistance for the Congo police force and a reorganized Force Publique, essentially because such help would be less likely to add to the disturbances than the deployment of Belgian troops.[15] On 10 July Lumumba, Kasavubu and 15 Cabinet members had a four-hour meeting with Ralph Bunche, the personal representative of the UN secretary-general, Dag Hammarskjöld, which resulted in an appeal to the UN for 'technical military assistance to help in organizing, strengthening and training the national forces of the Congo for purpose of defence and the maintenance of law and order'. This was to be endorsed by the impending UN Security Council meeting, and the emphasis was somewhat different to restoring order allegedly destroyed by the Cold War communist plot described by Wigny in order to conceal their main role in supporting secession.[16]

However, the focus of debate over the value of Belgian troops or UN assistance in dealing with Congo disturbances suddenly changed on 10 July – although this is often conveniently forgotten. It changed when Belgian troops arrived in Elizabethville Katanga from the base in Kamina, which was far from the area in which non-Africans had been attacked. The Congolese foreign minister, Bomboko, was informed Belgian troops from Kitona would also be dispatched to Matadi to protect the port installations there. They would relinquish the 'security responsibility' as soon as the Force Publique established control. A small detachment at Matadi arrested their European officers on 8 July, although Lumumba arriving the next day secured their release.[17] Communist plots were, in the opinion of some, clearly spreading. The real question was the extent of the Belgian wish to portray the disturbances as indicative of the Lumumba Government's inability to maintain law and order, and therefore to give Belgium reason to reassert some elements of European control. The purpose of the troops in Elizabethville, where there were no disturbances, was made clear the following day when Moishe Tshombe announced that, because of a 'neo-communist Congo government in Leopoldville', Katanga was seceding to become a separate independent state. The arrival of Belgian forces was to ensure Lumumba was less able to use force to prevent the secession that was clearly supported by the copper interests in the UMHK. In the event, Lumumba flew to Katanga to attempt to preserve the unity of the newly independent Congolese state, but was prevented by one of Tshombe's leading supporters, Gottfried Munongo, from disembarking from the aircraft.

Lumumba was now facing not just disturbances connected to the Force Publique mutiny, but a secession in Katanga, and possible one in the diamond-rich area Kasai, where there was ethnic conflict between the Baluba and Lulua. The incident at Matadi was particularly serious, as Belgian troops attacked Congolese members of the Force Publique, killing 12 of them. Despite Belgian claims of a communist plot, the disturbances reflected a series of localized African grievances, except in Katanga. Attacks on whites were used by the Belgians to justify providing troops to support the secession of Katanga and its considerable wealth from a state in which the elected leader was a radical left-wing African nationalist. Lumumba was always likely to oppose the way wealth was extracted by Europeans, operating similarly to the old state of King Leopold, especially if they were not going to pass the gains accruing to the Congolese state to the newly independent government. The humiliation the Lumumba Government was required to accept was made worse when on 12 July 1960 the first Belgian troops landed uninvited in Leopoldville as part of the reinforcements arriving from Belgium, and took over the airport the following day.[18]

In Leopoldville the British ambassador, with an overview of the disturbances, described them as definitely not an uprising of Africans against whites, but an uprising against Belgians, and particular the ones of Flemish origin. Ironically, this served as a catalyst for the continued involvement of Belgians, who were ill-disposed towards the Lumumba Government.[19] The fear and contempt such Belgians had of Africans, whom they would refer to as macaques, bred fear on the part of the Force Publique, according to the British ambassador. He discounted all talk of plots, Russian intrigue or other extraneous factors in the uprisings, which were not against foreigners but the Belgian colonial regime.[20] Scott thus refused to accept the 'deep laid communist plot' connection Wigny was trying to make out to be the cause of the disturbances.[21] Scott was quite clear in explaining to the Foreign Office that the Belgians were 'not willing to accept a transition to the sort of relationship that Britain now enjoys with its former dependent territories', although he offered no explanation of how this may have originated in the institutional connections between the profits of European enterprises and the Belgian colonial state.[22]

By the time Belgian reinforcements arrived in the Congo, the day after the first appeal to the UN, Khrushchev made a statement accusing the West of trying to re-impose colonialism on the Congo. This was the first indication for some in the West that the Cold War had arrived in the Congo. Such Soviet statements were regarded as more troublesome by some Westerners than the uninvited reappearance in the Congo of Belgian troops. It was as yet unclear whether the latter would herald the re-imposition of colonialism in a new guise or simply support the secession of Katanga to permit the interests of shareholders in the European companies to be protected.

Lumumba was now in a dilemma, but his pro-Western foreign minister had already chosen to react to the obvious need to avoid the re-imposition of colonialism by appealing for the dispatch of US troops. As this was being considered by Eisenhower, Bamboko showed Timberlake the telegrams he had sent to Ghana, the United Arab Republic, Sudan, Israel, Libya, Guinea, and Liberia, urging them to support the Congolese request for troops. Timberlake told Bomboko his personal view was that US troops could only be sent under UN auspices, but he urgently cabled Washington recommending the dispatch of two companies to stabilize the situation long enough to permit the peaceful entry of other forces.[23] This was rejected by Eisenhower in order to preserve the importance of using the UN as a more acceptable face of intervention and US influence in Africa.[24]

Lumumba's dilemma was that with the US ruling out intervention and the Soviet depiction of Belgian actions being too close to the truth for Western comfort, he would have to turn to the UN for help. Yet if that was not forthcoming he could well end up with a Cold War choice of accepting help from communist states and their supporters or the re-imposition of a form of colonialism over a failed Congolese centralized state. Lumumba and Kasavubu thus returned to the UN with a more urgent and appropriate request for assistance given the occupation of Njili airport in Leopoldville and the presence of troops in Katanga. The request to the UN on 13 July, therefore, was made not so much for help with law and order and the re-establishment of government authority, but in order to prevent aggression against a two-week-old UN member state. It was thus a request for UN intervention because of the

> dispatch to the Congo of Belgian troops in violation of the treaty of friendship of 29 June. Under the terms of that treaty, Belgian troops may only intervene at the express request of the Congo government [...]. We accuse the Belgian government of having carefully prepared the secession of the Katanga with a view to maintaining a hold on our country [...], The essential purpose of the requested military aid is to protect the national territory of the Congo against the present external aggression, which is a threat to international peace.[25]

Once the secession of Katanga had been announced on 11 July, moves were already under way to ensure Tshombe's new state received more European support. The chairman of Tanganyika Concessions and UMHK board member Charles Waterhouse, a backbench Tory MP, contacted the Foreign Office on 13 July. Until Alec Douglas-Home became foreign secretary on 27 July, after which Waterhouse could meet with the foreign secretary in a social setting, Waterhouse had to make do with officials. He met E. B. Boothby from the Foreign Office as Belgian troops were taking over the airport in Leopoldville, which Boothby thought was a mistake, noting that they should return to their bases as requested by Lumumba and Kasavubu. He also noted that the troops' purpose was not merely to protect lives, but to impose a Belgian solution on the Congo.[26]

Waterhouse informed Boothby that his Brussels contact was telling him the directors of the SGB, including most of the UMHK directors, had passed a unanimous resolution in favour of creating an independent Katanga as indispensable for the security of shareholders' interests. In London, Waterhouse was asking Boothby for Britain to put pressure on the Belgian government to act in accordance with the resolution of the SGB. Two days later, Wigny summoned the British, French, and American ambassadors in Brussels to tell them he hoped they would all give encouragement short of recognition to Tshombe's secessionist regime.[27]

Meanwhile, the UN Secretary-General, receiving the request from Kasavubu and Lumumba, called a meeting of the Security Council to consider it on the night of 13–14 July.[28] The Belgian representative did not simply argue that the intervention had been legal, but justified it on the basis of 'the total inability of the Congolese national authorities to ensure respect for rules that must be observed in any civilized community and by the Belgian government's sacred duty to take measures required by morality and by public international law'. He also pointed out the initial Congolese approval of the intervention of troops to protect the safety of people and property in Luluabourg Kasai, and the actions of Bomboko concerning the appeal to the US and other states to intervene. A Soviet amendment condemning the Belgians for armed aggression was rejected, but the original resolution was passed with Britain and France abstaining and the US and the Soviet Union voting with the majority.[29]

That resolution was abundantly clear in that it called for 'the government of Belgium to withdraw its troops from the territory of the Congo'. It was less clear about when and in authorizing the Secretary-General:

> to take the necessary steps, in consultation with the government of the Republic of the Congo, to provide the government with such

military assistance as may be necessary until, through the efforts of the Congolese government with the technical assistance of the UN, the national security forces may be able, in the opinion of the government, to meet fully their tasks.[30]

But the key and straightforward fact was that the position of the UN and the Security Council was on the line and dependent on Belgian compliance with it in the context of decolonization and neo-colonialism, whether or not Lumumba was 'mad'. Lumumba increased the tension on 15 July with a radio broadcast condemning Belgian aggression and calling for the withdrawal of Belgian troops in line with the UN resolution. At the UN, the Belgian reaction, given the real reason for their intervention, was to inform the Americans that to comply with the resolution on withdrawal would adversely affect NATO's interests in retaining the bases at Kitona and Kamina.[31]

The final component of the Cold War neo-colonial dilemma for the Americans – as opposed to securing the newly independent state's sovereignty entitlement that formed part of the dilemma facing Lumumba in the context of neo-colonialism and Cold War – was put in place after the Security Council resolution when Lumumba and Kasavubu appealed to Khrushchev to follow the situation from 'hour to hour'. They could be brought to ask for Soviet intervention 'if the Western camp does not stop its aggressive act against the sovereignty of the republic of Congo'.[32] Khrushchev replied by congratulating the UN Security Council on acting to end imperialist aggression and restore Congo's sovereignty by the withdrawal of Belgian troops. If, however, the aggression were to continue in defiance of the UN, the Soviets would be in favour of more effective measures on 'the part of the peace loving states'.[33] The Cold War aspect was again blown up by the Belgians as an obvious smoke screen for their Katangan intentions. Scheyven, in the Belgian embassy in Washington, argued that Khrushchev's response gave substance 'to this mounting Soviet threat' that could lead to the Third World War. Thus, according to Scheyven's argument, it would not be appropriate for the West to suppress the Katangan independence movement, as it might become the only part of the Congo available to the free world.[34]

The die was now completely cast as far as the Cold War–colonial dichotomy was concerned, with the issues unmistakably laid out. Would the Belgians and their African supporters under Tshombe be allowed to defy the UN and re-impose some degree of control over the mineral-rich Katanga, whatever the implications of their position as a member of the NATO alliance? Would the Soviet Union succeed in maintaining support for UN resolutions and defy the previous Western dominance of that organization in the years before 1960? Could the Soviets be successfully castigated for Cold War reasons when they were supporting UN resolutions that required actions to prevent the restoration of some elements of colonialism that a US ally was prepared to ignore? And what would Soviet support for the UN and the sovereignty of a newly independent African state actually involve? The icing on the cake highlighting such issues in a neo-colonial context was supplied by Belgian settlers at Njili airport who encountered Kasavubu and Lumumba on 15 July and greeted them with hissing and shouts of 'macaques'.[35]

Washington was of course eminently uncomfortable about the questions now being raised by the Congo situation, let alone by having to answer them. The issues of Belgian compliance with UN resolutions and Congo sovereignty were immediately discussed by the US National Security Council (NSC). The NSC was told that seven members of the Belgian Cabinet were supporting Katangan secession, but that the Belgian refusal to withdraw troops could reasonably be justified until UN forces were in position to take their place.[36] Unfortunately, the Belgians had no intention of doing that, which indicated the real Cold War problem, which of course would have to be presented as a Soviet not Western problem. As it was, the US had gone into the new decade with a belief that supporting the UN was a good international strategy for furthering its Cold War interests against communism. Now, all of a sudden supporting the UN placed the US fairly and squarely in opposition to a NATO state and on the same side as the UN-supporting Soviet Union. The US had hoped to work with the UN and international opinion in the cause of freedom and democracy, but the Congo, and Belgian defiance of the UN, was leading the US towards condoning Belgian neo-colonialism, which Lumumba was likely to broadcast throughout Africa with implications for the UN.

The most obvious line to take to obscure any support for something that would certainly be interpreted as neo-colonialism was the Soviet threat line, which would depend on Lumumba being portrayed as a communist and/or Soviet tool and detract from or justify Belgium's refusal to comply with UN resolutions. As UN troops began arriving in the Congo on the fateful day of 15 July, there was nothing but pessimism from the embassy in Leopoldville. Timberlake believed 'the present government has not the slightest idea of what is happening [...]. Some Belgians on the other hand, particularly the military, have become completely irrational and in many instances have behaved worse than the Congolese'. In Belgium, support for Tshombe was growing, and in Britain the pressure from Tanganyika Concessions was producing Conservative backbench support and government concern about the threat to investors that the use of UN troops in Katanga would present. Even worse was the possible involvement of settlers in the Central African Federation supporting Katangan secession.[37] For UK ministers, the financial threat to British interests that left-wing African nationalists presented was compounded by the fact that almost to a man the Conservative Party's chief financial backers were the principals in Tanganyika Concessions, who were on the board of UMHK.[38]

It was therefore no surprise when an official compromise line with consideration of British/Conservative Party interests was soon established by the Foreign Office in presenting British policy as aiming to achieve a settlement between the Congo and Katanga that would preserve Western, and especially British Conservative Party shareholder, interests. And of course, for the sake of stability, no UN troops should enter Katanga while law and order still prevailed.[39] Nothing was said about the original entry of Belgian troops into Katanga. As in Europe, it would be easier to preserve Western interests if a threat from the Soviet Union could be evoked. That way not only would the issue of neo-colonialism be avoided, but the economic links established by King Leopold's regime would not have to be unearthed. And who would be most likely to unearth them but a left-wing African nationalist like Patrice Lumumba?

The key thus became the role that could be created for Lumumba as 'mad' 'anti-Western' or 'communist stooge' aiming to increase communist influence in the Congo or allow it to be taken over by the Soviet Union. The US had already conflated communism and democratic left-wing ideas in Central America with the argument that advocates of the latter would, like past non-communist Popular Front members, be susceptible to being taken over and controlled by communists. In addition, Lumumba made it easier for his opponents to dress him in anti-Western clothes by his tactless behaviour when he visited the US. The Congolese leader's increasing hostility to the UN's failure to coordinate its policies with his government understandably continued to grow, but it was to have negative consequences for the preservation of Congo's territorial integrity against the reappearance of colonialism.

On 17 July, Lumumba issued an ultimatum to the British general commanding the Ghanaian contingent of UN forces, that if Belgian troops did not leave by 19 July he would call on the Soviets to intervene. The rationale was that the UN, acting through Ralph Bunche, had assured Lumumba that Belgian forces would leave as soon as UN troops arrived. They had been arriving since 15 July, but their very presence, according to the British general, was 'highly explosive'.[40] The Belgian foreign minister was now telling the Americans that Lumumba's recent activities made it clear the Congo problems 'must be looked at in the context of the East–West struggle', which meant the essential thing was to 'get rid of Lumumba', who would otherwise 'be an instrument for a Soviet takeover'.[41]

Meanwhile, back in Washington, on 19 July, Scheyven accepted Belgian troops would withdraw from Leopoldville, which was eventually carried out on 23 July in agreement with Bunche. However, the Belgians subsequently made clear that 'once the UN had restored order' meant 'the restoration of technical facilities and public services' – not much of which 50 years of Belgian colonialism had managed to put in place.[42] Moreover, the State Department was informed the Belgians also had every intention of keeping troops in their Congo bases.[43] It was thus no surprise the following day at a press conference when Lumumba said the UN resolution was not being carried out. It was obvious, according to a member of the embassy staff, that Lumumba regarded the Americans and the UN as co-operating with the Belgians against the Congolese, and that this was why he had read out a Cabinet decision that an appeal should be made to the Soviet Union or a country of the Afro-Asian bloc. Lumumba was increasingly losing patience with the UN, and with a meeting of the UN Security Council scheduled for 22 July its position on the resolution of eight days earlier would be significant for Lumumba in determining whether an appeal for assistance should be made to the Soviet Union or the Afro-Asian states.[44]

One day before that, the NSC had considered the continued Belgian defiance of the UN, and in particular Belgium's refusal to even state openly a willingness to withdraw her forces. Lumumba's response to this Belgian intransigence would obviously have to be considered in the context of the Cold War, and therefore the issue of whether Lumumba was in reality considered by those in the US or elsewhere to be a communist became significant. Prior to the meeting on 21 July, the US government had not specifically examined Lumumba's communist sympathies, but at the round table conference on independence in January 1960 Lumumba had insisted the Belgian communist advisers to one Congolese political party leave the conference. The ambassador in Brussels did, however, note Lumumba's 'unprincipled intelligence' that made him aware of what his listeners wanted to hear. There was also an inconsistency between Lumumba's own statements and the reports that he was receiving money from the Soviet bloc, although that could be explained by the receipt of money from Conakry or Accra that originated in Moscow.[45] As independence drew nearer, the retiring Belgian burgomaster of Leopoldville, George Depi, argued that both Lumumba and his left-wing ally Antoine Gizenga were not committed to the communist cause and could be worked with.[46]

When the NSC met, it was told that the Soviets had not received a request to send troops to the Congo, even assuming they were willing to do so, but there was now evidence, as Herter repeated to Eisenhower, that some Belgians were supporting Katangan efforts to achieve independence,[47] re-emphasizing why the Belgians were refusing to implement a clear Security Council resolution. A traditional Western opponent of colonialism was tacitly approving the actions of a member-state in the NATO alliance that was about to enter the neo-colonial dock. But could this be presented as preventing the expansion of communism by opposing Lumumba? At the NSC, Allen Dulles, head of the Central Intelligence Agency (CIA), was adamant Lumumba was a Castro or worse who had been bought by the Soviets either directly or through the United Arab Republic with a channel to Belgian communists. After the NSC meeting, the State Department Intelligence Bureau (INR) produced an assessment of Lumumba's communism that contradicted that given to the NSC by Dulles. It maintained there was nothing to substantiate the allegations Lumumba was a communist or a communist sympathizer, and that his own pronouncement that 'we are not communists, Catholics or socialist, we are African nationalists' was probably an accurate summary of his views.[48] Timberlake also informed Herter that Lumumba was an opportunist not a communist, which was more in line with his earlier assessment of the man as mad.[49]

Whatever the assessments, the deadlock continued as the Belgians refused to implement a UN resolution and sought to maintain Katangan secession, while Lumumba was threatening to ask the Soviets for support if the UN Secretary-General with troops at his disposal was unable to get a simple resolution carried out and enable the Congo to restore its independence as a unitary state. The deadlock was emphasized when the UN Security Council produced another resolution on 22 July after it was pointed out that the UN had 1,200 troops in Leopoldville, but not a single Belgian troop had withdrawn from the Congo. The resolution of 13–14 July was reaffirmed, with the demand that Belgians now withdraw 'speedily'. How could the US do anything but try and persuade a NATO ally to comply? The price for preventing an open breach within NATO seemed to be undermining the UN for the sake of tolerating actions that appeared to increasingly resemble neo-colonialism.

The UN under Secretary-General Dag Hammarskjöld could best be described as a neutral pro-West body, meaning that the neutralization of Soviet communism in Africa was the overriding goal for Hammarskjöld. The quid pro quo was that the West should behave reasonably and respect the emerging independent African states, while assisting them to become good democratic members of the Western world. The Belgians were doing none of those things. In the wake of the second resolution demanding their troops withdraw from the Congo, the Americans now pleaded with the Belgians to at least make a statement that some Belgian troops would leave the Congo as opposed to eventually returning to Kamina and Kitona. All to no avail, and Prime Minister Gaston Eyskens was quick to tell the Americans that such a statement was not possible for several days because of the inflamed state of public opinion.[50] The small ray of hope was that on 1 August the Belgians announced that they would withdraw 1,500 troops.[51] This was now ten days after the second resolution and just as the NSC in Washington was being informed all African states felt Tshombe was a creature of UMHK (in fact he was more a difficult but important ally). The Belgians had agreed not to exclude eventual withdrawal from the bases, but that would be something for future consideration. Meanwhile, the subversive Soviet provision of food had begun and was threatening to escalate into the sending of technicians.[52]

The whole situation was escalating, and the attempt of the French and the British to support the Belgian argument that withdrawal would create a precedent jeopardizing other foreign bases in Africa ('feeble', according to parts of the State Department) was going nowhere, despite Bureau of European Affairs insisting the bases were 'of enormous importance'. As was now noted in Washington, the Belgian position was becoming more and more untenable both legally and politically.[53] As the mad and irrational Lumumba informed Hammarskjöld that if the UN did not act it would be necessary to go to the Security Council for a third time, Hammarskjöld was very aware the crux of the problem was Katanga. If UN troops were to enter that territory, any excuse for the Belgian presence would be removed, along with the ultimate Cold War disaster for Hammarskjöld of the Soviets entering Africa. For Lumumba, this was secondary to the nightmare of colonialism returning to Africa, but he was informed on 2 August that UN troops would enter Katanga by 6 August. Lumumba was far from pleased as the first resolution required the Secretary-General to consult with his government and provide it with such military assistance as might be necessary. Hammarskjöld had not been doing this as, for him, preventing the Cold War reaching the Congo meant keeping the Soviets out. To place the UN on the side of Lumumba would involve supporting a left-wing leader who could increase Soviet involvement in the Congo. Precisely because Lumumba would oppose neo-colonialism and support compliance with UN resolutions, this made things worse as the Soviets were also urging the possibility of their assistance if the UN were to fail. Thus, at the start of August, the UN had to avoid aligning UN Security Council decisions with the Lumumba Government and the Soviets. Hammarskjöld also had to try and play a more neutral pro-Western role to avoid a member of the Western alliance being more effectively condemned without taking account of the Cold War.

Unfortunately, the idea of Hammarskjöld in a neutral role, getting the UN forces into Katanga and securing the withdrawal of Belgian troops, was prevented by Tshombe calling the use of UN troops in Katanga a 'declaration of war' and promising resistance by all means. Bunche's plane was fired on from the airport roof in Elizabethville on 5 August by a Belgian settler with a machine gun, and neither he nor any other UN personnel were permitted to leave the plane.[54] As the prospect of UN forces confronting Belgian troops and Tshombe's supporters loomed, Bunche telegraphed the UN pointing out that only the immediate withdrawal of Belgian troops could save the situation. The entry of UN troops into Katanga thus had to be postponed for fear they 'might be opposed by force', to the fury of Lumumba.[55] Lodge, the US ambassador to the UN, immediately told Wigny he had to announce an early date by which Belgian troops would leave the Congo. On being told this was impossible, Lodge pointed out that it was the only way of preventing a Soviet victory in Africa: that is by supporting the UN and opposing neo-colonialism. Wigny then claimed that to withdraw without the UN assuming responsibility for the safety of Europeans in Katanga 'would jeopardize his political career'.[56]

Thus, the UN Security Council met again and produced another withdrawal resolution, this time with 'immediately' replacing 'speedily' as it applied to the withdrawal of Belgian troops. And now it was clear that the entry of UN troops into Katanga would be necessary for the full implementation of the resolution. The UN would be off the hook without the risk of falling in with Lumumba if their troops went into Katanga and the Belgian troops left. Again, it was the Tshombe-Belgian-neo-colonial combo that was the main obstacle preventing this. Yet the final clause continued to muddy the water by reaffirming that the UN 'will not be a party to or anyway intervene in or be used to influence the outcome of any internal conflict, constitutional or otherwise', even though what was required from the Belgians was clear.[57]

For Lumumba, what was now clear was that the UN and Hammarskjöld were not going to support his government, despite the resolutions, and were certainly not going to enter Katanga forcefully. Hammarskjöld had to reconcile his commitment to an impartial UN with his partiality for the West and its values over communist ones, which required preventing an increase in Soviet influence in Africa in the face of neocolonialism. This could only be pulled off with enormous difficulty, but not if the West's values were embodied in a commitment to a version of colonialism sustained by uninvited Western forces that were defying UN resolutions. The stalemate could not be broken in the Cold War by the West sanctioning the West, but the longer it went on the more the reputation of the UN was tarnished and the more likely it became the Soviets would become involved in Africa.

The Congo leader then made two mistakes that sealed his fate. First, he made demands on the UN, including the provision of planes to enable him to transport forces to Katanga; second, and more importantly, in a letter one month after the first withdrawal resolution, he focused blame on Hammarskjöld and the UN for the failure to end Katangan secession. With the reappearance of a new form of Belgian control over part of the Congo, Lumumba accused Hammarskjöld of being a puppet of the Belgians just as the latter announced their troops would not evacuate their bases completely.[58] As a result, the Congo government declared it had lost confidence in the UN Secretary-General and called for his replacement.[59] By not concentrating on the failure of some nations to support or implement the resolutions of the Security Council, the result was that Hammarskjöld, not the failings of Belgium and the West, was central and the Secretary-General could more easily avoid a neutral Cold War role tied to support for Lumumba. Worse, problems within the Congo were growing, including the secession of Kasai, anti-Belgian actions, the arrival of communist diplomats, and the stopping and searching of US air force personnel. By condemning the UN and trying to avoid conflict with the US by giving a speech praising America, Lumumba was not only ignoring the US policy of working through the UN as a filter of American policy but transferring culpability onto the UN, which – correct or not – did not distinguish between the supporters of it and those who were reluctant to do so.[60] Hence, it was easier to sidestep reality and make the conflict more of an imaginary one between those supporting communism and the Soviet Union and those, including the Western alliance and the UN, who were against those forces. That was reflected in and reinforced in an 18 August NSC wishful-thinking meeting, which portrayed Lumumba simply as being in the pay of the Soviets.[61]

At yet another UN Security Council session later in the month, Hammarskjöld openly proclaimed UN neutrality. He argued it had no right to resist the Congo retaking Katanga or to assist it in doing so. It was thus no surprise that the Soviet involvement in the Congo moved from the provision of food aid to the offering of ten Ilyushin planes to transport Lumumba's Force Publique to Katanga. By now, more than 2,000 Belgian troops had left, but most Belgian forces remained in their Congo bases, prompting Hammarskjöld to announce that the UN would take them over, with Belgian officers remaining in a civilian capacity.[62]

What now made the situation critical for the West in Cold War terms was not the increase in Soviet aid, but the implications of the Hammarskjöld–Lumumba rift for the nightmare scenario for the US. That nightmare would arise if Lumumba next asked, as he was perfectly entitled to do, for the removal of UN forces. Not only would that end any possibility of the US working through the UN in the Cold War in support of newly independent African states, but it would hand the initiative in the emerging African world to Moscow, leaving the West clutching at some discredited version of colonialism. Hammarskjöld had already told the Americans that the 'UN effort could not continue with Lumumba in office – one or other would have to go'. Thus the issues arising from the Belgian refusal to comply with the UN, and the US and Hammarskjöld refusing to align with the Soviets in not condemning their non-compliance were crystal clear.[63] After the Security Council meeting on 22 August, Hammarskjöld reinforced the message that Lumumba must be broken,[64] essentially to preserve the West's Cold War position in the Congo that was being threatened, but not by the Soviets. Yet he was knocking on a door that Wigny had already opened. As Herter had pointed out in July, the Americans would look for a better alternative to Lumumba, despite the embassy in Leopoldville informing him Lumumba was not a communist and probably not communist-orientated. Thus it was doubtful if the Soviets could establish reliable continuing influence. That was now not the point, just as in the 2003 Iraq war weapons of mass destruction were not the point except for presentational purposes.[65] By late August, the NSC was being advised Lumumba's removal would open the way for 'new arrangements' and the Special Group or committee arising from Eisenhower's annual revision of US national security policy, which was now responsible in theory for supervising covert actions, was planning special operations against Lumumba.[66] Unlike action against Katanga, which would pose problems in terms of Belgian and British reactions, actions to eliminate Lumumba could be justified by his permitting Soviet interference in the Congo.

Ironically, it is highly unlikely the Soviets would have interfered, apart from their diplomatic representatives, however 'subversive' in Western eyes they may have been. Their 'interference' came later with money to Gizenga's regime in Stanleyville, a dubious investment if ever there was one, which the Soviets came to realize only after the CIA had managed to steal their money.[67] In any case, it was small beer compared to what the US provided to further assist the corruption present in the Congo. And that is without any money that may have been given to support the dismissal of Lumumba. Soviet interference was the provision of food aid and ten Ilyushins.

What had Lumumba done? Because of his objections to neo-colonialism he was preventing the US, Belgium, the West and the UN from presenting a united front in the Cold War against the Soviets, which for a brief moment was centred on winning the hearts and minds of the people and governments of the newly emerging African nations. Worse, he was doing it because the West and the UN were prepared to tolerate defiance of the UN Security Council, and oppose the apparent acceptance of an uninvited incursion of Belgian troops as part of that neo-colonialism that the secession of Katanga and the preservation of European capitalist interests represented. Sture Linner, a Swedish official acting as under-secretary to the secretary-general, had indicated the extent of this by relaying to Hammarskjöld an account of his meeting with 25 members of the Katangan business community, including the head of UMHK in Katanga. The group had greeted him with curses, spat at him, and accused him of being a criminal before spending time portraying the dire consequences of UN intervention in Katanga. Later that day, 21 members of the group returned and explained they were under strict instructions from Count Harold Aspremont, Eyskens's chief of staff, who had been on a special mission to the Congo in July, before resigning his position to become head of a technical assistance mission to Katanga in August, to ensure Europeans stayed at their posts. He had instructed them to sabotage the UN mission or they would be put in jail. In the first week of December he was appointed minister for African affairs in the Eyskens Government.[68]

Unfortunately, the more Lumumba was enraged by this and the more he complained – not about the ineffectiveness of the UN, but about Hammarskjöld's reluctant failure to act appropriately in a neutral Cold

War capacity – the more he was sealing his own fate. The latter was made more of a reality by Kasavubu's legally questionable decision to dismiss him on 5 September. When objections were made in the parliament it was replaced with a government of college commissioners appointed by the Force Publique (now the Congolese National Army [Armeé National Congolaise, ANC]) leader, Colonel Joseph Mobutu. As Lumumba was preparing to challenge his dismissal, the UN forces, unable to act in Katanga because of the resolution preventing them intervening or being 'used to influence the outcome of any internal conflict, constitutional or otherwise', acted to occupy Leopoldville airport and prevent forces supporting Lumumba landing from Stanleyville in Orientale province and Kasai. The final irony.

Lumumba was not a communist, even though for some he had to be made out to be one because their way of life, some of which involved making significant profits from European enterprises, had to be maintained. The Cold War socio-economic system that constituted that way of life in the West could not be readily handed over in the Congo in 1960, primarily because of the economic legacies of the Congo Free State and the politics of Belgian colonialism. Even though the Eisenhower Administration and Hammarskjöld did not share these views, they feared something worse replacing them, which had to be avoided by sacrificing victims like Lumumba on the altar of the Western alliance. The gods that received the sacrificial victim were not simply capitalism created in the old context of European exploitation of Africa, but the relatively new gods of internationalism and Cold War, as Lumumba was undoubtedly a victim of the Western Cold War colonial triangle of the US, Belgium, and the UN. Like much human destruction in the less developed world, from Guatemala to Vietnam, the sad ghosts of Soviet victims in Europe may have been present, but the real demons in the Congo were entirely of Western making.

Notes

1. FRUS 1958–60 XIV Africa Memcon Dillon and Wigny, Belgian foreign minister, 13 May 1959.
2. Ibid., 423rd NSC meeting, 5 November 1959.
3. National Archives and Records Administration (NARA), RG 59 755A:00, State Department memo, 'Analytical chronology of the Congo crisis', undated.
4. These questions, known as *contentieux*, were supposed to be resolved by negotiations that did not take place until Mobutu's second coup.
5. NARA RG 59 755A:00 1960–63 Box 1831. Memo by Hugh Cumming, INR, State Dept Bureau of Intelligence and Research, 17 June 1960; W. G. van der

Meersch, *Fin de la Souveraineté Belge au Congo*, Den Haag, Martinu Nijhoff, 1963, pp. 191–299.

6. NARA RG 59 755A:00 1960–63 Box 1831, Brussels to S. of S., 15 May 1960, with account of the ambassador's trip to the Congo, March 1960.
7. Ibid., Elizabethville to S. of S., 7 March 1960.
8. NARA RG 59 755A:00 1960–63 Box 1831, Memcon by Joseph Satterthwaite (AF), of call by Belgian ambassador, Louis Scheyven, 1 July 1960.
9. National Archives Kew (NA) FO371/146639, Report by Ian Scott, 5 July 1960.
10. Ibid., Telegram 302, Leopoldville to Foreign Office (FO), 19 July 1960.
11. Ibid., Telegram 224, Leopoldville to FO, 6 July 1960.
12. Ibid., J Nicholls (Brussels) to Fredrick Hoyer-Millar, FO.
13. Ibid., Leopoldville to FO, 19 July 1960.
14. M. Kalb, *The Congo Cables: The Cold War in Africa – from Eisenhower to Kennedy*, London, Macmillan, 1982, p. 6.
15. NARA RG 59 770G:00 1960–63 Box 1954, Telegram 88, Leopoldville to S. of S., 10 July 1960; RG 59 755A:00, State Department memo, Analytical chronology of the Congo Crisis,
16. Ibid.
17. NARA RG 59 755A:00, State Department memo, Analytical Chronology of the Congo Crisis; NA FO371/146442, Account by Jack Nicholls of the recent events in the Congo recorded in diary form in a letter to Hoyer-Millar, 19 August 1960.
18. Ibid.
19. Ibid., Scott to Hoyer-Millar, 2 August 1960.
20. NA FO371/146640, Leopoldville to FO, 18 July 1960.
21. Ibid., Leopoldville to FO, 22 July 1960.
22. NA FO371/146639, Leopoldville to FO, 20 July 1960.
23. NARA RG 59 755A:00, State Department memo, 'Analytical chronology of the Congo Crisis'.
24. FRUS, 1958–60 XIV, Africa Memcon Herter-Eisenhower, 12 July 1960; Assistant Staff Secretary to Assistant Secretary Goodpaster, 12 July 1960.
25. NARA RG 59 755A:00, State Department memo, 'Analytical Chronology of the Congo Crisis' undated.
26. NA FO371/146639. Minute by E. B. Boothby, 13 July.
27. NA FO371/146642, Account by Nicholls, 19 August 1960.
28. Article 99 of the UN Charter permits the secretary-general to bring an urgent problem to the Security Council, even if it has not been raised by a member-state. Hammarskjöld in 1960 was particularly keen to prevent the communist powers playing a role in Africa.
29. NARA RG 59 755A:00, State Department memo, Analytical Chronology of the Congo Crisis, undated.
30. www.un.org/documents/sc/res/1960/scres60.htm, Security Council Resolution 143, 14 July 1960, accessed 15 January 2014.
31. NARA RG 59 770G:00 1960–63 Box 1954, Telegram 74, USUN to S. of S., 15 July 1960.
32. Ibid., Telegram 136, State Dept to Brussels, 15 July 1960.
33. C. Hoskins, *The Congo since Independence, January 1960–December 1961*, London, Oxford University Press, 1965, p. 129, citing *Soviet News*, 18 July 1960. The American State Department memo 'Analytical Chronology of

the Congo Crisis' received a reply from Khrushchev on 15 July stating the Soviet Union would not shrink from 'resolute measures to curb the aggression'.

34. NARA RG 59 770G:00 1960–63 Box 1954, Telegram 137, State Dept to Brussels, 15 July 1960.
35. FRUS 1958–60 XIV, Africa, Telegram 106, Leopoldville to S. of S., 15 July 1960.
36. Ibid., Record of 451st NSC meeting, 15 July 1960.
37. NARA RG 59 770G:00 1960–63 Box 1954, Telegram 207, Brussels to S. of S., 16 July 1960; Telegram 27, London to S. of S., 15 July 1960; State Department memo, 'Analytical chronology of the Congo crisis', citing Telegram 125, Leopoldville to S. of S., 16 July 1960.
38. John F. Kennedy Library (JFKL), National Security Files, (NSF) Country Series Congo, Box 30, Telegram 3657, USUN to S. of S., 4 May 1962. The information was provided to the Americans by Sir Brian Urquhart, a British official attached to the UN staff.
39. NA FO371/146642, Account by Nicholls, 18 July.
40. NARA RG 59 770G:00 1960–63, Box 1954, Telegram 134, Leopoldville to S. of S., 18 July 1960; 755A:00, State Department memo, 'Analytical chronology of the Congo crisis'.
41. State Department memo, 'Analytical chronology of the Congo crisis', undated, citing Telegram 200, Brussels to S. of S., 16 July 1960.
42. FRUS 1958–60 XIV Africa, Memcon, Herter-Belgian Minister of State-Scheyven, 19 July 1960.
43. RG 59 755:00, State Department memo, 'Analytical chronology of the Congo crisis', undated.
44. NARA RG 59 770G:00, 1960–63, Box 1954, Telegram 166, USUN to S. of S., 21 July 1960; NARA RG 59 770G:00 1960–63, Box 1954, Telegram 178, Leopoldville to S. of S., 20 July 1960.
45. FRUS 1958–60 XIV Africa, Memcon US Ambassador Brussels (Burden)–Lumumba, 25 February 1960.
46. Ibid., Telegram 469, Leopoldville to S. of S., 14 June 1960.
47. Ibid., Memcon Herter-Eisenhower, 19 July 1960.
48. NARA RG 59 755A:00 1960–63 Box 1831, Intelligence memo, 'Communist influence in the Congo', by Hugh Cumming (INR), 25 July 1960.
49. FRUS 1958–60 XIV Africa, Telegram 235, USUN to S. of S., 26 July 1960; Kalb, The Congo Cables, 1982, pp. 36–39.
50. NARA RG 59 770G:00 1960–63 Box 1954, Telegram 237, State Department to Brussels, 22 July 1960.
51. NARA RG 59 755A:00 1960–63 Box 1831, Memo by Woodruff Wallner, International Organizations, 1 August 1960.
52. FRUS 1958–60 XIV Africa, Record of 454th NSC meeting, 1 August 1960.
53. NARA RG 59 755A:00, State Department, 'Analytical chronology of the Congo crisis', undated.
54. NARA RG 59 770G:00 1960–63 Box 1955, Telegram 300, USUN to S. of S., 3 August 1960.
55. FRUS 1958–60 XIV Africa, Memcon Herter-Scheyven, 5 August 1960.
56. NARA RG 59 770G:00 1960–63 Box 1955, Telegram 347, USUN to S. of S., 7 August 1960.

57. www.un.org/documents/sc/res/1960/scres60.htm, Security Council Resolution 146, 9 August 1960, accessed 13 April 2014.
58. NARA RG 59 770G:00 1960–63 Box 1955, Telegram 412, Leopoldville to S. of S., 16 August 1960.
59. NARA RG 59 770.G, State Department, 'Congo chronology', 2nd phase, August 1960.
60. NARA RG 59 755A:00, State Department, 'Analytical chronology of the Congo crisis', undated.
61. FRUS 1958–60 XIV Africa, 456th meeting, 18 August 1960.
62. Dwight D Eisenhower Library (DDEL), White House Office Files, Staff Secretary Goodpaster, International Series, Box 3, Situation Reports 35, 46 and 47, 19 August 1960.
63. Kalb, *The Congo Cables*,1982, p. 51.
64. NARA RG 59 755A:00, State Department, 'Analytical chronology of the Congo crisis', undated.
65. NARA RG 59 770G:00 1960–63 Box 1955, Telegram 438, State Department to Leopoldville, 12 August 1960.
66. FRUS 1958–60 XIV Africa, Record of 457th NSC meeting, 25 August 1960.
67. S Mazov, 'Soviet aid to the Gizenga Government in the former Belgian Congo, 1960–1961', *Cold War History*, 7, 3, 2007, pp. 425–37.
68. NARA RG 59 770G:00 1960–63 Box 1955, Telegram 349, USUN to S. of S., 7 August 1960.

10
The International Dimensions of Portuguese Colonial Crisis

Luís Nuno Rodrigues

Introduction

This chapter deals with the international dimensions of the Portuguese colonial crisis, focusing on the beginning of the war in Angola in early 1961, and on the reaction of several countries to the problems Portugal was facing in that territory and, in the following years, in Portuguese Guinea and Mozambique. It begins with a general overview of Portuguese colonialism in the context of the Cold War and then analyses the positions taken by the United States, the United Kingdom, France, and the Federal Republic of Germany in 1961 regarding Portuguese colonial crisis. The argument presented here is that Portugal was able to circumvent the difficulties felt in the United Nations (UN) and in the relationship with the United States by developing and strengthening its relations with the above mentioned European countries. Contrary to what Salazar, the leader of the Portuguese government, would claim in 1965, Portugal was not 'proudly alone' in its military efforts in Africa and diplomacy was playing a central role in the Portuguese strategy of resisting decolonization.

Portuguese colonialism and the Cold War

In the last years of the Second World War, the Portuguese government, led since 1932 by Salazar, had authorized the US and the UK to use air and naval facilities in the islands of the Azores. Portugal was officially a neutral country, but it signed agreements regarding the use of the Azores with the British in 1943 and with the Americans in 1944. This last agreement authorized the US to establish a military base in the strategically located island of Santa Maria, Azores.[1]

With the beginning of the Cold War, the Azores reinforced its strategic value as a transatlantic 'stepping stone', and therefore the US negotiated with Portugal for the maintenance of military facilities on the islands. The Portuguese government accepted the request and renewed US base rights in 1946, 1948, 1951, and 1957. These bilateral agreements marked the gradual integration of Portugal within the US 'sphere of influence' in Western Europe during the early years of the Cold War.[2] Multilaterally, Portugal was also invited to participate in the Marshall Plan and to be a founding member of the North Atlantic Treaty Organization (NATO). The Azores, the Marshall Plan, and NATO, therefore, were important instruments for the international acceptance of Salazar's authoritarian regime, following the veto of the Soviet Union, which denied Portugal UN membership in 1946.[3]

During the first decade of the Cold War, therefore, Portugal's allies never put any kind of pressure on Salazar's government: the political characteristics of the regime were tolerated and the reality of Portuguese colonial empire was ignored. The US, as the dominant power in the West, was concerned above all with the restoration of European prosperity and with the containment of the Soviet Union. Africa and the dismantlement of old European empires were left to a second plan. As Thomas Noer explained, American leaders feared a rapid decolonization would 'cripple European economic recovery (and the ability to resist communism) and produce weak and unstable African nations unable to prevent Soviet subversion'.[4] The new Cold War policy of containment was more important than any new initiative in Africa, and this set of assumptions clearly determined the position of the US regarding Portuguese colonialism.

In the 1950s, however, the situation would change. Gradually, European colonial empires in Africa began to disappear. The so-called third world emerged and became a decisive actor in international relations with the Banding Conference, the general condemnation of colonialism, and the 'global Cold War'.[5] The 'liberation phase' of the Cold War had begun. Events like the Suez Crisis and the beginning of the war in Algeria were two other important turning points in this process, and both superpowers were now actively trying to gain 'the loyalties of emerging peoples'.[6]

Portugal, however, remained immovable. The Portuguese government considered the maintenance of its colonial empire in Africa and Asia essential for the survival of the regime and also for Portugal's existence as an independent nation. In 1963 a long-serving US embassy officer in

Lisbon described the importance the Portuguese attached to the survival of the colonial empire:

> The Portugal of today is a small, poor, relatively impotent country. Its area and population are, however, vastly increased if to metropolitan Portugal there are added the overseas provinces and territories. The protected markets and the economic resources of those territories are a further factor in Portuguese thinking, as well as the open frontier and land holdings available to those Portuguese who now or at some time in the near future may wish to emigrate to the overseas territories. But in addition to their political and economic significance, Portugal's overseas holdings are enormously important to every Portuguese as a vestigial link with the glories of the past when Portugal was in every sense of the word a world power and a world leader. To us this may seem romantic and unrealistic, but I am not sure that it is so in terms of Portuguese psychology.[7]

According to these assumptions, and contrary to what happened with other European countries, the Portuguese government was not willing to negotiate or to consider alternatives to the existing colonial rule. Therefore, in the decades after the Second World War the regime used every means at its disposal to resist the 'wind of change': legally, by changing the constitution in 1951 in order to transform the colonies into overseas provinces, allegedly with the same political rights as the metropolitan provinces;[8] ideologically, by adopting the concept of lusotropicalism developed by Brazilian sociologist Gilberto Freyre, and arguing the Portuguese presence in the tropics represented a milder version of European colonialism due to the natural disposition of the Portuguese people to socialize with other peoples;[9] politically, by defeating domestic military and political factions that defended a political solution to the colonial conundrum;[10] and militarily, when all other strategies seemed to fail and Portugal was forced to face the liberation movements in Angola from 1961, in Guinea-Bissau from 1963, and Mozambique from 1964.[11]

Internationally, Portugal was finally accepted into the UN in December 1955 and, since then, this organization put colonialism in general, and Portuguese colonialism in particular, on the spot. As early as February 1956, the UN Secretary-General sent a letter to the Portuguese government inquiring about the existence of non-autonomous territories administered by Portugal. If Portugal was responsible for 'the administration of territories whose peoples have not yet reached a complete form of self-government', its government should, according to Article 73 of the UN Charter, send 'statistics or other technical data concerning the economic, social and educational conditions of the territories for which it is responsible' to the Secretary-General on a regular basis. The Portuguese government answered negatively, arguing that, according to the constitution of the country, Portugal had no colonies and did not administer non-autonomous territories. Its overseas provinces were an integral part of the Portuguese state in the same way that its continental provinces were.[12]

The 14th UN General Assembly (UNGA) of 1959 decided to set up a Committee of Six, in order to find a precise definition of non-autonomous territory. The UNGA also approved a resolution urging all member states 'responsible for non-autonomous territories' to transmit 'information under Article 73, including an indication of the time limits within which self-rule for such territories would be proclaimed'. The following year, the UNGA adopted the report of the Committee of Six, then incorporated into resolution 1541 of 15 December 1960. From this time on, the UN began to consider as non-autonomous those territories that were geographically separate and distinct ethnically and/or culturally from the country administering it, and any territory that was arbitrarily placed in a position or status of subordination. The report was approved by a large majority, although Portugal voted against it. The same General Assembly also adopted Resolution 1514, considering 'the subjection of peoples to alien subjugation, domination and exploitation' as a 'denial of fundamental human rights' and declaring that 'all peoples have the right to self-determination'. Finally, the UNGA approved Resolution 1542, which determined the applicability of the terms defined in the previous resolutions to the Portuguese colonial empire.[13]

Kennedy and the new African policy

This outlook was aggravated by the fact that a few months later Portugal faced, for the first time since the Second World War, outright US opposition to its colonial policy. The new Kennedy Administration decided to vote in favour of a UN Security Council resolution calling on the Portuguese government to 'urgently' introduce 'measures and reforms in Angola for the purpose of the implementation of General Assembly resolution 1514'.[14] The resolution received the favourable vote of the US delegation, although it was not approved. Moreover, it was discussed and voted on 15 March 1961, the day the nationalists of the Union of the People of Angola (União dos Povos de Angola, UPA) launched a major attack on Portuguese positions in northern Angola, starting a war that would last until 1974.[15]

Although the first signs of change in US policy were already visible during the Eisenhower Administration,[16] it was during Kennedy's tenure at the White House that the US radically altered its policy towards Africa. Even before he took office, JFK sent a task force to Africa to analyse the situation on the continent and make recommendations. The task force recommended sweeping changes in America's attitude towards Africa. The US should 'abandon its traditional fence-sitting – arising from links with the colonial powers – in favour of support for African nationalism'. The report argued American policy had failed to keep pace with events in Africa mainly because the US was 'accustomed to deal with Africa primarily through metropolitan powers that controlled the major part of the continent'. As far as the Portuguese territories were concerned, the report was particularly critical of American policy. It deplored the 'widespread impression that the US supports Portuguese colonialism in Angola, Mozambique and Portuguese Guinea', and described Portuguese rule in these places as intolerable. It traced this impression of American support to Portuguese membership in NATO and to the importance of the American base in the Azores. The report believed that 'silence on issues affecting Portuguese Africa is a liability far outweighing any short-term strategic considerations'.[17]

According to these recommendations, Kennedy decided the US delegation should vote favourably on the Security Council resolution of 15 March. This new policy regarding Portuguese colonialism continued through 1961 and early 1962. In the UN, the Americans voted in favour of resolutions concerning Portuguese colonialism in the General Assembly (April 1961), in the Security Council (June 1961), and again in the General Assembly (December 1961 and January 1962).

Moreover, the deterioration of Portuguese–American relations was aggravated by other policies that brought great distress to the Portuguese government. The American government intensified its contacts with Angolan nationalist groups, particularly the UPA which was led by Holden Roberto. The contacts with Roberto, which had already existed before the war, were significantly intensified from March 1961 onwards, with the Department of State instructing the embassy in Leopoldville (where the UPA was based) to maintain close contacts with this nationalist movement.[18] On the other hand, the Administration implemented a new arms policy towards Portugal, officially announced to the Portuguese government in August 1961. During this period the US refused to sell Portugal military equipment destined for non-NATO purposes, ruling out its use in Africa. As US ambassador in Lisbon, Charles Burke Elbrick stated, after informing the Portuguese government of this new arms policy, that this was indeed the 'latest nail in the coffin of United States–Portuguese relations'.[19]

Facing pressure from the US, the Portuguese government reacted with the diplomatic weapons at its disposal, namely the existence of the American military base in the Azores. The agreement, signed in 1957, was due to expire on 31 December 1962. Throughout the Kennedy years, the Pentagon constantly reminded the White House and the Department of State of the crucial military and strategic value of the base.[20] The Azores were defined as 'the single most valuable facility which the United States is authorized by a foreign power to use', essential 'to execute emergency or contingency plans requiring the rapid aerial deployment of ground or air force units to Europe, the Middle East or Africa'. Its loss would have 'the gravest military consequences' and would require a 'major overhaul of US wartime plans'.[21]

Aware of the importance of the base, Portuguese diplomacy played the Azorean 'trump card' shrewdly. In May 1962, Salazar gave an interview to the *Washington Evening Star* declaring he could not agree 'to a renewal of the Azores Base Agreement under the present circumstances'. The Portuguese, Salazar said, were fully aware of 'the treatment that the United States ha[d] given Portugal and would fail to understand if the government were to agree to renew the base rights'. The US had not behaved as an ally of Portugal and, therefore, the Portuguese government had 'no further interest in making the base facilities available'.[22]

Between the Azores and Angola, the Administration was caught in a real dilemma, summarized in the words of Kennedy's special assistant Arthur Schlesinger Jr: 'never enough for the nationalists in Africa and always too much for the Pentagon and Dr Salazar'.[23] Eventually, the arguments from the Pentagon and the Europeanists within the State Department would prevail. The year 1962 marked a new change in the direction of US foreign policy towards Portugal and Portuguese colonialism. In the summer of 1962, the US delegation in the UN (USUN) voted against two resolutions regarding Portuguese territories in the UN Decolonization Committee, and also against a 4th Committee (and then plenary) General Assembly resolution in late 1962. It also abstained on a Decolonization Committee resolution of April 1963 and on the Security Council resolution of July 1963. Finally, it abstained on a Fourth Committee (and then plenary) General Assembly resolution in late 1963. During this period, the only favourable vote on a resolution concerning Portuguese colonialism came in December 1963, on the most moderate Security Council resolution since March 1963. Likewise, the administration reversed its policy on the sale of military equipment to Portugal. Despite the official embargo, in 1962 and 1963 there were several sales of military equipment and a significant quantity of this equipment ended up in Africa, being used by the Portuguese in the colonial wars. Since Washington could base its decision for sale on a simple statement from the American military authorities in Lisbon that the arms were for NATO use, it did not require any official declaration from the Portuguese government on the end-use of these arms and equipment.

The contacts with the Angolan nationalists were also significantly reduced and the USUN and the Department of State were forbidden to receive Holden Roberto. This fact even led Holden Roberto to write directly to President Kennedy in late 1962. Roberto evoked the 'growing indignation of the Angolan people over the identification of US policies regarding Angola with the aims of those of Portugal', and said he was 'extremely disappointed at the stand of the US, which voted, together with Portugal and South Africa, against the overwhelming majority of the world's states'.[24]

Finally, in April 1962, the US made a major financial contribution to Portugal allowing the Export-Import Bank to provide about $55 million to 'finance the export of US steel' for the construction of a bridge across the Tagus in Lisbon.[25]

During the presidency of Lyndon Johnson, the behaviour of the US regarding Portuguese colonialism continued to follow the trend started in 1962. Gradually, the US ceased to exert any significant pressure on the Portuguese government to accept the principle of self-determination, and silence became the keyword as far as Portuguese colonialism was concerned, with the Administration completely absorbed and submerged by other problems, such as Vietnam.[26]

In sum, it is fair to say there was a significant change in terms of American policy towards Portugal, and especially towards Portuguese colonialism, in the early months of the Kennedy Administration. On the international level, Portugal felt strong difficulties. In the context of the Cold War, the major power of the Western world was now openly criticizing Portuguese colonialism, supporting liberation movements, and defending self-determination and independence in Portuguese Africa. The change in American policy towards Portugal was, however, short-lived. After 1962 another reversal in American behaviour took place. The USUN began to abstain or to vote against resolutions on Portuguese territories; the US authorized several sales of military equipment to Portugal; the contacts with the Angolan nationalists were significantly reduced and the USUN and the Department of State were forbidden from receiving Holden Roberto. Although neither Kennedy nor Johnson returned to a position of open support for the Portuguese presence in Africa, the importance of the military base in the Azores had convinced American leaders to moderate their stance towards Portuguese colonialism.

The oldest alliance

The position of the United Kingdom towards Portuguese colonialism was always more cautious than that adopted by the Kennedy Administration in 1961. When the US decided to change its policy towards Portugal, the USUN consulted with its British counterpart. The reaction from the British was one of scepticism and caution. Andrew Cohen, from the British delegation, stated the UK had already tried 'on a number of occasions at a pretty high level' to convince the Portuguese government of the need for change in its African policies. These conversations produced 'no results whatever.' Although the UK was 'increasingly embarrassed' by the situation in Portuguese Africa, Cohen noted that it was not 'realistic' to believe 'anything can be done about it'. He then asked the American representatives that 'whatever the US does vis-à-vis Portugal, please don't say the United Kingdom suggested it'.[27]

Therefore, when the Security Council voted the resolution on Angola, on 15 March, the UK abstained. The reasons behind the British attitude derived from its historic alliance with Portugal and the fact that the UK was itself a colonial power. Andrew Cohen expressed to the head of the American delegation, Adlai Stevenson, his 'great concern that decisions of this sort by the Security Council would open the way for similar intrusion of the UN into the political development of British East African territories during the next few critical years'.[28] While the Foreign Office agreed with the US 'on the general objective of securing some modification of Portuguese policies respecting their African territories', it also believed that in view of the Portuguese sensitivity 'great care should be exercised to avoid the impression of ganging up on Portugal and perhaps precipitating Portuguese withdrawal from NATO'.[29]

Two months later, Lord Home arrived in Lisbon for an official visit. Never mentioning in public the idea of self-determination, Home met with Salazar to discuss the situation in Portuguese Africa. He insisted on the importance of African nationalism and tried to convince the

Portuguese government to accept some degree of participation by Africans in local government. He also referred to the need to offer some positive signs to the Americans. Salazar, however, did not make any concessions and accused the US of being 'ignorant' about African affairs.[30] In early June, when the Security Council met again to discuss the situation in Angola, the UK abstained on a resolution deploring 'the large-scale killings and the severely repressive measures in Angola' and considering 'the continuance of the situation in Angola [...] likely to endanger the maintenance of international peace and security'.[31]

Gradually, however, the British felt compelled to change their policies towards Portugal and Portuguese colonialism. First, there was an acute awareness among British leaders of the importance of maintaining the special relationship with the new White House. The Kennedy Administration, moreover, was constantly requesting that the UK adopt a more forceful position with Salazar. Second, the ambiguity of the British government regarding Portuguese colonialism was also a matter of concern to some countries, members of the Commonwealth, who began to express their discontent with the policies followed by Downing Street.[32] Domestically, the Conservative Government also faced some criticism regarding its policy towards Portugal. The visit of HMS Leopard to Luanda on 15 May was discussed in the Parliament and mentioned in the London press. Members of the Labour Party sharply criticized the government for the decision to proceed with this visit, 'in face of the international criticism of Portugal and of the events taking place in Angola'. Denis Healey, the Labour spokesman on foreign affairs, urged Lord Home, the foreign secretary, to reconsider his planned trip to Lisbon.[33] Finally, Church groups were also very active in criticizing the government. On 5 July 1961, the Baptist Missionary Society presented a petition to the House of Commons asking that 'no military supplies be allowed to be sent from the United Kingdom of Great Britain and Northern Ireland to the Republic of Portugal and its overseas territories in Africa'.[34] The House of Commons held a long debate on the situation in Angola. The Labour Opposition used the testimony of the Baptist missionaries 'to indict Portugal for a policy of repression in Angola'. It criticized the British government for failing to take a 'strong stand against Portugal in this connection and, instead, for condoning Portuguese policy by recent actions, e.g. naval visits to Angola and sale of arms to Portugal'.[35]

In late June, the British government decided to adopt a new arms policy towards Portugal. Sales of military equipment destined for the Portuguese African territories were suspended for the time being.

The shipment of materiel for use in metropolitan Portugal continued to be allowed and the UK did not require any formal certification by the Portuguese government on the ultimate use of the equipment.[36] Moreover, in November 1961, the British delegation for the first time sided with the USUN by voting in favour of a resolution creating a special committee to examine the situation in the Portuguese territories and urging all UN members 'to deny Portugal all kind of aid and assistance that it could use to subjugate the populations in the territories that it administered'.[37]

Relations between Portugal and the UK were further disrupted by the annexation of the Portuguese enclaves of Goa, Damão, and Diu by Indian forces in late December 1961. Fearing the imminent military action, Portugal had requested British support on 10 December, officially evoking the 600-year-old Anglo-Portuguese alliance, and asking 'what means can the United Kingdom [...] put at the disposal of the Portuguese government in order to, in conjunction with the Portuguese means, frustrate the above mentioned aggression'. According to the Portuguese foreign minister Franco Nogueira, Portugal had 'no illusions on the final attitude of the British government'. Obviously, the British would not make 'a declaration of war on India'; however, Salazar and Nogueira hoped the British would feel compelled to press the Indian government to solve the problem by 'exclusively political means and to stop the imminent aggression'.[38] The British government replied, as expected, that it could not 'take sides against a Commonwealth member'.[39] Harold MacMillan wrote directly to Nehru, trying to deter him 'from what seemed an act of pure aggression' and 'to hold his hand and try to obtain his purposes by negotiation'. Nehru replied that 'after 14 years in which Indian public opinion had shown extraordinary patience he could now no longer hold his hand'.[40]

Following the invasion of Goa, the UK co-sponsored and supported a Security Council resolution condemning the action taken by the Indian government. The UK representative stated that 'while his government understood the desire of the Indian people to incorporate these territories and their impatience because Portugal had not followed the example of France and Great Britain, it deeply deplored India's decision to use military force to achieve its political objectives'.[41] Despite strong criticism from Salazar and public protests in Lisbon, the Goan affair did not cause any permanent damage to the relations between Portugal and the UK. Throughout 1962 and 1963, the British never voted against Portugal in the UN (with the exception of a UNGA resolution in January 1962) and they also eased their arms embargo. Particularly revealing was a conversation between Nogueira and the British ambassador in Lisbon, Archibald Ross, on 9 November 1962. Ross had just returned from a trip to Angola and Mozambique and was fascinated with what he had found in these two territories. Nogueira asked him if there were signs of 'extermination, oppression, threat to the world peace and security'. Ross replied that those accusations were 'ridiculous'. The British ambassador also declared that the UK was now ready to sell British aircraft to Portugal, and his government only wanted a 'guarantee from us, simply verbal and very vague, that we would not use the aircraft overseas'. Ross made this declaration 'smiling, suggesting that such a guarantee was a simple formality', and did not apply in the case of 'external aggression' in the Portuguese territories.[42]

A few years later there was another moment of tension in the relations between Britain and Portugal, but this was only indirectly related to Portuguese colonialism. The crisis was caused by the unilateral declaration of independence of Southern Rhodesia in November 1965 and Salazar's decision to help Ian Smith and his regime avoid or 'circumvent' the sanctions imposed by the UN. This decision was considered to be against British national interests and caused 'a sharp cooling of relations' with the British Labour Government.[43] Portugal was always supportive of the Rhodesian cause, and in the following years the Portuguese government developed even closer relations of co-operation with Rhodesia and South Africa. These relations eventually culminated in a military agreement signed by these three countries in October 1970.[44]

Nevertheless, it is safe to conclude that during the first phase of the Portuguese colonial wars, until the replacement of Salazar in 1968, Portugal did not feel strong pressure from the UK for it to change its colonial policies or for decolonization. There was a brief period of tension, with a couple of favourable votes in the UN, the announcement of the arms embargo and the Goan episode, but the British position in respect of Portuguese colonialism was marked above all else by 'ambivalence', combining 'complacency' and 'critical disengagement'.[45]

European complicities: Portugal and France

Portugal could also count on support from France and General de Gaulle regarding its colonial policy. Not only were the French sympathetic to Portuguese colonialism, they were also concerned with the possible results of a colonial crisis on Portuguese domestic politics. In August 1963, Marcello Mathias, the Portuguese ambassador to Paris, explained to American representatives that there were several reasons for French support for the Portuguese case in Africa. These reasons transcended the purely African aspect of problem. De Gaulle believed that 'if the Portuguese should lose Angola and Mozambique, the Salazar regime would fall and would be succeeded by a leftist or Castroist type of government'. This would provoke 'parallel upheaval in Spain with similar consequences'. France would then find itself with a 'most uncomfortable neighbour on the southern flank, to say nothing of a disrupted Nato'.[46] On the other hand, de Gaulle was also a persistent critic of American foreign policy. France was never the loyal helpmate the US expected during the Cold War, and instead its policies 'cut directly across US interests all along the board'.[47] Particularly worrisome to de Gaulle was the position of the US regarding the conflict in Algeria. In July 1961, he told Adlai Stevenson that France was counting on the US and 'if the Atlantic alliance abandons France in its efforts to resolve colonial problems the alliance will lose France'.[48]

The French applied the same analysis to the Portuguese problems. When the US ambassador in Paris informed Couve de Murville, the French foreign minister, the US was going to vote against Portugal in the UN resolution of March 1961, Murville merely replied that this American action would create 'one more crisis in the West'. He had already discussed the question of colonialism with the Portuguese government and realized the situation there was 'quite different' from the French one. Portugal was a small country, 'not possessing the prestige and affluence of France', and without its colonies it would be 'vulnerable to Spanish domination'. Murville had visited Portugal twice and he 'understood the Portuguese point of view and felt that they thought of themselves as a "colonial empire" and that to deny them that would completely change their philosophy, way of life, etc.'. Therefore, the French government believed the Western nations should not force the Portuguese to change their policies.[49] According to this position, the French government considered the March 1961 resolution on Angola as 'unreasonable, bad for Portugal, bad for the UN' and establishing an 'undesirable precedent'. The adoption of the resolution would encourage other countries 'to bring any purely propagandistic item before the Security Council'.[50] Reinforcing this position, on 6 April, Couve de Murville arrived at Lisbon for an official visit. The Portuguese press, jubilant, announced the visit as having a special meaning at a 'particularly delicate moment for Portugal'.[51]

On 4 May, in the tripartite meeting between representatives of the US, the UK, and France, the French representatives recognized the situation in the Portuguese colonies was grave, but they pointed out that the change in American policy had the opposite effect on Salazar. The Portuguese had confessed they were planning to introduce reforms in their African colonies, 'but had given up, at least temporarily, because of United States and UN pressure'. Regarding the discussion of Angola in the UN, the French said 'we must not give the impression that we are using the United Nations to put pressure on the Portuguese', and considered, just like their British counterparts, that such action would amount to intervening in Portugal's internal affairs. The French declared they would oppose the calling of a special session of the General Assembly. They believed that a UN intervention in Portuguese territories would only make matters there worse. They also suggested 'perhaps we should simply wait out developments and just ride out any storms which might be raised in the UN'.[52] Accordingly, France abstained on two resolutions on Angola: in April in the General Assembly, and in June in the Security Council.

On his European tour of 1961, President Kennedy met Charles de Gaulle on 1 June. Among other subjects, they discussed the situation in Portuguese Africa. De Gaulle told Kennedy that France was concerned with the Portuguese inflexibility regarding Angola. Portugal was 'making great mistakes and its thinking is not up to the present times'. De Gaulle also said that Portugal should move towards self-determination in its overseas territories and that France would do everything it could to bring about such a change. But the French president did not believe the policy followed by the US was correct and he argued: 'bullying is not the way [...] pushing the Portuguese too hard will only aggravate the problem [...]. Nothing can be done by humiliating the Portuguese'.[53]

Franco Nogueira commented upon the French attitude throughout this period in favourable terms. Despite their interests in Africa, the French did not succumb to what Nogueira called the 'psychological terrorism that characterized the environment in the UN' and were not intimidated by the 'spectacular gestures of the Third World'. Moreover, Nogueira pointed out, President de Gaulle had 'authority and prestige enough to impose moderation on the new French-speaking African countries'. De Gaulle wanted to maintain the connection between Europe and Africa and, in Nogueira's words, he opposed American penetration in that continent. Therefore, France never created any difficulties in the supply of armaments to Portugal and reaffirmed its political support of Portugal, despite American attempts to influence the French government.[54] At the end of 1961, in a rare interview to *Le Figaro*, Salazar praised the French government's 'chivalrous attitude' during the

Goa affair.[55] The French government had in fact declared it was opposed to the use of force in Goa and, after the invasion took place, it expressed its 'astonishment and regret'.[56]

This position remained unchanged in the following years and was visible both bilaterally and within the context of NATO and the UN, where the French always supported the Portuguese position. In December 1963, France was the only country to abstain in a moderate Security Council resolution on Portuguese territories. The French delegate explained to Charles Yost, from the USUN, that this had been a personal decision of de Gaulle. The French president believed the Portuguese government was 'vulnerable internally and its allies should take no step that might weaken it'. Moreover, de Gaulle considered that the Portuguese government 'had shown signs of good will vis-à-vis Africans and this was a good occasion for showing Africans that Portugal's allies would not let themselves be pushed too far on this subject'.[57]

France also became one of the most important suppliers of military equipment to Portugal, delivering 'on a great scale, warships, helicopters, tanks, rifles, guns and ammunition'.[58] This tendency was visible before the outbreak of the war in Angola, with negotiations in late 1960 for the acquisition of Nordatlas, Broussard and T-6 Harvard aircraft. A considerable part of the aircraft, however, would be delivered in late 1961 and 1962 when military operations in Angola were already in full-force.[59] In the following years, the purchases of military equipment from France continued. As an example, in March 1963, the Portuguese government purchased 15 Alouette helicopters. There was no doubt, according to the American embassy in Lisbon, that 'most of the new helicopters will be used in Angola'.[60] Even more important, in September 1964 both governments announced the conclusion of another agreement concerning 'the construction of Portuguese warships in French shipyards'. The agreement provided for the construction of eight vessels: 'four submarines and four frigates of over 2,000 tons each'.[61]

Another important signal of the military and political co-operation between the Portuguese and French governments was the agreement, signed in April 1964, permitting 'utilization by France for scientific purposes of [...] facilities and installations in the Azores archipelago'. The agreement provided for landing rights for aircraft and French vessels equipped with measurement instruments, and contemplated the installation of ballistic missile tracking station facilities. According to the Portuguese minister of foreign affairs, this agreement represented 'one more step in the reinforcement of the traditional ties of friendship between the two countries'.[62] *The New York Times* indicated that the base 'will be used to track ballistic missiles like Polaris, which are to be built in the second phase of France's nuclear arms programme'. The missiles, 'designed to be launched from atomic submarines, ultimately will be armed with thermonuclear warheads'.[63]

The German connection

One of the most important Portuguese diplomatic triumphs in the early 1960s was the development and reinforcement of the relationship with the Federal Republic of Germany (FRG). West Germany gradually became one of Portugal's most important allies, and to the dismay of the US government the Portuguese consciously played the German card when they faced the international difficulties of the early 1960s. Franco Nogueira justified the support Portugal received from FRG in this delicate context. First of all, the Germans were exempted from the debates in the UN and therefore from defining a clear position regarding Portuguese colonialism. Second, German commercial and economic interests in Portugal and in Africa were also considerable. and FRG was interested in developing training facilities for aviation in southern Portugal. Finally, according to Nogueira, German politicians – such as Adenauer, Erhard, and Strauss – had a genuine admiration for Salazar. Therefore, during the 1960s, West Germany maintained a friendly policy towards Portugal, opening financial credits in favourable conditions and increasing German imports from Portugal. The Germans also supplied, 'many times at symbolic prices [...] appropriate planes for the fight in Africa, telecommunications equipment, war material, military vehicles and others'. Nogueira emphasized the role of the German ambassador in Lisbon, Schaffarzyk, who 'believed in Portuguese policy' and whose 'reports and informations encouraged the German government'.[64]

The FRG government never criticized Portuguese colonial policy in public, especially after the beginning of the war in Angola. The official position of the Germans was one of 'total discretion'. But West Germany was equally cautious in not assuming a position of open support that might have caused some kind of embarrassment in its relations with the emerging third-world countries, where FRG had growing economic interests. Therefore, the West German government went so far as to authorize the creation, on German territory, of the Union of Students from Black Africa under Portuguese Colonial Domination, in September 1961, and the Committee for Angola, in March 1964.[65]

This was largely compensated for, however, by the establishment and maintenance of a high level of military co-operation with Portugal. German military support was indeed crucial for the Portuguese war effort in Africa. It should be noted that at least since 1959 the Germans had enjoyed special training facilities in Portugal at the Ota airbase, some 25 miles north of Lisbon.[66] In early 1960, following the visit to Portugal of West Germany's defence minister Franz Joseph Strauss, FRG expressed an interest in acquiring landing rights in the Beja area. The project for the construction of an airbase in Beja developed over the next three years. In January 1962, the US ambassador in Lisbon, Charles Elbrick, reported Strauss 'motoring in the neighbourhood of Beja,' and noted that for the second successive year the Portuguese budget 'contained an item of 50 million escudos (US $1.75 million) for the acquisition of lands for this base'.[67] Strauss himself reported his visit to the American embassy in Bonn, indicating he had met Salazar and discussed the 'bilateral question of Beja air base and small naval harbour that Germans desire to develop for joint use with Portuguese'.[68] A few months later the Portuguese press announced the bidding on the construction of eight hangars to be built at airbase 11, Beja, Portugal, would begin on 18 September. Reporting this information, Elbrick added that 'although it had been known for some time that the airfield facilities at Beja would be constructed, this is the first evidence that these plans were about to be carried out'. Elbrick recalled that 'the financing of this construction is being borne by the Federal German Republic, whose air force will enjoy facilities there'.[69]

More importantly, West Germany was also the main vendor of military equipment to Portugal during the 1960s. Luc Crollen noted that 'immediately after the beginning of the insurgency in Angola', West Germany had delivered 'tanks, machine guns and broadcasting equipment to Portugal with a total value of US $55 million'.[70] In terms of aircraft, FRG sold dozens of Dornier DO-27s and Harvard T-6s that would be used by the Portuguese armed forces in Africa. German technicians from the Dornier aircraft company were in Luanda in April 1961 to assemble the first aircraft to arrive in Angola. By October 1961 there were 16 DO-27s operating in Angola and 24 more were negotiated and sold by September 1962. In November 1963, the Portuguese minister of defence signed an agreement with his German colleague for the acquisition of 46 DO-27s and 70 Harvard T-6s. This last group of aircraft was partly paid for by providing maintenance services for German aircraft in Portuguese facilities. In 1966, 40 Fiat G-91s were also sold to Portugal and promptly transported to Portuguese Guinea.[71]

Other types of equipment were also important. In July 1961, the American embassy in Lisbon reported that the Portuguese air force had recently purchased twelve Saunders-Roe Skeeter helicopters from the West German government. Of these, ten were being assembled at Alverca and two 'were being shipped directly to Luanda for assembly and combat use'.[72] Portugal also became an important producer of the German G3 rifle, the weapon most widely used during the wars in Africa. The Germans ordered some 50,000 G-3s from Portugal, which allowed the Portuguese Fábrica Militar (Military Factory) to access the technology and know-how to produce those rifles for the Portuguese armed forces.[73] In the following years, Portugal also bought significant quantities of pistols and rifles, machine guns, military vehicles, and motorboats from West Germany, and more aircraft from Dornier, Nordatlas, Saber, and Fiat.[74]

Holden Roberto publicly denounced the sale of German military equipment to Portugal in a press conference in Leopoldville on 8 June 1961. He criticized West Germany 'for the alleged sale of 10,000 machine guns to Portugal'.[75] The German foreign office 'categorically denied the allegation', stating 'it is regular policy of the Federal Government to prevent weapons deliveries in areas of international tension'.[76] Officially, the West German government had decided to 'suspend action' on a number of 'pending licences covering export of weapons to Portugal' in view of 'recent reports that German military equipment has shown up in the hands of settlers and Portuguese forces in Angola'. The West German foreign office was now requesting that the Portuguese certify 'the arms are to be retained in Europe for the use of the Portuguese NATO forces'. The American embassy in Bonn was informed on 12 October 1961 that the Portuguese government had refused to provide these guarantees. The West German government asked the US embassy for advice, with American officials in Bonn informing them that the US had recently 'yielded on our decision to require certificates, but are instead requiring end-use investigation by our MAAG (Military Assistance Advisory Group) in Lisbon'.[77]

The military co-operation between Portugal and West Germany was further developed in late 1963 when the two governments concluded a military agreement on the use of the Beja airbase. On 14 October, the Portuguese defence minister issued an official communiqué stating that 'following negotiations with the minister of defence of the Federal Republic Germany,' Portugal granted, 'within the framework of NATO, training and logistics facilities to the German armed forces similar to those granted them by other NATO countries'. The agreement involved, specifically, the 'use of one national airbase, now under construction, for jet pilot training, with special emphasis on aspects of supersonic and low-altitude flight execution, which is difficult in the rest of Europe due to high population density'.[78]

In June 1964, the Portuguese defence minister, Gomes de Araújo, announced the finalization in Bonn of 'various details concerning instructional facilities and logistical matters' resulting from the Portuguese-German bilateral agreement signed in October 1963. Araújo confirmed the agreement was 'being implemented as planned' and that 'in addition to air training facilities at Beja, FRG ground forces will use some facilities at Santa Margarida for a short period each year'. Moreover, 'storage facilities for the peacetime stockpiling of military supplies' would be 'constructed and put in operation'. Araújo also announced that a new hospital to be located at Beja was only the first of several to be constructed, and that within the framework of the agreement, Portuguese wounded from Guinea and Angola are now receiving treatment in German hospitals. Finally, the Portuguese minister recognized that West Germany 'has made a great (and profitable) contribution to the Portuguese overseas military effort over the past two years, particularly through unrestricted sales sorely needed of vehicles and light aircraft'. Portugal was naturally grateful. In a telegram, the American army attaché in Lisbon said, 'Germany in military sense has largely filled vacuum created by the displacement since 1961 of US from number one position previously enjoyed here. Believe West German military activity and influence will continue grow and thrive'.[79]

Economic co-operation between Portugal and Germany also grew considerably during the early 1960s. Luc Crollen noted that 'next to the sale of military equipment, most of which has eventually been used in Africa, the Federal Republic has made substantial financial loans to Portugal'. Crollen mentioned the sums of $41.25 million in 1961, $37.12 million in 1962, and $13.75 million in 1963.[80] This financial and economic cooperation was announced in Portugal by Ludwig Erhard, the West German economy minister, who visited Lisbon in May 1961 accompanied by a large staff of advisors. On his arrival, Erhard 'praised Portuguese financial policies under Prime Minister Salazar' and stated that West Germany wanted to 'facilitate, by every means, the more rapid economic development of Portugal'.[81] At a press conference, Erhard said the West Germans were going to help Portugal in terms of 'material and financial assistance, as well as private investments in Portuguese industry'.[82] A few months later, the American embassy in Lisbon noted the German Krupp Company was already 'concluding negotiations for the investment of $45 million in the Lobito Mining Company in Angola'.[83]

In August 1962, Franco Nogueira met the West German ambassador to Lisbon. The ambassador had recently travelled to Bonn and he declared himself very happy with the situation he found. A year earlier, he had informed his government that Angola and Mozambique would not fall and that the political situation in Portugal would stabilize. His reports were initially received with some scepticism, but now the West German government concluded the ambassador was correct. Therefore, he was in a position to guarantee a loan from the Frankfurt Reconstruction Bank of DM100 million. He recommended the Portuguese government acquire this credit urgently.[84] In late July 1963, the vice-president of the Bundestag, Richard Jaeger, led a delegation of West German politicians and journalists on a trip that took in Lisbon, Luanda, and Lourenço Marques. The delegation met Salazar and other Portuguese officials. In statements to the press, Jaeger said 'this was the first visit anyone in his group had made to any part of Portugal, and expressed his admiration [...] of Portugal's "civilizing mission" in Africa'.[85]

Conclusions

With the change in US policy during the early days of the Kennedy Administration, the major concern of Portuguese diplomacy became the diversification of international contacts and the garnering of political and diplomatic support for the colonial policies of the country. Right up to the end of his rule in 1968, Salazar's Government responded to the frequent resolutions and condemnations in the UN and to the crisis in US–Portuguese relations in the early 1960s with a deliberate effort to improve relations with Portugal's NATO allies, such as the UK, France, and West Germany. The country's foreign minister, Franco Nogueira, defined the new orientation and strategy that governed Portuguese diplomacy since he took office in early May 1961. Facing hostility from Washington, he said Portugal should 'extend and increase its relations with some other countries'. It should play upon European rivalries, taking advantage of the divergences existing between other nations, and make the support obtained with some of them work as an 'encouragement' for their rivals. It should also prevent the powers controlling the 'centres of economic and political decision making' from simultaneously allying themselves against Portugal. Nogueira added that beyond the US there were other powers that counted in the international scene, such as the UK, West Germany, and France.[86]

The Portuguese government's policy of diversifying international alliances produced significant results. From March 1961, Portuguese diplomacy sought to guarantee the support of some of the most important European countries. In that same month, the leaders of French and Spanish foreign policy visited Lisbon. Two months later, Lord Home, the British foreign secretary, also travelled to Portugal. The support of the European allies was particularly welcome in the most critical areas of Portuguese–American relations: that is to say, in the UN and in the supply of military equipment to Portugal. In these two areas, the UK, France, and West Germany were always loyal to Portugal. They abstained or voted against almost all UN resolutions on Portuguese colonialism and, despite some public assurances to the contrary, they kept open the normal channels for the sale of military equipment. The Portuguese government also signed two important military agreements with France and West Germany, giving these countries facilities in the Azores and Beja. The US was never successful in developing a concerted strategy of pressure with these European countries. They always refused to work as a kind of common front in the effort to convince Salazar to change Portugal's colonial policy and exert combined pressure for Portuguese decolonization.

This narrative shows that the success of the Portuguese government in resisting decolonization came in part from its foreign policy and diplomacy. Portugal benefited from its long-time association with the British, from European and colonial complicities in the case of France, and from the desire of European powers, like West Germany, to assert their new role in international affairs during the 1960s. Resistance to decolonization, in the case of Portugal, was also possible due to the international context of the Cold War. The new approach adopted by the US during the first months of the Kennedy Administration was justified by the fear that African nationalism could gravitate exclusively to the Soviet or Chinese orbits. The US did not want to lose the Cold War in Africa and, therefore, channelled its support to the UPA, led by Holden Roberto, instead of the communist-supported Movement for the Liberation of Angola (Movimento para a Libertação de Angola, MPLA). However, this Cold War context, while decisive in promoting a new policy in the early days of the Kennedy Administration, would in the long run seriously hamper that same policy. It was the same background of pragmatic Cold War considerations that ultimately justified the abandonment of many of the fresh new African and third-world policies initiated by the Administration, namely the policy towards Portuguese colonialism. Waldemar Nielsen, in his analysis of American policy towards Africa during the Kennedy Administration, believed that from 1961 'events in other parts of the world – from the Bay of Pigs fiasco in Cuba in mid-April to ominous new tensions in Berlin after mid-year – tended to drive Africa once again into the background and to bring to the fore those political and strategic considerations that had been consistently dominant in American foreign policy since the end of the Second World War'.[87]

Notes

1. See also L. N. Rodrigues, *No Coração do Atlântico: Os Estados Unidos e os Açores, 1939–1948*, Lisbon, Prefácio, 2005.
2. L. N. Rodrigues, 'Crossroads of the Atlantic: Portugal, the Azores and the Atlantic community (1943–57)', in V. Aubourg, G. Bossuat and G. Scott-Smith, eds, *European Community, Atlantic Community?*, Paris, Soleb, 2008.
3. For Portugal and the Marshall Plan see F. Rollo, *Portugal e a Reconstrução Económica do Pós-Guerra: O Plano Marshall e a Economia Portuguesa dos Anos 50*, Lisbon, Instituto Diplomático, 2007. Portugal's participation in NATO is analysed by A. Telo, *Portugal e a Nato: O Reencontro da Tradição Atlântica*, Lisbon, Cosmos, 1996, and N. S. Teixeira, 'Da neutralidade ao alinhamento: Portugal na fundação do pacto do Atlântico', *Análise Social*, XXVIII, 120, 1993, pp. 55–80. Available at analisesocial.ics.ul.pt/documentos/122328980 8W3fUK8ss8Gz37OV3.pdf.
4. T. J. Noer, 'New frontiers and old priorities in Africa', in T. G. Paterson, ed., *Kennedy's Quest for Victory: American Foreign Policy, 1961–1963*, New York, NY, Oxford University Press, 1989, p. 254.
5. See O. A. Westad, *The Global Cold War*, Cambridge, Cambridge University Press, 2007, especially chapter 4.
6. J. Parker, 'Cold War II: The Eisenhower Administration, the Bandung Conference, and the reperiodization of the postwar era', *Diplomatic History*, 30 (5), 2006, p. 890.
7. National Archives and Records Administration (NARA), College Park, State Department Lot Files (SDLF) 68D401, Entry 5296, Box 3, 'Official-Informal' letter from Theodore Xanthaky to David Popper, 28 January 1963.
8. For the Constitutional revision of 1951 see A. E. D. Silva, 'Salazar e a política colonial do Estado Novo: O Acto Colonial, 1930–1951', in F. Rosas and J. M. Brandão de Brito, eds, *Salazar e o Salazarismo*, Lisbon, Dom Quixote, 1989.
9. On lusotropicalism see C. Castelo, *O Modo Português de Estar no Mundo: O Luso-Tropicalismo e a Ideologia Colonial Portuguesa (1933–1961)*, Lisbon, Afrontamento, 1998.
10. The failed coup d'état of April 1961 in Portugal is analysed by Rodrigues, *Marechal Costa Gomes*, 2008, chapter 2.
11. There is a vast literature on the Portuguese colonial wars. For a general overview, among others, see A. Afonso and C. de M. Gomes, *Os Anos da Guerra*

Colonial, 1961–1975, Matosinhos, QuidNovi, 2010; A. C. Pinto, *O Fim do Império Português: A Cena Internacional, a Guerra Colonial, e a Descolonização, 1961–1975*, Lisbon, Horizonte, 2001; J. P. Cann, *Contra-Insurreição em África: O Modo Português de Fazer a Guerra, 1961–1974*, Lisbon, Atena, 1998; and J. F. Antunes, *A Guerra de África, 1961–1974*, vols. 1–2, Lisbon, Círculo de Leitores, 1995.

12. J. C. de Magalhães, *Portugal e as Nações Unidas: A Questão Colonial, 1955–1974*, Lisbon, IEEI, 1996. On Portugal and the United Nations see also F. Martins, 'A política externa do Estado Novo, o Ultramar e a ONU, 1955–1968', *Penélope*, 18, pp. 189–206, 1998.

13. Documents available at www.un.org/documents/ga/res/15/ares15.htm.

14. *Department of State Bulletin*, 3 April 1961, p. 499.

15. On Kennedy's policy on Angola see L. N. Rodrigues, 'About-face: The United States and Portuguese colonialism in 1961', *E-Journal of Portuguese History*, 2, 1, 2004, available at www.brown.edu/Departments/Portuguese_Brazilian_Studies/ejph/html/issue3/pdf/lnrodrigues.pdf; L. N. Rodrigues, *Kennedy-Salazar: A Crise de uma Aliança: As Relações Luso-Americanas entre 1961 e 1963*, Lisbon, Notícias, 2002; W. Schneidman, *Engaging Africa: Washington and the Fall of Portugal's Colonial Empire*, New York, NY University Press of America, 2004; J. F. Antunes, *Kennedy e Salazar: O Leão e a Raposa*, Lisbon, Difusão Cultural, 1992.

16. See D. Marcos, 'Uma relação conturbada: Os americanos nos Açores e a questão colonial portuguesa nos anos 50', in P. A. Oliveira and M. I. Rezola, eds, *O Longo Curso: Estudos em Homenagem a José Medeiros Ferreira*, Lisbon, Tinta da China, 2010.

17. Arquivo Histórico-Diplomático (AHD), Lisbon, MNE-SE, PEA Conf., Box 15.

18. L. N. Rodrigues, 'Today's terrorist is tomorrow's statesman: The United States and Angolan nationalism in the early 1960s', *Portuguese Journal of Social Science*, 3, 2 , 2004, pp. 115–140.

19. NARA, State Department Central Files (SDCF), 1960–63, Box 1817, 'Lisbon 240', 16 August 1961.

20. L. N. Rodrigues, 'Azores or Angola? Military bases and self-determination during the Kennedy administration', in L. N. Rodrigues and S. Glebov, eds, *Military Bases: Historical Perspectives, Contemporary Challenges*, Amsterdam, IOS, 2009.

21. NARA, SDCF, 1960–63, Box 1816, 'Presidential Task Force on Portuguese Territories in Africa: Report', July 1961.

22. NARA, SDCF, 1960–63, Box 1815, 'Joint Weeka No 21, 25 May 1962'.

23. A. Schlesinger Jr., *A Thousand Days: John F. Kennedy in the White House*, Boston, MA, Houghton Mifflin, 1965, pp. 562–563.

24. NARA, SDLF 68D401, Entry 5296, Box 4.

25. NARA, SDLF, Entry 3093, Box 2, 'Financial Assistance to Portugal,' 23 March 1962.

26. T. Lyons, 'Keeping Africa off the agenda,' in W. Cohen and N. Bernkopf Tucker, eds, *Lyndon Johnson Confronts the World: American Foreign Policy, 1963–1968*, Cambridge: Cambridge University Press, 1994.

27. NARA, DSLF, Entry 3093, Box 1, 'Portugal and Angola and the UN, 23 February 1961'.

28. NARA, SDCF, 1960–63, Box 1821, 753n.00/3–1061, 'New York 2428, 10 March 1961'.
29. NARA, SDCF, 1960–63, Box 1821, 753n.00/3–1661, 'London 3721, 16 March 1961'.
30. P. Oliveira, *Os Despojos da Aliança: A Grã-Bretanha e a Questão Colonial Portuguesa, 1945–1975*, Lisbon, Tinta da China, 2007, p. 239.
31. *Department of State Bulletin*, 10 July 1961, p. 89.
32. Oliveira, *Os Despojos da Aliança*, 2007, pp. 230–231, 240.
33. NARA, SDCF, 1960–63, Box 1824, 753N.5841/5–2461, 'London G-1522, 24 May 1961'.
34. L. W. Henderson, *Angola: Five Centuries of Conflict*, Ithaca, NY, Cornell University Press, 1979, p. 237.
35. NARA, SDCF, 1960–63, Box 1822, 753N.00/7–861, 'London A-38, 8 July 1961'.
36. NARA, SDCF, 1960–63, Box 1817, 753.5 MSP/8–1861, 'Lisbon 252, 18 August 1961.' See also Oliveira, *Os Despojos da Aliança*, 2007, pp. 255–256.
37. R. N. Swift, *Annual Review of United Nations Affairs, 1961–1962*, New York, NY, Oceana, 1963, p. 147.
38. F. Nogueira, *Salazar*. Vol. V: *A Resistência (1958–1964)*, Oporto: Livraria Civilização, 1988, pp. 358–362.
39. NARA, SDCF, 1960–63, Box 1819, 753D.00/12–1361, 'London 2308, 14 December 1961'.
40. H. MacMillan, *At the End of the Day, 1961–1963*, London, Macmillan, 1973, pp. 225–226.
41. *United States Participation in the United Nations. Report by the President to the Congress for the Year 1961*, p. 102.
42. F. Nogueira, *Diálogos Interditos; Parte Primeira (1961–1962–1963)*, Lisbon, Intervenção, 1979, pp. 185–190.
43. N. MacQueen and P. A. Oliveira, '"Grocer meets butcher": Marcello Caetano's London visit of 1973 and the last days of Portugal's Estado Novo', *Cold War History*, 10, 1, 2010, p. 30.
44. For relations between Portugal and Rhodesia see L. Barroso, *Salazar e Ian Smith: O Apoio de Portugal à Rodésia (1964–1969)*, Lisbon, Instituto Diplomático, 2009.
45. Oliveira, *Os Despojos da Aliança*, 2007, p. 479.
46. NARA, SDCF, 1963, Box 3815, 'Lisbon 195, 22 August 1963'.
47. F. Costigliola, 'The pursuit of Atlantic community: Nuclear arms, dollars, and Berlin,' in T. G. Paterson, ed., *Kennedy's Quest for Victory: American Foreign Policy, 1961–1963*, New York, NY, Oxford University Press, 1989, pp. 33–34.
48. M. Connelly, *A Diplomatic Revolution: Algeria's Fight for Independence and the Origins of the Post-Cold War Era*, New York, NY, Oxford University Press, 2002, pp. 253–254.
49. NARA, SDCF, 1960–63, Box 1813, 753.00/3–861, 'Paris 3717, 8 March 1961'.
50. NARA, SDCF, 1960–63, Box 1821, 753n.00/3–1361, 'New York 2449, 13 March 1961'.
51. D. Marcos, *Salazar e de Gaulle: A França e a Questão Colonial Portuguesa (1958–1968)*, Lisbon, Instituto Diplomático, 2007, p. 82.
52. NARA DSLF, Entry 3093, Box 1, 'Tripartite Meeting on Angola, 4 May 1961'.

53. NARA, SDCF, 1960–63, Box 1816, 753.022/7–1361, 'Presidential Task Force on Portuguese Territories in Africa. Report. 12 July 1961'.
54. Nogueira, *A Resistência*, 1988, pp. 304–305.
55. NARA, SDCF, 1960–63, Box 1816, 753.13/12–2661, 'Lisbon 696, 26 December 1961'.
56. *The New York Times*, 19 December 1961, p. 16.
57. NARA, SDCF, 1963, Box 4020, 'New York 2474, 13 December 1963'.
58. L. Crollen, *Portugal, the United States and NATO*, Leuven, Leuven University Press, 1973, p. 130.
59. Marcos, *Salazar e de Gaulle*, 2007, pp. 110–114.
60. NARA, SDCF, 1963, Box 3737, 'Lisbon 684, 26 March 1963'.
61. NARA, SDCF, 1964–1966, Box 2598, 'Joint Weeka, 28 September 1964'.
62. NARA, DSLF 68D401, Entry 5296, Box 6, Telegram from USAIRA, Lisbon, to HQ DIA, Washington D.C., 9 April 1964.
63. *The New York Times*, 10 April 1964, pp. 1 and 8.
64. Nogueira, *A Resistência*, 1988, pp. 303–304.
65. A. M. Fonseca, *A Força das Armas: O Apoio da República Federal da Alemanha ao Estado Novo, 1958–1968*, Lisbon, Instituto Diplomático, 2007, pp. 94, 127–30.
66. NARA, SDCF, 1960–63, Box 1817, 753.563 62a/9–2060, 'Official-Informal' letter from John Goodyear to Russel Fessenden.
67. NARA, SDCF, 1960–63, Box 1815, 753.00 (w)/1–2662, 'Joint Weeka No 4, 26 January 1962'.
68. NARA, SDCF, 1960–63, Box 1819, 1960–63, 753N.00/1–3162, 'Bonn 1769, 31 January 1962'.
69. NARA, SDCF, 1960–63, Box 1815, 753.00 (w)/7–2162, 'Joint Weeka No 29, 21 July 1962'.
70. Crollen, *Portugal, the United States and NATO*, 1973, p. 131.
71. Fonseca, *A Força das Armas*, 2007, pp. 75–6, 161–9.
72. NARA, SDCF, 1960–63, Box 1814, 753.00 (w)/7–1461, 'Joint Weeka N° 28, 14 July 1961'.
73. Fonseca, *A Força das Armas*, 2007, p. 161.
74. See Fonseca, *ibid.*, p. 170; Crollen, *Portugal, the United States and Nato*, 1973, p. 132; and NARA, DSLF 68D401, Entry 5296, Box 6, 'USARMA, Lisbon C-20, 30 January 1964'.
75. NARA, SDCF, 1960–63, Box 1821, 753N.00/6–861, 'Leopoldville 2430, 8 June 1961'.
76. NARA, SDCF, 1960–63, Box 1821, 753N.00/6–961, 'Bonn 2067, 9 June 1961'.
77. NARA, SDCF, 1960–63, Box 1817, 753.56/10–1261, 'Bonn A-20, 12 October 1961'.
78. NARA, SDCF, 1963, Box 3737, 'Lisbon 343, 15 October 1963'.
79. NARA, DSLF 68D401, Entry 5296, Box 6, EUR/SPP, Message from USARMA, Lisbon to ACSI, DA, 19 June 1964. See also Crollen, *Portugal, the United States and Nato*, 1973, p. 132.
80. Ibid.
81. NARA, SDCF, 1960–63, Box 1814, 753.00 (w)/5–1261, 'Joint Weeka No 19, 12 May 1961'.

82. NARA, SDCF, 1960–63, Box 1814, 753.00 (w)/5–1961, 'Joint Weeka No 20, 19 May 1961'.
83. NARA, SDCF, 1960–63, Box 1814, 753.00 (w)/7–76, 'Joint Weeka Np 27, 7 July 1961'.
84. Nogueira, *Diálogos Interditos*, 1979, pp. 163–166.
85. NARA, SDCF, 1963. Box 4018, 'Joint Weeka, 25 July 1963'.
86. Nogueira, *A Resistência*, 1988, pp. 301–302. See also A. Telo, 'As guerras de África e a mudança nos apoios internacionais de Portugal', *Revista de História das Ideias*, 16, 1994, pp. 347–369; Pinto, *O Fim do Império Português*, 2001.
87. W. A. Nielsen, *The Great Powers and Africa*, New York, NY, Praeger, 1969, pp. 288–291.

Last Days of Empire

John Darwin

Sixty years after the headline events that the term 'decolonization' evokes, its historiography remains a work in progress. There are several reasons for this. Perhaps the first, and most material, is access to new sources, although what promises to be among the most revealing, the so-called 'migrated archive' of British colonial administrations for long discreetly lodged at Hanslope Park, has yet to yield up its secrets. The second influence at work is the startling series of geopolitical changes through which the world has moved since the 1960s and 1970s: the fall of one great imperial system and the consequent end of the Cold War; the rise of a new (potential) superpower; the political growth of fundamentalist Islam. The third is the emergence of new public (and therefore scholarly) concerns that have shaped our perception of the causes, course, and outcome of decolonization: perhaps most obviously the discourse of human rights, and a sensitivity, much less developed even twenty years ago, to the threat and use of violence for political purposes. The fourth is the discovery of a new relevance in the processes of decolonization, as international interventions, whether for humanitarian or geostrategic reasons, have proliferated. Staging the 'exit' (not least its rhetorical justification) has become a major new branch of statecraft. The fifth reflects the collapse of the old binary distinction between the 'third world' (largely but not exclusively composed of ex-colonial states) and the rest, on which much of the older literature on decolonization was implicitly constructed. The quite different trajectories of the third world's components – in Latin America, ex-colonial Asia, the Arab Middle East and sub-Saharan Africa – raise intriguing questions about the colonial legacy and the motives of withdrawal. Finally, we have had to take account of the 'globalizing' realities of our own times, chief amongst them the exceptional degree of demographic turbulence caused by economic migration, forced migrations, and the vast human tide of refugees escaping oppression or famine in their 'own' nation states. The world has clung to the fiction (for very good reasons) that decolonization transformed colonial states into nations. Contemplating the reality in many parts of the ex-colonial sphere, we might be tempted to ask: decolonization for whom?

Some of these points require a little further reflection. The issue of sources might be thought fundamental. A striking feature of several of the contributions in this volume is the heavy reliance upon American and British archives. This is hardly surprising since both offer the progressive disclosure of more recent records on a more or less predictable timetable and both are relatively easy to use ('relatively' might be the right term for the records at College Park, Maryland). The picture amongst the other ex-colonial powers is more variable: the Netherlands National Archive operates a 75-year rule with some exclusions; the Belgian National Archive website promised a guide to archives on the Congo and Rwanda-Urundi to be ready by 2012 – but no indication where it might be found. Outside the West, the picture is hardly encouraging. We may expect to wait quite a long time before Russian documentation on its rapid decolonization after 1989 becomes available. Anyone hoping to study China's recent colonial policies in Inner Asia will have to rely on a very long life expectancy indeed. There are a number of bright spots: the Kenya National Archives caters for a heavy traffic of foreign scholars; a recent user of the Ghanaian archives found access to Nkrumah's correspondence straightforward. Massive amounts of the documentation of India's freedom struggle have been published. But in many of the former colonial territories the public archive is difficult to access, or suffers from gross neglect, while the preservation of private archival material is either non-existent or patchy at best. The modern historiography of the Arab Middle East has been crippled by the inaccessibility of its archival collections. Why does all this matter? Because it reinforces to a disturbing degree the deeply ingrained tendency to view decolonization as a process decisively shaped by policymakers in Western capitals (a flattering delusion). Secondly, and perhaps more insidiously, it reduces the scope of decolonization as a world-historical transition to its most visible (but not necessarily its most important) dimension: the transfers of sovereignty. Outside the West (perhaps even inside it), this might be seen as an impoverished perspective on a much vaster change.

The supply of new sources is thus likely to exert an erratic and perhaps even restrictive effect on decolonization's historiography.

By contrast, the dramatic re-ordering of the geopolitical landscape should help to alleviate the tendency to imagine decolonization as a bilateral relationship between an imperial power and (one) colonial territory. With the indispensable benefit of hindsight, we can see how crucial it was that the transfers of sovereignty took place at the time when the bipolar rivalry of East and West was at its height. How different they might have been had the harmonious division of spheres between four 'world policemen', naively projected at the end of the Second World War, become a global reality. The wider point may be obvious. The meaning of 'independence' (a more exacting status than sovereignty) was bound to be in large part a function of the global distribution of power. Even within the Cold War era c.1948–89, we can see quite distinct phases when the scope and intensity of bipolar competition varied considerably. It was the sudden escalation of Soviet ambitions (as it was perceived in the West) in the late 1950s that shattered the nerves of policymakers in London and Washington, and raised the morale of nationalist politicians. American involvement in the Vietnamese quagmire, and the widespread belief by the mid-1970s that 'national liberation movements' were an unstoppable force, raised the bargaining power of new Afro-Asian regimes. The 'new cold war' after 1979 seemed to be sucking both superpowers into forward movements and raising the stakes where their spheres of interference collided. In more recent times, we have seen a no less sudden and unpredictable shift from the prospect of unipolar hegemony to an emerging multipolar world. In each of these phases, the meaning and content of post-colonial freedom (both external and internal) were liable to vary significantly as outside pressures to conform institutionally, ideologically, or commercially waxed and waned.

Yet perhaps it is the appearance of new concerns and preoccupations within Western societies that has played the largest part in revising the agenda of decolonization historiography, and is likely to change it still more in the future. The most salient of these is the protean idea of human rights, which has sensitized Western opinion more powerfully than ever before to the individual fates concealed behind news reports and economic statistics. Of all the infringements of human rights, it is state-sponsored violence that arouses the fiercest condemnation. So it is hardly surprising that it this dimension of decolonization that has attracted widespread attention, first of all among historians of France's 'dirty war' in Algeria, and increasingly among those scrutinizing the British record. By same token, however, the criteria of human rights have served to dispel the somewhat misty-eyed gaze with which some observers at least had regarded the building of new Afro-Asian nations. Criticism of the treatment of women, of male and female homosexuals, as well as of ethnic and religious minorities, in post-colonial societies, sometimes in association with local lobbies and pressure groups, has become part of the way in which they are now viewed in the West. It is no longer so easy to equate decolonization with liberation, or at least not without very large qualifications. Indeed, the failure of the colonial powers to address the problems of social, cultural, and sexual inequality before the handover of power may become part of a new arraignment of their record.

Lastly, several influences have converged to challenge the once conventional view that decolonization was a 'tryst with destiny' and the bringing to birth of an immanent nation. In a self-consciously 'global' age, we are less prone than we were to regard the building of nations as the universal desideratum of historical change – although in some parts of the world this belief remains stubbornly rooted. The intensity of globalization, in the realms of commerce and information technology most of all, has shattered the illusion (once remarkably prevalent) that new nations could aspire to a genuine economic and cultural independence. It is now widely believed in the West (much less elsewhere) that the claims of human rights transcend the jurisdiction of 'errant' nation states, and qualify their sovereignty. We are much more alert than we were a generation ago to the ethnic and religious diversity to be found within states, and to the oppressions to which this can give rise – a consequence in part of the astonishing proliferation of non-governmental organizations now active across the world, and furiously competing for funds and publicity. Above all, perhaps, the dramatic scale of the diasporas of economic migrants and refugees, from the 'South' to the 'North', has created a new awareness of the poverty, insecurity, and injustice that pervades many ex-colonial territories, even where, as in the case of Somalia, that state has not collapsed completely. At the very least, we are likely to question not whether decolonization was inevitable, nor the nobility of the ideals on which it was based, but rather the extent to which it might be counted a 'success' in the forms that it took.

At first sight, the chapters in this book address a well-worn theme: the making of policy in the capitals of the decolonizing powers and, in Washington, their overbearing protector. The appearance is deceptive since their real aim is to give more depth, substance, and subtlety to existing accounts of the policy-making process. In Crawford Young's analysis, it was the political systems of the three smaller colonial powers that constrained their ability to anticipate the breakdown of their imperial authority and extract themselves gracefully before the roof fell in. In the Netherlands and Belgium, the culprit was the clumsiness of multi-party democracy, which blocked the possibility of the pragmatic ruthlessness practised by Harold Macmillan and Charles de Gaulle, whose notorious promise to the Algerian *pieds noirs* 'je vous ai compris' might be best be translated as 'I've taken your measure'. In Portugal, it was an autocracy trapped in its conservative ideology, and fearful of any impression of weakness, that performed the same inflexible function. We might add to this the fact that both Britain and France enjoyed more geopolitical leeway in which to engineer their withdrawals, and that it required a new constitution before France could escape the institutional constraints that Young identifies. The British case is more curious. As Bruno Cardoso Reis points out, politicians might be hindered by, but could also exploit, the power of myth – in this case the prevailing myths of empire. Harold Macmillan, whose pragmatic foresight has been greatly exaggerated, was a dab hand at myth use and myth making. But he also enjoyed two enormous advantages in presenting Britain's colonial withdrawals as the masterly culmination of a long-matured programme (a shameless falsehood!). Firstly, he could exploit to the full the well-established myth of the Commonwealth as the shiny new vehicle for Britain's post-imperial influence, a quasi- empire populated with grateful self-governing clients. Timely generosity would ensure, so the argument ran, that the right kind of nationalists would inherit the new states, nationalists attuned to the Commonwealth's value. Secondly, Macmillan could deploy the charismatic power of the British monarchy, perhaps then at its height, to lend reassurance and dignity both to the Commonwealth (of which the British Crown was 'Head') and to the Disneyesque pageantry in which the transfers of power were artfully blanketed. Conservative opinion, if not reassured, would find it hard to attack a political process over which the prestige of the monarchy was so liberally spread.

A second theme that emerges powerfully though a number of chapters is the energy with which the imperial bureaucracies and their advisors sought to reinvent themselves and their role in the post-1945 world. As Fred Cooper describes it, there was much about the late colonial state that could be made to chime with the fashionable doctrines of 'modernization' theory. The late colonial state was committed to 'developmentalism': in part because of the material needs of the imperial metropole; in part out of deference to the social and economic deficiencies that colonial officialdom had acknowledged even before the Second World War. Casting aside the administrative theology of 'indirect rule', and the lethargy induced by the starvation diet of Depression finance, the late colonial state was a hyperactive, if somewhat febrile, phenomenon. But its declared preoccupations – economic planning and social welfare – were closely aligned with those that ruled in domestic politics. More to the point, they allowed colonial policymakers to claim that – far from presiding with passive indifference over the backwaters of the world – they were engaged in the business of spreading modernity where it was most urgently needed. This may help to explain why, in what appears in retrospect as the dying fall of the colonial age, the plans and projects of the colonial state were able to mobilize so much youthful idealism. Miguel Bandeira Jerónimo and António Costa Pinto's fascinating chapter on Portugal's late colonial state portrays a regime girding itself for action in a new and more challenging global environment. The old prescriptions of colonial subordination and fiscal self-sufficiency were cast aside. The colonies became 'provinces', now primed for development with funds from the centre and endowed with new infrastructures to make them more governable. The least acceptable face of old-style imperialism, the *indigenato* with its labour conscription and forced crop-growing rules, was abolished in 1961. Simultaneously, the reach of the political police was extended. New strategies of colonization were invented: the *colonato* – either ethnically mixed or Portuguese only – to promote the ideal of the small landed proprietor as the bulwark of the state. Here, in what is often thought of as the least progressive of Europe's colonial powers, was a pattern of bureaucratic activism comparable to that of the British or French. Why should it have been otherwise?

Perhaps the larger point is that accounts of colonialism that portray it as intellectually moribund after 1918 are far wide of the mark. Indeed, the accusation might carry much greater force (certainly for Africa) between the wars than after 1945. Colonialism was, paradoxically, at its most innovative and energetic, and most in tune with the 'mainstream' of intellectual inquiry, at the very moment when its political future was about to be foreshortened drastically. Indeed, even after the timetables for independence had shifted from 'a generation hence' to 'this time next year', plans and schemes for the preservation of 'influence' were being busily drafted. In Sarah Stockwell's chapter, we can see how seriously the British took the idea of implanting their 'ethos' in the post-colonial states in Africa. They hoped to maintain a 'public service' tradition by insulating the civil service from political 'interference', initially by key administrative personnel 'staying on'. They wanted to keep a close link between the new national armies and the British Army, ideally by the continuing employment of senior British officers. The Bank of England set itself to groom the new central banks with which ex-colonial states were endowed, and to supply their directors. Here the motive was partly to maintain the sterling link that was vital to hopes of revitalizing the pound as a global reserve currency, partly to help the City keep its financial foot in the ex-colonial door. Success was limited and relatively short-lived, perhaps because – as Stockwell points out – to a greater extent than they realized the British had ceded control over the levers of political power. Most of these links soon withered away. The British might have preferred 'informal' to 'formal' ties (perhaps as a way of limiting liability). But as they (and others) were to find, informal empires can be even more costly than the formal kind.

These and other initiatives are best understood in their geopolitical context. Indeed, the whole course of decolonization was decisively shaped by a double conjuncture: the 'internal' crisis of colonialism and the onset of the Cold War. Cold War considerations led Washington to force the Dutch to abandon their empire in Indonesia, and to pay the French to hang on to theirs in Indochina. Washington's heart may have been anti-colonial (its publicity machine certainly was), but its head was quite often imperial. Luís Nuno Rodrigues describes how President Kennedy's enthusiasm for the nationalist cause in Angola and Mozambique evaporated rapidly when Lisbon hinted that the huge American airbase in the Azores – the great Atlantic stepping stone in the age of air power – might be the price of such ideological purity. The British government performed (how independently is not clear) a similar somersault. Indeed, Bandeira Jerónimo and Costa Pinto's chapter tells us that American funding, public and private, was injected into Portuguese Africa in the later 1960s, while Portugal's experiments with whites-only *colonatos* received a favourable press across the Atlantic. But it was in the Congo that decolonization and Cold War became most closely entangled. In John Kent's account we can see how the conjunction could be turned to advantage by another small power. The Belgians had orchestrated their unexpectedly sudden departure on the premise that the new Congolese government would depend on them for advice, personnel, and technical assistance. They had also discreetly ensured that the investment income that had previously accrued to Leopoldville would be transferred to Brussels. When Patrice Lumumba emerged as the new Congo's premier to threaten these plans, the Belgian foreign minister skilfully exploited the paranoia in Washington to secure its antipathy to this 'agent' of communism. With Belgian complicity (at least), Lumumba was kidnapped and murdered. But, perhaps to Belgian dismay, the same geopolitical fears that had sanctioned Lumumba's erasure made the separation of Katanga, the copper-rich southern province that bordered (still colonial) Zambia, an intolerable risk. The forward march (as it seemed) of Soviet influence from the late 1950s, now in partnership with Colonel Nasser in Cairo, raised the spectre of a Congo divided between pro-Western and pro-Soviet successor states. So in a further twist, American and (much more reluctantly) British support was thrown behind the crushing of Katanga's independence. Katanga must die that the Congo might live.

It is curious how unanimous most commentators have been that Katanga's independence was an illegitimate enterprise. Those who denounced Belgian rule in the Congo were just as insistent that the bizarre construct that Leopold II had fashioned should be preserved intact. Of course, there were many tell-tale signs that Katanga's independence was supported by the great mining combine of Union Minière and sustained by white mercenaries. But Moise Tshombe, the Katanga premier, was a much more considerable figure than hostile propaganda allowed and not merely a puppet. Moreover, there is evidence that prior to its forced incorporation into Leopold's Congo, Katanga had enjoyed longstanding cultural and political autonomy. The 'Katanga syndrome' reminds us that the pattern of territorial decolonization across much of the world, with its rigid adherence to the colonial boundaries, had little to do with ethnic or cultural realities, let alone justice. It was at bottom a bargain between the leaders of successor regimes, eager to maximize the scope of their power, and colonial ex-rulers who expected those regimes to be their clients and allies, and feared that their balkanization would open the gate to 'unfriendly' influence. But the powerful condemnation that Katanga's bid for independence evoked points to another influential force – what might be called the 'sensibility' of the decolonizing era.

Three chapters in this book bring this out clearly. Ryan Irwin's account of the career of Enuga Reddy at the United Nations reminds us how the sudden enlargement of the number of 'non-white states' in the General Assembly transformed the ideological climate of the world organization as a whole after 1960. Martin Shipway's depiction of the French scholar-mandarin Robert Delavignette captures the moral dilemma of a self-consciously liberal imperialist. Delavignette had served time as a *commandant de cercle* in French West Africa. He had been a 'man on the spot'. But he had spent much of his career in Paris helping to refashion France's overseas empire as new pressures beat upon it. He taught at ENSOM, the prestigious *école* where colonial administrators were trained. In a cri de coeur written towards the end of his life, he denounced the habit of blaming the evils of colonialism upon settlers, administrators and missionaries by opinion in the metropole, which, he said, had forgotten who sent them. But Delavignette was appalled by the savage methods employed to repress the Algerian insurrection, by the evidence of torture and the gross irregularities practised in the name of the state. This was the same kind of reaction as that to be found in the Devlin Report on the Nyasaland disturbances of 1959. Here, too, the state, invested with the dignity of trusteeship and good government, had behaved in ways characteristic, as Devlin famously put it, of a 'police state'. His message was that the price of empire in the face of a local revolt would be morally higher than many at home would be willing to pay. The politics of this sensibility are neatly captured in Philip Murphy's analysis of the use and threat of violence in Britain's central African policy. British governments, and probably most British opinion, had been happy enough to turn a blind eye to the coercive tactics employed to establish the white-controlled Central African Federation (the Federation of Rhodesia and Nyasaland) in 1953 – perhaps because the concurrent Mau Mau emergency had discredited all forms of African resistance. At the time of the Nyasaland emergency in 1959, London fell back on the 'Mau Mau' argument to justify the severity of the Nyasaland government's actions, and showed little interest in restraining the zeal of its men on the spot, being willing even to sanction machine-gunning from the air. The Devlin Report and the public reaction in Britain changed the game completely. Henceforth, the repression of large-scale unrest in Africa became a political nightmare to be avoided at almost any cost. In the long-drawn-out negotiations over Northern Rhodesia's constitution in 1960–61, the British first advised Kenneth Kaunda, leader of the main African party, that violent unrest would make it hard for them to justify concessions to majority rule. Somewhat later, however, when an excuse was needed to renege on the promises made to the white settler party, Kaunda was given a nod and a wink that just such an outburst would be tactically useful – as indeed it was. The unspoken corollary was that the British themselves would not attempt to suppress it. Indeed, as the British moved (with extraordinary speed) from rulers to brokers in their central African dealings, the violent unrest that had once been anathema became a convenient lever with which to engineer their release from an unwelcome commitment.

Yet, as Murphy also records, the distaste for violence inflicted on Africans was far from wholehearted. Defending the Nyasaland government (privately) against the criticisms of the Devlin Report, the Cabinet secretary Sir Norman Brook remarked on the difficulty of maintaining order 'where a handful of white men are controlling hordes of primitive people'. It was 'rather jolting', remarks Murphy, to find 'this kind of Rider Haggard imagery as late as 1959'. But perhaps that is the point, and it goes far wider than the British reaction to events in Nyasaland. It is the business of historians to trace the roots of change. In the case of decolonization, it is easy to see 'straws in the wind' signalling the imminent fall of colonialism almost as far back as one cares to look. The year 1919 was once fashionable as the great turning point in the fate of empires. But sometimes this search for origins can be misleading. It can encourage the habit of denouncing the absence of 'foresight' by contemporary actors. The speed of change can sometimes be overwhelming and even disorienting. There is a powerful case for arguing that the (wholly unpredicted) events of 1959–60 – in the Congo, central Africa, south Africa, west Africa, and elsewhere – were transformative, not just at the level of policy making but also in terms of what could be thought of as morally defensible. The geopolitical assumptions and banal forms of racism that seemed plausible or acceptable before 1960 acquired *quite suddenly* an old-fashioned look and a reactionary character. Of course, the change in sensibility was much slower to become general, and was subject to wide local variation. Even at the end of the decade, rivers could still 'foam with much blood'. But the die had been cast. The world had been changed.

Index – Names*

A

Abrahams, Peter, 203
Adenauer, Konrad, 257
Alleg, Henri, 89, 90
Amery, Julian, 186
Anderson, David, 178
Andrews, Bill, 203
Antunes, Ernesto Melo (Major), 142, 143
Araújo, Manuel Gomes de, 260
Armitage, Robert Perceval (Sir), 187, 188
Aron, Raymond, 130, 133
Aspremont, Harold (Count), 238
Audin, Maurice, 90
Aussaresses, Paul, 90

B

Balandier, Georges, 38, 39, 40
Ball, George, 138
Banda, Hastings, 166, 179, 180, 186, 193
Barthes, R., 145
Baudouin of Belgium (King), 189
Bennett, John, 159
Benson, Arthur, 184, 192
Bilsen, A. A. J. Van, 110
Blum, Léon, 85
Bollardière, Jacques Pâris de, 90, 95
Bomboko, Justin Marie, 225, 227, 228
Boothby, E. B., 228
Bossa, José Ferreira, 56
Boumendjel, Ali, 90
Bourgès-Maunoury, Maurice, 90
Bouteille, Pierre, 82
Branche, Raphaëlle, 89
Brook, Norman (Sir), 180, 277
Bunche, Ralph, 225, 231, 232, 235
Burke, Roland, 199

C

Cabral, Amílcar, 118
Caetano, Marcelo, 57, 115, 117, 119, 139, 141
Caine, Sydney, 23
Cannadine, David, 132
Clarence-Smith, G., 116
Clayton, Anthony, 157, 158
Cohen, Andrew, 250
Cohen, William, 86
Colby, Geoffrey (Sir), 183, 184
Cooper, Frederick, 6, 199
Crollen, Luc, 258, 260
Cunha, J. Silva, 60
Curutchet, Lieutenant, 92, 93

D

Dadoo, Yusuf, 203
Daniel, Jean, 133
Darwin, John, 1, 5, 8, 127, 129
Davis, Merle, 20–1
De Gaulle, Charles, 89, 132, 133, 134, 135, 136, 140, 144, 253, 254, 255, 256, 265, 272
De La Rue, Napier of, 167
Defferre, Gaston, 82
Delafosse, Maurice, 20, 85
Delavignette, Robert, 6, 20, 81–98
Depi, George, 233
Devlin, Patrick (Lord), 179, 185, 187, 276
Dickson, Paul, 64
Dimier, Véronique, 85
Diop, Alioune, 39
Douglas-Home, Alec (Sir), 182, 228
Dulles, Allen, 233

E

Eckel, Jan, 199
Eden, Anthony (Sir), 122

---

*All the three indexes are compiled by Paula Gonçalves.

Index – Geo

Index – Analytic

Printed and bound by CPI Group (UK) Ltd, Croydon, CR0 4YY